Unless Recalled Earlier

DATE DUE

D1567612

THE SEARCH FOR SIMPLICITY

Essays in Parallel Programming

PER BRINCH HANSEN

IEEE Computer Society Press
Los Alamitos, California

Washington • Brussels • Tokyo

Library of Congress Cataloging-in-Publication Data

Brinch Hansen, Per, 1938–
    The search for simplicity: essays in parallel programming / Per
Brinch Hansen.
        p.   cm.
    Includes bibliographical references and index.
    ISBN 0-8186-7566-7
    1. Parallel programming (Computer science)   I. Title
QA76.642.B756   1996
005.2—dc20

                                                                                96-647
                                                                                CIP

IEEE Computer Society Press
10662 Los Vaqueros Circle
P.O. Box 3014
Los Alamitos, CA 90720-1264

IEEE Computer Society Press Order Number BP07566
Library of Congress Number 96-647
ISBN 0-8186-7566-7

Additional copies may be ordered from:

IEEE Computer Society Press
Customer Service Center
10662 Los Vaqueros Circle
P.O. Box 3014
Los Alamitos, CA 90720-1264
Tel: +1-714-821-8380
Fax: +1-714-821-4641
Email: cs.books@computer.org

IEEE Service Center
445 Hoes Lane
P.O. Box 1331
Piscataway, NJ 08855-1331
Tel: +1-908-981-1393
Fax: +1-908-981-9667
mis.custserv@computer.org

IEEE Computer Society
13, Avenue de l'Aquilon
B-1200 Brussels
BELGIUM
Tel: +32-2-770-2198
Fax: +32-2-770-8505
euro.ofc@computer.org

IEEE Computer Society
Ooshima Building
2-19-1 Minami-Aoyama
Minato-ku, Tokyo 107
JAPAN
Tel: +81-3-3408-3118
Fax: +81-3-3408-3553
tokyo.ofc@computer.org

Assistant Publisher: Matt Loeb
Acquisitions Assistant: Cheryl Smith
Advertising/Promotions: Tom Fink
Production Editor: Lisa O'Conner
Cover Design: Christa Schubert
Printed in the United States of America by Braun-Brumfield, Inc.

The Institute of Electrical and Electronics Engineers, Inc

In memory of
August and Alojzija Hrastar

Preface

More is in vain when less will serve.

Isaac Newton (1686)

Background

This is the first collection of my published papers on parallel programming. The book is intended for computer scientists and programmers who are interested in the programming principles of operating systems, parallel languages, and computational science.

Written over a period of thirty years, the papers describe a relentless search for simplicity exemplified by the RC 4000 multiprogramming system; the Solo operating system; the monitor notation for modular parallel programming; the parallel programming languages Concurrent Pascal, Edison, Joyce, and SuperPascal; and the scientific programs for parallel architectures.

These writings demonstrate my attempts to recognize the essence of complex software problems and express them in terms of a small number of abstract concepts. The technical ideas are now standard material in textbooks on operating systems and parallel programming.

By 1970 I had programmed operating systems in assembly language for several years and it seemed to me that it ought to be possible to write parallel software in high-level programming languages without machine-dependent features. This conviction became the driving force behind my work.

Those who are unfamiliar with the history of parallel programming may study these articles as stepping-stones towards parallel programming languages. If you already know the programming concepts, read these writings as reasoned essays on parallel programming practiced as an aesthetic craft.

The twenty-five articles appear in chronological order of publication. The scientific work described in these essays can be divided into three phases: operating system principles (1966–72), parallel programming languages (1972–88), and computational science (1988–95).

This is the first time I have had the opportunity to publish my best papers in one place. I will briefly place each paper in historical context. Apart from that I will let the papers speak for themselves. I hope that you will enjoy reading them.

Autobiographical Sketches

When I studied electrical engineering at the Technical University of Denmark, the most promising new field that was not yet being taught was computer programming. So that is what I decided to do.

After graduating in 1963 I joined the Danish computer company Regnecentralen. I taught myself to program as a member of a Cobol compiler group headed by Peter Naur and Jørn Jensen. I also discovered that writing is a rigorous test of simplicity: it is just not possible to write convincingly about ideas that cannot be understood.

You may well wonder why anyone would hire a systems programmer with no programming experience. At the time it seemed natural because compiler technology was still in its infancy and not yet described in textbooks. Since then, I have often worked in unfamiliar areas that neither I nor anyone else knew much about.

I left the computer industry in 1970 and became a university researcher in the United States.

Two *historical papers* describe my early career at Regnecentralen (1963–70) and my personal recollections of the birth of parallel programming languages (1971–90):

- Article 10: The Programmer as a Young Dog (1976).

- Article 21: Monitors and Concurrent Pascal: A Personal History (1993).

Operating System Principles

At Regnecentralen I was responsible for the architecture and software of the RC 4000 minicomputer. The *RC 4000 real-time control system* was my first experience with multiprogramming and semaphores:

- Article 1: The RC 4000 Real-time Control System at Pulawy (1967).

The project succeeded because we used the simplest possible techniques to solve an unfamiliar problem of modest size. I have tried to remain true to this ideal throughout my career.

The *RC 4000 multiprogramming system* introduced the novel idea of a system kernel for parallel processes and message communication that can be extended with a variety of operating systems:

- Article 2: The Nucleus of a Multiprogramming System (1970).

- Article 5: Testing a Multiprogramming System (1973).

The implementation techniques of operating systems were reasonably well understood in the late sixties. But most systems were too large and poorly described to be studied in detail. While Edsger Dijkstra had clarified fundamental aspects of process synchronization, most of the literature on operating systems emphasized implementation details of particular systems rather than general concepts. The terminology was unsystematic and incomplete.

At the time it was obvious to me (and others) that there really were no suitable textbooks on operating systems. Universities were therefore unable to teach core courses on the subject. In 1970 Alan Perlis invited me to spend a year at Carnegie-Mellon University where I wrote the first comprehensive textbook on the principles of operating systems:

- Article 3: An Outline of a Course on Operating System Principles (1971).

While writing the book I reached the conclusion that operating systems are not radically different from other programs. They are just large programs based on the principles of a more fundamental subject: parallel programming.

Starting from a concise definition of the purpose of an operating system, I divided the subject into five major areas. First, I presented the principles of parallel programming as the essence of operating systems. Then I described processor management, memory management, scheduling algorithms, and resource protection as techniques for implementing parallel processes.

I defined operating system concepts by algorithms written in Pascal extended with an (unimplemented) notation for structured multiprogramming. The book includes a concise vocabulary of operating system terminology, which is used consistently throughout the text.

Prentice-Hall published my book, *Operating System Principles*, in July 1973. It has since been translated into German, Czech, Polish, Serbo-Croatian, and Japanese.

Parallel Programming Languages

The steady work of Edsger Dijkstra, Tony Hoare, and me on programming notation for operating system concepts led to the initial development of parallel programming languages.

It began in 1971 with Hoare's notation for a *conditional critical region* that delays one or more processes until a Boolean expression is true. Unfortunately this elegant idea is inefficient since it requires periodic reevaluation of the expression as long as it is false.

One of my first papers on programming language concepts proposed an (equally inefficient) variant of conditional critical regions for priority scheduling. A more original idea was my introduction of *scheduling queues*, which eliminate superfluous evaluation (but complicate the programming somewhat):

- Article 4: Structured Multiprogramming (1972).

Dijkstra, Hoare and I suggested another parallel programming concept in 1971: the *monitor*, which combines synchronization procedures with the shared variables they operate on. My operating system book introduced a programming notation for monitors (*shared classes*), based on the class concept of Simula 67:

- Article 6: Shared Classes (1973).

Somewhat later, Tony Hoare published a similar notation for monitors. His proposal included a variant of my scheduling queues ("conditions").

By the fall of 1972 I was already committed to the goal of developing a parallel programming language with a modular ("object-oriented") notation for processes and monitors. At the California Institute of Technology I defined the programming language *Concurrent Pascal*, which supports monitors and parallel processes for implementation of modular operating systems:

- Article 7: The Programming Language Concurrent Pascal (1975).

Since synchronization errors can be extremely difficult to locate by program testing, Concurrent Pascal was designed to permit the detection of such errors during compilation. With the help of a couple of students, a portable implementation of the language was running on a PDP 11 minicomputer at the end of 1974.

Concurrent Pascal had obvious limitations by today's standards. But, in 1975, it laid the foundation for the development of programming languages with abstract concepts for parallelism.

I used Concurrent Pascal to program the portable operating system *Solo* as a realistic test of the new programming language. The most significant contribution of Solo was undoubtedly that the program text was short enough to be published in its entirety in a computer journal:

- Article 8: The Solo Operating System: A Concurrent Pascal Program (1976).

- Article 9: The Solo Operating System: Processes, Monitors, and Classes (1976).

The portable implementation of Concurrent Pascal and Solo was highly successful in spreading the software to almost 200 installations worldwide.

Now that Concurrent Pascal was running I knew that the time was ripe for a book about the principles of abstract parallel programming. I finished *The Architecture of Concurrent Programs* (1977) at the University of Southern California. It was published in English, German, and Japanese. The book includes the complete text of three model operating systems written in Concurrent Pascal:

- Article 11: Experience with Modular Concurrent Programming (1977).

- Article 12: Design Principles (1977).

My final Concurrent Pascal program implemented message communication in a *ring network* of minicomputers:

- Article 13: Network: A Multiprocessor Program (1978).

- Article 15: Reproducible Testing of Monitors (1978).

Technology was now moving from multiprocessors with shared memory towards multicomputers with distributed memory. For microcomputer networks I proposed a combination of processes and monitors: *Distributed processes*, which communicate by means of synchronized "remote procedure calls":

- Article 14: Distributed Processes: A Concurrent Programming Concept (1978).

In a *keynote address* delivered at the IEEE COMPSAC '78 I drew a parallel between the evolution of parallel programming concepts for shared memory machines and the next challenge of distributed computing:

- Article 16: A Keynote Address on Concurrent Programming (1979).

After Concurrent Pascal I designed the parallel programming languages, *Edison* and *Joyce*, to experiment with Hoare's concepts of conditional critical regions and synchronous message communication, respectively:

- Article 17: The Design of Edison (1981).

- Article 18: Joyce—A Programming Language for Distributed Systems (1987).

Computational Science

Prior to 1988 I only had access to sequential computers. Syracuse University made it possible for me to use *parallel architectures* for the first time:

- Article 19: A Multiprocessor Implementation of Joyce (1989).

At an interdisciplinary symposium I discussed the programming of parallel computers without going into technical details:

- Article 20: The Nature of Parallel Programming (1989).

In the 1990s the programming problems of operating systems have surfaced again in parallel scientific computing: there is a serious need for machine-independent programming languages and algorithms. To understand this challenge I spent five years writing portable multicomputer algorithms for typical problems in science and engineering. My book, *Studies in Computational Science* (1995), describes this work:

- Article 22: Model Programs for Computational Science: A Programming Methodology for Multicomputers (1993).

- Article 23: Parallel Cellular Automata: A Model Program for Computational Science (1993).

I also developed the programming language *SuperPascal* with message parallelism for publication of parallel scientific programs:

- Article 24: SuperPascal—A Publication Language for Parallel Scientific Computing (1994).

Dynamic memory allocation of parallel recursive processes has been a thorny problem, which most language designers wisely have ignored for twenty years. While implementing SuperPascal I discovered that the Quickfit scheme, used for heap allocation in the sequential language Bliss, can also be used as an efficient technique for implementing *parallel recursion*:

- Article 25: Efficient Parallel Recursion (1995).

Let me end on a philosophical note by quoting Albert Einstein: "In the light of knowledge attained, the happy achievement seems almost a matter of course, and any intelligent student can grasp it without too much trouble. But the years of anxious searching in the dark, with their intense longing, their alternations of confidence and exhaustion, and the final emergence into the light—only those who have experienced it can understand it."

Matters of Style

This book contains the original text of my articles retyped in LaTeX without any changes of grammar or punctuation. I have, however, used a uniform style of citations and references. Each article includes the original list of references, showing what was known to me at the time of writing. These lists include cross-references to the articles in this book, such as *Article 12*.

I write and rewrite my papers many times until they are as clear as I can make them. However, since I am not a native speaker, it is not always easy for me to formulate elegant thoughts in English. When I succeed, I sometimes fall for the temptation to repeat myself verbatim in later essays. You will find several examples in these articles, which were never intended to appear side by side. I regret the occasional repetition, which I cannot remove without rewriting my personal history.

Acknowledgements

These articles are reprinted by permission of Academic Press, Association for Computing Machinery, BIT, Institute of Electrical and Electronics Engineers, The MIT Press, Prentice Hall, John Wiley & Sons, and the author. A footnote on the title page of each paper gives full credit to the publication in which the work first appeared, including the owner's copyright notice.

PER BRINCH HANSEN
Syracuse University

Contents

The RC 4000 Real-time Control System at Pulawy[*]

(1967)

This paper describes a real-time control system implemented on the RC 4000 computer with an internal store of 4096 words. The system permits a number of independent programs to be executed periodically on a time-sharing basis. The first version of the system performs supervisory control of the ammonium nitrate plant Pulawy II in Poland. After a description of the Pulawy system, the choice of a time-sharing scheme and the handling of shared facilities are discussed. This is followed by an evaluation of the size and performance of the system.

1 Introduction

The multiprogramming system described in this paper was developed by Regnecentralen on contract with the Danish engineering company Haldor Topsøe. In connection with this project, Regnecentralen also developed a medium-sized computer, the RC 4000, which is specially suited for real-time control applications (Brinch Hansen 1967).

The system is implemented on the RC 4000 computer with an internal store of 4096 words (backing storage is not used). It permits a number of independent programs to be executed periodically under the real-time control of a monitor. For each program, the operator can select the start time of its first execution and the time interval between its subsequent executions. The programs are executed in a simple time-sharing scheme, in which each program in turn is allotted a small quantum of computing time. A critical feature of any multiprogramming system is the handling of shared

---

[*]P. Brinch Hansen, The RC 4000 real-time control system at Pulawy, *BIT* 7, 4 (1967), 279–288. Copyright © 1967, BIT. Reprinted by permission.

facilities. We have adopted the technique of binary semaphores suggested by E.W. Dijkstra (1965).

The first version of the system will be installed in 1967 in the ammonia nitrate plant Pulawy II, constructed by Haldor Topsøe in Poland. Here, the RC 4000 will perform regular alarm scanning, data logging, and evaluation of production and consumption figures.

In the following, we describe the supervision of the Pulawy plant in order to illustrate the requirements of a real-time control system and the difficulties of implementation. This is followed by a discussion of the time-sharing approach.

2   The RC 4000 Computer

The RC 4000 is a single-address, binary computer with typical instruction execution times from 2.5 to 5.5 microseconds. The following characteristics apply to the basic model used in the Pulawy plant.

Store: The internal store has a capacity of 4096 words. Each word contains 24 information bits, 1 parity bit, and 1 protection bit.

Registers: There are four working registers of 24 bits each. Three of these also function as index registers. The registers are addressable as the first four words of the internal store.

Addressing: Words of 24 bits and half-words of 12 bits are directly addressable. Address modification includes indexing, indirect addressing, and relative addressing.

Arithmetic: Integer arithmetic with operands of 12 and 24 bits is standard.

Input/Output: The standard data channel performs transfers of single words between low-speed devices and working registers under program control. Program execution continues while input/output operations are in progress.

Program Protection: In the RC 4000, the monitor program consists of all storage words in which the protection bits are set. A program stored in an unprotected area can neither alter nor jump to a protected area. All input/output operations as well as control of the interruption system and storage protection are handled by privileged instructions, which can only be executed within the monitor. Attempts to violate the protection system cause program interruption.

Program Interruption: The interruption system can register up to 24 signals simultaneously. These can be enabled and disabled individually. The interrupts are examined after each instruction; an enabled interrupt will transfer control from the current program to the monitor. All interrupts are disabled when the monitor is entered; they can be enabled again by a privileged instruction.

3   The Pulawy Installation

The Pulawy II plant consists of three units for the production of ammonia, nitric acid, and ammonium nitrate, respectively. The plant is operated manually under the supervision of the computer. This section describes the configuration of peripheral equipment at Pulawy.

The operator controls the operation of the system by means of a control typewriter. A paper tape reader and punch are provided for the assembly and loading of programs.

Real-time operation is controlled by two interval timers, which generate interrupts every 2.5 milliseconds and every 1 second, respectively.

The computer receives measurements from the plant in the form of 543 analog inputs and 127 digital inputs. The analog inputs are primarily measurements of temperatures, pressures, and flows expressed as voltages. The voltages are converted to decimal numbers by an analog/digital converter. The selection of input points is performed by a relay multiplexer with a switching rate of 30 points per second.

Digital inputs are discrete events registered as single bits in external registers: one type of digital input defines the status of alarm contacts in the plant; another collects single counting pulses from kilowatt-hour meters and bag-filling devices.

A digital output register controls a display panel that shows the operator in which part of the plant alarm conditions exist.

Regular alarm reports and log reports are printed on two strip printers and two typewriters.

4   Process Control Tasks

The computer examines the analog and digital inputs at regular intervals and produces balance evaluation reports, log reports, and alarm reports.

Balance Evaluation: Every 8 hours, a report on 135 material balances is printed on one of the log typewriters. This report shows the consumption of electricity and production of ammonium nitrate during the period. It also includes an evaluation of the total inflow and outflow of materials such as natural gas, steam, ammonia, and nitric acid. The information for this report is measured as follows: the digital pulses are input every second and accumulated in a table in the internal store; the analog flow values are measured every 5 minutes and accumulated in another table.

Data Logging: Every hour, two reports, each on approximately 275 analog values and 35 pulse counts, are printed simultaneously on the log typewriters. The log reports can be regarded as a snapshot of the operating state of the plant: the first report contains all data from the ammonia unit; the second covers the nitric acid and ammonium nitrate units.

Alarm Scanning: Every 5 minutes, the computer examines the state of 61 alarm contacts; at the same time, 188 analog variables are scanned and checked against alarm limits stored in a table. The operator is warned of alarm conditions by visible lamps and the printing of alarm messages on the strip printers.

Trend Logging: The operator can at any time request regular trend logging of a single analog variable on the strip printers.

Self-Checking: In the event of a computer malfunction, the plant can still be controlled manually while the system is being repaired. The computer must however be able to detect and report such malfunction; accordingly, in idle interals the computer performs checking of the instruction logic, the registers, the adder, and the analog/digital converter.

Operator Control: The operator can at any time type a command to the system on the control typewriter. The main options available to the operator are: selection of the start time and period of each process control task; exclusion of analog and digital inputs from one or more production lines; changing of scale factors and alarm limits of analog inputs; and selection of alternative output devices for the printing of balance and log reports.

5   Multiprogramming Approach

The table below summarizes the control tasks at Pulawy and their real-time requirements:

Task	Normal period	Completion time
Operator control	–	infinite
Pulse integration	1 second	2 milliseconds
Flow integration	5 minutes	10 seconds
Balance evaluation	8 hours	2.5 minutes
Data logging 1	1 hour	2.0 minutes
Data logging 2	1 hour	1.5 minutes
Alarm scanning	5 minutes	15 seconds
Trend logging	–	1 second
Self-checking	–	infinite

In the following discussion, it is important to note that several of the tasks use the same peripheral equipment: the analog/digital converter is used in all tasks except operator control and pulse integration; the log typewriters are shared in balance evaluation and data logging; the strip printers are used in both alarm scanning and trend logging.

From this description of the supervision of the Pulawy plant, we can draw a number of conclusions about the implementation of the real-time control system. We have a single computer that must perform a number of independent tasks, each with its own real-time requirements. The tasks are executed cyclically in periods determined by the operator. We have chosen to implement the tasks as separate programs, because they have individual and variable periods of execution. It is obvious, however, that we cannot fulfill the real-time requirements by executing one task program at a time: two task programs may well demand to be started at the same time; the time required for a single execution of a task program may also be longer than the time interval between successive executions of other task programs. Thus we are forced to introduce a multiprogramming scheme in which the computer performs rapid time-multiplexing among the task programs.

Ease of implementation requires that a task program can be programmed in as straightforward manner as in purely sequential programming; accordingly, time-sharing among task programs must be handled automatically by a monitor program activated regularly by interrupts from a clock.

For the sake of generality and simplicity, the individual task programs must be regarded as being independent of one another. In particular, we do not wish to impose any restrictions on the relative timing of programs. The operator must have complete freedom to change the frequency of task executions individually. He must even be able to stop one or more tasks completely for a period of time. The main problem introduced by this freedom is to find a general way to avoid conflicts about facilities shared among the task programs.

The solution to these problems is considered in the following sections.

6   Real-time Scheduling

The choice of a multiprogramming scheme must be based on the knowledge of the computing capacity required in worst-case situations. In a heavily loaded system, it may be necessary to establish a system of priorities among the task programs to ensure that the most urgent tasks are completed first. A simple estimate of the system load at Pulawy convinced us that a priority scheme would place unnecessary restrictions on the system. First, we have no backing store to slow down the execution of programs. Second, the majority of the tasks are limited by low-speed devices with input/output times of from 35 milliseconds (analog input) to 70 milliseconds (typewriter output). The programs use less than 1 millisecond each to process an input word or produce an output word; that is to say, a task program uses only 1/70 to 1/35 of the computing time. With only nine task programs, the load is so light that we can afford to serve all programs on equal terms.

The real-time operation of the monitor is controlled by an interval timer, which causes a program interruption every second. The monitor increments a clock counter by one, and examines a table defining the start time and period of each task program. If real-time exceeds the scheduled start time of a program, a flag bit is set and the start time is increased by the value of the period. When the scan of the time table is completed, the interrupted task program is resumed.

Time-sharing among active task programs is controlled by another interval timer as follows: every 2.5 milliseconds, the current task program is interrupted and the contents of the working registers and instruction counter are stored in a dump table. The monitor scans the flag bits cyclically until it finds another active task program, which is then started. After another 2.5 milliseconds, control is transferred to a third program, and so on.

When a task program is finished, it calls the monitor asking it to turn its flag bit off, after which the program does not receive computing time until the next scheduled run.

Switching from one task program to another is also performed, whenever a program must wait for the completion of an input/output operation or whenever a common facility is occupied by another program. Here the restart address in the dump table is adjusted to make the task program repeat the call of the input/output procedure or the reservation procedure the next time it receives a time quantum. Thus the monitor is relieved of having to keep track of queues of shared facilities.

The selection of a time quantum was influenced by the following considerations. The quantum had to be at least as great as the average response time required by a task program for a single input/output operation. At Pulawy this was about 1 millisecond. The upper limit was determined by the number of programs using the whole time quantum for computing. Too large a quantum would slow down the task programs limited by input/output, and thus degrade the performance of the low-speed devices. At Pulawy, the self-checking program was the only one of this type. Experiments showed that a time quantum 2–3 milliseconds resulted in the shortest completion time for all task programs.

7 Shared Facilities

We shall now consider the problem of mutual exclusion that arises, whenever two or more independent programs demand access to a common facility. Our understanding of this problem has been profoundly influenced by the monograph of E.W. Dijkstra (1965), *Cooperating Sequential Processes*. In the following we discuss his technique of binary semaphores as applied to our system.

The task programs at Pulawy can be regarded as independent programs, in as much they do not depend on explicit knowledge of one another's structures and speed ratios. The programs communicate with one another only for short intervals to ensure mutual exclusion from shared facilities. This communication implies inspection of and assignment to common booleans, called binary semaphores. Each semaphore is associated with a shared facility. It has the value zero if the facility is available, and one if it is busy.

When a program wishes to reserve a facility, it must inspect the corresponding semaphore. If the facility is available, the program will immediately occupy it by assigning the value one to the semaphore; otherwise the program must wait until the facility has been released. In the RC 4000 computer, this reservation can be made by the following sequence of instructions:

```
RESERVE:    LOAD, SEMAPHORE
            SKIP IF EQUAL TO, 0
            JUMP TO, RESERVE
            LOAD ADDRESS, 1
            STORE, SEMAPHORE
```

Consider now the case where program A is inspecting a semaphore. It may happen that the program is interrupted after the loading of the semaphore, but before inspection and assignment to it. The working register containing the value of the semaphore is then stored in the dump table within the monitor, and program B is started. B may load the same semaphore and find that the facility if available. Accordingly, B assigns the value one to the semaphore and starts using the facility. After a while B is interrupted, and at some later time A is restarted with the original contents of the working registers reestablished from the dump table. Program A continues the inspection of the original value of the semaphore and concludes erroneously that the facility is available.

This conflict arises because the task programs have no control over the interrupt system. The only indivisible operations available to the task programs are single instructions such as load, compare, and store. The reservation sequence can, however, be made an indivisible entity by incorporating it in the monitor program. The monitor is protected in the store and can only be called by a task program by provoking a program interruption (for example by executing a privileged instruction). This will transfer control to the monitor, with the interrupt system disabled. The monitor is now able to perform any sequence of instructions as an indivisible entity, before it reenables the interrupt system.

In our system, all semaphores are implemented as bits in a single storage word. The monitor can perform two primitive operations on the semaphores. The reservation procedure (called P by Dijkstra) examines a number of semaphores, selected by a mask, in parallel. If they are all zero, their values are changed to one, and a return is made to the calling program. If some of them are ones, the current task program is interrupted and another task program is started. When the interrupted program receives a new quantum of computing time, it repeats the call of the P procedure.

The releasing procedure (called V) sets a number of semaphores to zero, and starts another task program. The transfer of control is necessary to prevent a task program from monopolizing a facility. Most of the programs perform cyclic reservations of the same facility in the following way:

Program A: P(semaphore);
             critical section;
             comment: common facility reserved by A;
             V(semaphore);
             remainder of cycle;
             goto Program A;

At Pulawy, the probability of program A being interrupted in the remainder of the cycle before the next reservation is roughly equal to the execution time of about 100 instructions divided by the time quantum, i.e. 500 μsec/2.5 msec = 1/5. Thus program switching on the V function is vital for ensuring that the programs receive access to common facilities on equal terms.

In our system 13 semaphores are associated with common data tables, procedures, and input/output devices.

Two semaphores prevent the pulse and flow integration programs from updating the tables of integrated data, while they are used by the balance evaluation program.

To avoid a duplication of code, a number of procedures are shared by all task programs. They perform the control typewriter input/output and the input and conversion of analog values to proper engineering units. A shared procedure executes a normal P function on entry, and a modified V operation on exit. This V function ensures that the release of the procedure and the return jump are made an indivisible entity.

The remainder of the semaphores are associated with the log typewriters, the strip printers, and the paper tape punch.

8   Size and Performance

The time-sharing monitor and the process control programs for Pulawy were designed, programmed, and tested in 18 man-months. The size of the programs and the data tables are as follows:

	Words
Monitor	410
Common procedures	940
Operator control program	400
Pulse integration program	45
Flow integration program	45
Balance evaluation program	415
Log program 1	55
Log program 2	55
Alarm scan program	110
Trend log program	25
Self-check program	215
Data description tables	1000
Data integration tables	300
Total system	4015

The real-time performance of the multiprogramming system has been evaluated by measuring the execution times obtained by sequential and time-shared execution of the task programs. In the sequential run-mode, the computer executes one task program at a time. In the time-sharing mode, all task programs were executed simultaneously to obtain worst-case figures.

	Sequential execution (seconds)	Time-shared execution (seconds)
Pulse integration program	< 1	< 1
Flow integration program	9	21
Alarm scan program	13	32
Log program 2	94	105
Log program 1	120	128
Balance evaluation program	147	153
Operator control program	infinite	infinite
Self-check program	infinite	infinite

The log and balance evaluation programs are mainly limited by the speed of the typewriters. The multiprogramming system makes it possible to run these at 90–96 percent of their maximum speed.

The bottleneck of the system is the analog/digital converter. At present, this device is shared in a sequential maner among the flow, alarm, and log programs. The scanning rate of flows and alarms thus drops to 41–43 percent of the maximum speed.

In a system with a bigger internal store, this could have been improved by introducing another task program that would scan the analog variables and store them in a table, say, every five minutes. The other task programs would then reference this table instead of repeating the analog measurements.

Acknowledgements

The design of the time-sharing monitor for Pulawy is the work of Peter Kraft and the author. Later, we were joined by Karoly Simonyi, Jr., who contributed valuable ideas to the project and did the programming along with Peter Kraft. We are indebted to John Saietz of Haldor Topsøe for his continuous support in the specification of the process control tasks.

References

Brinch Hansen, P. 1967. The logical structure of the RC 4000 computer. *BIT 7*, 3, 191–199.

Dijkstra, E.W. 1965. Cooperating sequential processes. Technological University, Eindhoven, The Netherlands, (September).

2

The Nucleus of a
Multiprogramming System*

(1970)

This paper describes the philosophy and structure of a multiprogramming system that can be extended with a hierarchy of operating systems to suit diverse requirements of program scheduling and resource allocation. The system nucleus simulates an environment in which program execution and input/output are handled uniformly as parallel, cooperating processes. A fundamental set of primitives allows the dynamic creation and control of a hierarchy of processes as well as the communication among them.

1 Introduction

The multiprogramming system developed by Regnecentralen for the RC 4000 computer is a general tool for the design of operating systems. It allows the dynamic creation of a hierarchy of processes in which diverse strategies of program scheduling and resource allocation can be implemented.

For the designer of advanced information systems, a vital requirement of any operating system is that it allow him to change the mode of operation it controls; otherwise his freedom of design can be seriously limited. Unfortunately, this is precisely what present operating systems do not allow. Most of them are based exclusively on a single mode of operation, such as batch processing, priority scheduling, real-time scheduling, or conversational access.

When the need arises, the user often finds it hopeless to modify an operating system that has made rigid assumptions in its basic design about a

---

*P. Brinch Hansen, The nucleus of a multiprogramming system, *Communications of the ACM 13*, 4 (April 1970), 238–242. Copyright © 1970, Association for Computing Machinery, Inc. Reprinted by permission.

specific mode of operation. The alternative—to replace the original operating system with a new one—is in most computers a serious, if not impossible, matter because the rest of the software is intimately bound to the conventions required by the original system.

This unfortunate situation indicates that the main problem in the design of a multiprogramming system is not to define functions that satisfy specific operating needs, but rather to supply a system nucleus that can be extended with new operating systems in an orderly manner. This is the primary objective of the RC 4000 system.

In the following, the philosophy and structure of the RC 4000 multiprogramming system is explained. The discussion does not include details of implementation; size and performance are presented, however, to give an idea of the feasibility of this approach. The functional specifications of the multiprogramming system are described in detail in a report (Brinch Hansen 1969a) available from Regnecentralen.

2   System Nucleus

Our basic attitude during the designing was to make no assumptions about the particular strategy needed to optimize a given type of installation, but to concentrate on the fundamental aspects of the control of an environment consisting of parallel, cooperating processes.

Our first task was to assign a precise meaning to the process concept, i.e. to introduce an unambiguous terminology defining what a process is and how it is implemented on the actual computer.

The next step was to select primitives for the synchronization and transfer of information among parallel processes.

Our final decisions concerned the rules for the dynamic creation, control, and removal of processes.

The purpose of the system nucleus is to implement these fundamental concepts: simulation of processes; communication among processes; creation, control, and removal of processes.

3   Processes

We distinguish between internal and external processes, roughly corresponding to program execution and input/output.

More precisely, an *internal process* is the execution of one or more interruptable programs in a given storage area. An internal process is identified by a unique process name. Thus other processes need not be aware of the actual location of an internal process in the store, but can refer to it by name.

A sharp distinction is made between the concepts program and internal process. A *program* is a collection of instructions describing a computational process, whereas an internal process is the execution of these instructions in a given storage area.

In connection with input/output, the system distinguishes between peripheral devices, documents, and external processes.

A *peripheral device* is an item of hardware connected to the data channel and identified by a device number. A *document* is a collection of data stored on a physical medium, such as a deck of punched cards, a printer form, a reel of magnetic tape, or a file on the backing store.

An *external process* is the input/output of a given document identified by a unique process name. This concept implies that internal processes can refer to documents by name without knowing the actual devices on which they are mounted.

Multiprogramming and communication between internal and external processes is coordinated by the system nucleus—an interrupt response program with complete control of input/output, storage protection, and the interrupt system. We do not regard the system nucleus as an independent process, but rather as a software extension of the hardware structure, which makes the computer more attractive for multiprogramming. Its function is to implement our process concept and primitives that processes can invoke to create and control other processes and communicate with them.

So far we have described the multiprogramming system as a set of independent, parallel processes identified by names. The emphasis has been on a clear understanding of relationships among resources (store and peripherals), data (programs and documents), and processes (internal and external).

4   Process Communication

In a system of parallel, cooperating processes, mechanisms must be provided for the synchronization of two processes during a transfer of information.

Dijkstra (1965) has demonstrated that indivisible lock and unlock operations operating on binary semaphores are sufficient primitives from a logical point of view. We have been forced to conclude, however, that the sema-phore concept alone does not fulfill our requirements of safety and efficiency in a dynamic environment in which some processes may turn out to be black sheep and break the rules of the game.

Instead we have introduced message buffering within the system nucleus as the basic means of process communication. The system nucleus adminis-ters a common pool of *message buffers* and a *message queue* for each process.

The following primitives are available for communication between inter-nal processes:

> send message(receiver, message, buffer),
> wait message(sender, message, buffer),
> send answer(result, answer, buffer),
> wait answer(result, answer, buffer).

Send message copies a message into the first available buffer within the pool and delivers it in the queue of a named receiver. The receiver is acti-vated if it is waiting for a message. The sender continues after being informed of the identity of the message buffer.

Wait message delays the requesting process until a message arrives in its queue. When the process is allowed to proceed, it is supplied with the name of the sender, the contents of the message, and the identity of the message buffer. The buffer is removed from the queue and made ready to transmit an answer.

Send answer copies an answer into a buffer in which a message has been received and delivers it in the queue of the original sender. The sender of the message is activated if it is waiting for the answer. The answering process continues immediately.

Wait answer delays the requesting process until an answer arrives in a given buffer. On arrival, the answer is copied into the process and the buffer is returned to the pool. The result specifies whether the answer is a response from another process or a dummy answer generated by the system nucleus in response to a message addressed to a nonexisting process.

The procedure wait message forces a process to serve its queue on a first-come, first-served basis. The system, however, also includes two primitives that enable a process to wait for the arrival of the next message or answer and serve its queue in any order.

This communication system has the following advantages.

The multiprogramming system is dynamic in the sense that processes appear and disappear at any time. Therefore a process does not in general have a complete knowledge of the existence of other processes. This is reflected in the procedure wait message, which makes it possible for a process to be unaware of the existence of other processes until it receives messages from them.

On the other hand, once a communication has been established between two processes (i.e. by means of a message) they need a common identification of it in order to agree on when it is terminated (i.e. by means of an answer). Thus we can properly regard the selection of a buffer as the creation of an identification of a conversation. A happy consequence of this is that it enables two processes to exchange more than one message at a time.

We must be prepared for the occurrence of erroneous or malicious processes in the system (e.g. undebugged programs). This is tolerable only if the system nucleus ensures that no process can interfere with a conversation between two other processes. This is done by storing the identity of the sender and receiver in each buffer and checking it whenever a process attempts to send or wait for an answer in a given buffer.

Efficiency is obtained by the queueing of buffers, which enables a sending process to continue immediately after delivery of a message or an answer, regardless of whether or not the receiver is ready to process it.

To make the system dynamic, it is vital that a process can be removed at any time, even if it is engaged in one or more conversations. In this case, the system nucleus leaves all messages from the removed process undisturbed in the queues of other processes. When these processes answer them, the system nucleus returns the buffers to the common pool.

The reverse situation is also possible: during the removal of a process, the system nucleus finds unanswered messages sent to the process. These are returned as dummy answers to the senders.

The main drawback of message buffering is that it introduces yet another resource problem, since the common pool contains a finite number of buffers. If a process were allowed to empty the pool by sending messages to ignorant processes, which do not respond with answers, further communication within the system would be blocked. Consequently a limit is set to the number of messages a process can send simultaneously. By doing this, and by allowing a process to transmit an answer in a received buffer, we have placed the entire risk of a conversation on the process that opens it.

5   External Processes

Originally the communication primitives were designed for the exchange of messages between internal processes.   Later we also decided to use *send message* and *wait answer* for communication between internal and external processes.

For each kind of external process, the system nucleus contains a piece of code that interprets a message from an internal process and initiates input/output using a storage area specified in the message. When input/output is terminated by an interrupt, the nucleus generates an answer to the internal process with information about actual block size and possible error conditions. This is essentially the implementation of the external process concept.

We consider it to be an important aspect of the system that internal and external processes are handled uniformly as independent, self-contained processes. The difference between them is merely a matter of processing capability. A consequence of this is that any external process can be replaced by an internal process of the same name if more complex criteria of access and response become desirable.

External processes are created on request from internal processes. *Creation* is simply the assignment of a name to a particular peripheral device. To guarantee internal processes exclusive access to sequential documents, primitives are available for the *reservation* and *release* of external processes.

Typewriter consoles are the only external processes that can send messages to internal processes. The operator opens a conversation by pushing an interrupt key and typing the name of the internal receiver followed by a line of text.

A file on the backing store can be used as an external process by copying a description of the file from a catalog on the backing store into the system nucleus; following this, internal processes can initiate input/output by sending messages to the file process.

Real-time synchronization of internal processes is obtained by sending messages to a clock process. After the elapse of a time interval specified in the message, the clock returns an answer to the sending process.

In general, external processes can be used to obtain synchronization between internal processes and any signal from the external world. For example, an internal process may send a message to a watchdog process and receive an answer when a magnetic tape is mounted on a station. In response, the internal process can give the station a temporary name, identify the tape by reading its label, and rename the station accordingly.

6   Internal Processes

A final set of primitives in the system nucleus allows the creation, control, and removal of internal processes.

Internal processes are created on request from other internal processes. *Creation* involves the assignment of a name to a contiguous storage area selected by the parent process. The storage area must be within the parent's own area.

After creation, the parent process can load a program into the child process and *start* it. The child process now shares computing time with other active processes including the parent process.

On request from a parent process, the system nucleus waits for the completion of all input/output initiated by a child process and *stops* it. In the stopped state, the process can still receive messages and answers in its queue. These can be served when the process is restarted.

Finally, a parent process can *remove* a child process in order to assign its storage area to other processes.

According to our philosophy, processes should have complete freedom to choose their own strategy of program scheduling. The system nucleus only supplies the essential primitives for initiation and control of processes. Consequently, the concepts of program loading and swapping are not part of the nucleus. Time-sharing of a common storage area among children on a swapping basis is possible, however, because the system does not check whether internal processes overlap each other as long as they remain within the storage areas of their parents. Swapping from process A to process B can be implemented in a parent process as follows: stop(A); output(A); input(B); start(B).

7   Process Hierarchy

The idea of the system nucleus has been described as the simulation of an environment in which program execution and input/output are handled uniformly as parallel, cooperating processes. A fundamental set of primitives allows the dynamic creation and control of processes as well as communication among them.

For a given installation we still need, as part of the system, programs that control strategies of operator communication, program scheduling, and resource allocation; but it is essential for the orderly growth of the system that these *operating systems* be implemented as other programs. Since the difference between operating systems and production programs is one of jurisdiction only, this problem is solved by arranging the internal processes in a *hierarchy* in which parent processes have complete control over child processes.

After initial loading, the internal store contains the system nucleus and a basic operation system, S, which can create parallel processes, A, B, C, etc., on request from consoles. The processes can in turn create other processes, D, E, F, etc. Thus while S acts as a primitive operating system for A, B, and C, these in turn act as operating systems for their children, D, E, and F. This is illustrated by Fig. 1, which shows a family tree of processes on the left and the corresponding storage allocation on the right. This family tree of processes can be extended to any level, subject only to a limitation of the total number of processes.

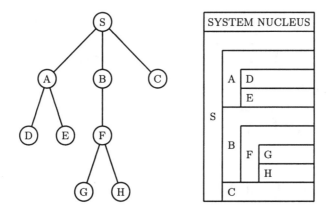

Figure 1 Process tree and storage allocation.

In this multiprogramming system, all privileged functions are implemented in the system nucleus, which has no built-in strategy. Strategies can be introduced at the various higher levels, where each process has the power to control the scheduling and resource allocation of its children. The only rules enforced by the nucleus are the following: A process can only allocate a subset of its own resources (including storage and message buffers) to its children; a process can only start, stop, and remove its own children (including their descendants). After removal of a process, its resources are returned to the parent process. Initially all system resources are owned by the basic operating system S. For details of process control and resource allocation, the reader should consult the manual of the system (Brinch Hansen 1969a).

We emphasize that the only function of the family tree is to define the rules of process control and resource allocation. Computing time is shared by round-robin scheduling among active processes regardless of their position in the hierarchy, and each process can communicate with all other processes.

Regarding the future development of operating systems, the most important characteristics of the system can now be seen as the following:

1. New operating systems can be implemented as other programs without modification of the system nucleus. In this connection, we should mention that the Algol and Fortran languages for the RC 4000 contain facilities for calling the nucleus and initiating parallel processes. Thus it is possible to write operating systems in high-level languages.

2. Operating systems can be replaced dynamically, thus enabling an installation to switch among various modes of operation; several operating systems can, in fact, be active simultaneously.

3. Standard programs and user programs can be executed under different operating systems without modification, provided there is common agreement on the possible communication between parents and children.

8   Implementation

The RC 4000 is a 24-bit, binary computer with typical instruction execution times of 4 microseconds (Brinch Hansen 1969b). It permits practically unlimited expansion of the internal store and standardized connection of all kinds of peripherals. Multiprogramming is facilitated by program interruption, storage protection, and privileged instructions.

The present implementation of the system makes multiprogramming feasible with a minimum store of 16K–32K words backed by a fast drum or disk. The system nucleus includes external processes for a real-time clock, typewriters, paper tape input/output, line printer, magnetic tape, and files on the backing store. The size of the nucleus and the basic operating system is as follows:

	words
primitives	2400
code for external processes	1150
process descriptions and buffers	1250
system nucleus	4800
basic operating system	1400
	6200

The communication primitives are executed in the uninterruptable mode within the system nucleus. The execution times of these set a limit to the system's response to real-time events:

	msec
send message	0.6
wait answer	0.4
wait message	0.4
send answer	0.6

An analysis shows that the 2 milliseconds required by a complete conversation (the sum of the four primitives) are used as follows:

	percent
validity checking	25
process activation	45
message buffering	30

This distribution is so even that one cannot hope to increase the speed of the system by introducing additional, ad hoc machine instructions. The only realistic solution is to make the hardware faster.

The primitives for creation, start, stop, and removal of processes are implemented in an anonymous internal process within the system nucleus to avoid intolerably long periods in the uninterruptable mode. Typical execution times for these are:

	msec
create process	3
start process	26
stop process	4
remove process	30

The excessive times for the start and removal of an internal process are due to the peculiar storage protection system of the RC 4000, which requires the setting of a protection key in every storage word of a process.

9   Conclusion

Ideas similar to those described here have been suggested by others (Harrison 1967; Huxtable 1967; Wichmann 1968). We have presented our system because we feel that, taken as a whole, it represents a systematic and practical approach to the design of replaceable operating systems. As an inspiration to other designers, it is perhaps most important that it illustrates a sequence of design steps leading to a general nucleus, namely, the definition of the process concept, the communication scheme, and the dynamic creation and structuring of processes.

We realize, of course, that a final evaluation of the system can only be made after it has been used to design a number of operating systems.

Acknowledgements

The design philosophy was developed by Jørn Jensen, Søren Lauesen, and the author. Leif Svalgaard participated in the implementation and testing of the final product.

Regarding fundamentals, we have benefited greatly from Dijkstra's analysis of cooperating sequential processes.

References

Brinch Hansen, P., Ed. 1969a. *RC 4000 Software: Multiprogramming System*. Regnecentralen, Copenhagen, Denmark, (April).

Brinch Hansen, P. Ed. 1969b. *RC 4000 Computer: Reference Manual*. Regnecentralen, Copenhagen, Denmark, (June).

Dijkstra, E.W. 1965. Cooperating sequential processes. Technological University, Eindhoven, The Netherlands, (September).

Harrison, M.C., and Schwartz, J.T. 1967. SHARER, a time sharing system for the CDC 6600. *Communications of the ACM 10*, 10 (October), 659–665.

Huxtable, D.H.R., and Warwick, M.T. 1967. Dynamic supervisors—their design and construction. *ACM Symposium on Operating System Principles*, Gatlinburg, TN, (October).

Wichmann, B.A. 1968. A modular operating system. *Proceedings of the IFIP Congress 68*, Edinburgh, United Kingdom. North Holland, Amsterdam, The Netherlands, 1969, 548–556.

3

An Outline of a Course on Operating System Principles[*]

(1971)

In 1970 the author began writing a comprehensive textbook on operating system principles. This is a description of its structure and how far it had progressed a year later.

Computer Science and Operating Systems

In November 1970 I began writing a textbook on operating system principles at Carnegie-Mellon University. This is a description of its structure and how far it has progressed.

The goal is to give students of computer science and professional programmers a general understanding of operating systems. The only background required is an understanding of the basic structure of computers and programming languages and some practical experience in writing and testing non-trivial programs. In a few cases a knowledge of elementary calculus and probability theory is also needed. The components of the course are well-known to a small group of designers, but most operating systems reveal an inadequate understanding of them.

The first and most obvious problem is to delimit the subject and consider its place in computer science education. I define an *operating system* as a set of manual and automatic procedures which enable a group of users to share a computer system efficiently. The keyword in this definition is *sharing*: it means competetion for the use of physical resources but also cooperation among users exchanging programs and data on the same computer system.

---

[*]P. Brinch Hansen, An outline of a course on operating system principles. In *Operating Systems Techniques*, Proceedings of a Seminar at Queen's University, Belfast, Northern Ireland, August–September 1971. C.A.R. Hoare and R.H. Perrott, Eds. Academic Press, New York (1972), 29–36. Copyright © 1972, Academic Press. Reprinted by permission.

All shared computer systems must *schedule* user computations in some order, *protect* them against one each other, and give them means of *long-term storage* of programs and data. They must also perform *accounting* of the cost of computing and *measure* the actual performance of the system.

In early computer systems, operators carried out most of these functions, but during the last fifteen years the programs that we call operating systems have gradually taken over these aspects of sharing.

Although most components of present computers are sequential in nature, they can work simultaneously to some extent. This influences the design of operating systems so much that the subject can best be described as the *management of shared multiprogramming systems.*

Operating systems are large programs developed and used by a changing group of people. They are often modified considerably during their lifetime. Operating systems must necessarily impose certain restrictions on all users. But this should not lead us to regard them as being radically different from other programs. They are just examples of large programs based on fundamental principles of computer science. The proper aim of education is to identify these fundamentals.

The student should realize that principles and methods of resource sharing have a general utility that goes beyond operating systems. Any large programming effort will be heavily influenced by the presence of several levels of storage, by the possibility of executing smaller tasks independently, and by the need for sharing a common set of data among such tasks. We find it convenient to distinguish between operating systems and user computations because the former can *enforce* certain rules of behavior on the latter. It is important, however, to realize that each level of programming solves some aspect of resource allocation.

I argue therefore that the study of operating systems leads to the recognition of general principles which should be taught as part of a core of computer science. Assuming that the student has an elementary background in *programming languages, data structures* and *computer organization,* the course concentrates on the following areas of computer science: *concurrent computations, resource sharing* and *program construction.*

Let us look at the course in some detail. It consists of eight parts which are summarized in the Appendix. The following is a more informal presentation of its basic attitude.

Technological Background

The necessity of controlling access to shared computer systems automatically is made clear by simple arguments about the poor utilization of equipment in an *open shop* operated by the users themselves, one at a time. As a first step in this direction, I describe the classical *batch processing system* which carries out computations on a main computer while a smaller computer prepares and prints magnetic tapes. The strict sequential nature of the processors and their backing storage in this early scheme made it necessary to prevent human interaction with computations and schedule them in their order of arrival inside a batch.

These restrictions on scheduling disappear to some extent with the introduction of multiprogramming techniques and large backing stores with random access. This is illustrated by two simple operating systems: the first one is a *spooling system* which handles a continuous stream of input, computation and output on a multiprogrammed computer with drum storage; the other is an *interactive system* in which main storage is shared cyclically among several computations requested from remote terminals.

Through a chain of simple arguments the student gradually learns to appreciate the influence of *technological constraints* on the service offered by operating systems.

The Similarity of Operating Systems

The main theme of the course is the similarity of problems faced by all operating systems. To mention one example: all shared computer systems must handle concurrent activities at some level. Even if a system only schedules one computation at a time, users can still make their requests simultaneously. This problem can, of course, be solved by the users themselves (forming a waiting line) and by the operators (writing down requests on paper). But the observation is important, since our goal is to handle the problems of sharing automatically.

It is also instructive to compare a batch processing and a spooling system. Both achieve high efficiency by means of concurrent activities: in a batch processing system independent programs work together; in a spooling system a single processor switches among independent programs. Both systems use backing storage (tape and drum) as a buffer to compensate for speed variations between the producers and consumers of data.

As another example, consider real-time systems for process control or conversational interaction. In these systems, concurrent processes must be able to exchange data in order to cooperate on common tasks. But again, this problem exists in all shared computer systems: in a spooling system user computations exchange data with concurrent input/output processes; and in a batch processing system we have another set of concurrent processes which exchange data by means of tapes mounted by operators.

So I find that all operating systems face a common set of problems. To recognize these we must reject the established classification of operating systems into batch processing, time sharing, and real time systems which stresses the dissimilarities of various forms of technology and user service. This does not mean that the problems of adjusting an operating system to the constraints of a certain environment are irrelevant. But the students will solve them much better when they have grasped the underlying common principles.

You will also look in vain for chapters on input/output and filing systems. For a particular operating system considerations about how these problems are handled are highly relevant; but again I have concentrated on the more elementary problems involved in these complicated tasks, namely, process synchronization, storage management and resource protection.

Sequential and Concurrent Computations

After this introduction, the nature of computations is described. A *computation* is a set of operations applied to a set of data in order to solve a problem. The operations must be carried out in a certain order to ensure that the results of some of them can be used by others. In a *sequential process* operations are carried out strictly one at a time. But most of our computational problems only require a partial ordering of operations in time: some operations must be carried out before others, but many of them can be carried out concurrently.

The main obstacles to the utilization of concurrency in computer systems are economy and human imagination. Sequential processes can be carried out cheaply by repeated use of simple equipment; concurrent computations require duplicated equipment and time-consuming synchronization of operations. Human beings find it extremely difficult to comprehend the combined effect of a large number of activities which evolve simultaneously with independent rates. In contrast, our understanding of a sequential process is independent of its actual speed of execution. All that matters is that operations are carried out one at a time with finite speed, and that certain relations hold between the data before and after each operation.

So sequential processes closely mirror our thinking habits, but a computer system is utilized better when its various parts operate concurrently. As a compromise, we try to partition our problems into a moderate number of sequential activities which can be programmed separately and then combined for concurrent execution. These processes are *loosely connected* in the sense that they can proceed simultaneously with arbitrary rates except for short intervals when they exchange data.

After a brief review of methods of structuring data and sequential programs, I consider the synchronizing requirements of *concurrent processes*. It is shown that the results of concurrent processes which share data cannot be predicted unless some operations exclude each other in time. Operations which have this property are called *critical regions*. Mutual exclusion can be controlled by a data structure, called a *semaphore*, consisting of a boolean, defining whether any process is inside its critical region, and a queue, containing the set of processes waiting to enter their regions.

A critical region is one example of a timing constraint or *synchronization* imposed on concurrent processes. Synchronization is also needed when some processes produce data which are consumed by other processes. The simplest *input/output relationship* is the exchange of *timing signals* between processes. The constraint here is that signals cannot be received faster than they are sent. This relationship can be represented by an integer semaphore accessed by *signal* and *wait* operations only.

Realistic *communication* between processes requires the exchange of data structures. This problem can be solved by synchronizing primitives operating on semaphores and data structures which are accessible to all the processes involved. It is tempting to conclude that critical regions, common data, and wait and signal operations are the proper concepts to include in a programming language. Experience shows that the slightest mistake in the use of these tools can result in erroneous programs which are practically impossible to correct because their behavior is influenced by external factors in a time-dependent, irreproducible manner.

A more adequate solution is to include *message buffers* as primitive data structures in the programming language and make them accessible only through well-defined *send* and *receive* operations. The crucial point of this language feature is that storage containing shared data (messages) is ac-

cessible to at most one process at a time. It has been proved that when
a set of smaller systems with time-independent behavior are connected by
means of message buffers only, the resulting system can also be made time-
independent in behavior.

The most general form of process interaction is one in which a process
must be delayed until another process has ensured that certain relationships
hold between the components of a shared data structure. This form of
synchronization can be expressed directly by means of *conditional critical
regions*.

The conceptual simplicity of simple and conditional critical regions is
achieved by ignoring the sequence in which waiting processes enter these
regions. This abstraction is unrealistic for heavily used resources. In such
cases, the operating system must be able to identify competing processes
and control the scheduling of resources among them. This can be done by
means of a *monitor*—a set of shared procedures which can delay and activate
individual processes and perform operations on shared data.

Finally, I consider the problems of *deadlocks* and their prevention by
hierarchical ordering of process interactions.

Resource Management

Most of the previous concepts are now widely used. Far more controversial
are the problems of how abstract computations are represented and man-
aged on physical systems with limited resources. At first sight, problems
caused by the physical constraints of computers seem to be of secondary
importance to the computational problems we are trying to solve. But in
practice most programming efforts are dominated by technological problems
and will continue to be so. It will always be economically attractive to share
resources among competing computations, use several levels of storage, and
accept occasional hardware malfunction.

It seems unrealistic to look for a unifying view of how different kinds of
technology are used efficiently. The student should realize that these issues
can only be understood in economic terms. What we can hope to do is to
describe the circumstances under which certain techniques will work well.

The implementation of the process concept is considered in two chapters
on *processor multiplexing* and *storage organization*. The first of these describes the representation of processes and scheduling queues at the lowest
level of programming and the implementation of synchronizing primitives.

Hardware registers, clocks and interrupts are treated as technological tools which in many cases can be replaced by more appropriate concepts at higher levels of programming. The second of these chapters discusses the compromises between associative and location-dependent addressing, and the dynamic allocation of fixed and variable-length data structures in storage with one or more levels.

Following this, I discuss the influence of various *scheduling algorithms*: first-come first-served, shortest job next, highest response ratio next, round robin, and so on, on the behavior of the system in terms of average response times to user request.

A Case Study

At the end of the course, the conceptual framework is used to describe an existing operating system in depth using a consistent terminology.

I have selected the RC 4000 multiprogramming system (Brinch Hansen 1970) as a case study, because it is the only one I know in detail, and is a small, consistent design which illustrates essential ideas of concurrent processes, message communication, scheduling and resource protection.

The Choice of a Description Language

So far nearly all operating systems have been written partly or completely in machine language. This makes then unnecessarily difficult to understand, test and modify. I believe it is desirable and possible to write efficient operating systems almost entirely in a *high-level language*. This language must permit *hierarchal structuring* of data and program, extensive *error checking* at compile time, and production of *efficient machine code*.

To support this belief, I have used the programming language *Pascal* (Wirth 1971) throughout the text to define operating system concepts concisely by algorithms. Pascal combines the clarity needed for teaching with the efficiency required for design. It is easily understood by programmers familiar with Algol 60 or Fortran, but is a far more natural tool than these for the description of operating systems because of the presence of data structures of type record, class and pointer.

At the moment, Pascal is designed for sequential programming only, but I extend it with a suitable notation for multiprogramming and resource sharing. I have illustrated the description of operating systems in Pascal elsewhere (Brinch Hansen 1971a, 1971b).

Status of the Course

I conceived the plan for the course in March 1970 and started to work on it in November 1970. Now, in November 1971, drafts have been written of parts 1–4, and 6 (see the Appendix). Most of the work on parts 5, and 7–8 remains to be done. It is unlikely that the structure of the course will change significantly, although the details certainly will.

Appendix: The Contents of the Course

1. An overview of operating systems

The purpose of an operating system. Technological background: manual scheduling, non-interactive scheduling with sequential and random access backing storage, interactive scheduling. The similarity of operating systems. Special versus general-purpose systems.

2. Sequential processes

Abstraction and structure. Data and operations. Sequential and concurrent computations. Methods of structuring data and sequential programs. Hierarchal program construction. Programming levels viewed as virtual machines. Our understanding and verification of programs.

3. Concurrent processes

Time-dependent programming errors in concurrent computations. Definition of functional behavior in terms of input/output histories. The construction of functional systems from smaller functional components. Concurrent systems with inherent time-dependent behavior: priority scheduling and shared processes.

Disjoint and interacting processes. Mutual exclusion of operations on shared data. Simple and conditional critical regions. Process communication by semaphores and message buffers. Explicit control of process scheduling by monitors.

The deadlock problem. Prevention of deadlocks by hierarchal ordering of process interactions.

4. Processor multiplexing

Short-term and medium-term scheduling. A computer system with identical processors connected to a single store. Peripheral versus central processors. Process descriptions, states and queues. Processor execution cycle. Scheduling of critical regions by means of a storage arbiter. Implementation of the scheduling primitives wait, signal, initiate and terminate process. Influence of critical regions on preemption. Processor multiplexing with static and dynamic priorities. Implementation details: hardware registers, clock, interrupts. Timing constraints.

5. Storage organization

Properties of abstract and physical storage. Methods of address mapping: searching, key transformation and base registers.

Single-level storage: fixed partitioning, dynamic allocation of fixed and variable-length data structures. Compacting and fragmentation.

Hierarchal storage: swapping, demand paging and extended storage. Locality principle. Prevention of thrashing. Placement and replacement strategies. Hardware support.

Influence of input/output, process communication, and scheduling on storage allocation.

6. Scheduling algorithms

Objectives of scheduling policies. Queueing models of user requests and computations. Performance measures. A conservation law for a class of priority scheduling algorithms.

Non-preemptive scheduling: fixed priorities, first-come first-served, shortest job next, and highest response ratio next.

Preemptive scheduling: round robin with swapping. Methods of reducing transfers between storage levels. Scheduling with performance feedback.

7. Resource protection

The concept of a process environment of shared objects. Requirements of naming and protection. Existing protection mechanisms: privileged execution state, storage protection, file systems with private and public data, user password identification, protection levels and process hierarchies.

8. A case study

A detailed analysis of the structure, size and performance of the RC 4000 multiprogramming system.

Acknowledgements

Without the encouragement of Alan Perlis this work would not have been undertaken. I am indebted to Nico Habermann, Anita Jones and Bill Wulf who read and criticized all or part of the manuscript. I learned much from discussions with Tony Hoare. It should also be mentioned that without the foundation of laid by Edsger Dijkstra (1965) we would still be unable to separate principles from their applications in operating systems. The idea of looking upon the management of shared computer systems as a general data processing problem was inspired by a smiliar attitude of Peter Naur (1966) towards program translation.

References

Brinch Hansen, P. 1970. The nucleus of a multiprogramming system. *Communications of the ACM 13*, 4 (April), 238–250. *Article 2.*

Brinch Hansen, P. 1971a. Short-term scheduling in multiprogramming systems. *3rd ACM Symposium on Operating System Principles*, Stanford University, Stanford, CA, (October), 101–105.

Brinch Hansen, P. 1971b. A comparison of two synchronizing concepts. (November). In *Acta Informatica 1*, 3 (1972), 190–199.

Dijkstra, E.W. 1965. Cooperating sequential processes. Technological University, Eindhoven, The Netherlands, (September).

Naur, P. 1966. Program translation viewed as a general data processing problem. *Communications of the ACM 9*, 3 (March), 176–179.

Wirth, N. 1971. The programming language Pascal. *Acta Informatica 1*, 1, 35–63.

4

Structured Multiprogramming*

(1972)

This paper presents a proposal for structured representation of multiprogramming in a high level language. The notation used explicitly associates a data structure shared by concurrent processes with operations defined on it. This clarifies the meaning of programs and permits a large class of time-dependent errors to be caught at compile time. A combination of critical regions and event variables enables the programmer to control scheduling of resources among competing processes to any degree desired. These concepts are sufficiently safe to use not only within operating systems but also within user programs.

1 Introduction

The failure of operating systems to provide reliable long-term service can often be explained by excessive emphasis on functional capabilities at the expense of efficient resource utilization, and by inadequate methods of program construction.

In this paper, I examine the latter cause of failure and propose a language notation for structured multiprogramming. The basic idea is to associate data shared by concurrent processes explicitly with operations defined on them. This clarifies the meaning of programs and permits a large class of time-dependent errors to be caught at compile time.

The notation is presented as an extension to the sequential programming language Pascal (Wirth 1971). It will be used in a forthcoming textbook to explain operating system principles concisely by algorithms (Brinch Hansen 1971). Similar ideas have been explored independently by Hoare. The conditional critical regions proposed in (Hoare 1971) are a special case of the ones introduced here.

---

*P. Brinch Hansen, Structured multiprogramming. *Communications of the ACM 15*, 7 (July 1972), 574–578. Copyright © 1972, Association for Computing Machinery, Inc. Reprinted by permission.

2   Disjoint Processes

Our starting point is the *concurrent statement*

$$\textbf{cobegin } S_1; \ S_2; \ \ldots; \ S_n \textbf{ coend}$$

introduced by Dijkstra (1965). This notation indicates that statements S_1, S_2, ..., S_n can be executed concurrently; when all of them are terminated, the following statement in the program (not shown here) is executed.

This restricted form of concurrency simplifies the understanding and verification of programs considerably, compared to unstructured *fork* and *join* primitives (Conway 1963).

Algorithm 1 illustrates the use of the concurrent statement to copy records from one sequential file to another.

```
var f, g: file of T;
  s, t: T; eof: Boolean;
begin
  input(f, s, eof);
  while not eof do
    begin t := s;
      cobegin
        output(g, t);
        input(f, s, eof);
      coend
    end
end
```

Algorithm 1 Copying of a sequential file.

The variables here are two sequential files, f and g, with records of type T; two buffers, s and t, holding one record each; and a Boolean, *eof*, indicating whether or not the end of the input file has been reached.

Input and output of single records are handled by two standard procedures. The algorithm inputs a record, copies it from one buffer to another, outputs it, and at the same time, inputs the next record. The copying, output, and input are repeated until the input file is empty.

Now suppose the programmer by mistake expresses the repetition as follows:

```
while not eof do
cobegin
  t := s;
  output(g, t);
  input(f, s, eof);
coend
```

The copying, output, and input of a record can now be executed concurrently. To simplify the argument, we will only consider cases in which these processes are arbitrarily *interleaved* but *not overlapped* in time. The erroneous concurrent statement can then be executed in six different ways with three possible results: (1) if copying is completed before input and output are initiated, the *correct* record will be output; (2) if output is completed before copying is initiated, the *previous* record will be output again; and (3) if input is completed before copying is initiated, and this in turn completed before output is initiated, the *next* record will be output instead.

This is just for a single record of the output file. If we copy a file of 10,000 records, the program can give of the order of $3^{10,000}$ different results!

The actual sequence of operations in time will depend on the presence of other (unrelated) computations and the (possibly time-dependent) scheduling policy of the installation. It is therefore very unlikely that the programmer will ever observe the same result twice. The only hope of locating the error is to study the program text. This can be very frustrating (if not impossible) when it consists of thousands of lines and one has no clues about where to look.

Multiprogramming is an order of magnitude more hazardous than sequential programming unless we ensure that the results of our computations are *reproducible in spite of errors*. In the previous example, this can easily be checked at compile time.

In the correct version of Algorithm 1, the output and input processes operate on disjoint sets of variables (g, t) and (f, s, eof). They are called *disjoint* or *noninteracting processes*.

In the erroneous version of the algorithm, the processes are not disjoint: the output process refers to a variable t changed by the copying process; and the latter refers to a variable s changed by the input process.

This can be detected at compile time if the following rule is adopted: a concurrent statement defines disjoint processes $S_1, S_2, \ldots, S_n$ which can be executed concurrently. This means that a variable v_i changed by statement S_i cannot be referenced by another statement S_j (where $j \neq i$). In other words, we insist that a variable subject to change by a process must be strictly *private* to that process; but disjoint processes can refer to *shared* variables not changed by any of them.

Throughout this paper, I tacitly assume that sequential statements and assertions made about them only refer to variables which are *accessible* to the statements according to the rules of disjointness and mutual exclusion. The latter rule will be defined in Section 3.

Violations of these rules must be detected at compile time and prevent execution. To enable a compiler to check the disjointness of processes the language must have the following property: it must be possible by simple inspection of a statement to distinguish between its constant and variable parameters. I will not discuss the influence of this requirement on language design beyond mentioning that it makes unrestricted use of *pointers* and *side-effects* unacceptable.

The rule of disjointness is due to Hoare (1971). It makes the *axiomatic property* of a concurrent statement S very simple: if each component statement S_i terminates with a result R_i provided a predicate P_i holds before its execution then the combined effect of S is the following:

$$\text{``}P\text{''} \ S \ \text{``}R\text{''}$$

where

$$P \equiv P_1 \ \& \ P_2 \ \& \ \cdots \ \& \ P_n$$
$$R \equiv R_1 \ \& \ R_2 \ \& \ \cdots \ \& \ R_n$$

As Hoare puts it: "Each S_i makes its contribution to the common goal."

3 Mutual Exclusion

The usefulness of disjoint processes has its limits. We will now consider *interacting processes*—concurrent processes which access shared variables.

A *shared variable* v of type T is declared as follows:

$$\textbf{var } v\text{: } \textbf{shared } T$$

Concurrent processes can only refer to and change a shared variable inside a structured statement called a *critical region*

$$\textbf{region } v \ \textbf{do } S$$

This notation associates a statement S with a shared variable v.

Critical regions referring to the same variable exclude each other in time. They can be arbitrarily interleaved in time. The idea of progressing towards a final result (as in a concurrent statement) is therefore meaningless. All one can expect is that each critical region leaves certain relationships among the components of a shared variable v unchanged. These relationships can be defined by an assertion I about v which must be true after initialization of v and before and after each subsequent critical region associated with v. Such an assertion is called an *invariant*.

When a process enters a critical region to execute a statement S, a predicate P holds for the variables accessible to the process outside the critical region and an invariant I holds for the shared variable v accessible inside the critical region. After the completion of S, a result R holds for the former variables and invariant I has been maintained. So a critical region has the following axiomatic property:

> "P"
> **region** v **do** "$P\&I$" S "$R\&I$";
> "R"

4   Process Communication

Mutual exclusion of operations on shared variables makes it possible to make meaningful statements about the effect of concurrent computations. But when processes cooperate on a common task they must also be able to wait until certain conditions have been satisfied by other processes.

For this purpose I introduce a synchronizing primitive, **await**, which delays a process until the components of a shared variable v satisfy a condition B:

> **region** v **do**
> **begin** ... **await** B; ... **end**

The await primitive must be textually enclosed by a critical region. If critical regions are nested, the synchronizing condition B is associated with the innermost enclosing region.

The await primitive can be used to define *conditional critical regions* of the type proposed in (Hoare 1971):

> "Consumer"   "Producer"
> **region** v **do**   **region** v **do** S_2
> **begin await** B; S_1 **end**

The implementation of critical regions and await primitives is illustrated in Fig. 1. When a process, such as the consumer above, wishes to enter a critical region, it enters a *main queue* Q_v associated with a shared variable v. After entering its critical region, the consumer inspects the shared variable to determine whether it satisfies a condition B. In that case, the consumer completes its critical region by executing a statement S_1; otherwise, the process leaves its critical region *temporarily* and joins an *event queue* Q_e associated with the shared variable.

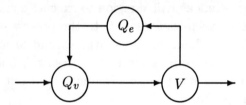

Figure 1 Scheduling of conditional critical regions V by means of process queues Q_v and Q_e.

All processes waiting for one condition or another on variable v enter the same event queue. When another process (here called the producer) changes v by a statement S_2 inside a critical region, it is possible that one or more of the conditions expected by processes in the event queue will be satisfied. So, after completion of a critical region, all processes in the event queue Q_e are transferred to the main queue Q_v to enable them to reenter their critical regions and inspect the shared variable v again.

It is possible that a *consumer* will be transferred in vain between Q_v and Q_e several times before its condition B holds. But this can only occur as frequently as *producers* change the shared variable. This controlled amount of *busy waiting* is the price we pay for the conceptual simplicity achieved by using arbitrary Boolean expressions as synchronizing conditions.

The desired *invariant I* for the shared variable v must be satisfied before an *await* primitive is executed. When the waiting cycle terminates, the assertion $B \ \& \ I$ holds.

As an example, consider the following resource allocation problem: two kinds of concurrent processes, called readers and writers, share a single resource. The readers can use the resource simultaneously, but the writers must have exclusive access to it. When a writer is ready to use the resource, it should be enabled to do so as soon as possible.

This problem is solved by Algorithm 2. Here variable v is a record consisting of two integer components defining the number of *readers* currently using the resource and the number of *writers* currently waiting for or using the resource. Both *readers* and *writers* are initialized to zero.

var v: **shared record** readers, writers: integer **end**
    w: **shared** Boolean;

"Reader"	"Writer"
region v **do**	**region** v **do**
begin	**begin**
await writers = 0;	writers := writers + 1;
readers := readers + 1;	**await** readers = 0;
end	**end**
read;	**region** w **do** write;
region v **do**	**region** v **do**
readers := readers − 1;	writers := writers − 1;

Algorithm 2 Resource sharing by readers and writers.

Mutual exclusion of readers and writers is achieved by letting readers wait until the number of writers is zero, and vice versa. Mutual exclusion of individual writers is ensured by the critical region on the Boolean w.

The priority rule is obeyed by increasing the number of writers as soon as one of them wishes to use the resource. This will delay subsequent reader requests until all pending writer requests are satisfied.

A correctness proof of Algorithm 2 is outlined in (Brinch Hansen 1972). In this paper I also point out the superiority of conditional critical regions over *semaphores* (Dijkstra 1965). Compared to the original solution to the problem (Courtois 1971) Algorithm 2 demonstrates the conceptual advantage of a structured notation.[†]

The conceptual simplicity of critical regions is achieved by ignoring details of scheduling: the programmer is unaware of the sequence in which

---

[†]The original solution includes the following refinement: when a writer decides to make a request at most one more reader can complete a request ahead of it. This can be ensured by surrounding the reader request in Algorithm 2 with an additional critical region associated with a shared Boolean r.

waiting processes enter critical regions and access shared resources. This assumption is justified for processes which are so *loosely connected* that simultaneous requests for the same resource rarely occur.

But in most computer installations *resources* are *heavily used* by a large group of users. In this situation, an operating system must be able to *control the scheduling of resources explicitly* among competing processes.

To do this a programmer must be able to associate an arbitrary number of event queues with a shared variable and control the transfers of processes to and from them. In general, I would therefore replace the previous proposal for conditional delays with the following one:

The declaration

$$\textbf{var } e\text{: } \textbf{event } v;$$

associates an event queue e with a shared variable v.

A process can leave a critical region associated with v and join the event queue e by executing the standard procedure

$$\text{await}(e)$$

Another process can enable all processes in the event queue e to reenter their critical regions by executing the standard procedure

$$\text{cause}(e)$$

A consumer/producer relationship must now be expressed as follows:

"Consumer"	"Producer"
region v **do**	**region** v **do**
begin	**begin**
while not B **do** await(e);	S_2;
S_1;	cause(e);
end	**end**

Although less elegant than the previous notation, the present one still clearly shows that the consumer is waiting for condition B to hold. And we can now control process scheduling to any degree desired.

To simplify explicit scheduling, I suggest that processes reentering their critical regions from event queues take priority over processes entering critical regions directly through a main queue (see Fig. 1). If the scheduling rule is completely unknown to the programmer as before, additional variables

```
var v: shared record
                available: set of R;
                requests: set of P;
                grant: array P of event v;
            end

procedure reserve(process: P; var resource: R);
region v do
begin
   while empty(available) do
   begin enter(process, requests);
      await(grant[process]);
   end
   remove(resource, available);
end

procedure release(resource: R);
var process: P;
region v do
begin enter(resource, available);
   if not empty(requests) then
   begin remove(process, requests);
      cause(grant[process]);
   end
end
```

Algorithm 3 Scheduling of heavily used resources.

are required to ensure that resources granted to waiting processes remain available to them until they reenter their critical regions.

Algorithm 3 is a simple example of completely controlled resource allocation. A number of processes share a pool of equivalent resources. Processes and resources are identified by indices of type P and R respectively. When resources are *available*, a process can *acquire* one immediately; otherwise, it must enter a request in a data structure of type *set of P* and wait until a resource is *granted* to it. It is assumed that the program controls the entry and removal of set elements completely.

5 Conclusion

I have presented structured multiprogramming concepts which have simple axiomatic properties and permit extensive compile time checking and generation of efficient machine code.

The essential properties of these concepts are:

1. A distinction between disjoint and interacting processes;

2. An association of shared data with operations defined on them;

3. Mutual exclusion of these operations in time;

4. Synchronizing primitives which permit partial or complete control of process scheduling.

These are precisely the concepts needed to implement *monitor procedures* such as the ones described in (Brinch Hansen 1970). They appear to be sufficiently safe to use not only within operating systems but also within user programs to control local resources.

References

Brinch Hansen, P. 1970. The nucleus of a multiprogramming system. *Communications of the ACM 13*, 4 (April), 238–250.

Brinch Hansen, P. 1971. An outline of a course on operating system principles. *International Seminar on Operating System Techniques*, Belfast, Northern Ireland, (August–September).

Brinch Hansen, P. 1972. A comparison of two synchronizing concepts. *Acta Informatica 1*, 190–199.

Conway, M.E. 1963. A multiprocessor system design. *Proc. AFIPS FJCC 24*, Spartan Books, New York, 139–146.

Courtois, P.J, Heymans, F., and Parnas, D.L. 1971. Concurrent control with "readers" and "writers." *Communications of the ACM 14*, 10 (October), 667–668.

Dijkstra, E.W. 1965. Cooperating sequential processes. Technological University, Eindhoven. Also in *Programming Languages*, F. Genyus, Ed. Academic Press, New York, 1968.

Hoare, C.A.R. 1971. Towards a theory of parallel programming. *International Seminar on Operating System Techniques*, Belfast, Northern Ireland, (August–September).

Wirth, N. 1971. The programming language Pascal. *Acta Informatica 1*, 35–63.

5

Testing a Multiprogramming System*

(1973)

A central problem in program design is to structure a large program such that it can be tested systematically by the simplest possible techniques. This paper describes the method used to test the RC 4000 multiprogramming system. During testing, the system records all transitions of processes and messages between various queues. The test mechanism consists of fifty machine instructions centralized in two procedures. By using this mechanism in a series of carefully selected test cases, the system was made virtually error free within a few weeks. The test procedure is illustrated by examples.

1 Introduction

This paper describes the method used to test the RC 4000 multiprogramming system (Brinch Hansen 1970). The system was built with the following *test criteria* in mind:

1. A large program should be structured such that it can be tested by the simplest possible techniques.

2. The documentation of a large program should include a systematic set of reproducible test cases.

The nucleus of the RC 4000 system is an interrupt response program of 4,800 machine words called the *monitor*. The monitor multiplexes a single processor among concurrent processes and implements a set of procedures which these processes can call to create other processes and send messages to them. Monitor procedures are executed in a non-interruptable, privileged

---

*P. Brinch Hansen, Testing a multiprogramming system, *Software—Practice and Experience 3*, 2 (April–June), 145–150. Copyright © 1973, John Wiley & Sons, Ltd. Reprinted by permission.

processor state; processes are executed in an interruptable, non-privileged state.

The monitor consists of five *programming layers* with the following tasks:

> processor multiplexing
> message buffering
> input/output operations
> process creation and termination
> file system

The layers were tested in that order starting with the bottom layer (processor multiplexing) working towards the top layer (file system).

2 Test Mechanism

The main difficulty in testing a (possibly erroneous) multiprogramming system is to prevent concurrent events from causing irreproducible, time-dependent test results.

During each test, the system was initialized with the monitor and a number of *test processes*. The simplest idea would have been to let a test process first call a monitor procedure and then examine various monitor variables (such as process descriptions and scheduling queues) to decide whether the call had the intended effect. Unfortunately, this idea does not work in a multiprogramming environment in which other events (caused by processor multiplexing) may change the internal state of the monitor before the result of a given monitor call has been recorded by a test process.

To make a test event well defined and reproducible, the execution of a monitor call and the recording of its result had to be an indivisible event. Mutual exclusion of test events was achieved by letting the monitor output test data on a typewriter in the non-interruptable processor state.

The hardest problem was to select a minimal set of monitor events that would give significant information about its handling of concurrent processes. It turned out to be sufficient to record all *transitions* of *processes* and *messages* among various queues. When a list element (representing a process or a message) is removed from or linked to a list (representing a queue), the monitor outputs the addresses of the list element and the head of the list plus a single character to distinguish removal from linking. The meaning of these addresses is defined by the assembly listing of the monitor program.

In the following, such test output is represented by more readable lines of the form:

take element from queue
put element in queue

This test mechanism, which adds fifty machine instructions to the monitor, is centralized in two local procedures, *take* and *put*. The following sections describe how it was used to test the monitor.

3   Processor Multiplexing

The processor is shared cyclically among all active processes. Every 25 msec, a clock interrupt causes the monitor to preempt a running process in favor of another process ready to run (Fig. 1).

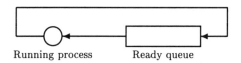

Running process   Ready queue

Figure 1 Processor multiplexing.

The monitor code for processor multiplexing can be represented as follows:

```
on clock interrupt do
begin
    put running process in ready queue;
    take another process from ready queue;
    continue that process;
end
```

To test processor multiplexing, the system was initialized with three processes P, Q and R in the ready queue (in that order). These processes cycled forever:

P: **repeat until** false;
Q: **repeat until** false;
R: **repeat until** false;

The clock was replaced by a manually operated *interrupt key*. During the test, the monitor produced the following output when processor multiplexing was correct:

```
         take P from ready queue
    *    put P in ready queue
         take Q from ready queue
    *    put Q in ready queue
         take R from ready queue
    *    put R in ready queue
         take P from ready queue
         . . .
```

The lines marked * are monitor responses to clock interrupts simulated by pushing the interrupt key.

As soon as processor multiplexing worked, the monitor procedures for process communication were tested.

4   Process Communication

Processes can exchange messages in buffer elements of fixed length stored within the monitor. A communication between two processes, S and R, takes place in four steps:

1. Process S sends a message M to process R in a buffer element B selected by the monitor by calling the procedure

$$\text{send message}(R, M, B)$$

2. Process R receives the message by calling the procedure

$$\text{wait message}(S, M, B)$$

3. Process R sends an answer A to process S in the same buffer element B by calling the procedure

$$\text{send answer}(A, B)$$

4. Process S receives the answer by calling the procedure

$$\text{wait answer}(A, B)$$

Figure 2 shows the life cycle of a buffer element. Available buffer elements are linked to a common *pool* within the monitor. The monitor also maintains a *message queue* for each process. A buffer element is linked to this queue when a message is sent to the corresponding process. The buffer element is removed from the queue when the message has been received. When the message has been answered, and the answer has been received, the buffer element is linked to the pool again.

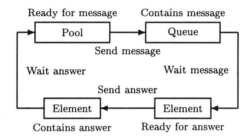

Figure 2 Message buffer states.

In a simplified form these monitor procedures can be represented as follows:

    send message:
        take buffer from pool;
        if message expected **then**
            put receiver in ready queue
        else put buffer in message queue;

    wait message:
        if message available **then**
            take buffer from message queue
        else
            begin
                indicate message expected;
                take another process from ready queue;
            end

    send answer:
        if answer expected **then**

```
      begin
        put buffer in pool;
        put receiver in ready queue;
      end

   wait answer:
     if answer available then
       put buffer in pool
     else
       begin
         indicate answer expected;
         take another process from ready queue;
       end
```

During testing a process can ask the monitor whether a message or an answer is available for it without being forced to wait for its arrival. A process can also ask the monitor whether another process is expecting a message or an answer.

To test process communication, the system was initialized with two processes, R and S, in the ready queue (in that order). The processes exchange messages and answers in two buffer elements B and B':

```
   R:   wait message(S, M, B);
        repeat until answer expected(S);
        send answer(A, B);
        repeat until message available(R);
        wait message(S, M', B');
        send answer(A', B');
        repeat until false;

   S:   repeat until message expected(R);
        send message(R, M, B);
        wait answer(A, B);
        send message(R, M', B');
        repeat until answer available(B');
        wait answer(A', B');
        repeat until false;
```

This test should produce the following output:

```
 1:       take R from ready queue
 2:       take S from ready queue
 3:       take B from buffer pool
 4:       put R in ready queue
 5:       take R from ready queue
 6:       put B in buffer pool
 7:       put S in ready queue
 8:   *   put R in ready queue
 9:       take S from ready queue
10:       take B' from buffer pool
11:       put B' in message queue(R)
12:   *   put S in ready queue
13:       take R from ready queue
14:       take B' from message queue(R)
15:   *   put R in ready queue
16:       take S from ready queue
17:       put B' in buffer pool
```

The output can be explained as follows:

Line 1: The monitor selects process R as the first process to run.

Line 2: While process R waits for nessage M, the monitor continues to run process S.

Lines 3–4: Process S sends message M to process R which in turn reenters the ready queue.

Line 5: While process S waits for answer A, the monitor continues to run process R.

Lines 6–7: Process R sends answer A to process S which in turn reenters the ready queue.

Lines 8–9: Process R continuously asks the monitor whether a message is available for it. A key interrupt preempts process R in favor of process S.

Lines 10–11: Process S sends message M' to process R.

Lines 12–13: Process S continuously asks the monitor whether an answer is available for it. A key interrupt preempts process S in favor of process R.

Line 14: Process R receives message M' and sends answer A' to process S.

Lines 15–16: Process R cycles indefinitely. A key interrupt preempts process R in favor of process S.

Line 17: Process S receives answer A'.

This test covers the eight relevant cases of process communication:

$$\left\{ \begin{array}{c} send \\ receive \end{array} \right\} \left\{ \begin{array}{c} expected \\ unexpected \end{array} \right\} \left\{ \begin{array}{c} message \\ answer \end{array} \right\}$$

5   Concluding Remarks

When the communication procedures worked, all possible interactions between processes and peripheral devices of various types were tested. Tests
concerning dynamic process creation and termination then followed. Finally,
the file system was tested.

The test output immediately revealed all serious synchronizing errors
within the monitor. Quite often, the output also led to the discovery of errors
in the test programs themselves. As a result of this systematic approach,
the monitor was virtually error free after a test period of a few weeks.

It is worth mentioning that the monitor program was written *after* the
test mechanism had been selected. If the test problem had been attacked
after the monitor was finished, the relevant test events (*take* and *put*) might
have been scattered all over the program as in-line code, thus making a
centralization of the test mechanism impossible without extensive study and
revision of the program text.

Acknowledgements

The author is indebted to Peter Naur (1963) for demonstrating the validity
of simple, systematic testing techniques for large, sequential compilers.

References

Brinch Hansen, P. 1970. The nucleus of a multiprogramming system. *Communications of
    the ACM 13*, 4 (April), 238–250. *Article 2.*
Naur, P. 1963. The design of the Gier Algol compiler. *BIT 3*, 2–3, 124–140 and 145–166.

6

Shared Classes*

(1973)

The author discusses the close relationship between data and operations and suggests that a compiler should be able to check that data structures are accessed by meaningful procedures only. This idea leads to the introduction of shared classes—a programming notation for the monitor concept. The notation is illustrated by a message buffer for concurrent processes.

We will discuss the close relationship between data and operations and use it to define a very important form of resource protection.

If we consider variables of *primitive types* such as *integer* and *boolean*, it is quite possible that values of different types will be represented by identical bit strings at the machine level. For example both the *boolean* value *true* and the *integer* value 1 might be represented by the bit string

$$000...001$$

in single machine words.

So data of different types are distinguished not only by the representation of their values, but also by the operations associated with the types. An *integer*, for example, is a datum subject only to arithmetic operations, comparisons, and assignments involving other data subject to the same restrictions.

Now consider *structured types*. Take for example a variable that represents a message buffer which contains a sequences of messages sent, but not yet received. A *static* picture of process communication can be defined by

---

*P. Brinch Hansen, *Operating System Principles*, Section 7.2 Class Concept, Prentice Hall, Englewood Cliffs, NJ, (July 1973), 226–232. Copyright © 1973, Prentice Hall. Reprinted by permission.

assertions about the relationships of the components of the message buffer. But to understand how and when messages are exchanged *dynamically,* one must also study the *send* and *receive* procedures defined for a message buffer. These operations in turn are only meaningful for the particular representation of the message buffer chosen and can only be understood precisely by studying its type definition.

These examples illustrate the point made by Dahl (1972): "Data and operations on data seem to be so closely connected in our minds, that it takes elements of both kinds to make any concept useful for understanding computing processes."

Simon (1962) has pointed out that the search for state and process descriptions of the same phenomenon is characteristic of problem solving: "These two modes of apprehending structure are the warp and weft of our experience. Pictures, blueprints, most diagrams, chemical structural formulae are state descriptions. Recipes, differential equations, equations for chemical reactions are process descriptions. The former characterize the world as sensed; they provide the criteria for identifying objects, often by modeling the objects themselves. The latter characterize the world as acted upon; they provide the means for producing or generating objects having the desired characteristics."

"The distinction between the world as sensed and the world as acted upon defines the basic condition for the survival of adaptive organisms. The organism must develop correlations between goals in the sensed world and actions in the world of process."

In Section 2.6 on program construction, I have illustrated this alternation between a refinement of data (representing states) and program (representing processes). The essence of this form of problem solving is the following:

When a programmer needs a concept such as process communication, he first postulates a set of operations (in this case, *send* and *receive*) that have the desired effect at his present level of thinking. Later, he chooses a specific representation of a data structure (a message buffer), that enables him to implement the operations efficiently on the available machine.

When the programmer is trying to convince himself of the correctness of a program (by formal proof or testing), he will tacitly assume that these operations (*send* and *receive*) are the only ones carried out on data structures of this type (*message buffers*).

If other statements in his program are able to operate on message buffers, he cannot make this assumption. The most extreme case is unstructured machine language, which potentially permits each statement to influence any other statement, intentionally or by mistake. This makes program verification an endless task since one can never be sure, when a new component is added to a large program, how this will influence previously tested components.

If, on the other hand, the previous assumption is justified, the programmer can convince himself of the correctness of process communication by studying only the type definition of a message buffer and the procedures *send* and *receive*. Once this program component has been shown to be correct, the designer can be confident that subsequent addition of other components will not invalidate this proof. This makes the task of verification grow linearly with the number and size of components—an essential requirement for the design of large, reliable programs.

According to the previous definition, it is an obvious protection problem to check that data are accessed by operations consistent with their type. To what extent do the structures of present high-level languages enable a compiler to do this?

A decent compiler for an algorithmic language such as *Fortran*, *Algol 60*, or *Pascal* will check the compatibility of data and operations on them for *primitive types* (Naur 1963). The compiler can do this because the permissible operations on primitive types are part of the language definition.

But in the case of *structured types*, only the most rudimentary kind of checking is possible with these languages. All the compiler can check is that data in assignment statements and comparisons for equality are of the same type. But, since the languages mentioned do not enable the programmer to associate a set of procedures with a type definition, the compiler cannot check whether the operations on a message buffer are restricted to *send* and *receive* procedures as intended by the programmer. This is a serious deficiency of most programming languages available today.

An exception is the *Simula 67* language (Dahl 1968), an extension of Algol 60 originally designed for simulation. In Simula 67, the definition of a structured data type and the meaningful operations on it form a single, syntactical unit called a class.[†]

I will briefly describe a simplified, restricted form of the Simula 67 class concept in a Pascal-inspired notation.

The notation

[†]Readers of the Pascal report by Wirth (1971) should notice that the Simula class concept is completely unrelated to the Pascal class concept.

class $T = v_1\colon T_1;\ v_2\colon T_2;\ \ldots;\ v_m\colon T_m;$

procedure $P_1(\ldots)$ **begin** S_1 **end**

$\ldots$

procedure $P_n(\ldots)$ **begin** S_n **end**

begin S_0 **end**

defines: (1) a data structure of type T consisting of the components v_1, v_2, $\ldots$, v_m of types T_1, T_2, $\ldots$, T_m; (2) a set of procedures (or functions), P_1, P_2, $\ldots$, P_n that operate on the data structure; and (3) a statement S_0 that can define its initial value.

A variable v of type T is declared as usual:

var $v\colon T$

Upon entry to the context in which the variable v is declared, storage is allocated for its components v_1, v_2, $\ldots$, v_m, and the initial statement S_0 is carried out for this variable.

A call of a procedure P_i on the variable v is denoted:

$$v.P_i(\ldots)$$

Procedure P_i can refer to the components v_1, v_2, $\ldots$, v_m of v, to its own local variables, and to the parameters of the given call. The operations P_1, P_2, $\ldots$, P_n are the only ones permitted on the variable v.

An obvious idea is to represent critical regions by the concept *shared class*, implying that the operations P_1, P_2, $\ldots$, P_n on a given variable v of type T exclude one another in time.

The concept *message buffering* is defined as a shared class in Algorithm 1. A buffer variable b and a message variable t are declared and accessed as follows:

var b: B; t: T;

b.send(t)   b.receive(t)

Strictly speaking, assignment to a message parameter m can only be made within the class B if its type T is primitive. But it seems reasonable to retain the simple type definition

type $T = \ <\text{type}>$

```
shared class B =
  buffer: array 0..max−1 of T;
  p, c: 0..max−1;
  full: 0..max;

procedure send(m: T);
begin
  await full < max;
  buffer[p] := m;
  p := (p + 1) mod max;
  full := full + 1;
end

procedure receive(var m: T);
begin
  await full > 0;
  m := buffer[c];
  c := (c + 1) mod max;
  full := full − 1;
end

begin p := 0; c := 0; full := 0 end
```

Algorithm 1 Representation of a
message buffer by a shared class.

to indicate that variables of this type can be accessed directly.

The class concept in Simula 67 has several other aspects, among them a mechanism for defining a hierarchy of classes (Dahl 1972). My main purpose here is to show a notation which explicitly restricts operations on data and enables a compiler to check that these restrictions are obeyed. Although such restrictions are not enforced by Simula 67, this would seem to be essential for effective protection.

Many computers support a restricted form of shared class at the machine level of programming. I am referring to the *basic monitor* procedures and data structures which control the sharing of processors, storage, and peripherals at the lowest level of programming. This class concept enforced at run time is implemented as follows: The address mapping performed by a central processor prevents computations from referring directly to data structures belonging to the basic monitor, but permits them to call a well-defined set of monitor procedures. Mutual exclusion in time of such calls is achieved by means of an arbiter and by delaying interrupt response. To prevent computations from bypassing the monitor and referring directly to physical resources, the central processor recognizes two states of execution: the *privileged state*, in which all machine instructions can be executed; and the *user state*, in which certain instructions cannot be executed (those that control program interruption, input/output, and address mapping). The privileged state is entered after a monitor call; the user state is entered after a monitor return.

In Chapter 1 I said "It is now recognized that it is desirable to be able to distinguish in a more flexible manner between many levels of protection (and not just two)." We have seen that it is indeed desirable to be able to enforce a separate set of access rules for each data type used. The class concept is a general structuring tool applicable at all levels of programming, sequential as well as concurrent.

The class concept was introduced here to protect *local* data structures within a program against inconsistent operations. But the concept is applicable also to data structures which are *retained* within the computer after the termination of computations.

One example of retained data structures are those used within an *operating system* to control resource sharing among unrelated computations. These data structures must be acessed only through well-defined procedures; otherwise, the operating system might crash. So an operating system defines a set of standard procedures which can be called by computations. Since these procedures remain unchanged over reasonable periods of time, a compiler should be able to use a description of them to perform type checking of calls of them within user programs in advance of their execution.

We are thus lead to the idea of maintaining *data structures defining environments of compilation and execution*. An environment defines a set of retained data structures and procedures accessible to a given computation.

Another example of retained data structures are files stored semipermanently on backing stores. In most present *file systems*, a computation can either be denied access to a given file or be permitted to *read*, *write*, or *execute* it. This seems a rather crude distinction. In most cases, a data file is intended to be used only in a particular manner; for example, a source text of a program is intended to be edited or compiled by a particular compiler; most other operations on it may be entirely meaningless from the user's point of view. To maintain the integrity of a file, its creator should therefore be able to associate it with a set of procedures through which it can be accessed in a meaningful manner. This is possible, for example, in the file system for the *B5500* computer (McKeag 1971).

Assuming that this set of procedures remains unchanged over reasonable periods of time, it would again be possible to check the consistency of references to files within user programs at compile time. The basic requirement is that the access rules remain fixed between compilation and execution of programs.

Such a system differs from the present ones in two aspects: (1) a program is compiled to be executed in a particular environment; and (2) a compiled program may become invalid if its environment changes. This is acceptable only if most programs are compiled shortly before execution or if they operate in a fairly constant environment. The benefits of this approach would be an early detection of program errors and a more efficient execution because fewer protection rules would have to be checked dynamically.

References

Dahl, O.-J., Myhrhaug, B., and Nygaard, K. 1968. Simula 67—common base language. Norsk Regnesentral, Oslo, Norway, (May).

Dahl, O.-J., and Hoare, C.A.R. 1972. Hierarchical program structures. In *Structured Programming*, O.-J. Dahl, E.W. Dijkstra, and C.A.R. Hoare, Eds., Academic Press, New York, 175–220.

McKeag, R.M. 1971. Burroughs B5500 master control program. In *Studies in Operating Systems*, R.M. McKeag and R. Wilson, Academic Press, New York, (1976), 1–66.

Naur, P. 1963. The design of the GIER Algol compiler. *BIT 3*, 2–3, 124–140 and 145–166.

Simon, H.A. 1962. The architecture of complexity. *Proceedings of the American Philosophical Society 106*, 6, 468–482.

Wirth, N. 1971. The programming language Pascal. *Acta Informatica 1*, 1, 35–63.

The Programming Language Concurrent Pascal*

(1975)

The paper describes a new programming language for structured programming of computer operating systems. It extends the sequential programming language Pascal with concurrent programming tools called processes and monitors. Part I explains these concepts informally by means of pictures illustrating a hierarchical design of a simple spooling system. Part II uses the same example to introduce the language notation. The main contribution of Concurrent Pascal is to extend the monitor concept with an explicit hierarchy of access rights to shared data structures that can be stated in the program text and checked by a compiler.

I. The Purpose of Concurrent Pascal

A. Background

Since 1972 I have been working on a new programming language for structured programming of computer operating systems. This language is called Concurrent Pascal. It extends the sequential programming language Pascal with concurrent programming tools called processes and monitors (Wirth 1971; Brinch Hansen 1973; Hoare 1974).

This is an informal description of Concurrent Pascal. It uses examples, pictures, and words to bring out the creative aspects of new programming concepts without getting into their finer details. I plan to define these concepts precisely and introduce a notation for them in later papers. This form of presentation may be imprecise from a formal point of view, but is perhaps more effective from a human point of view.

---

*P. Brinch Hansen, The programming language Concurrent Pascal, *IEEE Transactions on Software Engineering 1*, 2 (June 1975), 199–207. Copyright © 1975, Institute of Electrical and Electronics Engineers, Inc. Reprinted by permission.

B. Processes

We will study concurrent processes inside an operating system and look at one small problem only: How can large amounts of data be transmitted from one process to another by means of buffers stored on a disk?

Figure 1 shows this little system and its three components: A process that produces data, a process that consumes data, and a disk buffer that connects them.

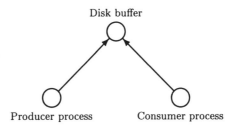

Figure 1 Process communication.

The circles are *system components* and the arrows are the *access rights* of these components. They show that both processes can use the buffer (but they do not show that data flows from the producer to the consumer). This kind of picture is an *access graph*.

The next picture shows a process component in more detail (Fig. 2).

Access rights
Private data
Sequential program

Figure 2 Process.

A *process* consists of a *private data* structure and a *sequential program* that can operate on the data. One process cannot operate on the private data of another process. But concurrent processes can share certain data structures (such as a disk buffer). The *access rights* of a process mention the shared data it can operate on.

C. Monitors

A disk buffer is a data structure shared by two concurrent processes. The details of how such a buffer is constructed are irrelevant to its users. All the processes need to know is that they can *send* and *receive* data through it. If they try to operate on the buffer in any other way it is probably either a programming mistake or an example of tricky programming. In both cases, one would like a compiler to detect such misuse of a shared data structure.

To make this possible, we must introduce a language construct that will enable a programmer to tell a compiler how a shared data structure can be used by processes. This kind of system component is called a monitor. A monitor can synchronize concurrent processes and transmit data between them. It can also control the order in which competing processes use shared, physical resources. Figure 3 shows a monitor in detail.

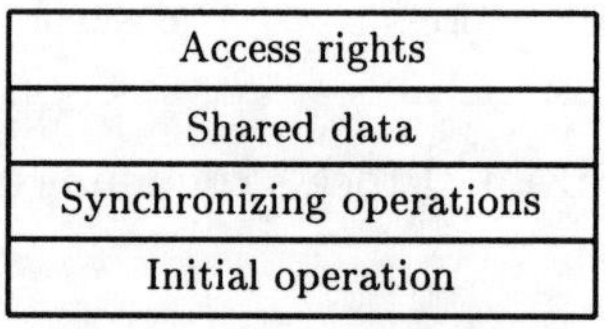

Access rights
Shared data
Synchronizing operations
Initial operation

Figure 3 Monitor.

A *monitor* defines a *shared data* structure and all the operations processes can perform on it. These synchronizing operations are called *monitor procedures*. A monitor also defines an *initial operation* that will be executed when its data structure is created.

We can define a *disk buffer* as a monitor. Within this monitor there will be shared variables that define the location and length of the buffer on the disk. There will also be two monitor procedures, *send* and *receive*. The initial operation will make sure that the buffer starts as an empty one.

Processes cannot operate directly on shared data. They can only call monitor procedures that have access to shared data. A monitor procedure is executed as part of a calling process (just like any other procedure).

If concurrent processes simultaneously call monitor procedures that operate on the same shared data these procedures will be executed strictly one at a time. Otherwise, the results of monitor calls would be unpredictable. This means that the machine must be able to delay processes for short periods of time until it is their turn to execute monitor procedures. We will not be concerned with how this is done, but will just notice that a monitor procedure has *exclusive access* to shared data while it is being executed.

So the (virtual) machine on which concurrent programs run will handle *short-term scheduling* of simultaneous monitor calls. But the programmer must also be able to delay processes for longer periods of time if their requests for data and other resources cannot be satisfied immediately. If, for example, a process tries to receive data from an empty disk buffer it must be delayed until another process sends more data.

Concurrent Pascal includes a simple data type, called a *queue*, that can be used by monitor procedures to control *medium-term scheduling* of processes. A monitor can either *delay* a calling process in a queue or *continue* another process that is waiting in a queue. It is not important here to understand how these queues work except for the following essential rule: A process only has exclusive access to shared data as long as it continues to execute statements within a monitor procedure. As soon as a process is delayed in a queue it loses its exclusive access until another process calls the same monitor and wakes it up again. (Without this rule, it would be impossible to enter a monitor and let waiting processes continue their execution.)

Although the disk buffer example does not show this yet, monitor procedures should also be able to call procedures defined within other monitors. Otherwise, the language will not be very useful for hierarchical design. In the case of the disk buffer, one of these other monitors could perhaps define simple input/output operations on the disk. So a monitor can also have *access rights* to other system components (see Fig. 3).

D. System Design

A process executes a sequential program—it is an active component. A monitor is just a collection of procedures that do nothing until they are called by processes—it is a passive component. But there are strong similarities between a process and a monitor: both define a data structure (private or shared) and the meaningful operations on it. The main difference between processes and monitors is the way they are scheduled for execution.

It seems natural therefore to regard processes and monitors as *abstract data types* defined in terms of the operations one can perform on them. If a compiler can check that these operations are the only ones carried out on data structures, then we may be able to build very reliable, concurrent programs in which *controlled access* to data and physical resources is guar-

anteed before these programs are put into operation. We have then to some
extent solved the *resource protection* problem in the cheapest possible manner (without hardware mechanisms and run time overhead).

So we will define processes and monitors as data types and make it
possible to use several instances of the same component type in a system.
We can, for example, use two disk buffers to build a *spooling system* with an
input process, a job process, and an output process (Fig. 4).

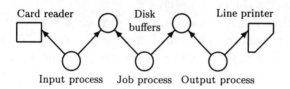

Figure 4 Spooling system.

I will distinguish between definitions and instances of components by
calling them *system types* and *system components*. Access graphs (such as
Fig. 4) will always show system components (not system types).

Peripheral devices are considered to be monitors implemented in hardware. They can only be accessed by a single procedure *io* that delays the
calling process until an input/output operation is completed. Interrupts are
handled by the virtual machine on which processes run.

To make the programming language useful for stepwise system design
it should permit the division of a system type, such as a disk buffer, into
smaller system types. One of these other system types should give a disk
buffer access to the disk. We will call this system type a *virtual disk*. It
gives a disk buffer the illusion that it has its own private disk. A virtual
disk hides the details of disk input/output from the rest of the system and
makes the disk look like a data structure (an array of disk pages). The only
operations on this data structure are *read* and *write* a page.

Each virtual disk is only used by a single disk buffer (Fig. 5). A system
component that cannot be called simultaneously by several other components will be called a *class*. A class defines a data structure and the possible
operations on it (just like a monitor). The exclusive access of class procedures to class variables can be guaranteed completely at compile time. The
virtual machine does not have to schedule simultaneous calls of class proce-

Figure 5 Buffer refinement.

dures at run time, because such calls cannot occur. This makes class calls considerably faster than monitor calls.

The spooling system includes two virtual disks but only one real disk. So we need a single *disk resource* monitor to control the order in which competing processes use the disk (Fig. 6). This monitor defines two procedures, *request* and *release* access, to be called by a virtual disk before and after each disk transfer.

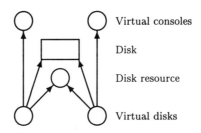

Figure 6 Decomposition of virtual disks.

It would seem simpler to replace the virtual disks and the disk resource by a single monitor that has exclusive access to the disk and does the input/output. This would certainly guarantee that processes use the disk one at a time. But this would be done according to the built-in short-term scheduling policy of monitor calls.

Now to make a virtual machine efficient, one must use a very simple short-term scheduling rule, such as first-come, first-served (Brinch Hansen 1973). If the disk has a moving access head this is about the worst possible algorithm one can use for disk transfers. It is vital that the language make it possible for the programmer to write a medium-term scheduling algorithm that will minimize disk head movement (Hoare 1974). The data type *queue* mentioned earlier makes it possible to implement arbitrary scheduling rules within a monitor.

The difficulty is that while a monitor is performing an input/output operation it is impossible for other processes to enter the same monitor and join the disk queue. They will automatically be delayed by the short-term scheduler and only allowed to enter the monitor one at a time after each disk transfer. This will, of course, make the attempt to control disk scheduling within the monitor illusory. To give the programmer complete control of disk scheduling, processes should be able to enter the disk queue during disk transfers. Since *arrival* and *service* in the disk queueing system potentially are simultaneous operations they must be handled by different system components, as shown in Fig. 6.

If the disk fails persistently during input/output this should be reported on an operator's console. Figure 6 shows two instances of a class type, called a *virtual console*. They give the virtual disks the illusion that they have their own private consoles.

The virtual consoles get exclusive access to a single, real console by calling a *console resource* monitor (Fig. 7). Notice that we now have a standard technique for dealing with virtual devices.

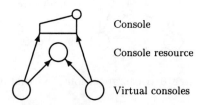

Console

Console resource

Virtual consoles

Figure 7 Decomposition of virtual consoles.

If we put all these system components together, we get a complete picture of a simple spooling system (Fig. 8). Classes, monitors, and processes are marked C, M, and P.

E. Scope Rules

Some years ago I was part of a team that built a multiprogramming system in which processes can appear and disappear dynamically (Brinch Hansen

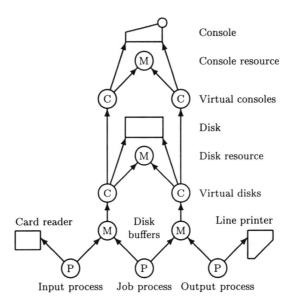

Figure 8 Hierarchical system structure.

1970). In practice, this system was used mostly to set up a fixed configuration of processes. Dynamic process deletion will certainly complicate
the semantics and implementation of a programming language considerably.
And since it appears to be unnecessary for a large class of real-time applications, it seems wise to exclude it altogether. So an operating system written
in Concurrent Pascal will consist of a fixed number of processes, monitors,
and classes. These components and their data structures will exist forever
after system initialization. An operating system can, however, be extended
by recompilation. It remains to be seen whether this restriction will simplify or complicate operating system design. But the poor quality of most
existing operating systems clearly demonstrates an urgent need for simpler
approaches.

In existing programming languages the data structures of processes, monitors, and classes would be called "global data." This term would be misleading in Concurrent Pascal where each data structure can be accessed by
a single component only. It seems more appropriate to call them *permanent
data structures*.

I have argued elsewhere that the most dangerous aspect of concurrent

programming is the possibility of *time-dependent programming errors* that
are impossible to locate by testing ("lurking bugs") (Brinch Hansen 1972,
1973, 1974b). If we are going to depend on real-time programming systems
in our daily lives, we must be able to find such obscure errors before the
systems are put into operation.

Fortunately, a compiler can detect many of these errors if processes and
monitors are represented by a structured notation in a high-level programming language. In addition, we must exclude low-level machine features
(registers, addresses, and interrupts) from the language and let a virtual
machine control them. If we want real-time systems to be highly reliable, we
must stop programming them in assembly language. (The use of hardware
protection mechanisms is merely an expensive, inadequate way of making
arbitrary machine language programs behave almost as predictably as compiled programs.)

A Concurrent Pascal compiler will check that the private data of a process
only are accessed by that process. It will also check that the data structure
of a class or monitor only is accessed by its procedures.

Figure 8 shows that *access rights* within an operating system normally
are not tree structured. Instead they form a directed graph. This partly
explains why the traditional scope rules of block-structured languages are
inconvenient for concurrent programming (and for sequential programming
as well). In Concurrent Pascal one can state the access rights of components
in the program text and have them checked by a compiler.

Since the execution of a monitor procedure will delay the execution of
further calls of the same monitor, we must prevent a monitor from calling
itself recursively. Otherwise, processes can become *deadlocked*. So the compiler will check that the access rights of system components are hierarchically
ordered (or, if you like, that there are no cycles in the access graph).

The *hierarchical ordering* of system components has vital consequences
for system design and testing (Brinch Hansen 1974a).

A hierarchical operating system will be tested component by component,
bottom up (but could, of course, be conceived top down or by iteration).
When an incomplete operating system has been shown to work correctly (by
proof or testing), a compiler can ensure that this part of the system will continue to work correctly when new untested program components are added
on top of it. Programming errors within new components cannot cause old
components to fail because old components do not call new components, and
new components only call old components through well-defined procedures

that have already been tested.

(Strictly speaking, a compiler can only check that single monitor calls are made correctly; it cannot check sequences of monitor calls, for example whether a resource is always reserved before it is released. So one can only hope for compile time assurance of *partial correctness*.)

Several other reasons besides program correctness make a hierarchical structure attractive:

1. A hierarchical operating system can be studied in a step-wise manner as a sequence of *abstract machines* simulated by programs (Dijkstra 1971).

2. A partial ordering of process interactions permits one to use *mathematical induction* to prove certain overall properties of the system, such as the absence of deadlocks (Brinch Hansen 1973).

3. *Efficient resource utilization* can be achieved by ordering the program components according to the speed of the physical resources they control, with the fastest resources being controlled at the bottom of the system (Dijkstra 1971).

4. A hierarchical system designed according to the previous criteria is often *nearly decomposable* from an analytical point of view. This means that one can develop stochastic models of its dynamic behavior in a stepwise manner (Simon 1962).

F. Final Remarks

It seems most natural to represent a hierarchical system structure, such as Fig. 8, by a two-dimensional picture. But when we write a concurrent program we must somehow represent these access rules by linear text. This limitation of written language tends to obscure the simplicity of the original structure. That is why I have tried to explain the purpose of Concurrent Pascal by means of pictures instead of language notation.

The class concept is a restricted form of the class concept of Simula 67 (Dahl 1972). Dijkstra (1971) suggested the idea of monitors. The first structured language notation for monitors was proposed in Brinch Hansen (1973), and illustrated by examples in Hoare (1974). The queue variables needed by monitors for process scheduling were suggested in Brinch Hansen (1972) and modified in Hoare (1974).

The main contribution of Concurrent Pascal is to extend monitors with explicit access rights that can be checked at compile time. Concurrent Pascal has been implemented at Caltech for the PDP 11/45 computer. Our system uses sequential Pascal as a job control and user programming language.

II. The Use of Concurrent Pascal

A. Introduction

In Part I the concepts of Concurrent Pascal were explained informally by means of pictures of a hierarchical spooling system. I will now use the same example to introduce the language notation of Concurrent Pascal. The presentation is still informal. I am neither trying to define the language precisely nor to develop a working system. This will be done in other papers. I am just trying to show the flavor of the language.

B. Processes

We will now program the system components in Fig. 8 one at a time from top to bottom (but we could just as well do it bottom up).

Although we only need one *input process*, we may as well define it as a general system type of which several copies may exist:

```
type inputprocess =
process(buffer: diskbuffer);
var block: page;
cycle
  readcards(block);
  buffer.send(block);
end
```

An input process has access to a *buffer* of type diskbuffer (to be defined later). The process has a private variable *block* of type page. The data type page is declared elsewhere as an array of characters:

$$\text{\textbf{type} page = \textbf{array} [1..512] \textbf{of} char}$$

A process type defines a *sequential program*—in this case, an endless cycle that inputs a block from a card reader and sends it through the buffer to another process. We will ignore the details of card reader input.

The *send* operation on the buffer is called as follows (using the block as a parameter):

buffer.send(block)

The next component type we will define is a *job process*:

```
type jobprocess =
process(input, output: diskbuffer);
var block: page;
cycle
  input.receive(block);
  update(block);
  output.send(block);
end
```

A job process has access to two disk buffers called *input* and *output*. It receives blocks from one buffer, updates them, and sends them through the other buffer. The details of updating can be ignored here.

Finally, we need an *output process* that can receive data from a disk buffer and output them on a line printer:

```
type outputprocess =
process(buffer: diskbuffer);
var block: page;
cycle
  buffer.receive(block);
  printlines(block);
end
```

The following shows a declaration of the main system components:

```
var buffer1, buffer2: diskbuffer;
    reader: inputprocess;
    master: jobprocess;
    writer: outputprocess;
```

There is an input process, called the *reader*, a job process, called the *master*, and an output process, called the *writer*. Then there are two disk buffers, *buffer1* and *buffer2*, that connect them.

Later I will explain how a disk buffer is defined and initialized. If we assume that the disk buffers already have been initialized, we can initialize the input process as follows:

init reader(buffer1)

The *init* statement allocates space for the *private variables* of the reader process and starts its execution as a sequential process with access to buffer1.

The *access rights* of a process to other system components, such as buffer1, are also called its *parameters*. A process can only be initialized once. After initalization, the parameters and private variables of a process exist forever. They are called *permanent variables*.

The init statement can be used to start concurrent execution of several processes and define their access rights. As an example, the statement

init reader(buffer1), master(buffer1, buffer2), writer(buffer2)

starts concurrent execution of the reader process (with access to buffer1), the master process (with access to both buffers), and the writer process (with access to buffer2).

A process can only access its own parameters and private variables. The latter are not accessible to other system components. Compare this with the more liberal scope rules of block-structured languages in which a program block can access not only its own parameters and local variables, but also those declared in outer blocks. In Concurrent Pascal, all variables accessible to a system component are declared within its type definition. This access rule and the init statement make it possible for a programmer to state access rights explicitly and have them checked by a compiler. They also make it possible to study a system type as a self-contained program unit.

Although the programming examples do not show this, one can also define constants, data types, and procedures within a process. These objects can only be used within the process type.

C. Monitors

The *disk buffer* is a monitor type:

```
type diskbuffer =
monitor(consoleaccess, diskaccess: resource;
    base, limit: integer);

var disk: virtualdisk; sender, receiver: queue;
    head, tail, length: integer;
```

```
procedure entry send(block: page);
begin
  if length = limit then delay(sender);
  disk.write(base + tail, block);
  tail := (tail + 1) mod limit;
  length := length + 1;
  continue(receiver);
end;

procedure entry receive(var block: page);
begin
  if length = 0 then delay(receiver);
  disk.read(base + head, block);
  head := (head + 1) mod limit;
  length := length - 1;
  continue(sender);
end;

begin "initial statement"
  init disk(consoleaccess, diskaccess);
  head := 0; tail := 0; length := 0;
end
```

A disk buffer has access to two other components, *consoleaccess* and *diskaccess*, of type resource (to be defined later). It also has access to two integer constants defining the *base* address and *limit* of the buffer on the disk.

The monitor declares a set of *shared variables*: The *disk* is declared as a variable of type virtualdisk. Two variables of type queue are used to delay the *sender* and *receiver* processes until the buffer becomes nonfull and nonempty. Three integers define the relative addresses of the *head* and *tail* elements of the buffer and its current *length*.

The monitor defines two *monitor procedures*, send and receive. They are marked with the word *entry* to distinguish them from local procedures used within the monitor (there are none of these in this example).

Receive returns a page to the calling process. If the buffer is empty, the calling process is *delayed* in the receiver queue until another process sends a page through the buffer. The receive procedure will then read and remove a page from the head of the disk buffer by calling a *read* operation defined within the virtualdisk type:

$$\text{disk.read(base + head, block)}$$

Finally, the receive procedure will *continue* the execution of a sending process
(if the latter is waiting in the sender queue).

Send is similar to receive.

The queueing mechanism will be explained in detail in the next section.

The *initial statement* of a disk buffer initializes its virtual disk with access
to the console and disk resources. It also sets the buffer length to zero.
(Notice, that a disk buffer does not use its access rights to the console and
disk, but only passes them on to a virtual disk declared within it.)

The following shows a declaration of two system components of type
resource and two integers defining the base and limit of a disk buffer:

```
var consoleaccess, diskaccess: resource;
    base, limit: integer;
    buffer: diskbuffer;
```

If we assume that these variables already have been initialized, we can
initialize a disk buffer as follows:

```
init buffer(consoleaccess, diskaccess, base, limit)
```

The *init* statement allocates storage for the parameters and shared variables
of the disk buffer and executes its initial statement.

A monitor can only be initialized once. After initialization, the parameters and shared variables of a monitor exist forever. They are called *permanent variables*. The parameters and local variables of a monitor procedure,
however, exist only while it is being executed. They are called *temporary
variables*.

A monitor procedure can only access its own temporary and permanent
variables. These variables are not accessible to other system components.
Other components can, however, call procedure entries within a monitor.
While a monitor procedure is being executed, it has *exclusive access* to the
permanent variables of the monitor. If concurrent processes try to call procedures within the same monitor simultaneously, these procedures will be
executed strictly one at a time.

Only monitors and constants can be permanent parameters of processes
and monitors. This rule ensures that processes only communicate by means
of monitors.

It is possible to define constants, data types, and local procedures within monitors (and processes). The local procedures of a system type can only be called within the system type. To prevent *deadlock* of monitor calls and ensure that access rights are hierarchical the following rules are enforced: A procedure must be declared before it can be called; procedure definitions cannot be nested and cannot call themselves; a system type cannot call its own procedure entries.

The absence of recursion makes it possible for a compiler to determine the store requirements of all system components. This and the use of permanent components make it possible to use *fixed store allocation* on a computer that does not support paging.

Since system components are permanent they must be declared as permanent variables of other components.

D. Queues

A monitor procedure can delay a calling process for any length of time by executing a *delay* operation on a queue variable. Only one process at a time can wait in a queue. When a calling process is delayed by a monitor procedure it loses its exclusive access to the monitor variables until another process calls the same monitor and executes a continue operation on the queue in which the process is waiting.

The *continue* operation makes the calling process return from its monitor call. If any process is waiting in the selected queue, it will immediately resume the execution of the monitor procedure that delayed it. After being resumed, the process again has exclusive access to the permanent variables of the monitor.

Other variants of process queues (called "events" and "conditions") are proposed in Brinch Hansen (1972) and Hoare (1974). They are multiprocess queues that use different (but fixed) scheduling rules. We do not yet know from experience which kind of queue will be the most convenient one for operating system design. A single-process queue is the simplest tool that gives the programmer complete control of the scheduling of individual processes. Later, I will show how multiprocess queues can be built from single-process queues.

A queue must be declared as a permanent variable within a monitor type.

E. Classes

Every disk buffer has its own virtual disk. A *virtual disk* is defined as a class type:

```
type virtualdisk =
class(consoleaccess, diskaccess: resource);

var terminal: virtualconsole; peripheral: disk;

procedure entry read(pageno: integer; var block: page);
var error: boolean;
begin
  repeat
    diskaccess.request;
    peripheral.read(pageno, block, error);
    diskaccess.release;
    if error then terminal.write('disk failure');
  until not error;
end;

procedure entry write(pageno: integer; block: page);
begin "similar to read" end;

begin "initial statement"
  init terminal(consoleaccess), peripheral;
end
```

A virtual disk has access to a console resource and a disk resource. Its permanent variables define a virtual console and a disk. A process can access its virtual disk by means of *read* and *write* procedures. These procedure entries *request* and *release* exclusive access to the real disk before and after each block transfer. If the real disk fails, the virtual disk calls its virtual console to report the error.

The *initial statement* of a virtual disk initializes its virtual console and the real disk.

Section II-C shows an example of how a virtual disk is declared and initialized (within a disk buffer).

A class can only be initialized once. After initialization, its parameters and private variables exist forever. A class procedure can only access its own temporary and permanent variables. These cannot be accessed by other components.

A class is a system component that cannot be called simultaneously by several other components. This is guaranteed by the following rule: A class must be declared as a permanent variable within a system type; a class can be passed as a permanent parameter to another class (but not to a process or monitor). So a chain of nested class calls can only be started by a single process or monitor. Consequently, it is not necessary to schedule simultaneous class calls at run time—they cannot occur.

F. Input/Output

The real *disk* is controlled by a class

type disk = **class**

with two procedure entries

read(pageno, block, error)
write(pageno, block, error)

The class uses a standard procedure

io(block, param, device)

to transfer a block to or from the disk device. The io parameter is a record

var param:
   record
      operation: iooperation;
      result: ioresult;
      pageno: integer
   end

that defines an input/output operation, its result, and a page number on the disk. The calling process is delayed until an io operation has been completed.

A *virtual console* is also defined as a class

type virtualconsole =
class(access: resource);
var terminal: console;

It can be accessed by read and write operations that are similar to each other:

```
        procedure entry read(var text: line);
        begin
            access.request;
            terminal.read(text);
            access.release;
        end
```

The real *console* is controlled by a class that is similar to the disk class.

G. Multiprocess Scheduling

Access to the console and disk is controlled by two monitors of type *resource*. To simplify the presentation, I will assume that competing processes are served in first-come, first-served order. (A much better disk scheduling algorithm is defined in Hoare (1974). It can be programmed in Concurrent Pascal as well, but involves more details than the present one.)

We will define a multiprocess queue as an array of single-process queues

$$\text{type multiqueue} = \textbf{array } [0..\text{qlength}-1] \textbf{ of } \text{queue}$$

where qlength is an upper bound on the number of concurrent processes in the system.

A first-come, first-served scheduler is now straightforward to program:

```
type resource =
monitor

var free: boolean; q: multiqueue;
    head, tail, length: integer;

procedure entry request;
var arrival: integer;
begin
    if free then free := false
    else
        begin
            arrival := tail;
            tail := (tail + 1) mod qlength;
```

```
        length := length + 1;
        delay(q[arrival]);
      end;
  end;


  procedure entry release;
  var departure: integer;
  begin
    if length = 0 then free := true
    else
      begin
        departure := head;
        head := (head + 1) mod qlength;
        length := length − 1;
        continue(q[departure]);
      end;
  end;


  begin "initial statement"
    free := true; length := 0;
    head := 0; tail := 0;
  end
```

H. Initial Process

Finally, we will put all these components together into a concurrent program. A Concurrent Pascal program consists of nested definitions of system types. The outermost system type is an anonymous process, called the *initial process*. An instance of this process is created during system loading. It initializes the other system components.

The initial process defines system types and instances of them. It executes statements that initializes these system components. In our example, the initial process can be sketched as follows (ignoring the problem of how base addresses and limits of disk buffers are defined):

```
type
  resource = monitor ... end;
  console = class ... end;
  virtualconsole = class(access: resource); ... end;
```

```
    disk = class ... end;
    virtualdisk = class(consoleaccess, diskaccess: resource); ... end;
    diskbuffer =
        monitor(consoleaccess, diskaccess: resource; base, limit: integer); ...
        end;
    inputprocess = process(buffer: diskbuffer); ... end;
    jobprocess = process(input, output: diskbuffer); ... end;
    outputprocess = process(buffer: diskbuffer); ... end;
var
    consoleaccess, diskaccess: resource;
    buffer1, buffer2: diskbuffer;
    reader: inputprocess;
    master: jobprocess;
    writer: outputprocess;
begin
    init consoleaccess, diskaccess,
        buffer1(consoleaccess, diskaccess, base1, limit1),
        buffer2(consoleaccess, diskaccess, base2, limit2),
        reader(buffer1),
        master(buffer1, buffer2),
        writer(buffer2);
end.
```

When the execution of a process (such as the initial process) terminates, its private variables continue to exist. This is necessary because these variables may have been passed as permanent parameters to other system components.

Acknowledgements

It is a pleasure to acknowledge the immense value of a continuous exchange of idea with C.A.R. Hoare on structured multiprogramming. I also thank my students L. Medina and R. Varela for their helpful comments on this paper.

References

Brinch Hansen, P. 1970. The nucleus of a multiprogramming system. *Communications of the ACM 13*, 4 (April), 238–250. *Article 2.*

Brinch Hansen, P. 1972. Structured multiprogramming. *Communications of the ACM 15*, 7 (July), 574–578. *Article 4*.

Brinch Hansen, P. 1973. *Operating System Principles*. Prentice-Hall, Englewood Cliffs, NJ, (July).

Brinch Hansen, P. 1974a. A programming methodology for operating system design. *Proceedings of the IFIP Congress 74*, Stockholm, Sweden, (August). North-Holland, Amsterdam, The Netherlands, 394–397.

Brinch Hansen, P. 1974b. Concurrent programming concepts. *ACM Computing Surveys 5*, 4 (December), 223–245.

Dahl, O.-J., and Hoare, C.A.R. 1972. Hierarchical program structures. In *Structured Programming*, O.-J. Dahl, E.W. Dijkstra, and C.A.R. Hoare, Eds. Academic Press, New York.

Dijkstra, E.W. 1971. Hierarchical ordering of sequential processes. *Acta Informatica 1*, 2, 115–138.

Hoare, C.A.R. 1974. Monitors: An operating system structuring concept. *Communications of the ACM 17*, 10 (October), 549–557.

Simon, H.A. 1962. The architeture of complexity. *Proceedings of the American Philosophical Society 106*, 6, 468–482.

Wirth, N. 1971. The programming language Pascal. *Acta Informatica 1*, 1, 35–63.

8

The Solo Operating System: A Concurrent Pascal Program*

(1976)

This is a description of the single-user operating system Solo written in the programming language Concurrent Pascal. It supports the development of Sequential and Concurrent Pascal programs for the PDP 11/45 computer. Input/output are handled by concurrent processes. Pascal programs can call one another recursively and pass arbitrary parameters among themselves. This makes it possible to use Pascal as a job control language. Solo is the first major example of a hierarchical concurrent program implemented in terms of abstract data types (classes, monitors and processes) with compile-time control of most access rights. It is described here from the user's point of view as an introduction to another paper describing its internal structure.

1 Introduction

This is a description of the first operating system *Solo* written in the programming language Concurrent Pascal (Brinch Hansen 1975). It is a simple, but useful single-user operating system for the development and distribution of Pascal programs for the PDP 11/45 computer. It has been in use since May 1975.

From the user's point of view there is nothing unusual about the system. It supports editing, compilation and storage of Sequential and Concurrent Pascal programs. These programs can access either console, cards, printer, tape or disk at several levels (character by character, page by page, file

*P. Brinch Hansen, The Solo operating system: A Concurrent Pascal program. *Software—Practice and Experience 6*, 2 (April–June 1976), 141–149. Copyright © 1975, Per Brinch Hansen. Also in P. Brinch Hansen, *The Architecture of Concurrent Programs*, Prentice Hall, Englewood Cliffs, NJ, (July 1977), 69–80. Copyright © 1977, Prentice Hall. Reprinted by permission.

by file, or by direct device access). Input, processing, and output of files are handled by concurrent processes. Pascal programs can call one another recursively and pass arbitrary parameters among themselves. This makes it possible to use Pascal as a job control language (Brinch Hansen 1976a).

To the system programmer, however, Solo is quite different from many other operating systems:

1. Less than 4 per cent of it is written in machine language. The rest is written in Sequential and Concurrent Pascal.

2. In contrast to machine-oriented languages, Pascal does not contain low-level programming features, such as registers, addresses and interrupts. These are all handled by the virtual machine on which compiled programs run.

3. System protection is achieved largely by means of compile-time checking of access rights. Run-time checking is minimal and is not supported by hardware mechanisms.

4. Solo is the first major example of a hierarchical concurrent program implemented by means of abstract data types (classes, monitors, and processes).

5. The complete system consisting of more than 100,000 machine words of code (including two compilers) was developed by a student and myself in less than a year.

To appreciate the usefulness of Concurrent Pascal one needs a good understanding of at least one operating system written in the language. The purpose of this description is to look at the Solo system from a user's point of view before studying its internal structure (Brinch Hansen 1976b). It tells how the user operates the system, how data flow inside it, how programs call one another and communicate, how files are stored on disk, and how well the system performs in typical tasks.

2   Job Control

The user controls program execution from a display (or a teletype). He calls a program by writing its name and its parameters, for example:

```
move(5)
read(maketemp, seqcode, true)
```

The first command positions a magnetic tape at file number 5. The second one inputs the file to disk and stores it as sequential code named maketemp. The boolean true protects the file against accidental deletion in the future.

Programs try to be helpful to the user when he needs it. If the user forgets which programs are available, he may for example type:

```
help
```

(or anything else). The system responds by writing:

```
not executable, try
list(catalog, seqcode, console)
```

The suggested command lists the names of all sequential programs on the console.

If the user knows that the disk contains a certain program, but is uncertain about its parameter conventions, he can simply call it as a program without parameters, for example:

```
read
```

The program then gives the necessary information:

```
try again
read(file: identifier; kind: filekind; protect: boolean)
using
filekind = (scratch, ascii, seqcode, concode)
```

Still more information can be gained about a program by reading its manual:

```
copy(readman, console)
```

A user session may begin with the input of a new Pascal program from cards to disk:

```
copy(cards, sorttext)
```

followed by a compilation:

pascal(sorttext, printer, sort)

If the compiler reports errors on the program listing:

pascal:
compilation errors

the next step is usually to edit the program text:

edit(sorttext)
. . .

and compile it again. After a successful compilation, the user program can now be called directly:

sort(. . .)

The system can also read job control commands from other media, for example:

do(tape)

A task is preempted by pushing the bell key on the console. This causes the system to reload and initialize itself. The command *start* can be used to replace the Solo system with any other concurrent program stored on disk.

3   Data Flow

Figure 1 shows the data flow inside the system when the user is processing a single text file sequentially by copying, editing, or compiling it.

The input, processing, and output of text take place simultaneously. Processing is done by a *job process* that starts input by sending an argument through a buffer to an input process. The argument is the name of the input device or disk file.

The *input process* sends the data through another buffer to the job process. At the end of the file the input process sends an argument through yet another buffer to the job process indicating whether transmission errors occurred during the input.

Output is handled similarly by means of an *output process* and another set of buffers.

In a single-user operating system it is desirable to be able to process a file continuously at the highest possible speed. So the data are buffered in core instead of on disk. The capacity of each buffer is 512 characters.

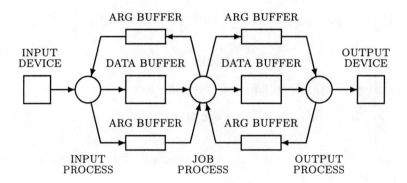

Figure 1 Processes and buffers.

4   Control Flow

Figure 2 shows what happens when the user types a command such as:

edit(cards, tape)

After system loading the machine executes a Concurrent Pascal program (Solo) consisting of three processes. Initially the input and output processes both load and call a sequential program *io* while the job process calls another sequential program *do*. The do program reads the user command from the console and calls the *edit* program with two parameters, *cards* and *tape*.

The editor starts its input by sending the first parameter to the io program executed by the input process. This causes the io program to call another program *cards* which then begins to read cards and send them to the job process.

The editor starts its output by sending the second parameter to the io program executed by the output process. The latter then calls a program *tape* which reads data from the job process and puts them on tape.

At the end of the file the cards and tape programs return to the io programs which then await further instructions from the job process. The editor returns to the do program which then reads and interprets the next command from the console.

It is worth observing that the operating system itself has no built-in drivers for input/output from various devices. Data are simply produced

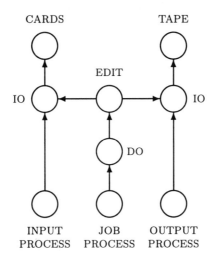

Figure 2 Concurrent processes and sequential programs.

and consumed by Sequential Pascal programs stored on disk. The operating system only contains the mechanism to call these. This gives the user complete freedom to supplement the system with new devices and simulate complicated input/output such as the merging, splitting and formatting of files without changing the job programs.

Most important is the ability of Sequential Pascal programs to call one another recursively with arbitrary parameters. In Fig. 2, for example, the do program calls the edit program with two identifiers as parameters. This removes the need for a separate (awkward) job control language. *The job control language is Pascal.*

This is illustrated more dramatically in Fig. 3 which shows how the command:

pascal(sorttext, printer, sort)

causes the do program to call the program *pascal*. The latter in turn calls seven compiler passes one at a time, and (if the compiled program is correct) *pascal* finally calls the filing system to store the generated code.

A program does not know whether it is being called by another program or directly from the console. In Fig. 3 the program *pascal* calls the filing sys-

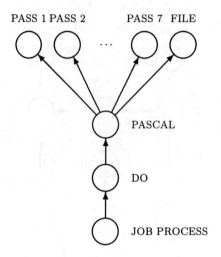

Figure 3 Compilation.

tem. The user, may, however, also call the file system directly, for example, to protect his program against accidental deletion:

file(protect, sort, true)

The Pascal *pointer* and *heap* concepts give programs the ability to pass arbitrarily complicated data structures among each other, such as symbol tables during compilation (Jensen 1974). In most cases, however, it suffices to be able to use identifiers, integers, and booleans as program parameters.

5   Store Allocation

The run-time environment of Sequential and Concurrent Pascal is a kernel of 4 K words. This is the only program written in machine language. The user loads the kernel from disk into core by means of the operator's panel. The kernel then loads the Solo system and starts it. The Solo system consists of a fixed number of processes. They occupy fixed amounts of core store determined by the compiler.

All other programs are written in Sequential Pascal. Each process stores the code of the currently executed program in a fixed core segment. After termination of a program called by another, the process reloads the previous program from disk and returns to it. The data used by a process and the programs called by it are all stored in a core resident stack of fixed length.

6 File System

The backing store is a slow *disk* with removable packs. Each user has his own disk pack containing the system and his private files. So there is no need for a hierarchical file system.

A disk pack contains a *catalog* of all files stored on it. The catalog describes itself as a file. A *file* is described by its name, type, protection and disk address. Files are looked up by hashing.

All system programs check the *types* of their input files before operating on them and associate types with their output files. The Sequential Pascal compiler, for example, will take input from an ascii file (but not from a scratch file), and will make its output a sequential code file. The possible file types are scratch, ascii, seqcode and concode.

Since each user has his own disk pack, files need only be *protected* against accidental overwriting or deletion. All files are initially unprotected. To protect one the user must call the file system from the console as described in Section 4.

To avoid compacting of files (lasting several minutes), file pages are scattered on disk and addressed indirectly through a *page map* (Fig. 4). A file is opened by looking it up in the catalog and bringing its page map into core.

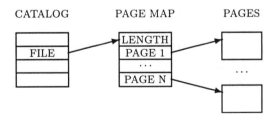

Figure 4 File system.

The resident part of the Solo system implements only the most frequently used file operations: lookup, open, close, get and put. A nonresident, sequential program, called *file*, handles the more complicated and less frequently used operations: create, replace, rename, protect, and delete file.

7   Disk Allocation

The disk always contains a scratch file of 255 pages called *next*. A program creates a new file by outputting data to this file. It then calls the file system to associate the data with a new name, a type, and a length (≤ 255). Having done this the file system creates a new instance of *next*.

   This scheme has two advantages:

1. All files are initialized with typed data.

2. A program creating a file need only call the nonresident file system once (after producing the file). Without the file *next* the file system would have to be called at least twice: before output to create the file, and after output to define its final length.

   The disadvantages of having a single file *next* is that a program can only create one file at a time.

   Unused disk pages are defined by a powerset of page indices stored on the disk.

   On a slow disk special care must be taken to make *program loading* fast. If program pages were randomly scattered on the disk it would take 16 seconds to load the compiler and its input/output drivers. An algorithm described in Brinch Hansen (1976c) reduces this to 5 seconds. When the system creates the file *next* it tries to place it on consecutive pages within neighboring cylinders as far as possible (but will scatter the pages somewhat if it has to). It then rearranges the page indices within the page map to minimize the number of disk revolutions and cylinder movements needed to load the file. Since this is done before a program is compiled and stored on disk it is called *disk scheduling at compile time*.

   The system uses a different allocation technique for the two temporary files used during compilation. Each pass of the compiler takes input from a file produced by its predecessor and delivers output to its successor on another file. A program *maketemp* creates these files and interleaves their page indices (making every second page belong to one file and every second one to the other). This makes the disk head sweep slowly across both files during a pass instead of moving wildly back and forth between them.

8   Operator Communication

The user communicates with the system through a console. Since a task (such as editing) usually involves several programs executed by concurrent processes these programs must identify themselves to the user before asking for input or making output:

```
do:
edit(cards, tape)
edit:
...

do:
...
```

Program identity is only displayed every time the user starts talking to a different program. A program that communicates several times with the user without interruption (such as the editor) only identifies itself once.

Normally only one program at a time tries to talk to the user (the current program executed by the job process). But an input/output error may cause a message from another process:

```
tape:
inspect
```

Since processes rarely compete for the console, it is sufficient to give a process *exclusive access* to the user for input or output of a single line. A conversation of several lines will seldom be interrupted.

A Pascal program only calls the operating system once with its identification. The system will then automatically display it when necessary.

9   Size and Performance

The Solo system consists of an operating system written in Concurrent Pascal and a set of system programs written in Sequential Pascal:

Program	Pascal lines	Machine words
operating system	1,300	4 K
do, io	700	4 K
file system	900	5 K
concurrent compiler	8,300	42 K
sequential compiler	8,300	42 K
editor	400	2 K
input/output programs	600	3 K
others	1,300	8 K
	21,800	110 K

(The two Pascal compilers can be used under different operating systems written in Concurrent Pascal—not just Solo.)

The amount of code written in different programming languages is:

Language	%
machine language	4
Concurrent Pascal	4
Sequential Pascal	92

This clearly shows that a good sequential programming language is more important for operating system design than a concurrent language. But although a concurrent program may be small it still seems worthwhile to write it in a high-level language that enables a compiler to do thorough checking of data types and access rights. Otherwise, it is far too easy to make time-dependent programming errors that are extremely difficult to locate.

The kernel written in machine language implements the process and monitor concepts of Concurrent Pascal and responds to interrupts. It is independent of the particular operating system running on top of it.

The Solo system requires a core store of 39 K words for programs and data:

Programs	K words
kernel	4
operating system	11
input/output programs	6
job programs	18
core store	39

This amount of space allows the Pascal compiler to compile itself.

The speed of text processing using disk input and tape output is:

Program	char/sec
copy	11,600
edit	3,300–6,200
compile	240

All these tasks are 60–100 per cent disk limited. These figures do not distinguish between time spent waiting for peripherals and time spent executing operating system or user code since this distinction is irrelevant to the user. They illustrate an overall performance of a system written in a high-level language using straightforward code generation without any optimization.

10   Final Remarks

The compilers for Sequential and Concurrent Pascal were designed and implemented by Al Hartmann and me in half a year. I wrote the operating system and its utility programs in 3 months. In machine language this would have required 20–30 man-years and nobody would have been able to understand the system fully. The use of an efficient, abstract programming language reduced the development cost to less than 2 man-years and produced a system that is completely understood by two programmers.

The low cost of programming makes it acceptable to throw away awkward programs and rewrite them. We did this several times: An early 6-pass compiler was never released (although it worked perfectly) because we found its structure too complicated. The first operating system written in Concurrent Pascal (called *Deamy*) was used only to evaluate the expressive power of the language and was never built (Brinch Hansen 1974). The second one (called *Pilot*) was used for several months but was too slow.

From a manufacturer's point of view it is now realistic and attractive to replace a huge ineffective "general-purpose" operating system with a range of small, efficient systems for special purposes.

The kernel, the operating system, and the compilers were tested very systematically initially and appear to be correct.

Acknowledgements

The work of Bob Deverill and Al Hartmann in implementing the kernel and compiler of Concurrent Pascal has been essential for this project. I am also grateful to Gilbert McCann for his encouragement and support.

Stoy and Strachey (1972) recommend that one should learn to build good operating systems for single-users before trying to satisfy many users simultaneously. I have found this to be very good advice. I have also tried to follow the advice of Lampson (1974) and make both high- and low-level abstractions available to the user programmer.

The Concurrent Pascal project is supported by the National Science Foundation under grant number DCR74–17331.

References

Brinch Hansen, P. 1974. Deamy—A structured operating system. Information Science, California Institute of Technology, (May), (out of print).

Brinch Hansen, P. 1975. The programming language Concurrent Pascal. *IEEE Transactions on Software Engineering 1*, 2 (June), 199–207. *Article 7.*

Brinch Hansen, P. 1976a. The Solo operating system: Job interface. *Software—Practice and Experience 6*, 2 (April–June), 151–164.

Brinch Hansen, P. 1976b. The Solo operating system: Processes, monitors amd classes. *Software—Practice and Experience 6*, 2 (April–June), 165–200. *Article 9.*

Brinch Hansen, P. 1976c. Disk scheduling at compile-time. *Software—Practice and Experience 6*, 2 (April–June), 201–205.

Jensen, K., and Wirth, N. 1974. Pascal–User manual and report. *Lecture Notes in Computer Science 18*, Springer-Verlag, New York.

Lampson, B.W. 1974. An open operating system for a single-user machine. In *Operating Systems, Lecture Notes in Computer Science 16*, 208–217.

Stoy, J.E., and Strachey, C. 1972. OS6—An experimental operating system for a small computer. *Computer Journal 15*, 2.

9

The Solo Operating System: Processes, Monitors, and Classes*

(1976)

This paper describes the implementation of the Solo operating system written in Concurrent Pascal. It explains the overall structure and details of the system in which concurrent processes communicate by means of a hierarchy of monitors and classes. The concurrent program is a sequence of nearly independent components of less than one page of text each. The system has been operating since May 1975.

1 Introduction

This is a description of the program structure of the Solo operating system. Solo is a single-user operating system for the PDP 11/45 computer written in the programming language Concurrent Pascal (Brinch Hansen 1976a, 1976b).

The main idea in Concurrent Pascal is to divide the global data structures of an operating system into small parts and define the meaningful operations on each of them. In Solo, for example, there is a data structure, called a resource, that is used to give concurrent processes exclusive access to a disk. This data structure can only be accessed by means of two procedures that request and release access to the disk. The programmer specifies that these are the only operations one can perform on a resource, and the compiler checks that this rule is obeyed in the rest of the system. This approach to program reliability has been called *resource protection at compile-time*

*P. Brinch Hansen, The Solo operating system: Processes, monitors, and classes. *Software—Practice and Experience 6*, 2 (April–June 1976), 165–200. Copyright © 1975, Per Brinch Hansen. Also in P. Brinch Hansen, *The Architecture of Concurrent Programs*, Prentice Hall, Englewood Cliffs, NJ, (July 1977), 98–142. Copyright © 1977, Prentice Hall. Reprinted by permission.

(Brinch Hansen 1973). It makes programs more reliable by detecting incorrect interactions of program components before they are put into operation. It makes them more efficient by reducing the need for hardware protection mechanisms.

The combination of a data structure and the operations used to access it is called an *abstract data type*. It is abstract because the rest of the system need only know what operations one can perform on it but can ignore the details of how they are carried out. A Concurrent Pascal program is constructed from three kinds of abstract data types: processes, monitors and classes. *Processes* perform concurrent operations on data structures. They use *monitors* to synchronize themselves and exchange data. They access private data structures by means of *classes*. Brinch Hansen (1975a) is an overview of these concepts and their use in concurrent programming.

Solo is the first major example of a hierarchical concurrent program implemented in terms of abstract data types. It has been in use since May 1975. This is a complete, annotated program listing of the system. It also explains how the system was tested systematically.

2 Program Structure

Solo consists of a hierarchy of *program layers*, each of which controls a particular kind of computer resource, and a set of concurrent processes that use these resources (Fig. 1):

- *Resource management* controls the scheduling of the operator's console and the disk among concurrent processes.

- *Console management* lets processes communicate with the operator after they have gained access to the console.

- *Disk management* gives processes access to the disk files and a catalog describing them.

- *Program management* fetches program files from disk into core on demand from processes that wish to execute them.

- *Buffer management* transmits data among processes.

These facilities are used by seven concurrent processes:

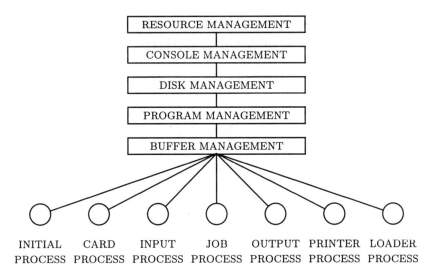

Figure 1 Program layers and processes.

- A *job process* executes Pascal programs upon request from the operator.

- Two *input/output processes* produce and consume the data of the job process.

- A *card process* feeds punched cards to the input process which then removes trailing blanks from them and packs the text into blocks.

- A *printer process* prints lines that are unpacked from blocks and sent to it by the output process.

- A *loader process* preempts and reinitializes the operating system when the operator pushes the bell key on the console.

- An *initial process* starts up the rest of the system after system loading.

The term *program layer* is only used as a convenient way of explaining the gross division of labor within the system. It cannot be represented by any language notation in Concurrent Pascal.

3   Abstract Data Types

Each program layer consists of one or more abstract data types (monitors and classes).

Resource management

A *fifo* class implements a first-in, first-out queue that is used to maintain multiprocess queues and message buffers.

A *resource* monitor gives processes exclusive access to a computer resource. It is used to control disk access.

A *typewriter resource* monitor gives processes exclusive access to a console and tells them whether they need to identify themselves to the operator.

Console management

A *typewriter* class transmits a single line between a process and a console (but does not give a process exclusive access to it).

A *terminal* class gives a process the illusion that it has its own private console by giving it exclusive access to the operator for input or output of a single line.

A *terminal stream* makes a terminal look character oriented.

Disk management

A *disk* class can access a page anywhere on disk (but does not give a process exclusive access to it). It uses a terminal to report disk failure.

A *disk file* can access any page belonging to a particular file. The file pages, which may be scattered on disk, are addressed indirectly through a page map. The disk address of the page map identifies the file. It uses a disk to access the map and its pages.

A *disk table* class makes a disk catalog of files look like an array of entries, some of which describe files, and some of which are empty. The entries are identified by numeric indices. It uses a disk file to access the catalog page by page.

A *disk catalog* monitor can look up files in a disk catalog by means of their names. It uses a resource to get exclusive acess to the disk and a disk table to scan the catalog.

A *data file* class gives a process access to a named disk file. It uses a resource, a disk catalog, and a disk file to access the disk.

Program management

A *program file* class can load a named disk file into core when a process wishes to execute it. It uses a resource, a disk catalog, and a disk file to do this.

A *program stack* monitor keeps track of nested program calls within a process.

Buffer management

The *buffer* monitors transmit various kinds of messages between processes: arguments (scalars or identifiers), lines, and pages.

The following defines the purpose, specification, and implementation of each of these abstract data types.

4   Input/output

The following data types are used in elementary input/output operations:

```
type iodevice =
  (typedevice, diskdevice, tapedevice, printdevice, carddevice);

type iooperation = (input, output, move, control);

type ioarg = (writeeof, rewind, upspace, backspace);

type ioresult =
  (complete, intervention, transmission, failure,
  endfile, endmedium, startmedium);

type ioparam =
  record
    operation: iooperation;
    status: ioresult;
    arg: ioarg
  end;

  const nl = '(:10:)'; ff = '(:12:)'; cr = '(:13:)'; em = '(:25:)';
```

```
const linelength = 132;
type line = array [1..linelength] of char;

const pagelength = 512;
type page = array [1..pagelength] of char;
```

They define the identifiers of peripheral devices, input/output operations and their results as well as the data types to be transferred (printer lines or disk pages). The details of input/output operations are explained in Brinch Hansen (1975b).

5   Fifo Queue

type fifo = class(limit: integer)

A fifo keeps track of the length and the head and tail indices of an array used as a first-in, first-out queue (but does not contain the queue elements themselves). A fifo is initialized with a constant that defines its range of queue indices 1..limit. A user of a fifo must ensure that the length of the queue remains within its physical limit:

$$0 \leq \text{arrivals} - \text{departures} \leq \text{limit}$$

The routines of a fifo are:

function arrival: integer

Returns the index of the next queue element in which an arrival can take place.

function departure: integer

Returns the index of the next queue element from which a departure can take place.

function empty: boolean

Defines whether the queue is empty (arrivals = departures).

function full: boolean

Defines whether the queue is full (arrivals = departures + limit).

Implementation:

A fifo queue is represented by its head, tail and length. The Concurrent Pascal compiler will ensure that these variables are only accessed by the routines of the class. In general, a class variable can only be accessed by calling one of the routines associated with it (Brinch Hansen 1975a). The final statement of the class is executed when an instance of a fifo queue is declared and initialized.

```
type fifo =
class(limit: integer);

var head, tail, length: integer;

function entry arrival: integer;
begin
   arrival := tail;
   tail := tail mod limit + 1;
   length := length + 1;
end;

function entry departure: integer;
begin
   departure := head;
   head := head mod limit + 1;
   length := length − 1;
end;

function entry empty: boolean;
begin empty := (length = 0) end;

function entry full: boolean;
begin full := (length = limit) end;

begin head := 1; tail := 1; length := 0 end;
```

6   Resource

type resource = monitor

A resource gives exclusive access to a computer resource (but does not perform any operations on the resource itself). A user of a resource must request it before using it and release it afterwards. If the resource is released within a finite time it will also become available to any process requesting it within a finite time. In short, the resource scheduling is fair.

procedure request

Gives the calling process exclusive access to the resource.

procedure release

Makes the resource available for other processes.

Implementation:

A resource is represented by its state (free or used) and a queue of processes waiting for it. The multiprocess queue is represented by two data structures: an array of single-process queues and a fifo to keep track of the queue indices.

The initial statement at the end of the monitor sets the resource state to free and initializes the fifo variable with a constant defining the total number of processes that can wait in the queue.

The compiler will ensure that the monitor variables only can be accessed by calling the routine entries associated with it. The generated code will ensure that at most one process at a time is executing a monitor routine (Brinch Hansen 1975a). The monitor can delay and (later) continue the execution of a calling process.

A routine associated with a class or monitor is called by mentioning the class or monitor variable followed by the name of the routine. As an example

next.arrival

will perform an arrival operation on the fifo variable next.

```
const processcount = 7;
type processqueue = array [1..processcount] of queue;
```

```
type resource =
monitor

  var free: boolean; q: processqueue; next: fifo;

  procedure entry request;
  begin
    if free then free := false
    else delay(q[next.arrival]);
  end;

  procedure entry release;
  begin
    if next.empty then free := true
    else continue(q[next.departure]);
  end;

  begin free := true; init next(processcount) end;
```

7   Typewriter Resource

type resource = monitor

A typewriter resource gives processes exclusive access to a typewriter console. A calling process supplies an identification of itself and is told whether it needs to display it to the operator. The resource scheduling is fair as explained in Section 6.

procedure request(text: line; var changed: boolean)

Gives the calling process exclusive access to the resource. The process identifies itself by a text line. A boolean changed defines whether this is the same identification that was used in the last call of request (in which case there is no need to display it to the operator again).

procedure release

Makes the resource available again for other processes.

Implementation:

```
type typeresource =
monitor

var free: boolean; q: processqueue; next: fifo; header: line;

procedure entry request(text: line; var changed: boolean);
begin
   if free then free := false
   else delay(q[next.arrival]);
   changed := (header <> text);
   header := text;
end;

procedure entry release;
begin
   if next.empty then free := true
   else continue(q[next.departure]);
end;

begin
   free := true; header[1] := nl;
   init next(processcount);
end;
```

8   Typewriter

type typewriter = class(device: iodevice)

A typewriter can transfer a text line to or from a typewriter console. It does not identify the calling process on the console or give it exclusive access to it. A typewriter is initialized with the identifier of the device it controls.

A newline character (nl) terminates the input or output of a line. A line that exceeds 73 characters is forcefully terminated by a newline character.

procedure write(text: line)

Writes a line on the typewriter.

procedure read(var text: line)

Rings the bell on the typewriter and reads a line from it. Single characters or the whole line can be erased and retyped by typing *control c* or *control l*. The typewriter responds to erasure by writing a question mark.

Implementation:

The procedure writechar is not a routine entry; it can only be called within the typewriter class. The standard procedure io delays the calling process until the transfer of a single character is completed.

```
type typewriter =
class(device: iodevice);

const linelimit = 73;
   cancelchar = '(:3:)'; "control c"
   cancelline = '(:12:)'; "control l"

procedure writechar(x: char);
var param: ioparam; c: char;
begin
   param.operation := output;
   c := x;
   io(c, param, device);
end;

procedure entry write(text: line);
var param: ioparam; i: integer; c: char;
begin
   param.operation := output;
   i := 0;
   repeat
      i := i + 1; c := text[i];
      io(c, param, device);
   until (c = nl) or (i = linelimit);
   if c <> nl then writechar(nl);
end;

procedure entry read(var text: line);
```

```
const bel = '(:7:)';
var param: ioparam; i: integer; c: char;
begin
  writechar(bel);
  param.operation := input;
  i := 0;
  repeat
    io(c, param, device);
    if c = cancelline then
      begin
        writechar(nl);
        writechar('?');
        i := 0;
      end
    else if c = cancelchar then
      begin
        if i > 0 then
          begin
            writechar('?');
            i := i - 1;
          end
      end
    else
      begin i := i + 1; text[i] := c end
  until (c = nl) or (i = linelimit);
  if c <> nl then
    begin
      writechar(nl);
      text[linelimit + 1] := nl;
    end;
end;

begin end;
```

9   Terminal

type terminal = class(access: typeresource)

A terminal gives a single process exclusive access to a typewriter, identifies the process to the operator and transfers a line to or from the device. The terminal uses a typewriter resource to get exclusive access to the device.

procedure read(header: line; var text: line)

Writes a header (if necessary) on the typewriter and reads a text line from it.

procedure write(header, text: line)

Writes a header (if necessary) followed by a text line on the typewriter.

The header identifies the calling process. It is only output if it is different from the last header output on the typewriter.

Implementation:

A class or monitor can only call other classes or monitors if they are declared as variables within it or passed as parameters during initialization (Brinch Hansen 1975a). So a terminal can only call the monitor *access* and the class *unit*. These access rights are checked during compilation.

```
type terminal =
class(access: typeresource);

var unit: typewriter;

procedure entry read(header: line; var text: line);
var changed: boolean;
begin
    access.request(header, changed);
    if changed then unit.write(header);
    unit.read(text);
    access.release;
end;
```

```
procedure entry write(header, text: line);
var changed: boolean;
begin
  access.request(header, changed);
  if changed then unit.write(header);
  unit.write(text);
  access.release;
end;

begin init unit(typedevice) end;
```

10   Terminal Stream

type terminalstream = class(operator: terminal)

A terminal stream enables a process to identify itself once and for all and then proceed to read and write single characters on a terminal. A terminal stream uses a terminal to input or output a line at a time.

procedure read(var c: char)

Reads a character from the terminal.

procedure write(c: char)

Writes a character on the terminal.

procedure reset(text: line)

Identifies the calling process.

Implementation:

The terminal stream contains two line buffers for input and output.

```
type terminalstream =
class(operator: terminal);

const linelimit = 80;
```

```
var header: line; endinput: boolean;
  inp, out: record count: integer; text: line end;

procedure initialize(text: line);
begin
  header := text;
  endinput := true;
  out.count := 0;
end;

procedure entry read(var c: char);
begin
  with inp do
    begin
      if endinput then
        begin
          operator.read(header, text);
          count := 0;
        end;
      count := count + 1;
      c := text[count];
      endinput := (c = nl);
    end;
end;

procedure entry write(c: char);
begin
  with out do
    begin
      count := count + 1;
      text[count] := c;
      if (c = nl) or (count = linelimit) then
        begin
          operator.write(header, text);
          count := 0;
        end;
    end;
end;
```

```
   procedure entry reset(text: line);
   begin initialize(text) end;

   begin initialize('unidentified:(:10:)') end;
```

11   Disk

type disk = class(typeuse: typeresource)

A disk can transfer any page to or from a disk device. A disk uses a typewriter resource to get exclusive access to a terminal to report disk failure. After a disk failure, the disk writes a message to the operator and repeats the operation when he types a newline character.

procedure read(pageaddr: integer; var block: univ page)

Reads a page identified by its absolute disk address.

procedure write(pageaddr: integer; var block: univ page)

Writes a page identified by its absolute disk address.

A page is declared as a universal type to make it possible to use the disk to transfer pages of different types (and not just text).

Implementation:

The standard procedure io delays the calling process until the disk transfer is completed (Brinch Hansen 1975b).

```
   type disk =
   class(typeuse: typeresource);

   var operator: terminal;

   procedure transfer(command: iooperation;
     pageaddr: univ ioarg; var block: page);
   var param: ioparam; response: line;
   begin
```

```
  with param, operator do
    begin
      operation := command;
      arg := pageaddr;
      io(block, param, diskdevice);
      while status <> complete do
        begin
          write('disk:(:10:)', 'error(:10:)');
          read('push return(:10:)', response);
          io(block, param, diskdevice);
        end;
    end;
end;


procedure entry read(pageaddr: integer; var block: univ page);
begin transfer(input, pageaddr, block) end;

procedure entry write(pageaddr: integer; var block; univ page);
begin transfer(output, pageaddr, block) end;

begin init operator(typeuse) end;
```

12   Disk File

type diskfile = class(typeuse: typeresource)

A disk file enables a process to access a disk file consisting of a fixed number of pages (≤ 255). A disk file uses a typewriter resource to get exclusive access to the operator after a disk failure.

The disk file is identified by the absolute address of a page map that defines the length of the file and the disk addresses of its pages. To a calling process the pages of a file are numbered 1, 2, ..., length.

Initially, the file is closed (inaccessible). A user of a file must open it before using it and close it afterwards. Read and write have no effect if the file is closed or if the page number is outside the range 1..length.

procedure open(mapaddr: integer)

Makes a disk file with a given page map accessible.

procedure close

Makes the disk file inaccessible.

function length: integer

Returns the length of the disk file (in pages). The length of a closed file is zero.

procedure read(pageno: integer; **var** *block:* **univ** *page)*

Reads a page with a given number from the disk file.

procedure write(pageno: integer; **var** *block:* **univ** *page)*

Writes a page with a given number on the disk file.

Implementation:

The variable *length* is prefixed with the word *entry*. This means that its value can be used directly outside the class. It can, however, only be changed within the class. So a *variable entry* is similar to a function entry. Variable entries can only be used within classes.

```
const maplength = 255;
type filemap =
  record
    filelength: integer;
    pageset: array [1..maplength] of integer
  end;

type diskfile =
class(typeuse: typeresource);

var unit: disk; map: filemap; opened: boolean;

entry length: integer;

function includes(pageno: integer): boolean;
begin
  includes := opened &
```

```
      ( 1 <= pageno) & (pageno <= length);
end;

procedure entry open(mapaddr: integer);
begin
   unit.read(mapaddr, map);
   length := map.filelength;
   opened := true;
end;

procedure entry close;
begin
   length := 0;
   opencd := false;
end;

procedure entry read(pageno: integer; var block: univ page);
begin
   if includes(pageno) then
      unit.read(map.pageset[pageno], block);
end;

procedure entry write(pageno: integer; var block: univ page);
begin
   if includes(pageno) then
      unit.write(map.pageset[pageno], block);
end;

begin
   init unit(typeuse);
   length := 0;
   opened := false;
end;
```

13   Catalog Structure

The disk contains a catalog of all files. The following data types define the
structure of the catalog:

```
const idlength = 12;
type identifier = array [1..idlength] of char;

type filekind = (empty, scratch, ascii, seqcode, concode);

type fileattr =
  record
    kind: filekind;
    addr: integer;
    protected: boolean;
    notused: array [1..5] of integer
  end;

type catentry =
  record
    id: identifier;
    attr: fileattr;
    key, searchlength: integer
  end;

const catpagelength = 16;
type catpage = array [1..catpagelength] of catentry;

const cataddr = 154;
```

The catalog is itself a file defined by a page map stored at the *catalog address*. Every *catalog page* contains a fixed number of catalog entries. A *catalog entry* describes a file by its identifier, attributes and hash key. The search length defines the number of files that have a hash key equal to the index of this entry. It is used to limit the search for a non-existing file name.

The *file attributes* are its kind (empty, scratch, ascii, sequential or concurrent code), the address of its page map, and a boolean defining whether it is protected against accidental deletion or overwriting. The latter is checked by all system programs operating on the disk, but not by the operating system. Solo provides a mechanism for protection, but does not enforce it.

14   Disk Table

type disktable = class(typeuse: typeresource; cataddr: integer)

A disk table makes a disk catalog look like an array of catalog entries identified by numeric indices 1, 2, ..., length. A disk table uses a typewriter resource to get exclusive access to the operator after a disk failure and a catalog address to locate a catalog on disk.

function length: integer

Defines the number of entries in the catalog.

procedure read(i: integer; var elem: catentry)

Reads entry number i in the catalog. If the entry number is outside the range 1..length the contents of the entry is undefined.

Implementation:

A disk table stores the most recently used catalog page to make a sequential search of the catalog fast.

```
type disktable =
class(typeuse: typeresource; cataddr: integer);

var file: diskfile; pageno: integer; block: catpage;

entry length: integer;

procedure entry read(i: integer; var elem: catentry);
var index: integer;
begin
   index := (i − 1) div catpagelength + 1;
   if pageno <> index then
     begin
       pageno := index;
       file.read(pageno, block);
     end;
   elem := block[(i − 1) mod catpagelength + 1];
end;
```

```
begin
  init file(typeuse);
  file.open(cataddr);
  length := file.length * catpagelength;
  pageno := 0;
end;
```

15   Disk Catalog

type diskcatalog =
monitor(typeuse: typeresource; diskuse: resource; cataddr: integer)

The disk catalog describes all disk files by means of a set of named entries
that can be looked up by processes. A disk catalog uses a resource to get
exclusive access to the disk during a catalog lookup and a typewriter resource
to get exclusive access to the operator after a disk failure. It uses a catalog
address to locate the catalog on disk.

procedure lookup(id: identifier; var attr: fileattr; var found: boolean)

Searches for a catalog entry describing a file with a given identifier and
indicates whether it found it. If so, it also returns the file attributes.

Implementation:

A disk catalog uses a disk table to make a cyclical search for an identifier.
The initial catalog entry is selected by hashing. The search stops when the
identifier is found or when there are no more entries with the same hash
key. The disk catalog has exclusive access to the disk during the lookup to
prevent competing processes from causing disk arm movement.

```
type diskcatalog =
monitor(typeuse: typeresource; diskuse: resource; cataddr: integer);

var table: disktable;

function hash(id: identifier): integer;
var key, i: integer; c: char;
begin
```

```
      key := 1; i := 0;
      repeat
        i := i + 1; c := id[i];
        if c <> ' ' then
          key := key * ord(c) mod table.length + 1;
      until (c = ' ') or (i = idlength);
      hash := key;
    end;

  procedure entry lookup(id: identifier;
    var attr: fileattr; var found: boolean);
  var key, more, index: integer; elem: catentry;
  begin
    diskuse.request;
    key := hash(id);
    table.read(key, elem);
    more := elem.searchlength;
    index := key; found := false;
    while not found & (more > 0) do
      begin
        table.read(index, elem);
        if elem.id = id then
          begin attr := elem.attr; found := true end
        else
          begin
            if elem.key = key then more := more - 1;
            index := index mod table.length + 1;
          end;
      end;
    diskuse.release;
  end;

begin init table(typeuse, cataddr) end;
```

16   Data File

type datafile =
class(typeuse: typeresource; diskuse: resource; catalog: diskcatalog)

A data file enables a process to access a disk file by means of its name in a diskcatalog. The pages of a data file are numbered 1, 2, ..., length. A data file uses a resource to get exclusive access to the disk during a page transfer and a typewriter resource to get exclusive access to the operator after disk failure. It uses a catalog to look up the the file.

Initially a data file is inaccessible (closed). A user of a data file must open it before using it and close it afterwards. If a process needs exclusive access to a data file while using it, this must be ensured at higher levels of programming.

procedure open(id: identifier; var found: boolean)

Makes a file with a given identifier accessible if it is found in the catalog.

procedure close

Makes the file inaccessible.

procedure read(pageno: integer; var block: univ page)

Reads a page with a given number from the file. It has no effect if the file is closed or if the page number is outside the range 1..length.

procedure write(pageno: integer; var block: univ page)

Writes a page with a given number on the file. It has no effect if the file is closed or if the page number is outside the range 1..length.

function length: integer

Defines the number of pages in the file. The length of a closed file is zero.

Implementation:

```
type datafile =
class(typeuse: typeresource; diskuse: resource; catalog: diskcatalog);
```

```
var file: diskfile; opened: boolean;

entry length: integer;

procedure entry open(id: identifier; var found: boolean);
var attr: fileattr;
begin
   catalog.lookup(id, attr, found);
   if found then
     begin
       diskuse.request;
       file.open(attr.addr);
       length := file.length;
       diskuse.release;
     end;
   opened := found;
end;


procedure entry close;
begin
   file.close;
   length := 0;
   opened := false;
end;


procedure entry read(pageno: integer; var block: univ page);
begin
   if opened then
     begin
       diskuse.request;
       file.read(pageno, block);
       diskuse.release;
     end;
end;


procedure entry write(pageno: integer; var block: univ page);
begin
```

```
      if opened then
        begin
          diskuse.request;
          file.write(pageno, block);
          diskuse.release;
        end;
    end;

    begin
      init file(typeuse);
      length := 0;
      opened := false;
    end;
```

17   Program File

type progfile =
class(typeuse: typeresource; diskuse: resource; catalog: diskcatalog)

A program file can transfer a sequential program from a disk file into core. The program file is identified by its name in a disk catalog. A program file uses a resource to get exclusive access to the disk during program loading and a typewriter resource to get exclusive access to the operator after disk failure. It uses a disk catalog to look up the file.

procedure open(id: identifier; var state: progstate)

Loads a program with a given identifier from disk and returns its state. The program state is one of the following: ready for execution, not found, the disk file is not sequential code, or the file is too big to be loaded into core.

function store: progstore

Defines the variable in which the program file is stored. A program store is an array of disk pages.

Implementation:

A program file has exclusive access to the disk until it has loaded the entire program. This is to prevent competing processes from slowing down program loading by causing disk arm movement.

```
type progstate = (ready, notfound, notseq, toobig);

const storelength1 = 40;
type progstore1 = array [1..storelength1] of page;

type progfile1 =
class(typeuse: typeresource; diskuse: resource; catalog: diskcatalog);

var file: diskfile;

entry store: progstore1;

procedure entry open(id: identifier; var state: progstate);
var attr: fileattr; found: boolean; pageno: integer;
begin
  catalog.lookup(id, attr, found);
  with diskuse, file, attr do
    if not found then state := notfound
    else if kind <> seqcode then state := notseq
    else
      begin
        request;
        open(addr);
        if length <= storelength1 then
          begin
            for pageno := 1 to length do
              read(pageno, store[pageno]);
            state := ready;
          end
        else state := toobig;
        close;
        release;
      end;
end;

begin init file(typeuse) end;
```

Solo uses two kinds of program files (progfile1 and progfile2); one for large programs and another one for small ones. They differ only in the dimension of the program store used. The need to repeat the entire class definition to handle arrays of different lengths is an awkward inheritance from Pascal.

18   Program Stack

type progstack = monitor

A program stack maintains a last-in, first-out list of identifiers of programs that have called one another. It enables a process to keep track of nested calls of sequential programs.

For historical reasons a program stack was defined as a monitor. In the present version of the system it might as well have been a class.

function space: boolean

Tells whether there is more space in the program stack.

function any: boolean

Tells whether the stack contains any program identifiers.

procedure push(id: identifier)

Puts an identifier on top of the stack. It has no effect if the stack is full.

procedure pop(var line, result: univ integer)

Removes a program identifier from the top of the stack and defines the line number at which the program terminated as well as its result. The result either indicates normal termination or one of several run-time errors as explained in the Concurrent Pascal report (Brinch Hansen 1975b).

procedure get(var id: identifier)

Defines the identifier stored in the top of the stack (without removing it). It has no effect if the stack is empty.

Implementation:

A program stack measures the extent of the heap of the calling process before pushing an identifier on the stack. If a pop operation shows abnormal program termination, the heap is reset to its original point to prevent the calling process from crashing due to lack of data space.

The standard routines, *attribute* and *setheap*, are defined in the Concurrent Pascal report.

```
type resulttype =
    (terminated, overflow, pointererror, rangeerror, varianterror,
    heaplimit, stacklimit, codelimit, timelimit, callerror);


type attrindex =
    (caller, heaptop, progline, progresult, runtime);


type progstack =
monitor


const stacklength = 5;


var stack:
  array [1..stacklength] of
    record progid: identifier; heapaddr: integer end;
  top: 0..stacklength;


function entry space: boolean;
begin space := (top < stacklength) end;


function entry any: boolean;
begin any := (top > 0) end;


procedure entry push(id: identifier);
begin
  if top < stacklength then
    begin
      top := top + 1;
      with stack[top] do
        begin
          progid := id;
```

```
            heapaddr := attribute(heaptop);
        end;
    end;
end;

procedure entry pop(var line, result: univ integer);
const terminated = 0;
begin
  line := attribute(progline);
  result := attribute(progresult);
  if result <> terminated then
    setheap(stack[top].heapaddr);
  top := top − 1;
end;

procedure entry get(var id: identifier);
begin
  if top > 0 then id := stack[top].progid;
end;

begin top := 0 end;
```

19   Page Buffer

type pagebuffer = monitor

A page buffer transmits a sequence of data pages from one process to another. Each sequence is terminated by an end of file mark.

procedure read(var text: page; var eof: boolean)

Receives a message consisting of a text page and an end of file indication.

procedure write(text: page; eof: boolean)

Sends a message consisting of a text page and an end of file indication.

   If the end of file is true then the text page is empty.

Implementation:

A page buffer stores a single message at a time. It will delay the sending process as long as the buffer is full and the receiving process until it becomes full $(0 \leq \text{writes} - \text{reads} \leq 1)$.

```
type pagebuffer =
monitor

var buffer: page; last, full: boolean;
    sender, receiver: queue;

procedure entry read(var text: page; var eof: boolean);
begin
   if not full then delay(receiver);
   text := buffer; eof := last; full := false;
   continue(sender);
end;

procedure entry write(text: page; eof: boolean);
begin;
   if full then delay(sender);
   buffer := text; last := eof; full := true;
   continue(receiver);
end;

begin full := false end;
```

Solo also implements buffers for transmission of arguments (enumerations and identifiers) and lines. They are similar to the page buffer (but use no end of file marks). The need to duplicate routines for each message type is an inconvenience caused by the fixed data types of Pascal.

20   Character Stream

type charstream = class(buffer: pagebuffer)

A character stream enables a process to communicate with another process character by character. A character stream uses a page buffer to transmit one page of characters at a time from one process to another.

A sending process must open its stream for writing before using it. The last character transmitted in a sequence should be an end of medium (em). A receiving process must open its stream for reading before using it.

procedure initread

Opens a character stream for reading.

procedure initwrite

Opens a character stream for writing.

procedure read(var c: char)

Reads the next character from the stream. The effect is undefined if the stream is not open for reading.

procedure write(c: char)

Writes the next character in the stream. The effect is undefined if the stream is not open for writing.

Implementation:

```
type charstream =
class(buffer: pagebuffer);

var text: page; count: integer; eof: boolean;

procedure entry read(var c: char);
begin
  if count = pagelength then
    begin
      buffer.read(text, eof);
      count := 0;
    end;
  count := count + 1;
  c := text[count];
  if c = em then
    begin
```

```
        while not eof do buffer.read(text, eof);
          count := pagelength;
      end;
  end;


  procedure entry initread;
  begin count := pagelength end;


  procedure entry write(c: char);
  begin
    count := count + 1;
    text[count] := c;
    if (count = pagelength) or (c = em) then
      begin
        buffer.write(text, false); count := 0;
        if c = em then buffer.write(text, true);
      end;
  end;


  procedure entry initwrite;
  begin count := 0 end;


  begin end;
```

21   Tasks and Arguments

The following data types are used by several processes:

```
  type taskkind = (inputtask, jobtask, outputtask);

  type argtag = (niltype, booltype, inttype, idtype, ptrtype);
    argtype = record tag: argtag; arg: identifier end;

  const maxarg = 10;
  type arglist = array [1..maxarg] of argtype;

  type argseq = (inp, out);
```

The *task kind* defines whether a process is performing an input task, a job task, or an output task. It is used by sequential programs to determine whether they have been loaded by the right kind of process. As an example, a program that controls card reader input can only be called by an input process.

A process that executes a sequential program can pass a list of arguments to it. A program *argument* consists of a tag field defining its type (boolean, integer, identifier, or pointer) and another field defining its value. (Since Concurrent Pascal does not include the variant records of Sequential Pascal one can only represent a program argument by the largest one of its variants—an identifier.)

A job process is connected to two input and output processes by *argument buffers* called its input and output sequences.

22   Job Process

type jobprocess =
process
    (typeuse: typeresource; diskuse: resource;
    catalog: diskcatalog; inbuffer, outbuffer: pagebuffer;
    inrequest, inresponse, outrequest, outresponse: argbuffer;
    stack: progstack)
"program data space" +16000

A job process executes Sequential Pascal programs that can call one another recursively. Initially, it executes a program called *do* with console input. A job process also implements the interface between sequential programs and the Solo operating system as defined in Brinch Hansen (1976b).

A job process needs access to the operator's console, the disk, and its catalog. It is connected to an input and an output process by two page buffers and four argument buffers as explained in Brinch Hansen (1976a). It uses a program stack to handle nested calls of sequential programs.

It reserves a data space of 16,000 bytes for user programs and a code space of 20,000 bytes. This enables the Pascal compiler to compile itself.

Implementation:

The private variables of a job process give it access to a terminal stream, two character streams for input and output, and two data files. It uses a large program file to store the currently executed program. These variables are inaccessible to other processes.

The job process contains a declaration of a sequential program that defines the types of its arguments and the variable in which its code is stored (the latter is inaccessible to the program). It also defines a list of interface routines that can be called by a program. These routines are implemented within the job process. They are defined in Brinch Hansen (1976b).

Before a job process can call a sequential program it must load it from disk into a program store and push its identifier onto a program stack. After termination of the program, the job process pops its identifier, line number, and result from the program stack, reloads the previous program from disk and returns to it.

A process can only interact with other processes by calling routines within monitors that are passed as parameters to it during initialization (such as the catalog declared at the beginning of a job process). These access rights are checked at compile-time (Brinch Hansen 1975a).

```
type jobprocess =
process
   (typeuse: typeresource; diskuse: resource;
   catalog: diskcatalog; inbuffer, outbuffer: pagebuffer;
   inrequest, inresponse, outrequest, outresponse: argbuffer;
   stack: progstack);
"program data space" +16000


const maxfile = 2;
type file = 1..maxfile;


var operator: terminal; opstream: terminalstream;
   instream, outstream: charstream;
   files: array [file] of datafile;
   code: progfile1;


program job(var param: arglist; store: progstore1);
entry read, write, open, close, get, put, length,
   mark, release, identify, accept, display, readpage,
   writepage, readline, writeline, readarg, writearg,
   lookup, iotransfer, iomove, task, run;
```

```
procedure call(id: identifier; var param: arglist;
   var line: integer; var result: resulttype);
var state: progstate; lastid: identifier;
begin
  with code, stack do
    begin
      line := 0;
      open(id, state);
      if (state = ready) & space then
        begin
          push(id);
          job(param, store);
          pop(line, result);
        end
      else if state = toobig then result := codelimit
      else result := callerror;
      if any then
        begin get(lastid); open(lastid, state) end;
    end;
end;

procedure entry read(var c: char);
begin instream.read(c) end;

procedure entry write(c: char);
begin outstream.write(c) end;

procedure entry open(f: file; id: identifier; var found: boolean);
begin files[f].open(id, found) end;

procedure entry close(f: file);
begin files[f].close end;

procedure entry get(f: file; p: integer; var block: page);
begin files[f].read(p, block) end;

procedure entry put(f: file; p: integer; var block: page);
begin files[f].write(p, block) end;
```

```
function entry length(f: file): integer;
begin length := files[f].length end;

procedure entry mark(var top: integer);
begin top := attribute(heaptop) end;

procedure entry release(top: integer);
begin setheap(top) end;

procedure entry identify(header: line);
begin opstream.reset(header) end;

procedure entry accept(var c: char);
begin opstream.read(c) end;

procedure entry display(c: char);
begin opstream.write(c) end;

procedure entry readpage(var block: page; var eof: boolean);
begin inbuffer.read(block, eof) end;

procedure entry writepage(block: page; eof: boolean);
begin outbuffer.write(block, eof) end;

procedure entry readline(var text: line);
begin end;

procedure entry writeline(text: line);
begin end;

procedure entry readarg(s: argseq; var arg: argtype);
begin
   if s = inp then inresponse.read(arg)
   else outresponse.read(arg);
end;

procedure entry writearg(s: argseq; arg: argtype);
```

```
begin
  if s = inp then inrequest.write(arg)
  else outrequest.write(arg);
end;


procedure entry lookup(id: identifier;
  var attr: fileattr; var found: boolean);
begin catalog.lookup(id, attr, found) end;

procedure entry iotransfer(device: iodevice;
  var param: ioparam; var block: page);
begin
  if device = diskdevice then
    begin
      diskuse.request;
      io(block, param, device);
      diskuse.release;
    end
  else io(block, param, device);
end;


procedure entry iomove(device: iodevice; var param: ioparam);
begin io(param, param, device) end;

function entry task: taskkind;
begin task := jobtask end;


procedure entry run(id: identifier; var param: arglist;
  var line: integer; var result: resulttype);
begin call(id, param, line, result) end;


procedure initialize;
var i: integer; param: arglist; line: integer; result: resulttype;
begin
  init operator(typeuse), opstream(operator),
    instream(inbuffer), outstream(outbuffer);
  instream.initread; outstream.initwrite;
  for i := 1 to maxfile do
```

```
      init files[i](typeuse, diskuse, catalog);
    init code(typeuse, diskuse, catalog);
    with param[2] do
       begin tag := idtype; arg := 'console      ' end;
    call( 'do           ', param, line, result);
    operator.write('jobprocess:(:10:)', 'terminated (:10)');
  end;


  begin initialize end;
```


23   IO Process

type ioprocess =
process
   (typeuse: typeresource; diskuse: resource;
   catalog: diskcatalog; slowio: linebuffer;
   buffer: pagebuffer; request, response: argbuffer;
   stack: progstack; iotask: taskkind)
"program data space" +2000

An io process executes Sequential Pascal programs that produce or consume data for a job process. It also implements the interface between these programs and the Solo operating system.

An io process needs access to the operator, the disk, and the catalog. It is connected to a card reader (or a line printer) by a line buffer and to a job process by a page buffer and two argument buffers. It uses a program stack to handle nested calls of sequential programs.

It reserves a data space of 2,000 bytes for input/output programs and a code space of 4,000 bytes.

Initially, it executes a program called *io*

Implementation:

The implementation details are similar to a job process.

```
  type ioprocess =
  process
     (typeuse: typeresource; diskuse: resource;
     catalog: diskcatalog; slowio: linebuffer;
```

```
      buffer: pagebuffer; request, response: argbuffer;
      stack: progstack; iotask: taskkind);
   "program data space" +2000

   type file = 1..1;

   var operator: terminal; opstream: terminalstream;
      iostream: charstream; iofile: datafile;
      code: progfile2;

   program driver(var param: arglist; store: progstore2);
   entry read, write, open, close, get, put, length,
      mark, release, identify, accept, display, readpage,
      writepage, readline, writeline, readarg, writearg,
      lookup, iotransfer, iomove, task, run;

   procedure call(id: identifier; var param: arglist;
      var line: integer; var result: resulttype);
   var state: progstate; lastid: identifier;
   begin
      with code, stack do
        begin
          line := 0;
          open(id, state);
          if (state = ready) & space then
            begin
              push(id);
              driver(param, store);
              pop(line, result);
            end
          else if state = toobig then result := codelimit
          else result := callerror;
          if any then
            begin get(lastid); open(lastid, state) end;
        end;
   end;

   procedure entry read(var c: char);
```

begin iostream.read(c) **end**;

procedure entry write(c: char);
begin iostream.write(c) **end**;

procedure entry open(f: file; id: identifier; **var** found: boolean);
begin iofile.open(id, found) **end**;

procedure entry close(f: file);
begin iofile.close **end**;

procedure entry get(f: file; p: integer; **var** block: page);
begin iofile.read(p, block) **end**;

procedure entry put(f: file; p: integer; **var** block: page);
begin iofile.write(p, block) **end**;

function entry length(f: file): integer;
begin length := iofile.length **end**;

procedure entry mark(**var** top: integer);
begin top := attribute(heaptop) **end**;

procedure entry release(top: integer);
begin setheap(top) **end**;

procedure entry identify(header: line);
begin opstream.reset(header) **end**;

procedure entry accept(**var** c: char);
begin opstream.read(c) **end**;

procedure entry display(c: char);
begin opstream.write(c) **end**;

procedure entry readpage(**var** block: page; **var** eof: boolean);
begin buffer.read(block, eof) **end**;

```
procedure entry writepage(block: page; eof: boolean);
begin buffer.write(block, eof) end;

procedure entry readline(var text: line);
begin slowio.read(text) end;

procedure entry writeline(text: line);
begin slowio.write(text) end;

procedure entry readarg(s: argseq; var arg: argtype);
begin request.read(arg) end;

procedure entry writearg(s: argseq; arg: argtype);
begin response.write(arg) end;

procedure entry lookup(id: identifier;
   var attr: fileattr; var found: boolean);
begin catalog.lookup(id, attr, found) end;

procedure entry iotransfer(device: iodevice;
   var param: ioparam; var block: page);
begin
   if device = diskdevice then
     begin
       diskuse.request;
       io(block, param, device);
       diskuse.release;
     end
   else io(block, param, device);
end;

procedure entry iomove(device: iodevice; var param: ioparam);
begin io(param, param, device) end;

function entry task: taskkind;
begin task := iotask end;

procedure entry run(id: identifier; var param: arglist;
```

```
   var line: integer; var result: resulttype);
begin call(id, param, line, result) end;


procedure initialize;
var param: arglist; line: integer; result: resulttype;
begin
  init operator(typeuse), opstream(operator),
    iostream(buffer), iofile(typeuse, diskuse, catalog),
    code(typeuse, diskuse, catalog);
  if iotask = inputtask then iostream.initwrite
  else iostream.initread;
  call( 'io          ', param, line, result);
  operator.write('ioprocess:(:10:)', 'terminated (:10)');
end;


begin initialize end;
```

24   Card Process

type cardprocess =
process(typeuse: typeresource; buffer: linebuffer)

A card process transmits cards from a card reader through a line buffer to an input process. The card process can access the operator to report device failure and a line buffer to transmit data. It is assumed that the card reader is controlled by a single card process. As long as the card reader is turned off or is empty the card process waits. It begins to read cards as soon as they are available in the reader. After a transmission error the card process writes a message to the operator and continues the input of cards.

Implementation:

The standard procedure *wait* delays the card process one second (Brinch Hansen 1975b). This reduces the processor time spent waiting for operator intervention.

```
type cardprocess =
process(typeuse: typeresource; buffer: linebuffer);
```

```
    var operator: terminal; param: ioparam;
        text: line; ok: boolean;
    begin
      init operator(typeuse);
      param.operation := input;
      cycle
        repeat
          io(text, param, carddevice);
          case param.status of
            complete:
              ok := true;
            intervention:
              begin ok := false; wait end;
            transmission, failure:
              begin
                operator.write('cards:(:10:)', 'error(:10:)');
                ok := false;
              end
          end
        until ok;
        buffer.write(text);
      end;
    end;
```

25   Printer Process

type printerprocess =
process(typeuse: typeresource; buffer: linebuffer)

A printer process transmits lines from an output process to a line printer.
The printer process can access the operator to report device failure and a
line buffer to receive data. It is assumed that the line printer is controlled
only by a single printer process. After a printer failure the printer process
writes a message to the operator and repeats the output of the current line
until it is successful.

Implementation:

```
type printerprocess =
process(typeuse: typeresource; buffer: linebuffer);

var operator: terminal; param: ioparam; text: line;
begin
  init operator(typeuse);
  param.operation := output;
  cycle
    buffer.read(text);
    io(text, param, printdevice);
    if param.status <> complete then
      begin
        operator.write('printer:(:10:)', 'inspect(:10:)');
        repeat
          wait;
          io(text, param, printdevice);
        until param.status = complete;
      end;
  end;
end;
```

26   Loader Process

type loaderprocess =
process(diskuse: resource)

A loader process preempts the operating system and reinitializes it when
the operator pushes the *bell* key (*control g*) on the console. A loader process
needs access to the disk to be able to reload the system.

Implementation:

A control operation on the typewriter delays the loader process until the
operator pushes the bell key (Brinch Hansen 1975b).

The operating system is stored on consecutive disk pages starting at
the *Solo address*. It is loaded by means of a control operation on the disk
as defined in Brinch Hansen (1975b). Consecutive disk pages are used to

make the system kernel of Concurrent Pascal unaware of the structure of a particular filing system (such as the one used by Solo). The disk contains a sequential program *start* that can copy the Solo system from a concurrent code file into the consecutive disk segment defined above.

```
type loaderprocess =
process(diskuse: resource);

const soloaddr = 24;
var param: ioparam;

procedure initialize(pageno: univ ioarg);
begin
  with param do
    begin
      operation := control;
      arg := pageno;
    end;
end;

begin
  initialize(soloaddr);
  "await bel signal"
  io(param, param, typedevice);
  "reload solo system"
  diskuse.request;
  io(param, param, diskdevice);
  diskuse.release;
end;
```

27 Initial Process

The initial process initializes all other processes and monitors and defines their access rights to one another. After initialization the operating system consists of a fixed set of components: a card process, an input process, a job process, an output process, a printer process, and a loader process. They have access to an operator, a disk, and a catalog of files. Process communication takes place by means of two page buffers, two line buffers and four argument buffers (see also Fig. 1).

Implementation:

When a process, such as the initial process, terminates its execution, its variables continue to exist (because they may be used by other processes).

```
var
    typeuse: typeresource;
    diskuse: resource; catalog: diskcatalog;
    inbuffer, outbuffer: pagebuffer;
    cardbuffer, printerbuffer: linebuffer;
    inrequest, inresponse, outrequest, outresponse: argbuffer;
    instack, outstack, jobstack: progstack;
    reader: cardprocess; writer: printerprocess;
    producer, consumer: ioprocess; master: jobprocess;
    watchdog: loaderprocess;
begin
    init
        typeuse, diskuse,
        catalog(typeuse, diskuse, cataddr),
        inbuffer, outbuffer,
        cardbuffer, printerbuffer,
        inrequest, inresponse, outrequest, outresponse,
        instack, outstack, jobstack,
        reader(typeuse, cardbuffer),
        writer(typeuse, printerbuffer),
        producer(typeuse, diskuse, catalog, cardbuffer,
            inbuffer, inrequest, inresponse, instack, inputtask),
        consumer(typeuse, diskuse, catalog, printerbuffer),
            outbuffer, outrequest, outresponse, outstack, outputtask),
        master(typeuse, diskuse, catalog, inbuffer, outbuffer,
            inrequest, inresponse, outrequest, outresponse,
            jobstack),
        watchdog(diskuse);
end;
```

28   Conclusion

The Solo system consists of 22 line printer pages of Concurrent Pascal text divided into 23 component types (10 classes, 7 monitors, and 6 processes). A

typical component is less than one page long and can be studied in isolation
as an (almost) independent piece of program. All program components called
by a given component are explicitly declared within that component (either
as permanent variables or a parameters to it). To understand a component
it is only necessary to know *what* other components called by it do, but *how*
they do it is irrelevant.

The entire system can be studied component by component as one would
read a book. In that sense, Concurrent Pascal supports *abstraction* and
hierarchical structuring of concurrent programs very nicely.

It took 4 compilations to remove the formal programming errors from
the Solo system. It was then tested systematically from the bottom up by
adding one component type at a time and trying it by means of short test
processes. The whole program was tested in 27 runs (or about 1 run per
component type). This revealed 7 errors in the test processes and 2 trivial
ones in the system itself. Later, about one third of it was rewritten to speed
up program loading. This took about one week. It was then compiled and
put into operation in one day and has worked ever since.

I can only suggest two plausible explanations for this unusual testing
experience. It seems to be vital that the compiler prevents new components
from destroying old ones (since old components cannot call new ones, and
new ones can only call old ones through routines that have already been
tested). This strict checking of hierarchical access rights makes it possible
for a large system to evolve gradually through a sequence of intermediate,
stable subsystems.

I am also convinced now that the use of abstract data types which hide
implementation details within a fixed set of routines encourages a clarity of
design that makes programs practically correct before they are even tested.
The slight inconvenience of strict type checking is of minor importance compared to the advantages of instant program reliability.

Although Solo is a small concurrent program of only 1,300 lines it does
implement a virtual machine that is very convenient to use for program development (Brinch Hansen 1976a). The availability of cheap microprocessors
will put increasing pressure on software designers to develop special-purpose
operating systems at very low cost. Concurrent Pascal is one example of a
programming tool that may make this possible.

Acknowledgements

The development of Concurrent Pascal and Solo has been supported by the National Science Foundation under grant number DCR74-17331.

References

Brinch Hansen, P. 1973. *Operating System Principles*, Chapter 7. Resource Protection. Prentice-Hall, Englewood Cliffs, NJ (July).

Brinch Hansen, P. 1975a. The programming language Concurrent Pascal. *IEEE Transactions on Software Engineering 1*, 2 (June), 199–207. *Article 7.*

Brinch Hansen, P. 1975b. Concurrent Pascal report. Information Science, California Institute of Technology, Pasadena, CA, (June).

Brinch Hansen, P. 1976a. The Solo operating system: A Concurrent Pascal program. *Software—Practice and Experience 6*, 2 (April–June), 141–149. *Article 8.*

Brinch Hansen, P. 1976b. The Solo operating system: Job interface. *Software—Practice and Experience 6*, 2 (April–June), 151–164.

10

The Programmer as a Young Dog*

(1976)

This autobiographical sketch describes the beginning of the author's career at the Danish computer company Regnecentralen from 1963 to 1970. (The title is inspired by James Joyce's "A Portrait of the Artist as a Young Man" and Dylan Thomas's "Portrait of the Artist as a Young Dog.") After three years in Regnecentralen's compiler group, the author got the chance to design the architecture of the RC 4000 computer. In 1967, he became Head of the Software Development group that designed the RC 4000 multiprogramming system. The article was written in memory of Niels Ivar Bech, the dynamic director of Regnecentralen, who inspired a generation of young Danes to make unique contributions to computing.

I came to Regnecentralen in 1963 to work with Peter Naur and Jørn Jensen. The two of them worked so closely together that they hardly needed to say anything to solve a problem. I remember a discussion where Peter was writing something on the blackboard, when Jørn suddenly said "but Peter ..." and immediately was interrupted with the reply "yes, of course, Jørn." I swear that nothing else was said. It made quite an impression on me, especially since I didn't even know what the discussion was about in the first place.

After a two-year apprenticeship as a systems programmer, I wanted to travel abroad and work for IBM in Winchester in Southern England. At that time Henning Isaksson was planning to build a process control computer for Haldor Topsøe, Ltd. Henning had asked Niels Ivar Bech for a systems

*P. Brinch Hansen, Programmøren som hvalp. In *Niels Ivar Bech—en epoke i edb-udviklingen i Danmark*, P. Sveistrup, P. Naur, H.B. Hansen, and C. Gram, Eds., (In Danish), Data, Copenhagen, Denmark, (1976), 65–68. English translation by the author. Copyright © 1995, Per Brinch Hansen. Reprinted by permission.

programmer for quite some time. Since I was thinking about leaving anyhow, Bech felt that I might as well move to Isaksson's department in Valby. So it was not because of my vast experience that I got the opportunity to design the RC 4000 computer.

Henning was an efficient manager and very pleasant to work for. Our programming group consisted of Peter Kraft, Charles Simonyi, and me. Peter was an experienced programmer, who had learned his craft during the Gier-Algol project. Charles was a long-haired teenager, a refugee from Hungary who was fascinated by everything in the western world. Later he went to the United States and worked for Xerox in California.

It was in an old cozy villa in Valby that I defined the instruction set of the RC 4000 computer. It became a nice, uninspired copy of the IBM 360. However, one thing set the RC 4000 apart from other computers: its function was concisely defined in the programming language Algol 60 before it was built. It was no doubt the only computer in the world that made it possible for the user to predict the result, bit by bit, of dividing two non-normalized floating-point numbers!

One of Isaksson's young engineers, Allan Giese, was inspired by this to extend Algol 60 so it could also be used to describe the internal structure of the RC 4000 (the microprogram).

At the same time, Peter Kraft developed our first process control program for a chemical plant in Poland. A few years later, Peter continued this pioneering work and (together with others) produced RC 4000 software for real-time supervision of two Danish power plants, Vestkraft and Nordkraft.

Our group was also joined by a student, Leif Svalgaard, who became so absorbed in programming the RC 4000 for the Meteorological Institute in Copenhagen that he forgot to take his final exam. Leif liked to show off. Once he told us that he had a new theory of the magnetic fields of the sun and earth. That made us smile a bit. Later, I met Leif in the United States. He was then working at Stanford University and his theory was world-famous.

Early on, Henning Isaksson realized that our new computer would become the successor of the Gier, and that we had to start thinking about developing software for it. But first it had to be named. I suggested calling it the RC 4000, since "who would buy an RC 3 for a million kroner when you can buy an RC 3000 for a lot less?" So RC 4000 it was.[†]

I now returned to the Rialto Center as Head of Systems Programming.

[†]The RC 4000 was Regnecentralen's third computer architecture. The RC 3000 was a special-purpose device for data conversion.

Bech's directive was rather amazing. His only request was: "I need something new in multiprogramming!"

In my opinion Niels Ivar Bech was somewhat of a gambler and showman. He could rarely resist the temptation to do the unexpected. I once participated in a negotiation between Bech and a customer about the sale of an RC 4000 in the middle of a noisy discotheque. Perhaps it is true that unconventional acts rarely succeed in business (we did not sell a machine that evening), but they almost always work in research.

Research is gambling at the highest level. A cautious effort only leads to uninteresting results. A research director must have a sense of which problem to attack next and the courage to give his collaborators the freedom to solve it without imposing narrow constraints. The talent for inspiring his associates to create new things of world-wide renown was one that Bech possessed in the highest degree. Once you have known a leader who has this intellectual courage, it is quite depressing to realize how extremely rare this quality is.

Niels Ivar Bech was a dreamer in the most creative sense of the word. His time scale was longer than the one I adopted as a young, impatient engineer. I found it unreasonable that he gave Regnecentralen's senior people time to write textbooks on computer science without considering how this would influence the future of the company. That was short-sighted of me. While Bech gave his younger colleagues the chance to create new things, he gave Peter Naur, Christian Gram and Henning B. Hansen the opportunity to lay the foundation of computer science education in Denmark.

It wasn't easy for me to measure up to the standard of excellence set by the Gier-Algol compiler (Edsger Dijkstra called it a masterpiece). The instant rivalry between Søren Lauesen and me did not improve matters either. Søren and I were both "promising" and ambitious, and no room was big enough for the two of us. However, we had no choice but to cooperate and try to match the achievements of the compiler group.

In such a creative environment only personal ability counted. Unfortunately, it seemed that none of us had any original ideas whatsoever about multiprogramming. Finally, I went to Bech and said: "We aren't getting anywhere. Is it all right with you if Jørn, Søren, and I stay at a country inn for a weekend?" I wanted us to discuss the software issues in depth in cozy surroundings to give ourselves one last chance. We had already agreed that we would either return with new ideas or give up and settle for copying the best ideas we could find elsewhere. Bech immediately agreed (he had done the same thing when Regnecentralen's Cobol project had come to a stand-still). And it worked! The thought of returning to Regnecentralen without new ideas was simply unacceptable to us.

Out of that weekend came the first seminal ideas for the RC 4000 monitor (the nucleus of a multiprogramming system). Four years later, the U.S. National Academy of Engineering published a report about the need for courses on operating system design. It stated that in the whole world there were only three operating systems that were so simple and completely described that they could be used for teaching. The first one mentioned was the one that enabled the RC 4000 computer to do many things simultaneously. The accolade was a letter from Edsger Dijkstra expressing his admiration for our system.

Denmark has made four world-class contributions to data technology: Peter Naur's Algol 60 report, which Tony Hoare called a considerable improvement over its successors; the Gier-Algol compiler, which has never been surpassed; the world's fastest paper tape reader, the RC 2000 (which Bech gave a co-worker money to design at home, because his manager didn't believe in the idea); and, finally, the RC 4000 monitor, which has been imitated by other computer companies.

Each of these products combined radically new ideas, which were years ahead of their time (and therefore could not be motivated by an immediate "need"). Without Niels Ivar Bech's brilliant sense of innovation, a Danish company could probably not have attracted so many outstanding young computer scientists and be at the cutting edge of programming technology for more than a decade.

In 1970, I left Regnecentralen and moved to the United States. At that time, Niels Ivar Bech was already showing signs of illness. Since then I only saw him briefly at a conference in Yugoslavia. There was one thing I would have liked to tell him. I have lectured at most of the leading universities and research centers in the United States. But only at Carnegie-Mellon University and Xerox Research Center have I found programming groups that measured up to Regnecentralen's.

With Niels Ivar Bech's death, Denmark lost its leading role in the development of programming technology. Since then I have met some of the most creative computer scientists and outstanding leaders in the computer industry. But no other human being has had a deeper impact on my work and given it a broader perspective than Niels Ivar.

Acknowledgements

I thank Thomas Brinch Hansen, Erik Hemmingsen, Skip Mattson and Peter O'Hearn for their helpful comments on the English translation of this essay.

References (added 1995)

Brinch Hansen, P., and House, R. 1966. The Cobol compiler for the Siemens 3003. *BIT 6*, 1, 1–23.

Brinch Hansen, P. 1967a. The logical structure of the RC 4000 computer. *BIT 7*, 3, 191–199.

Brinch Hansen, P. 1967b. The RC 4000 real-time control system at Pulawy. *BIT 7*, 4, 279–288. *Article 1*.

Brinch Hansen, P. 1970. The nucleus of a multiprogramming system. *Communications of the ACM 13*, 4 (April), 238–242. *Article 2*.

Brinch Hansen, P. 1973. *Operating System Principles*, Chapter 8 A Case Study: RC 4000. Prentice Hall, Englewood Cliffs, NJ, (July), 237–286.

Cosine Committee. 1971. *An Undergraduate Course on Operating Systems Principles*. Commission on Education, National Academy of Engineering, Washington, DC, (June).

Dijkstra, E.W. 1969. Letter to the author, (August 1).

Hoare, C.A.R. 1974. Hints on programming language design. In *Computer Systems Reliability*, C. Bunyan, Ed., State of the Art Report 20, Infotech International, Berkshire, England, 505–534.

Naur, P., Ed. 1960. Report on the algorithmic language Algol 60. *Communications of the ACM 3*, 6 (June), 299–314.

Naur, P. 1963. The design of the Gier Algol compiler. *BIT 3*, 2–3, 123–140 and 145–166.

Naur, P. 1966. Data translation viewed as a general data processing problem. *Communications of the ACM 9*, 3 (March), 176–179.

Naur, P. 1974. *Concise Survey of Computer Methods*. Petrocelli/Charter, New York.

Sveistrup, P., Naur, P., Hansen, H.B., and Gram, C., Eds. 1976. *Niels Ivar Bech—An Era in Danish Computer Development*. (In Danish), Data, Copenhagen, Denmark.

11

Experience with
Modular Concurrent Programming*

(1977)

This paper summarizes the initial experience with the programming language
Concurrent Pascal in the design of three model operating systems. A Concurrent Pascal program consists of modules called processes, monitors, and
classes. The compiler checks that the data structures of each module are
accessed only by the operations defined in the module. The author empha-
sizes that the creative aspect of program construction is the initial selection
of modules and the connection of them into hierarchical structures. By comparison the detailed implementation of each module is straightforward. The
most important result is that it is possible to build concurrent programs of
one thousand lines out of one-page modules that can be comprehended at a
glance.

1 Introduction

This paper summarizes the initial experience with the abstract programming language *Concurrent Pascal* in the design of three model operating
systems. A Concurrent Pascal program consists of *modules* called processes,
monitors, and classes (Brinch Hansen 1975a). The compiler checks that the
data structures of each module are accessed only by the operations defined
in the module. *The most important result so far is that it is possible to build
a concurrent program of one thousand lines of text out of one-page modules
that can be comprehended at a glance* (Brinch Hansen 1976b).

When this research project was started four years ago we had four main
goals:

---

*P. Brinch Hansen, Experience with modular concurrent programming, *IEEE Transac-
tions on Software Engineering 3*, 2 (March 1977), 156–159. Copyright © 1977, Institute
of Electrical and Electronics Engineers, Inc. Reprinted by permission.

1. To develop an effective method for constructing large, reliable concurrent programs from trivial modules that can be defined, programmed, tested, and described one at a time.

2. To design an abstract programming language that supports a precise form of modularity and hides irrelevant machine detail.

3. To make a compiler that checks whether program modules use one another properly (in a restricted sense).

4. To build useful minicomputer operating systems exclusively by means of this abstract programming language.

The first attempt by Hoare and myself to invent a structured language for concurrent programs led to a notation for shared variables, critical regions, and scheduling queues (Hoare 1972a; Brinch Hansen 1972). In 1972 we combined these concepts into a single program module called a *shared class* (Brinch Hansen 1973) or a *monitor* (Hoare 1974). This was inspired by Dahl's *class* module (Dahl 1972; Hoare 1972b) and Dijkstra's *secretaries* (1971).

To experiment with these ideas on modularity I designed the programming language Concurrent Pascal (Brinch Hansen 1975b). It extends the sequential language Pascal (Wirth 1971) with processes, monitors, and classes. A Concurrent Pascal compiler for the PDP 11/45 computer (written in Pascal) was completed in January 1975 (Hartmann 1975).

A Concurrent Pascal program consists of a fixed number of processes executed simultaneously. Each process performs a sequence of operations on a data structure that is inaccessible to other processes. Processes can only communicate by means of monitors. A monitor is a module that defines all the possible operations on a shared data structure. It can, for example, define the *send* and *receive* operations on a message buffer. Finally, a class is a module that defines all the possible operations on a data structure used by a single process only. It can, for example, define the *open*, *close*, *read*, and *write* operations on a disk file.

The compiler checks that the data structures of each process, monitor, and class are accessed only by the operations defined within that module. The controlled access to data structures tends to confine programming errors within single modules and prevent them from causing obscure effects in other modules. This makes systematic testing of modules fast and effective.

Concurrent Pascal has been used to write three model operating systems: a single-user operating system (Solo), a job stream system for small jobs, and a real-time scheduler for process control (Brinch Hansen 1975d, 1976a, 1976b). They have been running successfully on a PDP 11/45 computer for more than a year.

The following describes the modular structure of these operating systems. I hope to show that *the creative aspect of concurrent programming is the initial selection of modules and the connection of them into hierarchical structures. The detailed implementation of each module is quite straightforward.* These details are described in the three papers mentioned above.

2   Program Modules

I will begin with an example from the *job stream system* which compiles and executes a stream of Pascal jobs. Input, execution, and output take place simultaneously using large buffers stored on disk.

Figure 1 shows two processes in the job stream system connected by a disk buffer. The circles are program modules (processes, monitors, and classes); the arrows show how they call one another.

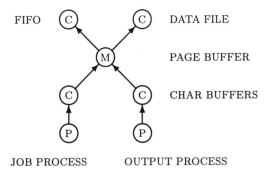

Figure 1 Job stream system.

A *job process* sends one character at a time to a *character buffer* module which assembles them into disk pages. When a page is full, the character buffer sends it through a *page buffer* module which in turn calls a *data file* module to store the page in a disk file of fixed length. The disk file is used as a cyclical buffer. The page buffer uses a *fifo* (first-in, first-out) module to keep track of the order in which pages are transferred to and from the disk file.

An *output process* receives one character at a time from another character buffer which calls the page buffer when it needs another page from the disk.

Each of the modules consists of a data structure and the possible operations on it. Take for example the *page buffer*,

```
type pagebuffer =
monitor
var ...

procedure send(block: page)
begin ... end

procedure receive(var block: page)
begin ... end

begin initialize buffer end
```

It is defined as a *data type* that can be used to transmit pages from one process to another by means of *send* and *receive* operations.

A page buffer is represented by a *data file* and a *fifo* sequence. It also uses two *queues* to delay the sending and receiving processes when the buffer is full or empty:

```
var file: datafile; next: fifo;
    sender, receiver: queue
```

These variables are declared within the module and are not accessible outside it. They can only be used by the routines of the modules, for example

```
procedure receive(var block: page)
begin
  if next.empty then delay(receiver);
  file.read(next.departure, block);
  continue(sender)
end
```

This page buffer routine in turn calls other routines

```
next.empty    next.departure    file.read
```

defined within the fifo and data file modules, *next* and *file*.

A particular page buffer can be declared and used as follows by two processes:

var buffer: pagebuffer; text1, text2: page;

buffer.send(text1)   buffer.receive(text2)

3   Hierarchical Structures

The job stream module that implements data files on disk was borrowed from the *Solo* operating system. Figure 2 shows the hierarchical structure of the Solo filing system (simplified a bit).

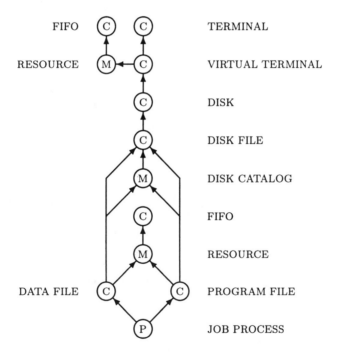

Figure 2 Solo system.

The heart of Solo is a *job process* that compiles and executes programs. It can access disk files through *data* and *program file* modules. Since there are other processes in the system, the file modules must use a *resource* module to get exclusive access to the disk during page transfers. *Disk catalog* and *disk file* modules are used to locate a named file and its pages on the disk. A *disk* module handles the details of transferring a single page to or from the device. If the disk fails this is reported to the operator through a *virtual terminal*. Each process has its own virtual terminal. They all use the same resource module to get exclusive access to a single real *terminal*. A resource module uses a *fifo* module to implement first-come, first-served scheduling.

The Solo system was written eight months before the job stream system. It was a pleasant surprise to discover that 14 modules from Solo could be used unchanged in the job stream system. This may be the first example of different kinds of operating systems using the same modules.

Figure 3 shows the structure of another concurrent program. This is the *real-time scheduler* which executes a fixed number of task processes regularly with frequencies chosen by an operator. It is based on an existing process control system (Brinch Hansen 1967).

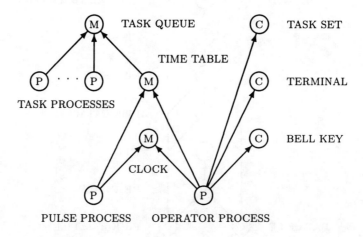

Figure 3 Real-time scheduler.

Each *task* is a cyclical process that waits inside a *task queue* module until a timing signal from a *time table* module wakes it up. After performing its task the process waits for the next signal. The time table defines the start time and frequency of each task. A *pulse process* updates a *clock* module every second and calls the time table which then starts all tasks that are due.

The operator contacts the scheduler by pushing the *bell key* on a terminal. This wakes up an *operator process* which then accepts a command from the operator through a *terminal* module. The command may cause the operator process to either set the clock or change the time table. The scheduler uses a *task set* to keep track of task names.

4   Program and Module Size

The model operating systems illustrate how one can build a concurrent program as a hierarchy of modules. Each module implements a data type and its operations. Other modules can use these operations, but cannot access the components of the data type directly.

So modules "know" very little about each other. This makes it possible to program them one at a time. The programming experience with Concurrent Pascal illustrates the success of this approach.

	Solo	Job Stream	Real Time
Lines	1300	1400	600
Modules	23	24	13
Lines/Module	57	58	46
Routines/Module	5	4	4
Lines/Routine	11	15	12

The table shows that each of the model operating systems is a Concurrent Pascal program of about 1000 lines of text divided into 15–25 modules. A module is roughly one page of text (50–60 lines) with about 5 routines of 10–15 lines each.

These three examples consistently show that it is possible to compose nontrivial concurrent programs of very simple modules that can be studied one page at a time as one reads a book. This must surely be the main goal of structured programming on a larger scale.

Each of the model operating systems corresponds to an assembly language program of about 4000 machine instructions. But fortunately they are written in an abstract programming language that hides machine detail, such as registers, addresses, bit patterns, interrupts, store allocation, and processor multiplexing. As a result it was possible for me to design, program, test, and describe each of these programs in a matter of weeks. Compared to assembly language, Concurrent Pascal has reduced my design effort for concurrent programs by an order of magnitude and has made them so simple that a journal could publish the complete text of a 1300 line program (Brinch Hansen 1976b).

5   Reliability and Efficiency

The integrity of modules enforced during compilation tends to make programs practically correct before they are even tested. The modules of a concurrent program are tested one at a time starting with those that do not depend on other modules. Each module is tested by means of a short test process that calls the module and makes it execute all its statements. A detailed example of how this is done is described in Brinch Hansen (1975d).

When a module works, another one is tested on top of it. The compiler now makes sure that the new (untested) module only uses the routines of the old (tested) module. Since these routines already work, the new module cannot make the old one fail. This makes it quite easy to locate errors during testing.

Although systematic testing theoretically does not guarantee correctness it is very successful in practice. The Solo system was tested in 27 test runs during April 1975. It has since been used daily without software failure. The job stream system and the real-time scheduler were tested in 10 and 21 test runs. So the initial experience has been that *a concurrent program of one thousand lines requires a couple of compilations followed by one test run per component. And then it works.*

The checking of access rights to data structures is almost exclusively done during compilation. It is not supported by hardware protection mechanisms during execution. The elimination of consistency checks at run time makes routine calls between modules about as fast as routine calls within modules:

	μs
simple routine call	60
class routine call	80
monitor routine call	200

The static allocation of store among a fixed number of processes also contributes to efficiency (Brinch Hansen 1975c).

The Solo and job stream systems compile programs at the speed of the line printer (10 lines/s) and are not limited by the speed of the computer.

6   Final Remarks

As the first abstract language for modular concurrent programming Concurrent Pascal will no doubt turn out to have deficiences in detail, but the overall modular approach to program design by means of processes, monitors, and classes seems to be a fertile direction for further research.

Since a concurrent program can be composed of semi-independent modules of one page each, there is reason to believe that verification techniques for small, sequential programs can be extended to concurrent programs as well. Some of this work has already been started by Hoare (1972a, 1972b, 1974), Howard (1976), and Owicki and Gries (1976). It would be a worthy achievement to verify parts of a working operating system, such as Solo.

The greatest value of a formal approach to correctness is probably the extreme rigor and structure that it must impose on the design process from the beginning to be succesful. This cannot fail to improve our informal understanding of programs as well.

References

Brinch Hansen, P. 1967. The RC 4000 real-time control system at Pulawy. *BIT 7*, 4, 279–288. *Article 1*.

Brinch Hansen, P. 1972. Structured multiprogramming. *Communications of the ACM 15*, 7 (July), 574–578. *Article 4*.

Brinch Hansen, P. 1973. *Operating System Principles*. Prentice Hall, Englewood Cliffs, NJ, (July).

Brinch Hansen, P. 1975a. The programming language Concurrent Pascal. *IEEE Transactions on Software Engineering 1*, 2 (June), 199–207. *Article 7*.

Brinch Hansen, P. 1975b. Concurrent Pascal report. Information Science, California Institute of Technology, Pasadena, CA, (June).

Brinch Hansen, P. 1975c. Concurrent Pascal machine. Information Science, California Institute of Technology, Pasadena, CA, (October).

Brinch Hansen, P. 1975d. A real-time scheduler. Information Science, California Institute of Technology, Pasadena, CA, (November).

Brinch Hansen, P. 1976a. The job stream system. Information Science, California Institute of Technology, Pasadena, CA, (January).

Brinch Hansen, P. 1976b. The Solo operating system. *Software—Practice and Experience 6*, 2 (April–June), 141–205. *Articles 8–9*.

Dahl, O.-J., Dijkstra, E.W., and Hoare, C.A.R. 1972. *Structured Programming*. Academic Press, New York.

Dijkstra, E.W. 1971. Hierarchical ordering of sequential processes. *Acta Informatica 1*, 115–138.

Hartmann, A.C. 1975. A Concurrent Pascal compiler for minicomputers. Information Science, California Institute of Technology, Pasadena, CA, (September).

Hoare, C.A.R. 1972a. Towards a theory of parallel programming. In *Operating Systems Techniques*, C.A.R. Hoare and R.H. Perrott, Eds., Academic Press, New York.

Hoare, C.A.R. 1972b. Proof of correctness of data representations. *Acta Informatica 1*, 271–281.

Hoare, C.A.R. 1974. Monitors: An operating system structuring concept. *Communications of the ACM 17*, 10 (October), 549–557.

Howard, J.H. 1976. Proving monitors. *Communications of the ACM 19*, 5 (May), 273–279.

Owicki, S., and Gries, D. 1976. Verifying properties of parallel programs: An axiomatic approach. *Communications of the ACM 19*, 5 (May), 279–285

Wirth, N. 1971. The programming language Pascal. *Acta Informatica 1*, 35–63.

12

Design Principles*

(1977)

This is the opening chapter of the author's book on concurrent programming. The essay describes the fundamental principles of programming which guided the design and implementation of the programming language Concurrent Pascal and the model operating systems written in that language.

This book describes a method for writing concurrent programs of high quality. Since there is no common agreement among programmers about the qualities a good program should have, I will begin by describing my own requirements.

1 Program Quality

A good program must be *simple*, *reliable*, and *adaptable*. Without simplicity one cannot expect to understand the purpose and details of a large program. Without reliability one cannot seriously depend on it. And without adaptability to changing requirements a program eventually becomes a fossil.

Fortunately, these essential requirements go hand in hand. Simplicity gives one the confidence to believe that a program works and makes it clear how it can be changed. Simplicity, reliability, and adaptability make programs *manageable*.

In addition, it is desirable to make programs that can work efficiently on several different computers for a variety of similar applications. But *efficiency*, *portability*, and *generality* should never be sought at the expense of simplicity, reliability, and adaptability, for only the latter qualities make

---

*P. Brinch Hansen, *The Architecture of Concurrent Programs*, Chapter 1 Design Principles, Prentice Hall, Englewood Cliffs, NJ, (July 1977), 3–14. Copyright © 1977, Prentice Hall. Reprinted by permission.

it possible to understand what programs do, depend on them, and extend their capabilities.

The poor quality of much existing software is, to a large extent, the result of turning these priorities upside down. Some programmers justify extremely complex and incomprehensible programs by their high efficiency. Others claim that the poor reliability and efficiency of their huge programs are outweighed by their broad scope of application.

Personally I find the efficiency of a tool that nobody fully understands irrelevant. And I find it difficult to appreciate a general-purpose tool which is so slow that it cannot do anything well. But these are matters of taste and style and are likely to remain so.

Whenever program qualities appear to be in conflict with one another I shall consistently settle the issue by giving first priority to manageability, second priority to efficiency, and third priority to generality. This boils down to the simple rule of limiting our computer applications to those which programmers fully understand and which machines can handle well. Although this is too narrow a view for experimental computer usage it is sound advice for professional programming.

Let us now look more closely at these program qualities to see how they can be achieved.

2 Simplicity

We will be writing concurrent programs which are so large that one cannot understand them all at once. So we must reason about them in smaller *pieces*. What properties should these pieces have? Well, they should be so small that any one of them is trivial to understand in itself. It would be ideal if they were no more than *one page* of text each so that they can be comprehended at a glance.

Such a program could be studied page by page as one reads a book. But in the end, when we have understood what all the pieces do, we must still be able to see what their combined effect *as a whole* is. If it is a program of many pages we can only do this by ignoring most of our detailed knowledge about the pieces and relying on a much simpler description of what they do and how they work together.

So our program pieces must allow us to make a clear separation of their detailed behavior and that small part of it which is of interest when we consider combinations of such pieces. In other words, we must distinguish between the *inner and outer behavior* of a program piece.

Program pieces will be built to perform well-defined, simple functions. We will then combine program pieces into larger *configurations* to carry out more complicated functions. This design method is effective because it splits a complicated task into simpler ones: First you convince yourself that the pieces work individually, and then you think about how they work together. During the second part of the argument it is essential to be able to forget how a piece works in detail—otherwise, the problem becomes too complicated. But in doing so one makes the fundamental assumption that the piece always will do the same when it carries out its function. Otherwise, you could not afford to ignore the detailed behavior of that piece in your reasoning about the whole system.

So *reproducible behavior* is a vital property of program pieces that we wish to build and study in small steps. We must clearly keep this in mind when we select the kind of program pieces that large concurrent programs will be made of. The ability to repeat program behavior is taken for granted when we write sequential programs. Here the sequence of events is completely defined by the program and its input data. But in a concurrent program simultaneous events take place at rates not fully controlled by the programmer. They depend on the presence of other jobs in the machine and the scheduling policy used to execute them. This means that a conscious effort must be made to design concurrent programs with reproducible behavior.

The idea of reasoning first about *what* a piece does and then studying *how* it does it in detail is most effective if we can repeat this process by explaining each piece in terms of simpler pieces which themselves are built from still simpler pieces. So we shall confine ourselves to *hierarchical structures* composed of *layers* of program pieces.

It will certainly simplify our understanding of hierarchical structures if each part only depends on a small number of other parts. We will therefore try to build structures that have *minimal interfaces* between their parts.

This is extremely difficult to do in *machine language* since the slightest programming mistake can make an instruction destroy any instruction or variable. Here the *whole store* can be the interface between any two instructions. This was made only too clear in the past by the practice of printing the contents of the entire store just to locate a single programming error.

Programs written in *abstract languages* (such as Fortran, Algol, and Pascal) are unable to modify themselves. But they can still have broad interfaces in the form of *global variables* that can be changed by every statement (by intention or mistake).

We will use a programming language called *Concurrent Pascal*, which makes it possible to divide the global variables into smaller parts. Each of these is accessible to a small number of statements only.

The main contribution of a good programming language to simplicity is to provide an abstract *readable notation* that makes the parts and structure of a program obvious to a reader. An abstract programming language *suppresses machine detail* (such as addresses, registers, bit patterns, interrupts, and sometimes even the number of processors available). Instead the language relies on *abstract concepts* (such as variables, data types, synchronizing operations, and concurrent processes). As a result, program texts written in abstract languages are often an order of magnitude shorter than those written in machine language. This *textual reduction* simplifies program engineering considerably.

The fastest way to discover whether or not you have invented a simple program structure is to try to *describe* it in completely readable terms—adopting the same standards of clarity that are required of a survey paper published by a journal. If you take pride in your description you have probably invented a good program structure. But if you discover that there is no simple way of describing what you intend to do, then you should probably look for some other way of doing it.

Once you appreciate the value of description as an early warning signal of unnecessary complexity it becomes self-evident that program structures should be described (without detail) *before* they are built and should be described by the *designer* (and not by anybody else). *Programming is the art of writing essays in crystal clear prose and making them executable.*

3   Reliability

Even the most readable language notation cannot prevent programmers from making mistakes. In looking for these in large programs we need all the help we can get. A whole range of techniques is available

correctness proofs
proofreading
compilation checks
execution checks
systematic testing

With the exception of correctness proofs, all these techniques played a vital role in making the concurrent programs described in this book work.

Formal proofs are still at an experimental stage, particularly for concurrent programs. Since my aim is to describe techniques that are immediately useful in professional software development, I have omitted proofs here.

Among the useful verification techniques, I feel that those that reveal errors at the earliest possible time during the program development should be emphasized to achieve reliability as soon as possible.

One of the primary goals of Concurrent Pascal is to push the role of *compilation checks* to the limit and reduce the use of *execution checks* as much as possible. This is not done just to make compiled programs more efficient by reducing the overhead of execution checks. In program engineering, compilation and execution checks play the same roles as preventive maintenance and flight recorders do in aviation. The latter only tell you why a system crashed; the former prevents it. This distinction seems essential to me in the design of real-time systems that will control vital functions in society. Such systems must be highly reliable *before* they are put into operation.

Extensive compilation checks are possible only if the language notation is *redundant.* The programmer must be able to specify important properties in at least two different ways so that a compiler can look for possible inconsistencies. An example is the use of declarations to introduce variables and their types before they are used in statements. The compiler could easily derive this information from the statements—provided these statements were always correct.

We shall also follow the crucial principle of language design suggested by Hoare: *The behavior of a program written in an abstract language should always be explainable in terms of the concepts of that language and should never require insight into the details of compilers and computers.* Otherwise, an abstract notation has no significant value in reducing complexity.

This principle immediately rules out the use of machine-oriented features in programming languages. So I shall assume that *all programming will take place in abstract programming languages.*

Dijkstra has remarked that *testing* can be used only to show the presence of errors but never their absence. However true that may be, it seems very worthwhile to me to show the presence of errors and remove them one at a time. In my experience, the combination of careful proofreading, extensive compilation checks, and systematic testing is a very effective way to make a program so dependable that it can work for months without problems. And that is about as reliable as most other technology we depend on. I do not know of better methods for verifying large programs at the moment.

I view programming as the art of building *program pyramids* by adding one brick at a time to the structure and making sure that it does not collapse in the process. The pyramid must remain *stable* while it is being built. I will regard a (possibly incomplete) program as being stable as long as it behaves in a predictable manner.

Why is program testing so often difficult? Mainly, I think, because the addition of a new program piece can spread a burst of errors throughout the rest of a program and make previously tested pieces behave differently. This clearly violates the sound principle of being able to assume that when you have built and tested a part of a large program it will continue to behave correctly *under all circumstances*.

So we will make the strong requirement that *new program pieces added on top of old ones must not be able to make the latter fail.* Since this property must be verified before program testing takes place, it must be done by a compiler. We must therefore use a language notation that makes it clear what program pieces can do to one another. This strong *confinement of program errors* to the part in which they occur will make it much easier to determine from the behavior of a large program where its errors are.

4 Adaptability

A large program is so expensive to develop that it must be used for several years to make the effort worthwhile. As time passes the users' needs change, and it becomes necessary to modify the program somewhat to satisfy them. Quite often these modifications are done by people who did not develop the program in the first place. Their main difficulty is to find out how the program works and whether it will still work after being changed.

A small group of people can often succeed in developing the first version of a program in a low-level language with little or no documentation to support them. They do it by talking to one another daily and by sharing a mental picture of a simple structure.

But later, when the same program must be extended by other programmers who are not in frequent contact with the original designers, it becomes painfully clear that the "simple" structure is not described anywhere and certainly is not revealed by the primitive language notation used. It is important to realize that *for program maintenance a simple and well-documented structure is even more important than it is during program development.* I will not talk about the situation in which a program that is neither simple nor well documented must be changed.

There is an interesting relationship between programming errors and changing user requirements. Both of them are sources of *instability* in the program construction process that make it difficult to reach a state in which you have complete confidence in what a program does. They are caused by our inability to fully comprehend at once what a large program is supposed to do in detail.

The relative frequencies of program errors and changing requirements are of crucial importance. If programming introduces numerous errors that are difficult to locate, many of them may still be in the program when the user requests changes of its function. And when an engineer constantly finds himself changing a system that he never succeeded in making work correctly in the first place, he will eventually end up with a very unstable product.

On the other hand, if program errors can be located and corrected at a much faster rate than the system develops, then the addition of a new piece (or a change) to the program will soon lead to a stable situation in which the current version of the program works reliably and predictably. The engineer can then, with much greater confidence, adapt his product to slowly changing needs. This is a strong incentive to make program verification and testing fast.

A hierarchical structure consists of program pieces that can be studied one at a time. This makes it easier to read the program and get an initial understanding of what it does and how it does it. Once you have that insight, the consequences of changing a hierarchical program become clear. When you change a part of a program pyramid you must be prepared to inspect and perhaps change the program parts that are on top of it (for they are the only ones that can possibly depend on the one you changed).

5   Portability

The ability to use the same program on a variety of computers is desirable for economic reasons: Many users have different computers; sometimes they replace them with new ones; and quite often they have a common interest in sharing programs developed on different machines.

Portability is only practical if programs are written in abstract languages that hide the differences between computers as much as possible. Otherwise, it will require extensive rewriting and testing to move programs from one machine to another. Programs written in the same language can be made portable in several ways:

1. by having *different compilers* for different machines. This is only practical for the most widespread languages.

2. by having a *single compiler* that can be modified to generate code for different machines. This requires a clear separation within the compiler of those parts that check programs and those that generate code.

3. by having a *single computer* that can be simulated efficiently on different machines.

The Concurrent Pascal compiler generates code for a simple machine tailored to the language. This machine is simulated by an assembly language program of 4 K words on the PDP 11/45 computer. To move the language to another computer one rewrites this interpreter. This approach sacrifices some efficiency to make portability possible. The loss of efficiency can be eliminated on a microprogrammable machine.

6 Efficiency

Efficient programs save time for people waiting for results and reduce the cost of computation. The programs described here owe their efficiency to

> special-purpose algorithms
> static store allocation
> minimal run-time checking

Initially the loading of a large program (such as a compiler) from disk took about 16 sec on the PDP 11/45 computer. This was later reduced to 5 sec by a disk allocation algorithm that depends on the special characteristics of program files (as opposed to data files). A scheduling algorithm that tries to reduce disk head movement in general would have been useless here. The reasons for this will be made clear later.

Dynamic store algorithms that move programs and data segments around during execution can be a serious source of inefficiency that is not under the programmer's control. The implementation of Concurrent Pascal does not require garbage collection or demand paging of storage. It uses static allocation of store among a fixed number of processes. The store requirements are determined by the compiler.

When programs are written in assembly language it is impossible to predict what they will do. Most computers depend on hardware mechanisms to prevent such programs from destroying one another or the operating system. In Concurrent Pascal most of this protection is guaranteed by the compiler and is not supported by hardware mechanisms during execution. This drastic reduction of run-time checking is only possible because all programs are written in an abstract language.

7 Generality

To achieve simplicity and reliability we will depend exclusively on a machine-independent language that makes programs readable and extensive compilation checks possible. To achieve efficiency we will use the simplest possible store allocation.

These decisions will no doubt reduce the usefulness of Concurrent Pascal for some applications. But I see no way of avoiding that. To impose *structure* upon yourself is to impose *restrictions* on your freedom of programming. You can no longer use the machine in any way you want (because the language makes it impossible to talk directly about some machine features). You can no longer delay certain program decisions until execution time (because the compiler checks and freezes things much earlier). But the freedom you lose is often illusory anyhow, since it can complicate programming to the point where you are unable to cope with it.

This book describes a range of small operating systems. Each of them provides a special service in the most efficient and simple manner. They show that Concurrent Pascal is a useful programming language for minicomputer operating systems and dedicated real-time applications. I expect that the language will be useful (but not sufficient) for writing large, general-purpose operating systems. But that still remains to be seen. I have tried to make a programming tool that is very convenient for many applications rather than one which is tolerable for all purposes.

8 Conclusion

I have discussed the programming goals of

simplicity
reliability
adaptability
efficiency
portability

and have suggested that they can be achieved by careful design of program structure, language notation, compiler, and code interpreter. The properties that we must look for are the following:

structure: hierarchical structure
              small parts
              minimal interfaces
              reproducible behavior
              readable documentation

notation: abstract and readable
              structured and redundant

compiler: reliable and fast
              extensive checking
              portable code

interpreter: reliable and fast
              minimal checking
              static store allocation

This is the philosophy we will follow in the design of concurrent programs.

9   Literature

For me the most enjoyable thing about computer programming is the insight it gives into problem solving and design. The search for simplicity and structure is common to all intellectual disciplines.

Here are a historian and a biologist talking about the importance of recognizing structure:

"It is a matter of some importance to link teaching and research, even very detailed research, to an acceptable architectonic vision of the whole. Without such connections, detail becomes mere antiquarianism. Yet while history without detail is inconceivable, without an organizing vision it quickly

becomes incomprehensible ... What cannot be understood becomes meaning-less, and reasonable men quite properly refuse to pay attention to meaningless matters."

William H. McNeill (1974)

"There have been a number of physicists who suggested that biological phenomena are related to the finest aspects of the constitution of matter, in a manner of speaking below the chemical level. But the evidence, which is almost too abundant, indicates that biological phenomena operate on the 'systems' level, that is, above chemistry."

Walter M. Elsasser (1975)

A linguist, a psychologist, and a logician have this to say about writing and notation:

"Omit needless words. Vigorous writing is concise. A sentence should contain no unnecessary words, a paragraph no unnecessary sentences, for the same reason that a drawing should have no unnecessary lines and a machine no unnecessary parts. This requires not that the writer make all his sentences short, or that he avoid all detail and treat his subject only in outline, but that every word tell."

William Strunk, Jr. (1959)

"How complex or simple a structure is depends critically upon the way in which we describe it. Most of the complex structures found in the world are enormously redundant, and we can use this redundancy to simplify their description. But to use it, to achieve the simplification, we must find the right representation."

Herbert A. Simon (1969)

"There is something uncanny about the power of a happily chosen ideo-graphic language; for it often allows one to express relations which have no names in natural language and therefore have never been noticed by anyone. Symbolism, then, becomes an organ of discovery rather than mere notation."

Susanne K. Langer (1967)

An engineer and an architect discuss the influence of human errors and cultural changes on the design process:

"First, one must perform perfectly. The computer resembles the magic of legend in this respect, too. If one character, one pause, of the incantation

is not strictly in proper form, the magic doesn't work. Human beings are not accustomed to being perfect, and few areas of human activity demand it. Adjusting to the requirement for perfection is, I think, the most difficult part of learning to program."

Frederick P. Brooks, Jr. (1975)

"Misfit provides an incentive to change ... However, for the fit to occur in practice, one vital condition must be satisfied. It must have time to happen. The process must be able to achieve its equilibrium before the next culture change upsets it again. It must actually have time to reach its equilibrium every time it is disturbed—or, if we see the process as continous rather than intermittent, the adjustment of forms must proceed more quickly than the drift of the culture context."

Christopher Alexander (1964)

Finally, here are a mathematician and a physicist writing about the beauty and joy of creative work:

"The mathematician's patterns, like the painter's or the poet's, must be beautiful; the ideas, like the colours or the words, must fit together in a harmonious way. Beauty is the first test: there is no permanent place in the world for ugly mathematics."

G.H. Hardy (1967)

"The most powerful drive in the ascent of man is his pleasure in his own skill. He loves to do what he does well and, having done it well, he loves to do it better. You see it in his science. You see it in the magnificence with which he carves and builds, the loving care, the gaiety, the effrontery. The monuments are supposed to commemorate kings and religions, heroes, dogmas, but in the end the man they commemorate is the builder."

Jacob Bronowski (1973)

References

Alexander, C. 1964. *Notes on the Synthesis of Form.* Harvard University Press, Cambridge, MA.

Bronowski, J. 1973. *The Ascent of Man.* Little, Brown and Company, Boston, MA.

Brooks, F.P. 1975. *The Mythical Man-Month. Essays on Software Engineering.* Addison-Wesley, Reading, MA.

Elsasser, W.M. 1975. *The Chief Abstractions of Biology.* American Elsevier, New York.

Hardy, G.H. 1967. *A Mathematician's Apology*. Cambridge University Press, New York.
Langer, S.K. 1967. *An Introduction to Symbolic Logic*. Dover Publications, New York.
McNeill, W.H. 1974. *The Shape of European History*. Oxford University Press, New York.
Simon, H.A. 1969. *The Sciences of the Artificial*. The MIT Press, Cambridge, MA.
Strunk, W., and White, E.B. 1959. *The Elements of Style*. Macmillan, New York.

13

Network: A Multiprocessor Program[*]

(1978)

This paper explores the problems of implementing arbitrary forms of process communication on a multiprocessor network. It develops a Concurrent Pascal program that enables distributed processes to communicate on virtual channels. The channels cannot deadlock and will deliver all messages within a finite time. The operation, structure, text, and performance of this program are described. It was written, tested, and described in two weeks and it worked immediately.

1 Introduction

As an industrial programmer, I discovered that *real-time applications* require a much greater variety of process interactions than any "general-purpose" operating system can support. This experience led to the development of *Concurrent Pascal*—a programming language that makes it possible to implement arbitrary forms of process communication and resource scheduling by means of *monitors* (Brinch Hansen 1973, 1975; Hoare 1974).

Concurrent Pascal has been available on the PDP 11/45 computer since January 1975. It has been used to write three model operating systems for a single processor (Brinch Hansen 1976, 1977a, 1977b). This paper describes the first Concurrent Pascal program that controls process communication in a *multiprocessor network*.

The *Network* program enables distributed processes to communicate on virtual channels. These channels cannot deadlock and will deliver all messages within a finite time. The paper describes the operation, structure, text, and performance of this program. It was written, tested, and described in two weeks and it worked immediately.

[*]P. Brinch Hansen, Network: A multiprocessor program, *IEEE Transactions on Software Engineering 4*, 3 (May 1978), 194–199. Copyright © 1978, Institute of Electrical and Electronics Engineers, Inc. Reprinted by permission.

2   Multiprocessor System

The multiprocessor system consists of a fixed number of processor *nodes* connected cyclically by unidirectional *bus links* (Fig. 1). Each node can receive input from its predecessor on one bus link and can send output to its successor on another bus link. An output operation in one node is delayed until its neighbor starts an input operation on the same bus link, and vice versa. (It is a sad comment on the complexity of the hardware that 500 words of machine code had to be added to the Concurrent Pascal kernel to implement these simple input/output operations.)

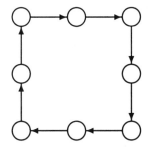

Figure 1 Data flow between processors connected by bus links.

The Network program assumes optimistically that the hardware works correctly.

3   Virtual Channels

The program uses the bus links to implement a fixed number of *virtual channels* connecting a fixed number of processes (Fig. 2). Each channel can transmit one data item at a time from a single sender process to a single receiver process. The sender and receiver processes of a channel may reside in the same or in different network nodes. The distribution of processes among the nodes and the connection of these processes by channels is fixed during program initialization. The restriction of one sender and one receiver per channel is assumed but is not enforced by the program.

Figure 3 shows an example of four processes *A*, *B*, *C*, and *D* connected by channels 1, 2, 3, and 4. Process *A* produces input for processes *B* and *C* which, in turn, deliver output to process D. This abstract process configuration can be distributed in several ways. Figure 4 shows one possibility.

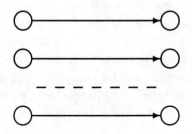

SENDERS   CHANNELS   RECEIVERS

Figure 2 Data flow between processes connected by virtual channels.

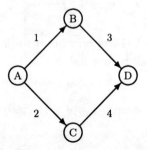

Figure 3 An example of processes connected by channels.

The Network program implements two operations

$$\text{send(channel, item)} \qquad \text{receive(channel, item)}$$

A *send* operation on a channel delays the calling process until another process performs a *receive* operation on the same channel, and vice versa.

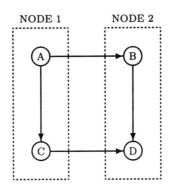

Figure 4 An example of a process distribution
in a network with two nodes.

4   Network Operation

When two processes communicate on a virtual channel, the receiving node
transmits a *request* to the sending node which then *responds* by transmitting
a data item on the network (Fig. 5). So *a transmission on the network causes
a message to pass through all nodes once*. The message begins as a request
and ends as a response.

Transmission only takes place when a receiver is waiting for a message.
Since each channel has only one receiver, it follows that *each channel can
transmit only one message at a time*.

*Each node is a first-come, first-served queuing system with a finite buffer
capacity*. A node receives input both from itself and its predecessor. The
node accepts some of these messages as input to itself and outputs the rest
to the next node (Fig. 6).

*As long as its buffer is not full, a node will continue to receive input
from itself and its predecessor in fair order. As long as a node is not delayed
indefinitely by its successor, it will continue to output messages from its
buffer in fair order* (first come, first served).

5   Network Properties

The network has several pleasant properties:

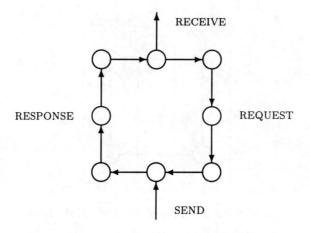

Figure 5 Transmission of a request and a response on the network.

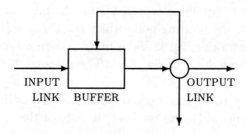

Figure 6 A network node viewed as a queuing system.

1. *No transmission takes place unless it is requested.* This means that the network only consumes machine time when processes are using it.

2. *Messages are never discarded due to buffer overflow.* A message cannot be sent until a process has provided a variable in which it can be stored and is waiting to receive it.

3. *The network cannot deadlock.* Each channel can transmit only one message at a time. If there are more buffer slots than channels in the network there will always be one or more empty buffer slots somewhere. So when there are messages on the net, at least one of the nodes will

always be able to receive a message from its predecessor and move it forwards towards its destination within a finite time.

4. *All messages are delivered within a finite time.* Suppose that a message M waits forever in a node N and is constantly being overtaken by other messages. Now, if the node is able to move some messages forward, it will do so in first-come, first-served order. And, if it continues to do so, it will eventually move the message M also. So, if one message gets stuck in a node, all messages arriving in that node will eventually get stuck there.

Since all messages pass through all nodes, they would all sooner or later be stuck in the node N. But this cannot happen since we have shown that at least one message always can make progress somewhere. So the original assumption must be wrong: a message cannot wait forever in a node.

The network will move each message forward with positive speed. And since a message passes through a finite number of nodes with finite buffer capacities it must arrive at its destination within a finite time. The network is fair.

5. *Transmission times are uniform.* All messages travel the same distance through all nodes. The uniform transmission times simplify the distribution of processes among the nodes.

The only exception is a transmission between two processes in the same node. In this case, the request and the response both pass through all nodes.

6. *Space and time requirements are proportional to the size of the network.* Let n, c, and b be the number of nodes, channels, and buffer slots in the whole network. To avoid deadlock we must have $b > c$. The simplest choice is to give each node $c/n + 1$ slots, making

$$b = c + n$$

Let t be the service time per message in a single node and let T be the total transmission time of a message on a single channel. Since a message must pass through all nodes once, we have $T \geq nt$. In the worst case, all channels may transmit simultaneously from the same

node. It will then take nt for the first message to pass through all
nodes. In addition, it will take the last node $(c-1)t$ to process the
other $c-1$ messages. So we have

$$nt \leq T \leq (c+n-1)t$$

6 Program Structure

Each node contains a copy of the Network program that implements the
virtual channels. The program consists of a fixed number of processes that
communicate by monitors (Fig. 7).

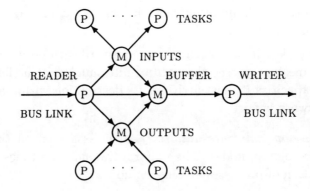

Figure 7 Data flow among processes
and monitors in a single network node.

The *task* processes in a node will vary from one application to another.
The other program components are fixed. A task process calls a local *input*
monitor when it wishes to *receive* data on a channel. A *request* is now sent
through the network to the other end of that channel and the process is
delayed until a response comes back.

A task process calls a local *output* monitor when it wishes to *send* data
on a channel. The process is delayed until a request for data arrives on that
channel. A *response* is then sent through the network to the other end of
the channel.

Each node contains a *reader* process that receives messages from the
previous node through a *bus link*. If a message is a request or a response

intended for its own node, the reader delivers it to the local output or input monitor. The remaining transit messages are sent directly to a local *buffer* monitor.

A *writer* process transmits messages from the local buffer through another *bus link* to the next node.

The Appendix contains the complete text of the Network program written in Concurrent Pascal.

7   Size and Performance

The Network program is about 250 lines long. It was written in less than a week and was tested systematically in another week using a method described in Brinch Hansen (1977b). No errors were found during testing. This paper was written in a few days making the total programming effort about two weeks.

The program has been running on two PDP 11/45 computers connected by bus links. It requires about 2900 words of core store in each computer (code 900 words and data 2000 words).

With 500 char/message the network has a maximum throughput of 30000 char/s. This rate is achieved only when the nodes spend all their time transmitting data. In practice, the speed of this multiprocesor system will be limited by the processing of messages performed by the task processes. The performance is also influenced by the configuration of processes and channels and their distribution among the network nodes.

8   Final Remarks

Many of these ideas are probably already described in the literature on computer networks (with which I am not familiar). The purpose of this paper, however, is not to advocate a particular method of network transmission. On the contrary, there are good reasons to believe that real-time programming can be simplified if process interactions can be tailored to the specific needs of each application.

To illustrate this point: It may be necessary to add recovery procedures to the present program to cope with transient hardware errors. Additional buffers must be added to make it possible for a process to poll several channels. And channels with many senders are much more convenient to use if distributed resources are scheduled among distributed processes. Finally, it

seems clear that a completely different approach is needed to achieve high
performance and cope with persistent hardware errors. This all depends on
the requirements of particular applications.

This uncertainty about future needs makes it essential to have a methodology for the design of many different network programs. This paper shows
one example of how such programs can be made simple and reliable at low
cost by using an abstract language for modular multiprogramming.

Appendix: Program Text

This Appendix is intended for readers who are already familiar with the
literature on Concurrent Pascal (Brinch Hansen 1975, 1976, 1977a, 1977b).

The Network program identifies procesor *nodes* and *virtual channels* by
unique indices

$$\textbf{type } \text{node} = 1..\text{nmax}; \text{ channel} = 1..\text{cmax}$$

The channels that originate or terminate in a node are identified by
channel sets

$$\textbf{type } \text{channelset} = \textbf{set of } \text{channel}$$

The number of nodes and channels available and the type of data items
transmitted through them may vary from one application to another

$$\textbf{const } \text{nmax} = \ldots; \text{ cmax} = \ldots$$
$$\textbf{type } \text{item} = \ldots$$

A network *message* is either a request or a response for a particular
channel. If it is a response, the message includes a data item

```
type message = record
                kind: (a_request, a_response);
                link: channel;
                contents: item
               end
```

A *task process* can *send* and *receive* data items on one or more more
channels. These operations are implemented by output and input monitors
described later.

```
type taskprocess =
process(inp: inputs; out: outputs; ...);
var a, b: channel; x, y: item;
begin
    ... inp.receive(a, x) ...
    ... out.send(b, y) ...
end
```

A *reader process* inputs one message at a time from the previous node through a bus link.

```
type readerprocess =
process(inpset, outset: channelset;
    inp: inputs; out: outputs;
    buf: buffer);
var m: message;
begin
  cycle
    input_from_buslink(m);
    with m do
      if (kind = a_response) & (link in inpset)
        then inp.response(m)
      else if (kind = a_request) & (link in outset)
        then out.request(m)
        else buf.send(m)
  end
end
```

The reader uses two constants defining the set of input channels and the set of output channels used by its node. If the node is the destination of a message, the reader performs a *response* or *request* operation on it. Otherwise, it *sends* the message through a local buffer to the next node. These operations are implemented by input, output, and buffer monitors. The details of input/output are described elsewhere (Brinch Hansen 1977b).

A *writer process* receives one message at a time from a local buffer and outputs it to the next node through a bus link.

```
type writerprocess =
process(buf: buffer);
var m: message;
begin
```

```
cycle
  buf.receive(m);
  output_to_buslink(m)
end
end
```

A *buffer monitor* implements two operations: *Send* delays a calling process as long as the buffer is full. It then puts a message into the buffer
and continues the execution of another process (if there are any) waiting to
receive the message. *Receive* delays a calling process as long as the buffer is
empty. It then gets a message from the buffer and continues the execution
of another process (if there are any) waiting to send a message.

Sequences and queues with several processes waiting to send or receive
messages are not primitive concepts in Concurrent Pascal, but can be implemented in the language (Brinch Hansen 1977b).

```
type buffer =
monitor
const bmax = ... "cmax/nmax + 1";
var buf: sequence [bmax] of message;
  sender, receiver: queue;

procedure entry send(m: message);
begin
  if buf.full then delay(sender);
  buf.put(m);
  continue(receiver)
end;

procedure entry receive(var m: message);
begin
  if buf.empty then delay(receiver);
  buf.get(m);
  continue(sender)
end;

begin buf.reset end
```

An *input monitor* implements two operations: *Receive* sends a request
through a local buffer and delays a calling process until a response arrives on

a given channel. *Response* delivers a data item on a channel and continues the process that is waiting to receive it.

```
type inputs =
monitor(buf: buffer);
var receiver: array [channel] of queue;
   this: message;

procedure entry receive(c: channel; var v: item);
begin
   with this do
      begin kind := a_request; link := c end;
   buf.send(this); delay(receiver[c]);
   v := this.contents
end;

procedure entry response(m: message);
begin
   this := m; continue(receiver[m.link])
end;

begin end
```

An *output monitor* implements two operations: *Send* delays a calling process until a given channel is ready for transmission. It then sends a data item through a local buffer. *Request* makes a channel ready to send and continues a process (if there are any) waiting to send on that channel. *Initially* no channels are ready.

```
type outputs =
monitor(buf: buffer);
var list: array [channel] of
            record ready: boolean; sender: queue end;
   c: channel; this: message;

procedure entry send(c: channel; v: item);
begin
   with list[c] do
      if not ready then delay(sender);
   with this do
```

```
    begin
       kind := a_response; link := c;
       contents := v
    end;
  buf.send(this);
  list[c].ready := false
end;

procedure entry request(m: message);
begin
  with list[m.link] do
    begin ready := true; continue(sender) end
end;

begin
  for c := 1 to cmax do list[c].ready := false
end
```

All instances of these program components are declared and initialized by an *initial process* shown below. The definitions of channel sets and task processes may vary from node to node.

```
var inpset, outset: channelset;
    buf: buffer;
    inp: inputs; out: outputs;
    reader: readerprocess;
    writer: writerprocess;
    task1, task2, ... : taskprocess
begin
  inpset := [...]; outset := [...];
  init buf, inp(buf), out(buf),
    reader(inpset, outset, inp, out, buf),
    writer(buf),
    task1(inp, out, ...),
    task2(inp, out, ...),
    ...
end
```

Acknowledgements

The ideas in this paper were developed in discussions with B. Heidebrecht, D. Heimbigner, F. Stepczyk, and R. Vossler of TRW Systems, Redondo Beach, CA. The program was tested at TRW's Signal Processing Facility.

References

Brinch Hansen, P. 1973. *Operating System Principles.* Prentice Hall, Englewood Cliffs, NJ, (July).

Brinch Hansen, P. 1975. The programming language Concurrent Pascal. *IEEE Transactions on Software Engineering 1*, 2 (June), 199–207. *Article 7.*

Brinch Hansen, P. 1976. The Solo operating system. *Software—Practice and Experience 6*, 2 (April–June), 141–205. *Articles 8–9.*

Brinch Hansen, P. 1977a. Experience with modular concurrent programming. *IEEE Transactions on Software Engineering 3*, 2 (March), 156–159. *Article 11.*

Brinch Hansen, P. 1977b. *The Architecture of Concurrent Programs.* Prentice Hall, Englewood Cliffs, NJ, (July).

Hoare, C.A.R. 1974. Monitors: An operating system structuring concept. *Communications of the ACM 17*, 10 (October), 549–557.

14

Distributed Processes: A Concurrent Programming Concept[*]

(1978)

A language concept for concurrent processes without common variables is introduced. These processes communicate and synchronize by means of procedure calls and guarded regions. This concept is proposed for real-time applications controlled by microcomputer networks with distributed storage. The paper gives several examples of distributed processes and shows that they include procedures, coroutines, classes, monitors, processes, semaphores, buffers, path expressions, and input/output as special cases.

1 Introduction

This paper introduces *distributed processes*—a new language concept for concurrent programming. It is proposed for real-time applications controlled by microcomputer networks with distributed storage. The paper gives several examples of distributed processes and shows that they include procedures, coroutines, classes, monitors, processes, semaphores, buffers, path expressions and input/output as special cases.

Real-time applications push computer and programming technology to its limits (and sometimes beyond). A real-time system is expected to monitor simultaneous activities with critical timing constraints continuously and reliably. The consequences of system failure can be serious.

Real-time programs must achieve the ultimate in simplicity, reliability, and efficiency. Otherwise one can neither understand them, depend on them, nor expect them to keep pace with their environments. To make real-time

---

[*]P. Brinch Hansen, Distributed processes: A concurrent programming concept, *Communications of the ACM 21*, 11 (November 1978), 934–941. Copyright © 1978, Association for Computing Machinery, Inc. Reprinted by permission.

programs manageable it is essential to write them in an abstract programming language that hides irrelevant machine detail and makes extensive compilation checks possible. To make real-time programs efficient at the same time will probably require the design of computer architectures tailored to abstract languages (or even to particular applications).

From a language designer's point of view, real-time programs have these characteristics:

1. A real-time program interacts with an environment in which many things happen simultaneously at high speeds.

2. A real-time program must respond to a variety of *nondeterministic requests* from its environment. The program cannot predict the order in which these requests will be made but must respond to them within certain time limits. Otherwise, input data may be lost or output data may lose their significance.

3. A real-time program controls a computer with a fixed configuration of processors and peripherals and performs (in most cases) a fixed number of concurrent tasks in its environment.

4. A real-time program never terminates but continues to serve its environment as long as the computer works. (The occasional need to stop a real-time program, say at the end of an experiment, can be handled by ad hoc mechanisms, such as turning the machine off or loading another program into it.)

What is needed then for real-time applications is the ability to specify a fixed number of concurrent tasks that can respond to nondeterministic requests. The programming languages *Concurrent Pascal* and *Modula* come close to satisfying the requirements for abstract concurrent programming (Brinch Hansen 1975, 1977; Wirth 1977). Both of them are based on the *monitor* concept (Brinch Hansen 1973; Hoare 1974). Modula, however, is primarily oriented towards multiprogramming on a single processor. And a straightforward implementation of Concurrent Pascal requires a single processor or a multiprocessor with a common store. In their present form, these languages are not ideal for a microcomputer network with distributed storage only.

It may well be possible to modify Concurrent Pascal to satisfy the constraints of distributed storage. The ideas proposed here are more attractive, however, because they unify the monitor and process concepts and result in more elegant programs. The new language concepts for real-time applications have the following properties:

1. A real-time program consists of a fixed number of concurrent processes that are started simultaneously and exist forever. Each process can access its *own variables* only. There are no common variables.

2. A process can call *common procedures* defined within other processes. These procedures are executed when the other processes are waiting for some conditions to become true. This is the only form of process communication.

3. Processes are synchronized by means of nondeterministic statements called *guarded regions* (Hoare 1972; Brinch Hansen 1978).

These processes can be used as program modules in a multiprocessor system with common or distributed storage. To satisfy the real-time constraints each processor will be dedicated to a single process. When a processor is waiting for some condition to become true then its processor is also waiting until an external procedure call makes the condition true. This does not represent a waste of resources but rather a temporary lack of useful work for that processor. Parameter passing between processes can be implemented either by copying within a common store or by input/output between separate stores.

The problems of designing verification rules and computer architectures for distributed processes are currently being studied and are not discussed. This paper also ignores the serious problems of performance evaluation and fault tolerance.

2   Language Concepts

A concurrent program consists of a fixed number of sequential processes that are executed simultaneously. A *process* defines its own variables, some common procedures, and an initial statement

```
process name
own variables
common procedures
initial statement
```

A process may only access its *own variables*. There are no common variables. But a process may call *common procedures* defined either within itself or within other processes. A procedure call from one process to another is called an *external request*.

A process performs two kinds of *operations* then: the *initial statement* and the *external requests* made by other processes. These operations are executed one at a time by *interleaving*. A process begins by executing its initial statement. This continues until the statement either terminates or waits for a condition to become true. Then another operation is started (as the result of an external request). When this operation in turn terminates or waits the process will either begin yet another operation (requested by another process) or it will resume an earlier operation (as the result of a condition becoming true). This interleaving of the initial statement and the external requests continues forever. If the initial statement terminates, the process continues to exist and will still accept external statements.

So the interleaving is controlled by the program (and *not* by clock signals at the machine level). A process switches from one operation to another only when an operation terminates or waits for a condition within a guarded region (introduced later).

A process continues to execute operations except when all its current operations are delayed within guarded regions or when it makes a request to another process. In the first case, the process is idle until another process calls it. In the second case, the process is idle until the other process has completed the operation requested by it. Apart from this nothing is assumed about the order in which a process performs its operations.

A process guarantees only that it will perform *some* operations as long as there are any unfinished operations that can proceed. But only the programmer can ensure that *every* operation is performed within a finite time.

A *procedure* defines its input and output parameters, some local variables perhaps, and a statement that is executed when it is called.

> **proc** name(input param#output param)
> local variables
> statement

A process P can call a procedure R defined within another process Q as follows:

> **call** $Q.R$(expressions, variables)

Before the operation R is performed the expression values of the call are assigned to the *input* parameters. When the operation is finished the values of the *output* parameters are assigned to the variables of the call. Parameter passing between processes can therefore be implemented either by copying within a common store or by input/output between processors that have no common store.

In this paper processes can call procedures within one another without any restrictions. In a complete programming language additional notation would be added to limit the access rights of individual processes. It may also be necessary to eliminate recursion to simplify verification and implementation. But these are issues that will not concern us here.

Nondeterminism will be controlled by two kinds of statements called *guarded commands* and *guarded regions*. A guarded region can delay an operation, but a guarded command cannot.

A guarded command (Dijkstra 1975) enables a process to make an arbitrary choice among several statements by inspecting the current state of its variables. If none of the alternatives are possible in the current state the guarded command cannot be executed and will either be skipped or cause a program exception.

The guarded commands have the following syntax and meaning:

$$\textbf{if } B_1 \colon S_1 \mid B_2 \colon S_2 \mid \ldots \textbf{ end}$$

$$\textbf{do } B_1 \colon S_1 \mid B_2 \colon S_2 \mid \ldots \textbf{ end}$$

If statement: If some of the conditions B_1, B_2, ..., are true then select one of the true conditions B_i and execute the statement S_i that follows it; otherwise, stop the program.

(If the language includes a mechanism whereby one process can detect the failure of another process, it is reasonable to let an exception in one process stop that process only. But, if recovery from programming errors is not possible then it is more consistent to stop the whole program. This paper does not address this important issue.)

Do statement: While some of the conditions are true, select one of them arbitrarily and execute the corresponding statement.

A guarded region (Hoare 1972; Brinch Hansen 1978) enables a process to wait until the state of its variables makes it possible to make an arbitrary choice among several statements. If none of the alternatives are possible in the current state the process postpones the execution of the guarded region.

The guarded regions have the following syntax and meaning:

$$\textbf{when } B_1\colon S_1 \mid B_2\colon S_2 \mid \ldots \textbf{ end}$$

$$\textbf{cycle } B_1\colon S_1 \mid B_2\colon S_2 \mid \ldots \textbf{ end}$$

When statement: Wait until one of the conditions is true and execute the corresponding statement.

Cycle statement: Endless repetition of a when statement.

If several conditions are true within a guarded command or region it is unpredictable which one of the corresponding statements the machine will select. This uncertainty reflects the nondeterministic nature of real-time applications.

The *data types* used are either integers, booleans, or characters, or they are finite sets, sequences, and arrays with at most n elements of some type T:

$$\text{int} \quad \text{bool} \quad \text{char} \quad \textbf{set}[n]T \quad \textbf{seq}[n]T \quad \textbf{array}[n]T$$

The following statement enumerates all the elements in a data structure:

$$\textbf{for } x \textbf{ in } y\colon S \textbf{ end}$$

For statement: For each element x in the set or array y execute the statement S. A for statement can access and change the values of array elements but can only read the values of set elements.

Finally, it should be mentioned that the empty statement is denoted *skip* and the use of semicolons is optional.

3   Process Communication

The following presents several examples of the use of these language concepts in concurrent programming. We will first consider communication between processes by means of procedure calls.

Example: Semaphore

A general semaphore initialized to zero can be implemented as a process *sem* that defines *wait* and *signal* operations.

```
process sem
s: int
proc wait when s > 0: s := s − 1 end
proc signal; s := s + 1
s := 0
```

The initial statement assigns the value zero to the semaphore and terminates. The process, however, continues to exist and can now be called by other processes

call sem.wait   call sem.signal

Example: Message buffer

A buffer process stores a sequence of characters transmitted between processes by means of *send* and *receive* operations.

```
process buffer
s: seq[n]char
proc send(c: char) when not s.full: s.put(c) end
proc rec(#v: char) when not s.empty: s.get(v) end
s := [ ]
```

The initial statement makes the buffer empty to begin with. The buffer operations are called as follows:

call buffer.send(x)   call buffer.rec(y)

The semaphore and buffer processes are similar to *monitors* (Brinch Hansen 1973; Hoare 1974): They define the representation of a shared data structure and the meaningful operations on it. These operations take place one at a time. After initialization, a monitor is idle between external calls.

Example: Character stream

A process inputs punched cards from a card reader and outputs them as a sequence of characters through a buffer process. The process deletes *spaces* at the end of each card and terminates it by a *newline* character.

```
process stream
b: array[80]char; n, i: int
do true:
   call cardreader.input(b)
   if b = blankline: skip |
      b ≠ blankline: i := 1; n := 80;
         do b[n] = space: n := n − 1 end
         do i ≤ n: call buffer.send(b[i]); i := i + 1 end
   end
   call buffer.send(newline)
end
```

This use of a process is similar to the traditional *process* concept: the process executes an initial statement only. It calls common procedures within other processes, but does not define any within itself. Such a process does not contain guarded regions because other processes are unable to call it and make the conditions within it true.

The example also illustrates how *peripheral devices* can be controlled by distributed processes. A device (such as the card reader) is associated with a single process. Other processes can access the device only through common procedures. So a peripheral device is just another process.

While a process is waiting for input/output, no other operations can take place within it. This is a special case of a more general rule: When a process P calls a procedure R within another process Q then R is considered an indivisible operation within process P, and P will not execute any other operation until R is finished (see Section 2).

Notice, that there is no need for *interrupts* even in a real-time language. Fast response to external requests is achieved by dedicating a processor to each critical event in the environment and by making sure that these processors interact with a small number of neighboring processors only (to prevent them from being overloaded with too many requests at a time).

Exercise: Write a process that receives a sequence of characters from a buffer process and outputs them line by line to a printer. The process should output a *formfeed* after every 60 lines.

4   Resource Scheduling

We will now look at a variety of scheduling problems solved by means of guarded regions. It should perhaps be mentioned that resource schedulers are by nature *bottlenecks*. It would therefore be wise in a real-time program to make sure that each resource either is used frequently by a small number of processes or very infrequently by a larger number of processes. In many applications it is possible to avoid resource scheduling altogether and dedicate a resource to a single process (as in the card reader and line printer examples).

Example: Resource scheduler

A set of user processes can obtain exclusive access to an abstract resource by calling request and release operations within a scheduling process.

```
process resource
free: bool
proc request when free: free := false end
proc release if not free: free := true end
free := true
```

```
call resource.request ... call resource.release
```

The use of the boolean *free* forces a strict alternation of request and release operations. The program stops if an attempt is made to release a resource that is already free.

In this example, the scheduler does not know the identity of individual user processes. This is ideal when it does not matter in which order the users are served. But, if a scheduler must enforce a particular scheduling policy (such as *shortest job next*) then it must know the identity of its users to be able to grant the resource to a specific user. The following example shows how this can be done.

Example: Shortest job next scheduler

A scheduler allocates a resource among n user processes in shortest job next order. A request enters the identity and service time of a user process in a queue and waits until that user is selected by the scheduler. A release makes the resource available again.

The scheduler waits until one of two situations arises:

1. A process enters or leaves the queue: The scheduler will scan the queue and select the next user (but will not grant the resource to it yet).

2. The resource is not being used and the next user has been selected: The scheduler will grant the resource to that user and remove it from the queue.

User processes identify themselves by unique indices 1, 2, ..., n. The constant *nil* denotes an undefined process index.

The scheduler uses the following variables:

queue	the indices of waiting processes
rank	the service times of waiting processes
user	the index of the current user (if any)
next	the index of the next user (if any)

```
process sjn
queue: set[n]int; rank: array[n]int
user, next, min: int

proc request(who, time: int)
begin queue.include(who); rank[who] := time
  next := nil; when user = who: next := nil end
end

proc release; user := nil

begin queue := [ ]; user := nil; next := nil
  cycle
    not queue.empty & (next = nil):
      min := maxinteger
      for i in queue:
        if rank[i] > min: skip |
          rank[i] ≤ min: next := i; min := rank[i]
        end
      end|
    (user = nil) & (next ≠ nil):
      user := next; queue.exclude(user)
  end
end
```

In a microprocessor network where each processor is dedicated to a single process it is an attractive possibility to let a process carry out computations *between* external calls of its procedures. The above scheduler takes advantage of this capability by selecting the next user while the resource is being used by the present user. It would be simpler (but less efficient) to delay the selection of the next user until the previous one has released the resource.

The scheduling of individual processes is handled completely by means of guarded regions without the use of synchronizing variables, such as semaphores or event queues.

The periodic reevaluation of a synchronizing condition, such as

$$\text{user} = \text{who}$$

might be a serious load on a *common* store shared by other processors. But it is quite acceptable when it only involves the *local* store of a single processor that has nothing else to do. This is a good example of the influence of hardware technology on abstract algorithms.

Exercise: Write a first-come, first-served scheduler.

Example: Readers and writers

Two kinds of processes, called readers and writers, share a single resource. The readers can use the resource simultaneously, but each writer must have exclusive access to it. The readers and writers behave as follows:

call resource.startread	**call** resource.startwrite
read	write
call resource.endread	**call** resource.endwrite

A variable s defines the current resource *state* as one of the following:

$$s = 0 \quad \text{1 writer uses the resource}$$
$$s = 1 \quad \text{0 processes use the resource}$$
$$s = 2 \quad \text{1 reader uses the resource}$$
$$s = 3 \quad \text{2 readers use the resource}$$
$$\ldots \qquad \ldots$$

This leads to the following solution (Brinch Hansen 1978):

```
process resource
s: int
proc startread when s ≥ 1: s := s + 1 end
proc endread if s > 1: s := s − 1 end
proc startwrite when s = 1: s := 0 end
proc endwrite if s = 0: s := 1 end
s := 1
```

Exercise: Solve the same problem with the additional constraint that further reader requests should be delayed as long as some writers are either waiting for or are using the resource.

Example: Alarm clock

An alarm clock process enables user processes to wait for different time intervals. The alarm clock receives a signal from a timer process after each time unit. (The problems of representing a clock with a finite integer are ignored here.)

```
process alarm
time: int

proc wait(interval: int)
due: int
begin due := time + interval
   when time = due: skip end
end

proc tick; time := time + 1

time := 0
```

5 Process Arrays

So far we have only used one instance of each process. The next example uses an array of n identical processes (Hoare 1978):

$$\textbf{process } \text{name}[n]$$

A standard function *this* defines the identity of an individual process within the array $(1 \leq \text{this} \leq n)$.

Example: Dining philosophers

Five philosophers alternate between thinking and eating. When a philosopher gets hungry, he joins a round table and picks up two forks next to his plate and starts eaiting. There are, however, only five forks on the table. So a philosopher can eat only when none of his neighbors are eating. When a philosopher has finished eating he puts down his two forks and leaves the table again.

```
process philosopher[5]
do true: think
   call table.join(this); eat; call table.leave(this)
end

process table
eating: set[5]int
proc join(i: int)
when([i ⊖ 1, i ⊕ 1] & eating) = [ ]: eating.include(i) end
proc leave(i: int); eating.exclude(i)
eating := [ ]
```

This solution does not prevent two philosophers from starving a philosopher between them to death by eating alternately.

Exercise: Solve the same problem without starvation.

Example: Sorting array

A process array sorts m data items in order $O(m)$. The items are input through sort process 1 that stores the smallest item input so far and passes the rest to its successor sort process 2. The latter keeps the second smallest item and passes the rest to its successor sort process 3, and so on. When the m items have been input they will be stored in their natural order in sort processes 1, 2, ..., m. They can now be output in increasing order through sort process 1. After each output the processes receive the remaining items from their successors.

A user process behaves as follows:

```
A: array[m]int
for x in A: call sort[1].put(x) end
for x in A: call sort[1].get(x) end
```

The sorting array can sort n elements or less ($m \leq n$). A sorting process is in equilibrium when it holds one item only. When the equilibrium is disturbed by its predecessor, a process takes the following action:

1. If the process holds two items, it will keep the smallest one and pass the largest one to its successor.

2. If the process holds no items, but its successor does, then the process will fetch the smallest item from its successor.

A sorting process uses the following variables:

here	the items stored in this process ($0 \leq$ here.length ≤ 2)
rest	the number of items stored in its successors

A standard function *succ* defines the index of the successor process (succ = this + 1).

```
process sort[n]
here: seq[2]int; rest, temp: int
proc put(c: int) when here.length < 2: here.put(c) end
proc get(#v: int) when here.length = 1: here.get(v) end

begin here := [ ]; rest := 0
  cycle
    here.length = 2:
      if here[1] ≤ here[2]: temp := here[2]; here := [here[1]] |
         here[1] > here[2]: temp := here[1]; here := [here[2]]
      end
      call sort[succ].put(temp); rest := rest + 1 |
    (here.length = 0) & (rest > 0):
      call sort[succ].get(temp); rest := rest − 1
      here := [temp]
  end
end
```

A hardware implementation of such a sorting array could be used as a very efficient form of priority scheduling queue.

Exercise: Program a process array that contains $N = 2^n$ numbers to begin with and which will add them in time $O(\log_2 N)$.

Since a process can define a common procedure it obviously includes the *procedure* concept as a special case. Hoare (1978) shows that a process array also can simulate a *recursive* procedure with a fixed maximum depth of recursion.

Exercise: Write a process array that computes a Fibonacci number by recursion.

6   Abstract Data Types

A process combines a data structure and all the possible operations on it into a single program module. Since other processes can perform these operations only on the data structure, but do not have direct access to it, it is called an *abstract* data structure.

We have already seen that a process can function as a *monitor*—an abstract data type that is shared by several processes. The next example shows that a process also can simulate a *class*—an abstract data type that is used by a single process only.

Example: Vending machine

A vending machine accepts one coin at a time. When a button is pushed the machine returns an item with change provided there is at least one item left and the coins cover the cost of it; otherwise, all the coins are returned.

```
process vending_machine
items, paid, cash: int
proc insert(coin: int) paid := paid + coin
proc push(#change, goods: int)
if (items > 0) & (paid ≥ price)
    change := paid − price; cash := cash + price
    goods := 1; items := items − 1; paid := 0 |
  (items = 0) or (paid < price):
    change := paid; goods := 0; paid := 0
end
begin items := 50; paid := 0; cash := 0 end
```

7 Coroutines

Distributed processes can also function as coroutines. In a coroutine relationship between two processes P and Q only one of them is running at a time. A resume operation transfers control from one process to the other. When a process is resumed it continues at the point where it has transferred control to another process.

```
process P
go: bool
proc resume; go := true

begin go := false
    ...
    call Q.resume
    when go: go := false end
    ...
end
```

Process Q is very similar.

8 Path Expressions

Path expressions define meaningful *sequences* of operations P, Q, ..., (Campbell 1974). A path expression can be implemented by a scheduling process that defines the operations P, Q, ..., as procedures and uses a state variable s to enforce the sequence in which other processes may invoke these procedures.

Suppose, for example, that the operation P only can be followed by the operation Q as shown by the graph below:

$$\rightarrow P \rightarrow Q \rightarrow$$

To implement this path expression one associates a distinct state a, b, and c with each arrow in the graph and programs the operations as follows:

proc P **if** $s = a$: ... $s := b$ **end**

proc Q **if** $s = b$: ... $s := c$ **end**

If P is called in the state $s = a$ it will change the state to $s = b$ and make Q possible. Q, in turn, changes the state from b to c. An attempt to perform P or Q in a state where they are illegal will cause a program exception (or a delay if a *when* statement is used within the operation).

The next path expression specifies that either P or Q can be performed. This is enforced by means of two states a and b.

proc P **if** $s = a$: ... $s := b$ **end**

proc Q **if** $s = a$: ... $s := b$ **end**

If an operation P can be performed zero or more times then the execution of P leaves the state $s = a$ unchanged as shown below.

proc P **if** $s = a$: ... **end**

The simple resource scheduler in Section 4 implements a composite path expression in which the sequence *request* ... *release* is repeated zero or more times.

The readers and writers problem illustrates the use of a state variable to permit some operations to take place *simultaneously* while other operations are temporarily *excluded* (in this case, simultaneous reading by several processes excludes writing). Each simultaneous operation P is surrounded by a pair of scheduling operations, *startP* and *endP*. The state variable counts the number of P operations in progress.

9 Implementation Hints

The following outlines the general nature of an implementation of distributed processes but ignores the details which are currently being studied.

In a well-designed concurrent program one may assume that each process communicates with a small number of neighboring processes only. For if the interactions are not strongly localized one cannot expect to gain much from concurrency. (A few resource schedulers may be an exception to this rule.)

Each processor will contain a distributed process P and a small, fixed number of anonymous processes which are the *representatives* of those distributed processes that can call process P. Additional notation in the language should make it possible for a compiler to determine the number of processes which call a particular process.

Whenever a processor is idle it activates a local representative which then waits until it receives a request with input data from another processor. The representative now calls the local procedure requested with the available input. When the procedure terminates, its output data are returned to the other processor and the representative becomes passive again. The switching from one *quasiconcurrent* process to another within a processor takes place as described in Section 2.

Since processes are permanent and procedures are nonrecursive, a compiler can determine the maximum storage required by a distributed process and the local representatives of its environment. So the storage allocation is *static* within each processor.

The parameter passing between two processors requires a single *input* operation before a procedure is executed and a single *output* operation when it terminates.

The speed of process switching within a single processor will probably be crucial for its real-time response.

The technique of representing the environment of a processor by local processes synchronized with external processes seems conceptually attractive. Although these processes are anonymous in this proposal one could design a language in which the store of a single process is shared by quasiconcurrent processes which communicate with nonlocal processes by input/output only.

10 Final Remarks

It would certainly be feasible to adapt the processes and monitors of Concurrent Pascal to multiprocessor networks with distributed storage by restricting the parameter passing mechanism as proposed here. All the examples discussed here could then be programmed in that language—but not nearly as elegantly!

What then are the merits of distributed processes? Primarily, that they are a combination of *well-known* programming concepts (processes, procedures, and conditional critical regions) which *unify* the class, monitor, and process concepts. They include a surprising number of basic programming concepts as special cases:

> procedures
> coroutines
> classes
> monitors
> processes
> semaphores
> buffers
> path expressions
> input/output

Since there is a common denominator for all these concepts, it may well be possible to develop common proof rules for them. The use of a single concept will certainly simplify the language implementation considerably.

The Concurrent Pascal machine distinguishes between 15 virtual instructions for classes, monitors, and processes. This number would be reduced by a factor of three for distributed processes. In addition, numerous special cases would disappear in the compiler.

It is also encouraging that distributed processes can be used to write elegant algorithms both for the more well-known concurrent problems and for some new ones that are nontrivial.

A recent proposal by Hoare (1978) has the same pleasant properties. Both proposals attack the problem of concurrency without shared variables and recognize the need for nondeterminacy within a single process.

Hoare's *communicating sequential processes* can be created and terminated dynamically. A single data transfer from one process to another is the communication mechanism. A process synchronizes itself with its environment by guarded input commands which are executed when a boolean expression is true *and* input is available from another process. The relationships between two communicating processes is symmetrical and requires both of them to name the other. The brief and nonredundant notation does not require declarations of communication channels but depends (conceptually) on dynamic type checking to recognize matching input and output commands in two processes.

In their present form communicating sequential processes seem well-suited to a theoretical investigation of concurrency and as a concise specification language that suppresses minor details, However, as Hoare points out, the language concepts and the notation would have to be modified to make them practical for program implementation.

The proposal for *distributed processes* is intended as a first step toward a practical language for networks. The proposal recognizes that the exchange of input and output in one operation is a frequent case, particularly for peripheral devices which return a result after each operation. The notation is redundant and enables a compiler to determine the number of processes and their storage requirements. The relationship between two communicating processes is asymmetrical and requires only that the caller of an operation name the process that performs it. This asymmetry is useful in hierarchical systems in which servants should be unaware of the identities of their masters.

Distributed processes derive much of their power from the ability to delay process interactions by means of boolean expressions which may involve both the global variables of a process *and* the input parameters from other processes (as illustrated by the *sjn* scheduler and the alarm clock). The price for this flexibility is the need for quasiconcurrent processes in the implementation. A more restricted form of Hoare's proposal might be able to implement process synchronization by the simpler method of polling a number of data channels until one of them transmits data.

But more work remains to be done on verification rules and network architectures for these new concepts. And then the ideas must be tested in *practice* before a final judgment can be made.

Acknowledgements

I am grateful to Nissim Francez, Wolfgang Franzen, Susan Gerhart, Charles Hayden, John Hennessy, Tony Hoare, David Lomet, David MacQueen, Johannes Madsen, David Musser, Michel Sintzoff, Jørgen Staunstrup and the referees for their constructive comments.

References

Brinch Hansen, P. 1973. *Operating System Principles*. Prentice Hall, Englewood Cliffs, NJ.

Brinch Hansen, P. 1975. The programming language Concurrent Pascal. *IEEE Transactions on Software Engineering 1*, 2 (June), 199–207. Article 7.

Brinch Hansen, P. 1977. *The Architecture of Concurrent Programs*. Prentice Hall, Englewood Cliffs, NJ.

Brinch Hansen, P., and Staunstrup, J. 1978. Specification and implementation of mutual exclusion. *IEEE Transactions on Software Engineering 4*, 4 (September), 365–370.

Campbell, R.H., and Habermann, A.N. 1974. The specification of process synchronization by path expressions. *Lecture Notes in Computer Science 16*, 89–102.

Dijkstra, E.W. 1975. Guarded commands, nondeterminacy, and formal derivation of programs. *Communications of the ACM 18*, 8 (August), 453–457.

Hoare, C.A.R. 1972. Towards a theory of parallel programming. In *Operating Systems Techniques*, C.A.R. Hoare and R.H. Perrott, Eds., Academic Press, New York.

Hoare, C.A.R. 1974. Monitors: An operating system structuring concept. *Communications of the ACM 17*, 10 (October), 549–557.

Hoare, C.A.R. 1978. Communicating sequential processes. *Communications of the ACM 21*, 8 (August), 666–677.

Wirth, N. 1977. Modula: A programming language for modular multiprogramming. *Software—Practice and Experience 7*, 1 (January), 3–35.

15

Reproducible Testing of Monitors*

(1978)

This paper describes a systematic method for testing monitor modules which control process interactions in concurrent programs. A monitor is tested by executing a concurrent program in which the processes are synchronized by a clock to make the sequence of interactions reproducible. The method separates the construction and implementation of test cases and makes the analysis of a concurrent experiment similar to the analysis of a sequential program. The implementation of a test program is almost mechanical. The method, which is illustrated by an example, has been used successfully to test a multicomputer network program written in Concurrent Pascal.

1 Introduction

Some computer scientists feel that testing is a futile effort since it can never convince one that a program is absolutely correct. My experience has been that systematic testing can be remarkably successful in practice for both sequential and concurrent programs (Naur 1963; Brinch Hansen 1973, 1977). I am sure that there are good theoretical reasons for this which could be uncovered if researchers would take a fresh look at the problem.

The purpose of this paper is to describe a method for testing monitor modules which control the interactions of processes in concurrent programs. The testing of a monitor involves several steps:

1. For each monitor operation the programmer identifies a set of preconditions that will cause each branch of the operation to be executed at least once.

---

*P. Brinch Hansen, Reproducible testing of monitors, *Software—Practice and Experience* 8, 6 (November–December), 721–729. Copyright © 1978, John Wiley & Sons, Ltd. Reprinted by permission.

2. The programmer then constructs a sequence of monitor calls that will try each operation under each of its preconditions.

3. The programmer now constructs a set of test processes that will interact exactly as defined above. These processes are scheduled by means of a clock monitor used for testing only.

4. Finally, the test program is executed and its output is compared with the predicted output.

This method makes it possible to test a monitor module by means of a reproducible sequence of operations without changing the monitor. The method has been used successfully to test a network program for a multi-computer system (Brinch Hansen 1978). The test example described in this paper was carried out successfully on a PDP 11/55 computer.

2 An Example: The Asymmetric Buffer

Figure 1 shows an example of two processes that communicate by means of a buffer monitor.

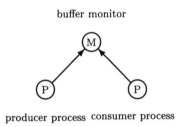

Figure 1 A concurrent program.

The arrows indicate that these processes have access to that monitor. A producer process inputs one *line* at a time from a card reader and sends it through a buffer. A consumer process receives one *character* at a time from the buffer. The buffer has a capacity of one line. When the buffer is full, 80 receive operations must be performed before another send operation can take place. The characters in each line must be received in their natural order (from left to right).

In the programming language *Concurrent Pascal* (Brinch Hansen 1977) this buffer can be programmed as follows:

```
type buffer=
monitor
var contents: line; length: integer;
    sender, receiver: queue;

procedure entry send(x: line);
begin
  if length > 0 then delay(sender);
  contents := x; length := 80;
  if not empty(receiver) then
     continue(receiver)
end;

procedure entry receive(var y: char);
begin
  if length = 0 then delay(receiver);
  y := contents[length]; length := length − 1;
  if not empty(sender) & (length = 0) then
     continue(sender)
end;

begin length := 0 end
```

The monitor defines a data structure representing the buffer and two operations, *send* and *receive*, on the buffer. An initial statement at the end of the monitor makes it empty to begin with.

The data structure represents the buffer *contents* (a single line) and its current *length* in characters ($0 \leq \text{length} \leq 80$). Two queue variables are used to delay the *sender* and the *receiver* processes (if necessary).

The send operation delays the producer process until the buffer is empty. It then puts a new line into the buffer. If the consumer process is waiting in the receiver queue its execution is continued.

The receive operation delays the consumer process until the buffer is nonempty. It then gets the next character from the buffer. If the buffer becomes empty and the producer process is waiting in the sender queue its execution is continued.

In Concurrent Pascal a *continue* operation has no effect if a queue is *empty*. It is therefore unnecessary to examine whether a queue is empty before performing a continue operation on it. The continue operations are nevertheless made conditional in this monitor to make it clear that they should be tested in two cases: when the queues are empty and also when they are not empty.

Processes can perform the send and receive operation on the buffer but cannot access the data structure representing it directly. This is guaranteed by the compiler.

The operations on a monitor take place strictly one at a time. When a process performs a monitor operation the computer will automatically delay further operations on the same monitor until the current operation is either finished or delayed explicitly in a queue variable. In the latter case, the delayed operation is resumed when another monitor operation performs a continue operation on the same queue.

(When I first wrote this paper the buffer monitor was programmed exactly as shown here. The test described in the following revealed a programming error. I found this very appropriate in a paper on systematic testing and decided to postpone the correction of the error until the end of the paper.)

3   Planning a Test Sequence

When a monitor has been programmed it must be tested systematically. The first step is to identify the *test cases* that must be tried experimentally.

In the buffer example both procedures may or may not delay the calling process and may or may not continue the other process. These are the only choices. So the following are the necessary *preconditions* that will ensure that all statements within the monitor procedures are executed at least once:

test cases (send)	*preconditions*
sender is delayed	S_1: length > 0
sender is not delayed	S_2: length $= 0$
receiver is continued	S_3: **not** empty(receiver)
receiver not continued	S_4: empty(receiver)

test cases (receive)	*preconditions*
receiver is delayed	R_1: length $= 0$
receiver is not delayed	R_2: length > 0
sender is continued	R_3: **not** empty(sender) & length $= 1$
sender is not continued	R_4: empty(sender) **or**
	R_5: length > 1

These preconditions must hold upon entry to the send and receive procedures.

It may be helpful to outline briefly how these test cases were identified. The aim of the testing is to try each branch of the monitor procedures at least once. Take, for example, the receive procedure. Its first *if* statement must be tried both when the condition (length = 0) is true and when it is false. This observation immediately defines the preconditions R_1 and R_2.

The next two statements are assignments. Since they are executed unconditionally, it is not necessary to plan special test cases for these statements. They will always be executed.

The final *if* statement should be tried both when the compound condition is true and when each of its terms is false. This defines test cases R_3–R_5.

The test cases for the send procedure were found by similar reasoning.

One may ask if it is sufficient to test each branch once instead of testing all combinations of all branches. The answer is that exhaustive testing of all the possible paths through a program normally is impractical. As usual, one must depend on insight into the program structure to reduce the number of test cases drastically.

Now, after the first *if* statement in the receive procedure it turns out to be irrelevant whether or not the calling process was delayed. In both cases the buffer will eventually end up in the same state (length > 0). So, at this point, the state of the monitor variables is independent of the actual path of program execution. This "memoryless" property is characteristic of well-structured programs. If it is carried far enough it is indeed sufficient to consider the two conditional statements as separate (unrelated) test cases.

The *path independence* of structured programs applies not only to statements (including loops), but also to procedures, monitors, and entire programs. It is not necessary to test all possible sequences of monitor operations. All that is needed is one *representative sequence* of operations that covers the relevant state transitions.

The study of the programming principles that make systematic testing possible is a fascinating research area that has barely been touched yet. It is not the purpose of this paper to discuss these issues. We will merely point out that whenever it is difficult to identify relevant test cases in a system program one can safely assume that this is due to poor structuring. The planning of test cases can therefore serve as an indication of unnecessary complexity.[†]

[†]In designing and testing a total of 5000 lines of Concurrent Pascal programs I have

In the following we will take it for granted that one can identify a small number of relevant test cases for a monitor. Our main concern then is to plan an experiment that will cover all the test cases once they have been identified.

We will therefore try to construct a set of processes that will test the buffer monitor systematically. To begin with we will, however, ignore these processes and focus our attention on what should happen within the monitor when it is being tested.

Since monitor operations are carried out strictly one at a time one can plan a sequence of operations that will force the monitor to go through all the test cases. One can then take the operations of this *test sequence* and distribute them among a set of test processes and make these processes perform the monitor operations in exactly the same order. Such a test will be both systematic and reproducible.

In practice, it is fairly easy to construct a test sequence by trial and error. The following shows one of the possible test sequences for the asymmetric buffer. The line length has been reduced to two characters for testing purposes. The producer process sends two lines consisting of the strings 'ab' and 'cd'. The state of the monitor variables before and after each operation are defined by *test assertions*. The assertions are labeled S_1, S_2 and so forth, to indicate which test cases they imply. The test sequence covers all the nine test cases described earlier.

> $\{R_1, R_4$: contents $= [\ ]$, empty(receiver), empty(sender)$\}$
>   receive( )
> $\{S_2, S_3$: contents $= [\ ]$, **not** empty(receiver), empty(sender)$\}$
>   send('ab')
> $\{$contents $=$ 'ab', empty(receiver), empty(sender)$\}$
>   receive( ) continued
> $\{S_1, S_4$: contents $=$ 'b', empty(receiver), empty(sender)$\}$
>   send('cd')
> $\{R_2, R_3$: contents $=$ 'b', empty(receiver), **not** empty(sender)$\}$
>   receive( )
> $\{$contents $= [\ ]$, empty(receiver), empty(sender)$\}$
>   send('cd') continued
> $\{R_2, R_5$: contents $=$ 'cd', empty(receiver), empty(sender)$\}$
>   receive( )

---

not yet found it necessary to write a monitor that exceeds one page of text.

$\{R_4$: contents = 'd', empty(receiver), empty(sender)$\}$
     receive( )
$\{$contents = [ ], empty(receiver), empty(sender)$\}$

4 Implementing a Test Sequence

Although the approach taken here is informal one could use verification techniques to show that the test sequence has the effect defined by the assertions.
In the present example, the result of the test seems fairly obvious. But, even
if formal techniques are used, typing mistakes can still be made when the
program text is entered into the computer. So one must still execute the
test sequence.

In a concurrent program the relative progress of processes will normally
be influenced by numerous unpredictable and irreproducible events, such as
the exact timing of interrupts, the presence of other (perhaps unrelated) processes, the occurrence of transient input/output errors, and the speed with
which operators interact with the program. The exact timing of operations
will therefore, in general, vary somewhat from one execution of the program
to another of a concurrent program even though the input remains the same!

During testing, however, we must be able to control precisely the sequence in which two or more processes interact with a monitor. Otherwise,
we cannot be sure that all the test cases have been tried.

We will therefore assume that the processes synchronize themselves by
means of an abstract clock during testing. This *test clock* is incremented
by one after each operation (or partial operation) in the test sequence. The
partial operations are the ones that are split into pieces by means of delay
operations.

With this idea in mind we now rewrite the test sequence and attach a
unique time value t_1, t_2 and so on to each operation:

$$
\begin{aligned}
&t_1: \quad \text{receive( )} \\
&t_2: \quad \text{send('ab')} \\
&t_3: \quad \text{receive( ) continued} \\
&t_4: \quad \text{send('cd')} \\
&t_5: \quad \text{receive( )} \\
&t_6: \quad \text{send('cd') continued} \\
&t_7: \quad \text{receive( )} \\
&t_8: \quad \text{receive( )}
\end{aligned}
$$

The test clock is a standard monitor that implements an operation clock.await(t)

which delays a test process until the time is t.

The *test processes* that implement the previous sequence of operations can now be programmed as follows:

```
producer:
  process(buf: buffer; clock: testclock);
  begin
    with buf, clock do
    begin
      await(2); send('ab');
      await(4); send('cd');
      await(6)
    end
  end


consumer:
  process(buf: buffer; clock: testclock;
    terminal: display);
  var c: char;
  begin
    with buf, clock, terminal do
    begin
      await(1); receive(c);
      await(3); print(c);
      await(5); receive(c); print(c);
      await(7); receive(c); print(c);
      await(8); receive(c); print(c)
    end
  end
```

The consumer process uses another standard monitor to print the characters it receives on a *display*. Notice that the construction of the test processes on the basis of the previous time sequence is an almost clerical task.

5   The Test Clock

The test clock is a monitor that implements two operations. An *await* operation delays the calling process until the clock reaches a certain value. A *tick* operation increments the clock by one and wakes up the process (if any) that is waiting for the new time value.

The current time is represented by an integer. Each instant of time is the starting time of a single monitor operation performed by a single process. Consequently, each time value in the test sequence can be represented by a queue variable that permits one (and only one) process to wait for that moment. The whole test sequence can therefore be represented by an array of queues.

```
type testclock =
monitor
var time: integer;
   sequence: array [1..steplimit] of queue;

procedure entry await(when: integer);
begin delay(sequence[when]) end;

procedure entry tick;
begin
   time := time + 1;
   continue(sequence[time]);
end;

begin time := 0 end;
```

How does one control the passage of time? The simplest idea is to let the test processes make the clock tick after each monitor operation. But this would not work since a process can be delayed by a test operation before it gets a chance to call *tick*. Since our purpose is to test the buffer monitor *as it is* we rule out the possibility of putting additional clock statements within it. (This idea would not have worked either since the language does not make it possible to combine a *delay* and a *tick* into a single indivisible operation.)

The progression of time must therefore be controlled by a separate process that makes the test clock tick at regular intervals. A clock interval of 3 seconds is used. This is an order of magnitude longer than the slowest operation in the test program (in this case, the printing of a single character on the display). Consequently, one test operation will always be completed before the next one begins.

```
timer:
    process(clock: testclock);
    var step, sec: integer;
    begin
      for step := 1 to steplimit do
      begin
        for sec := 1 to 3 do
            wait "one second";
        clock.tick
      end
    end
```

Since a test process only waits for times that are in the future and since the clock continues to increase (thanks to the timer), the test clock will eventually terminate the waiting of any test process and enable it to perform its next operation. The whole test sequence will therefore be carried out as planned.

6 A Complete Test Program

The buffer monitor is tested by means of the concurrent program shown in Fig. 2. The program consists of three processes (the producer, the consumer and the timer) and three monitors (the buffer, the test clock and the display controller). The arrows show how the modules call one another.

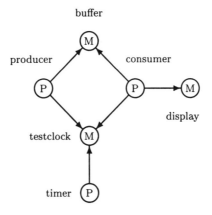

Figure 2 Test program.

The modules are initialized and linked to one another by an *initial statement* in the program:

```
var buf: buffer; clock: testclock; terminal: display;
begin
    init buf, clock, terminal, timer(clock),
        producer(buf, clock),
        consumer(buf, clock, terminal)
end
```

When the test program was executed on the PDP 11/55 computer it printed the output 'badc' instead of the expected 'abcd'. An examination of the receive operation on the buffer made it clear that the statement

$$y := contents[length]$$

should have been

$$y := contents[linelength - length + 1]$$

After this correction the test gave the correct output.

7   Final Remarks

Since the operations on a monitor can only take place one at a time, one can construct a sequence of monitor operations that will make the monitor variables go through all the states which the programmer wishes to test.

One can then assign consecutive time values to these operations and construct a set of processes that will perform the operations in the specified order. These processes are synchronized by a clock that is very slow compared to the monitor operations being tested.

This method separates the construction and implementation of test cases and makes the analysis of a concurrent experiment similar to the analysis of a sequential program. The implementation of a test program is almost mechanical in nature.

If an experiment tests all possible process interactions that can occur within a monitor then that monitor will continue to behave correctly when it is used in a concurrent program in which the precise timing of events is not controlled by a central clock.

The task of constructing a separate test program for each module in a concurrent program is much simpler than one might imagine. The resulting reliability of programs makes it an essential and worthwhile effort. A detailed example of the test programs for a *real-time scheduler* is included in Brinch Hansen (1977). The *network program* described in Brinch Hansen (1978) also worked immediately after being tested by this method.

Systematic testing deserves to be studied more carefully by computer scientists. Such an effort could lead to a theory that would point out precisely under which circumstances program testing can be successful. It seems plausible that the program structures which simplify formal verification will also simplify testing. Verification and testing would then emerge as complementary methods for obtaining program correctness. This important point was also made in Goodenough (1977).

Acknowledgements

I wish to thank Roger Vossler of TRW Systems, Redondo Beach, California, for providing the opportunity to develop the testing method described here. The Network program was originally tested at TRW's Signal Processing Facility. I also thank Nissim Francez, Charles Hayden and Jørgen Staunstrup for their constructive criticism of this paper.

References

Brinch Hansen, P. 1973. Testing a multiprogramming system. *Software—Practice and Experience 3*, 2 (April–June), 145–150. *Article 5.*

Brinch Hansen, P. 1977. *The Architecture of Concurrent Programs*, Prentice Hall, Englewood Cliffs, NJ, (July).

Brinch Hansen, P. 1978. Network: a multiprocessor program. *IEEE Transactions on Software Engineering 4*, 3 (May), 194–199. *Article 13.*

Goodenough, J.B., and Gerhart, S.L. 1977. Toward a theory of testing: data selection criteria. In *Current Trends in Programming Methodology II*, R.T. Yeh, Ed., Prentice Hall, Englewood Cliffs, NJ.

Naur, P. 1963. The design of the Gier Algol compiler. *BIT 3*, 2–3, 124–143 and 145–166.

16

A Keynote Address
on Concurrent Programming*

(1979)

Delivered at COMPSAC '78, this address draws a parallel between the major development phases of the first 20 years of concurrent programming and the present challenge of distributed computing.

Introduction

This keynote address summarizes the highlights of the first 20 years of concurrent programming (1960–80) and takes a look at the next 20 years (1980–2000).

A concurrent program is one that enables a computer to do many things simultaneously. Concurrent programming is used to increase computer efficiency and cope with environments in which many things need attention at the same time. Although there are good economic and conceptual reasons for being interested in concurrent programs there are major difficulties in making these programs reliable.

The slightest programming mistake can make a concurrent program behave in an irreproducible, erratic manner that makes program testing impossible. The following describes how this problem was gradually solved by software engineers and computer scientists. This development is seen as an initial hardware challenge followed by a software crisis, a conceptual innovation, and language development which in turn led to formal understanding and hardware refinement. The paper draws a parallel between this evolution of ideas and the present challenge of distributed computing.

---

*P. Brinch Hansen, A keynote address on concurrent programming. Keynote address for the IEEE Computer Software & Applications Conference, Chicago, IL, November 1978. *Computer 12*, 5 (May 1979), 50–56. Copyright © 1979, Institute of Electrical and Electronics Engineers, Inc. Reprinted by permission.

The Development Cycle

When you look at concurrent programming on a time-scale of decades you will see that it went through several stages of development, each lasting about 5 years:

Hardware challenge	(1955–60)
Software crisis	(1960–65)
Conceptual innovation	(1965–70)
Language development	(1970–75)
Formal understanding	(1975–)
Hardware refinement	(1980–)

At the beginning of this period new hardware developments make concurrent programming both possible and essential. As programmers experiment with this new idea they are gradually led to the development of extremely complicated systems without much of a conceptual basis to rely on. Not too surprisingly these systems soon become so unreliable that the phrase "software crisis" is coined by their designers. By then the importance of the problem is recognized by computer scientists, who start a seach for abstract concepts that will simplify the understanding of concurrent programs. Once the essence of the problem is understood a notation is invented for the basic concepts, and it now becomes possible to define them so precisely that they can be incorporated into new programming languages. This language notation in turn enables theoreticians to develop a more formal understanding of the problem. At the same time, the new language concepts inspire innovative computer designers.

At this point (if not sooner) new hardware possibilities start another development cycle. One must indeed agree with Alan Perlis that "hardware drives the field," but one must also add that abstractions make it manageable.

We will look at each of the stages that concurrent programming went through and see what the next challenge is likely to be.

The Hardware Challenge

Around 1955 computer architecture changed drastically with the invention of *large magnetic core stores* and *asynchronously operating peripheral devices*. It now became possible to write large programs of 10,000–1,000,000 machine instructions. At the same time interrupts made it possible to write concurrent programs that could switch a fast processor among its much slower peripheral devices and make them operate simultaneously.

The intellectual challenge of this technological revolution was formidable. For the first time programs became too large to be understood completely by a single programmer. In response to this challenge computer programmers invented the first abstract programming languages, Fortran and Algol 60, and made their compilers some of the best understood and most reliable system programs we know. All this happened in less than 10 years—a most impressive achievement (Wexelblat 1978).

The capabilities for simultaneous execution of several tasks on one computer did, however, create a serious problem that took much longer to solve: Programming errors could now cause a concurrent program to behave in an erratic, time-dependent manner. These errors were extremely difficult to find since their effect varied from one execution to the next even when the input data remained the same. It has taken 20 years to cope with this problem of concurrency.

If you look at computers from a programmer's point of view the main problem is to master the complexity of the hardware innovations that were introduced two decades ago. By comparison mini- and microcomputers are not revolutionary at all. Their economic impact and the numerous possibilities for new applications are far reaching. But they have not, so far, posed new programming problems of the same difficulty (thank heaven).

The Software Crisis

The slowness of peripheral devices made asynchronous operation essential for efficient computer operation. But the pitfalls of concurrency made it equally important to present the user with a simple, sequential interface to the machine. The new system programs that were supposed to make a concurrent computer system simple, reliable, and efficient were called *operating systems.*

Some of the early batch processing systems, such as Atlas (1961) and Exec II (1962), were both efficient and simple. But they were not entirely reliable. In looking back Bill Lynch (1972) observed that "several problems remained unsolved with the Exec II operating system and had to be avoided by one *ad hoc* means or another. The problem of deadlocks was not at all understood in 1962 when the system was designed. As a result several annoying deadlocks were programmed into the system."

The early timesharing systems, such as CTSS (1962) and SDC Q-32 (1964) were also of modest size.

Now, when faced with a new idea, programmers have an irresistable urge to push it to its natural limits and then beyond. The operating systems of the next generation were complex beyond human comprehension. The Multics system (1965) required 200 man-years of development effort, and OS360 (1966) a staggering 5000 man-years. Because of its size OS360 became quite unreliable. In 1969 Hopkins said this: "We face a fantastic problem in big systems. For instance, in OS360 we have about 1000 errors in each release and this number seems to be reasonably constant" (Naur 1969).

At this point it had become common for large operating systems to fail daily, and it was doubtful whether they were achieving their original aim of ensuring efficient, reliable computer operation. There was a clear feeling at this point that it was just not possible to design these large programs without some conceptual basis that would make them more understandable.

The importance (and failure) of operating systems had by now become clear to computer scientists who, like all other computer users, were forced to depend on these systems in their own computing centers. And so the search for abstractions began.

The Conceptual Innovation

Seen in retrospect this development was clearly a search for concepts that would make it possible to divide a concurrent program into smaller *asynchronous modules* with *time-independent behavior*.

The idea of dividing a concurrent program into *sequential processes* that are executed asynchronously was by far the most important innovation. This idea and its implementation were pioneered at MIT in the CTSS project (Saltzer 1966).

A process is a program module that consists of a data structure and a sequence of statements that operates on it. If each process only operates on its own data then it will behave in a completely predictable manner each time it is executed with the same data. Hardware protection mechanisms can prevent processes from referring to each other's data structures by mistake.

It now became possible to perform unrelated tasks simultaneously without time-dependent interference. However, if processes share computer resources or cooperate on common tasks then they must also be able to share data in a controlled manner. During the late sixties the main focus was the invention of safe methods for synchronizing processes which share data.

Dijkstra's THE system (1968a, 1968b, 1971) is the milestone of this era. It introduced most of the concepts on which our present understanding of concurrent programming rests. Dijkstra noticed that all communication among processes boils down to performing operations on common data. But if several processes operate simultaneously on the same variables at unpredictable speeds, the result will be unpredictable since none of the processes have any way of knowing what the others are doing to the variables. Dijkstra therefore concluded that it is essential to perform the operations on the common variables strictly one at a time. If one process is operating on common variables then the machine must delay further operations on the same variables until the present operation is finished. Dijkstra introduced the name *critical region* for operations on common variables which take place one at a time.

Critical regions only prevent competing processes from using common variables simultaneously. But they do not help in transmitting data correctly from one process to another. In looking at the problem of process communication, Dijkstra began by studying the simplest possible case in which timing signals are sent from one process to another. For this purpose he invented a data type, called a *semaphore*.

A signal operation permits a process to transmit a timing signal through a semaphore variable to another process which receives the signal by performing a wait operation. In a concurrent system, the programmer cannot predict the relative speeds of asynchronous processes. It is therefore impossible to know whether one process will try to send a signal before another is ready to receive it (or vice versa). Dijkstra removed this problem by defining the semaphore operations in such a way that it doesn't matter in which order they are initiated. If a process tries to receive a timing signal before it is available, the wait operation will simply delay the process until another process sends the next signal. Conversely, if signals temporarily are being sent faster than they can be received, they will simply be stored in the semaphore variable until they are needed.

The *commutativity* of semaphore operations made process synchronization time-independent. Dijkstra then went on to show how critical regions and message buffers can be implemented by means of semaphores.

Dijkstra's multiprogramming system also illustrated the conceptual clarity of *hierarchical structure*. His system consisted of several program layers which gradually transform the physical machine into a more pleasant abstract machine that simulates several processes which share a large, homogeneous store and several virtual devices. These program layers can be designed and studied one at a time.

His co-worker Habermann (1967) showed that a hierarchical ordering of resource requests and message communication also can prevent deadlocks.

Around 1970 researchers began to invent language notation for these powerful new concepts.

Language Development

The invention of precise terminology and notation plays a major role not only in the sciences but in all creative endeavors.

When a programming concept is understood informally it would seem to be a trivial matter to invent a language notation for it. But in practice this is hard to do. The main problem is to replace an intuitive, vague idea with a precise, unambiguous definition of its meaning and restrictions. The mathematician Polya (1957) was well aware of this difficulty:

"An important step in solving a problem is to choose the notation. It should be done carefully. The time we spend now on choosing the notation may well be repaid by the time we save later by avoiding hesitation and confusion. Moreover, choosing the notation carefully, we have to think sharply of the elements of the problem which must be denoted. Thus, choosing a suitable notation may contribute essentially to understanding the problem."

A programming language concept must represent a *general idea* that is used very often. Otherwise, it will just increase the complexity of the language at no apparent gain. The meaning and rules of a programming language concept must be *precisely defined*. Otherwise, the concept is meaningless to a programmer. The concept must be represented by a *concise notation* that makes it easy to recognize the elements of the concept and their relationships. Finally, it should be possible by simple techniques to obtain a *secure, efficient implementation* of the concept. The compiler should be able to check that the rules governing the use of the concept are satisfied, and the programmer should be able to predict the speed and size of any program that uses the concept by means of performance measurements of its implementation.

As long as nobody studies your programs their readability may not seem to be much of a problem. But as soon as you write a description for a wider audience the usefulness of notation that suppresses irrelevant detail immediately becomes obvious. So, although Dijkstra's THE system was implemented in assembly language, he found it helpful to invent a language notation for concurrent processes in his description (Dijkstra 1968a).

The following example of Dijkstra's *concurrent statement* shows two sequential statements that are executed simultaneously:

> **var** this, next: line
> **cobegin** consume(this); input(next) **coend**

While one statement is consuming a line of text, called *this*, another statement is inputting the *next* line. The concurrent statement terminates when all the component statements are terminated.

Hoare (1972a) pointed out that the concurrent statement only has a predictable effect if the statements within it operate on different variables. In this example, the consumer and the input statements refer to different variables (this and next). If the programmer by mistake lets both statements refer to the same variable, the effect of the concurrent statement will be time-dependent.

To prevent time-dependent programming errors a compiler should be able to recognize the *private variables* of a process and make them inaccessible to other processes. Unfortunately, this is difficult to do in more complicated examples involving procedures and global variables. The solution to this problem will be described later.

Although it is essential to make some variables accessible to one process only, it is also necessary to enable processes to share other variables to make cooperation and communication possible.

In 1971–72 notations were proposed for associating a *shared variable* with the *critical regions* that operate on it (Hoare 1972a; Brinch Hansen 1972). A shared integer used as a clock is a good example:

> **var** clock: **shared** integer

Processes can either increment or read this clock by statements of the form:

> tick: **region** clock **do**
>   clock := (clock + 1) **mod** max
>
> read(x):   **region** clock **do** x := clock

The compiler checks that a shared variable is accessed only within critical regions. The computer guarantees that these regions are executed one at a time without overlapping.

Hoare also invented the beautiful concept of a *conditional critical region* which is delayed until a shared variable satisfies some condition (defined by a boolean expression). A good example is a message buffer consisting of a single line *slot* and a boolean indicating whether or not it is *full*:

var buffer: **shared record**
slot: line
full: boolean
end

The send operation is a conditional critical region that is executed when the buffer is empty:

send(m):   **region** buffer **when not** full **do**
begin slot := m; full := true **end**

The receive operation is similar:

receive(m):   **region** buffer **when** full **do**
begin m := slot; full := false **end**

At that time it did not seem possible to implement conditional critical regions efficiently on a single processor. The problem was to limit the repeated evaluation of boolean expressions until they become true. As a compromise between elegance and efficiency process *queues* (also called "events" or "conditions") associated with shared variable were proposed (Brinch Hansen 1972).

At that time Dijkstra (1971) suggested that the meaning of process interactions could be further clarified by combining all operations on a shared data structure into a single program module (instead of scattering them throughout the program text).

In 1973 a language notation for this *monitor* concept was proposed (Brinch Hansen 1973). The data representation of a message buffer together with the send and receive operations on it now looked like this:

```
monitor buffer
var slot: line; full: boolean

procedure send(m: line)
when not full do
begin slot := m; full := true end

procedure receive(var m: line)
when full do
begin m := slot; full := false end

begin full := false end
```

The monitor includes an initial statement that makes the buffer empty to begin with. In a later paper Hoare (1974) also described the monitor concept and illustrated it with examples.

A central theme in this development was an attempt to replace earlier hardware protection mechanisms by compilation checks. The monitor concept enables a compiler to check that send and receive are the only operations performed on a message buffer. Once the buffer monitor has been tested systematically the compiler prevents other program modules from using it incorrectly. This tends to localize errors in new, untested modules and prevent them from causing obscure effects in old, tested modules.

The elimination of execution checks was not done just to make compiled programs more efficient. In program engineering, compilation and execution checks play the same roles as preventive maintenance and flight recorders do in aviation. The latter only tell you why a system crashed; the former prevents it. This distinction is essential in real-time systems that control vital functions in society. Such systems must be highly reliable *before* they are put into operation.

The monitor concept solved the problem of *controlled access* to shared variables. The earlier problem of controlling the access to private variables was solved by declaring each process and its local variables as a separate program module:

```
process producer
var next: line
cycle input(next); buffer.send(next) end

process consumer
var this: line
cycle buffer.receive(this); consume(this) end
```

This language notation makes it obvious to the program reader and the compiler that the variable *next* only can be used within the producer process.

The first programming language based on processes and monitors was *Concurrent Pascal.* It was defined and implemented in 1974 (Brinch Hansen 1975). By the end of 1975 Concurrent Pascal had been used to write three minicomputer operating systems of 600–1400 lines each. The development and documentation effort of each system only took a few weeks (Brinch Hansen 1976, 1977). A later language, *Modula* (Wirth 1977), is also based on the process and monitor concepts.

These language concepts had a dramatic impact on the structure of concurrent programs. It now became natural to build a concurrent program out of modules of one page each. Since each module defines all the meaningful operations on a single data structure (private or shared), the modules can be studied and tested one at a time. As a result these concurrent programs became more reliable than the hardware they ran on. And their simplicity made it possible to publish the entire text of a concurrent program of 1300 lines (Brinch Hansen 1976).

It is interesting that sequential programmers independently were led to the discovery of program modules which combine data repesentations and procedures into units (Hoare 1972b). But although the two developments led to the same conclusions the motivations were different: concurrent programmers were gradually led to modularity simply by their desire to master synchronization and prevent race conditions. These problems do not occur in sequential programs. Sequential programmers were motivated by more abstract concerns for clarity and the desire to make program verification simpler.

Formal Understanding

Once you have a notation for a concept it becomes possible to refine it further and get a more formal understanding of its properties. The impact of notation on discovery has been expressed very well by Susanne Langer (1967):

"There is something uncanny about the power of happily chosen ideographic language; for it often allows one to express relations which have no names in natural language and therefore have never been noticed by anyone. Symbolism, then, becomes an organ of discovery rather than mere notation."

It is no coincidence therefore that the development of language notation for concurrent programming immediately inspired theoretical work on program verification. Hoare's first paper on concurrent programming (1972a) contains axiomatic definitions of the meaning of concurrent statements and critical regions. A later paper by Hoare (1974) defines the effect of queue manipulation within monitors. The development of verification rules for concurrent programs with conditional critical regions was carried further by Owicki and Gries (1976).

It remains to be seen what effect these theories will have on language refinement and program reliability. Most researchers would agree that our theoretical understanding of concurrency is still in its infancy. A successful approach in this area will almost certainly require that computer scientists go beyond well-understood exercises and concern ourselves with model systems of a non-trivial size.

Hardware Refinement

The trend of decreasing hardware costs and increasing software costs is likely to continue due to better production methods and continued inflation. At the moment the use of abstract programming languages is the only effective way of reducing software costs. Unfortunately, present computer architectures do not support abstract languages efficiently compared to machine language. A real-time programmer is therefore faced with a meaningless choice among cost, reliability, and efficiency. The solution is quite obvious: we must build computer architectures that support our programming concepts directly.

A few years after the invention of the block and procedure concepts of Algol 60 the first stack computers appeared. It did, however, take more than a decade for this idea to be generally adopted by most computer manufacturers.

A similar development is now taking place in concurrent programming. The microprocessor technology makes it possible to build computer architectures that will support the process and monitor concepts directly. A recent proposal envisions a computer with 10 microprocessors. Each processor has a local store dedicated to a single process. The processors share a common store that contains the monitors. The computer has no interrupts and does not multiplex its processors among several processes (Brinch Hansen 1978b).

I would expect an increasing number of computer architectures to be oriented towards the support of concurrent programming languages for real-time applications.

For applications that are of interest to a large number of people it will be economical to specialize the hardware even further. In those cases it seems very attractive to write a concurrent program in an abstract language that hides machine detail, test it on an existing machine, and then derive the most straightforward specialized architecture from the program itself.

Like the development of our theoretical understanding, the design of new computer architectures for concurrent programming has started and will probably continue for another decade.

The Next Challenge: Computer Networks

It has taken 20 years to design reliable computer systems in which concurrent processes share storage. And now hardware technology has provided another challenge: microcomputer networks in which processors communicate by input/output only (without any common storage). This seems a natural approach to real-time applications in which geographically distributed functions must be coordinated.

Anyone who took the word "abstraction" to mean "machine-independent" suddenly discovered that abstract programming languages merely hide the irrelevant differences between similar computer architectures. The procedure concept is still fundamentally tied to the existence of a common store for parameter passing. And the people who developed monitors for concurrent programming also took this assumption for granted.

Now it may seem that the solution to the distributed processing problem is simple: message passing between processors connected by cables is all that is needed. And message passing (one of the oldest ideas in concurrent programming) we surely understand very well. Unfortunately, it is not that easy.

What we do understand is *deterministic message passing* in which a receiving process waits until another process sends a message on a given line. In such a system each process performs a completely predictable transformation of its input to its output. The analysis of individual processes must be supplemented with a global analysis of termination (or absence of deadlocks). This can be guaranteed by a hierarchical ordering of processes into "masters" and "servants."

A recent paper by Hoare (1978), however, makes it clear that one must also include *nondeterministic message passing*—a far more complex problem.

An obvious example is a process that functions as a buffer between two other processes. The buffer process cannot predict whether its environment will ask it to receive or send a message next. Consequently, it cannot commit itself to waiting until it receives a message on the input line, for this would make it unable to respond to a request for sending a message on the output line. Conversely, it cannot commit itself to wait until it is asked to send a message either, for this would make it unable to receiver further messages in the meantime, thereby slowing down the producer process unnecessarily.

What is needed therefore is the ability of a process to delay itself until it receives either a request for sending or receiving. It must then be able to perform one of two actions depending on what it was asked to do.

The problem is further complicated by the finite storage capacity of a buffer process. When the buffer is full, the process cannot accept further input; and when it is empty, the process cannot deliver further output. Hoare is therefore led to introducing a non-deterministic statement of the form:

> **when**
>   **not** full(buffer) & input(x): put(x, buffer)
>   **not** empty(buffer) & output(x): get(x, buffer)
> **end**

These *communicating sequential processes* seem somewhat inconvenient for the programming of processes that schedule other processes. To handle this problem the concept of *distributed processes* has been proposed (Brinch Hansen 1978a). It combines the process and monitor concepts and enables one process to call a procedure within another process when the latter process is waiting for some condition to be satisfied by its own variables. The parameter passing between processes can be done by a single input operation before a process interaction followed by a single output operation afterwards.

The practicality of these recent proposals has not yet been established. They have not even been implemented and are not understood formally. Their main value is to make it clear that distributed computing will require new concepts.

If the history of concurrent programming is about to repeat itself we should expect the new hardware challenge to lead to a software crisis as the technology is being used in real-time applications by means of *ad hoc* programming techniques. The search for concepts, languages, and theory will then start again. This will take longer than we may think. I would expect distributed computing to be reasonably well understood by the year 2000.

Acknowledgements

This work was supported by the Office of Naval Research under contract number NR049-415.

References

Brinch Hansen, P. 1972. Structured multiprogramming. *Communications of the ACM 15*, 7 (July), 574–578. *Article 4.*

Brinch Hansen, P. 1973. *Operating System Principles*. Prentice Hall, Englewood Cliffs, NJ, (July).

Brinch Hansen, P. 1975. The programming language Concurrent Pascal. *IEEE Transactions on Software Engineering 1*, 2 (June), 199–207. *Article 7.*

Brinch Hansen, P. 1976. The Solo operating system. *Software—Practice and Experience 6*, 2 (April–June), 141–205. *Articles 8–9.*

Brinch Hansen, P. 1977. *The Architecture of Concurrent Programs*. Prentice Hall, Englewood Cliffs, NJ, (July).

Brinch Hansen, P. 1978a. Distributed Processes—A concurrent programming concept. *Communications of the ACM 21*, 11 (November), 934–941. *Article 14.*

Brinch Hansen, P. 1978b. Multiprocessor architectures for concurrent programs. *Proceedings of the ACM 78 Conference*, Washington, DC, (December), 317–323.

Dijkstra, E.W. 1968a. Cooperating sequential processes. In *Programming Languages*, F. Genuys, Ed., Academic Press, New York, 43–112.

Dijkstra, E.W. 1968b. The structure of the "THE"-multiprogramming system. *Communications of the ACM 11*, 5 (May), 341–346.

Dijkstra, E.W. 1971. Hierarchical ordering of sequential processes. *Acta Informatica 1*, 115–138.

Habermann, A.N. 1967. On the harmonious cooperation of abstract machines. Technological University, Eindhoven, The Netherlands.

Hoare, C.A.R. 1972a. Towards a theory of parallel programming. In *Operating Systems Techniques*, C.A.R. Hoare and R.H. Perrott, Eds., Academic Press, New York, 61–71.

Hoare, C.A.R. 1972b. Proof of correctness of data representations. *Acta Informatica 1*, 271–281.

Hoare, C.A.R. 1974. Monitors: An operating system structuring concept. *Communications of the ACM 17*, 10 (October), 549–557.

Hoare, C.A.R. 1978. Communicating sequential processes. *Communications of the ACM 21*, 8 (August), 666–677.

Langer, S.K. 1967. *An Introduction to Symbolic Logic*. Dover Publications, New York.

Lynch, W.C. 1972. An operating system design for the computer utility environment. In *Operating Systems Techniques*, C.A.R. Hoare and R.H. Perrott, Eds., Academic Press, New York, 341–350.

Naur. P, and Randell, B., Eds. 1969. *Software Engineering*. NATO Scientific Affairs Division, Brussels, Belgium, (October), 20.

Owicki, S., and Gries, D. 1976. Verifying properties of parallel programs: An axiomatic approach. *Communications of the ACM 19*, 5 (May), 279–288.

Polya, G. 1957. *How to Solve It*. Doubleday, Garden City, NY.

Saltzer, J.H. 1966. Traffic control in a multiplexed computer system. Massachusetts Institute of Technology, Cambridge, MA, (July).

Wexelblat, R.L., Ed. 1978. *ACM Conference on the History of Programming Languages*, (Preprints), Los Angeles, CA, (June). In *SIGPLAN Notices 13*, 8 (August).

Wirth, N. 1977. Modula: A language for modular multiprogramming. *Software—Practice and Experience 7*, 1 (January–February), 3–35.

17

The Design of Edison[*]

(1981)

This paper describes the considerations behind the design of the programming
language Edison including the reasons why a large number of well-known language features were excluded. It also discusses the linguistic problems of
writing a concise language report.

1 Themes

This paper describes the considerations behind the design of the programming language Edison (Brinch Hansen 1981). Edison is deeply influenced
by the advances made by Pascal (Wirth 1971) and its successors Concurrent
Pascal (Brinch Hansen 1975) and Modula (Wirth 1977). In my attempt to
learn from these previous efforts and improve on them I had to focus on
both the virtues and defects of these languages. The criticism may appear
very unfair coming from a programmer who has benefited immensely from
the innovations of Pascal ten years ago. But such criticism is necessary to
gain a clearer perspective of a programming tradition that has become so
natural to me that it inhibits my ability to search for better methods.

In designing the programming language Edison I tried to do two things:
(1) to achieve simplicity by questioning the necessity of a number of well-known language concepts, and (2) to gain new insight by deliberately approaching language design with a philosophy that is completely different
from the spirit in which Concurrent Pascal was designed.

The first viewpoint gradually led to the omission of many language features that I had previously thought were valuable features of the programming languages Pascal and Concurrent Pascal, namely

---

[*]P. Brinch Hansen, The Design of Edison. *Software—Practice and Experience 11*, 4
(April 1981), 363–396. Copyright © 1981, Per Brinch Hansen. Reprinted by permission.

    reals
    subrange types
    variant records
    files
    pointers
    unnamed types
    goto statements
    case statements
    repeat statements
    for statements
    with statements
    cycle statements
    init statements
    multiple class instances
    parameterized classes
    monitors
    process modules
    process queues

If I were to do it again, I would go further and eliminate functions as well.

When you see the list of what is not in the language, you may wonder what is left. The answer is—not much!

The process of eliminating language features took place over a period of more than a year and was not an easy one. Old habits are hard to break! What took the longest though was the simple discovery of new syntactical structures for well-known concepts, such as type declarations. The experience of using a good programming tool tends to make one unable to discover better ones.

The search for a different design philosophy can best be illustrated by contrasting Concurrent Pascal and Edison.

In Concurrent Pascal, program modularity is supported by the rather complicated concepts of processes (which combine modularity and concurrent execution) and monitors (which combine modularity and synchronized execution). A large class of time-dependent programming errors are eliminated at compile-time by checking that processes do not refer directly to the same variables. The only form of communication among processes is by means of monitor procedure calls. Within monitors another class of synchronization error is automatically eliminated by a mutual exclusion of monitor calls enforced during program execution. In addition, the compiler detects recursive calls to prevent deadlocks.

This rigorous approach to security was based on the belief that race conditions would be extremely difficult to locate at run-time due to their irreproducible nature, and that they must be detected by a compiler before a concurrent program is even tested. The resulting programs have been simple enough to publish and have been more reliable than the hardware they run on (Brinch Hansen 1977).

The security of Concurrent Pascal was achieved by careful selection of a small number of complicated concepts. Although this approach can be quite successful in practice, it is not without pitfalls. It requires a great deal of practical experience in operating system design and a gambler's instincts to select the combination of shared variables, synchronized procedure calls, and the Simula class concept as the only possible mechanism of process communication in a programming language—when the much simpler concept of a semaphore (in theory) suffices. If you make the right guess, fine— otherwise, such a language will be of little practical use.

The RC 4000 multiprogramming system had the conceptual advantage of a clear and consistent structure, but it was not always successful in practice. When the system was ready, it soon became apparent that the transmission of small messages of fixed length was not enough to support the design of a general operating system. Since this was the only form of communication available to concurrent processes, system programmers began in some cases to ignore the system by using a single process to simulate several coroutines for which they could design more suitable forms of interaction (Brinch Hansen 1970).

Another (somewhat unexpected) consequence of careful *ad hoc* design is that the number of specialized mechanisms tends to multiply to cover the programming needs. In Concurrent Pascal, modules occur in three varieties (processes, monitors, and classes), and in Modula there are four kinds (processes, interface modules, device modules, and other modules).

These observations led to a separation of the concepts of modularity, concurrency, and synchronization in Edison. The result is a more flexible language based on fewer concepts in which one can achieve the same security as in Concurrent Pascal by adopting a programming style that corresponds to the processes and monitors of Concurrent Pascal. Or one can use the language to express entirely different concepts. On the other hand, it is also possible to break the structuring rules and write meaningless programs with a very erratic behavior. I have adopted this more general and less secure approach to programming to learn from it. It is still too early to make firm conclusions about consequences of such a compromise.

The desire to replace specialized mechanisms with more general ones that can be combined freely led to the adoption of the following rule: Whenever a mechanism is needed for a particular purpose the most general variant of that mechanism will be selected.

An example is provided by the well-known need to enable programs to call certain procedures implemented by an operating system, for example to access files. In Sequential Pascal the headings and parameter types of such procedures are described by a prefix to every program. When an operating system (written in Concurrent Pascal) calls a program (written in Sequential Pascal) an anonymous table with the addresses of these procedures is automatically generated for the program. The program prefix is the only mechanism for using procedures as parameters in Sequential Pascal.

In Edison the same problem is solved more generally by allowing procedures to be parameters of other procedures and by letting library programs in Edison take the form of procedures.

The more general approach has already paid off. The Mono operating system written in Concurrent Pascal includes procedures for writing integers and text on a variety of media. Each of these procedures in turn calls another procedure to write a single character on a given medium. Since the latter procedure varies from medium to medium it was necessary to write a different version of the former procedure for each kind of medium. When this operating system was rewritten in Edison it was sufficient to program one version of each procedure and pass as a parameter to that procedure another procedure for writing single characters on the desired medium. Generality pays off in unexpected ways!

Another example of the preference for generality in Edison is the general nesting of procedures and modules which is already supported by Pascal and Modula, but is forbidden in Concurrent Pascal. I find nested procedures as hard to read as prose that makes frequent use of parenthetic remarks. Such procedures were therefore outlawed in Concurrent and Sequential Pascal. The compilers took advantage of the exclusive use of two block levels by generating efficient instructions for the addressing of local and global variables.

In designing Edison I found that this restriction made it impossible to describe the effect of library programs by the simple rule of conceptually inserting the program text where the corresponding program declaration appears in the calling program. Since both the calling program and the library program could use two levels of nesting this textual substitution might create an invalid program with three levels of nesting. So general nesting was allowed merely as a means of simplifying the language description. Once this decision was made I discovered the obvious: the compiler can still recognize references to variables in a local block and the immediately surrounding block and generate special instructions for addressing them.

It is with both regret and delight that I finally in 1980 find myself appreciating language concepts that were obvious to the designers of Algol 60 twenty years ago (Naur 1962). In the following, a number of other design decisions are explained in some detail.

2   Abstract Data Types

The invention of syntactic structures to describe self-contained parts of larger programs is one of the major achievements of the last decade. In Concurrent Pascal, these structures are called processes, monitors, and classes. In Modula and Edison they are known as modules.

One of the main purposes of a program module is to implement the concept of an abstract data type—a data type that can only be operated upon by a fixed set of operations. In Concurrent Pascal, abstract data types are implemented by means of a secure variant of Simula classes (Dahl 1972). In Edison I decided to use a very different idea inspired by Modula.

Consider the problem of unpacking integer values from a sequence of disk pages. In Modula this can be done by means of the following module (Algorithm 1). The define clause shows that the module exports an entity named next to the surrounding block. The use clause indicates that the module uses (or imports) entities named page, pagelength, and get from the surrounding block.

The data structure of the module consists of two local variables which assume the value of a disk page and the index of the last value unpacked from that page.

The procedure called next gets another disk page from the disk (if necessary) and unpacks the next integer value from the page. The initial operation described at the end of the module gets the first page from the disk and sets the index to zero.

The compiler ensures that the only operation performed on the data structure (following the initial operation) is the well-defined operation called next. This kind of module is appealing because it ensures the integrity of the data structure entirely by means of scope rules: the variables named data

and index are local to the module and are unknown outside the module.
The protection of the data structure is achieved at compile-time without
run-time support.

```
module symbolinput;
  define next;
  use page, pagelength, get;

  var data: page; index: integer;

  procedure next(var value: integer);
  begin
    if index = pagelength then
      get(data); index := 0
    end;
    index := index + 1;
    value := data[index]
  end next;

begin get(data); index := 0
end symbolinput
```

Algorithm 1

In Edison the same module looks as follows (Algorithm 2). The define
clause has been replaced by an asterisk in front of the exported procedure
(a notation borrowed from Pascal Plus; see Welsh 1980). This simplifies the
visual image of the module a bit and makes it unnecessary for the compiler
to check whether all entities mentioned in the define list are indeed declared
within the module. On the negative side one must now scan the module
visually to discover the operations it implements. The imported entities are
known simply by virtue of the ordinary scope rules of nested blocks. So
there is no use clause either in Edison.

This kind of module is an ideal structuring tool when it controls the
access to a single instance of a data structure that is hidden inside the
module as in the previous example. The initial operation ensures that the
data structure is brought into a consistent, initial state before it is operated
upon by the surrounding block. The module concept is less convenient when
several instances of an abstract data type are needed. The following example
shows an Edison module that implements push and pop operations on stacks

of integer values (Algorithm 3).

```
              module "symbol input"
                var data: page; index: int

            *  proc next(var value: int)
                begin
                  if index = pagelength then
                    get(data); index := 0
                  end;
                  index := index + 1;
                  value := data[index]
                end

              begin get(data); index := 0 end
```

Algorithm 2

In the surrounding block one or more stacks can be declared

var s, t: stack

and used as follows

push(s, 15)   pop(t, value)

The initial operation of the module can no longer guarantee that all stacks are empty to begin with (since the stacks are declared in the surrounding block after the module). The surrounding block must do that by performing the operations

newstack(s)   newstack(t)

on the stacks before using them to push and pop integer values.

Now, if the asterisk in front of the record type named stack would export not only the record type, but also its field, then it would be possible to perform meaningless operations on stacks outside the module, for example

s.size := −3

```
module
  array table[1:100](int)
* record stack(contents: table; size: int)

* proc push(var x: stack; y: int)
  begin x.size := x.size + 1;
    x.contents[x.size] := y
  end

* proc pop(var x: stack; var y: int)
  begin y := x.contents[x.size];
    x.size := x.size - 1
  end

* proc newstack(var x: stack)
  begin x.size := 0 end

begin skip end
```

Algorithm 3

The rule that record fields cannot be exported from modules was introduced in the language to ensure that the module procedures describe the only possible operations on stacks (apart from assignments and comparisons of the values of whole stacks).

In Concurrent Pascal, a stack can be described more elegantly by the following type declaration (Algorithm 4). An instance of this data type is declared and used as follows:

var s: stack

init s   s.push(15)   s.pop(value)

But the class concept is more complicated both to explain and implement because it combines the concepts of data types, procedures, and modules into a single, indivisible unit. By contrast, the module concept of Edison merely modifies the scopes of a set of named entities of any kind. With the exception of fields, any named entity can be exported from a module by placing an asterisk in front of its declaration.

```
type stack =
class
   var contents: array [1..100] of integer;
      size: 0..100;

   procedure entry push(y: integer);
   begin size := size + 1;
      contents[size] := y
   end;

   procedure entry pop(var y: integer);
   begin y := contents[size];
      size := size − 1
   end;

begin size := 0 end
```

Algorithm 4

3 Monitors

The significance of the monitor concept was that it imposed modularity on synchronizing operations used by concurrent processes. A monitor introduces an abstract data type and describes all the operations on it by means of procedures that can be called by concurrent processes. If several processes attempt to execute monitor procedures simultaneously these procedures will be executed one at a time (Brinch Hansen 1973; Hoare 1974).

In Concurrent Pascal, a message buffer for transmitting characters from one process to another can be declared as follows (Algorithm 5). The buffer is represented by a message slot of type character and a boolean indicating whether it is full or empty. Two variables of type queue are used to delay the sending and receiving processes until the buffer is empty and full, respectively.

Initially, the buffer is empty. The procedure named put delays the calling process (if necessary) until there is room in the buffer for another message. When that condition is satisfied, a character is placed in the buffer making it full. Finally, the receiving process is continued if it is waiting for the message. (If the receiver queue is empty the continue operation has no effect.)

The get operation is similar to the put operation.

```
type buffer =
monitor
  var slot: char; full: boolean;
      sender, receiver: queue;

  procedure entry put(c: char);
  begin if full then delay(sender);
      slot := c; full := true;
      continue(receiver)
  end;

  procedure entry get(var c: char);
  begin if not full then delay(receiver);
      c := slot; full := false;
      continue(sender)
  end;

begin full := false end
```

Algorithm 5

Since only one operation must be performed at a time on the monitor variables the following rules apply to operations on queues: When a process delays its completion of a monitor operation another monitor operation can be performed by another process, and, when a process continues the execution of a delayed process, the former process automatically returns from the monitor procedure in which it executed the continue operation.

The whole monitor concept is a very intricate combination of shared variables, procedures, process scheduling, and modularity.

Here is Modula's variant of the monitor concept for a single buffer instance (Algorithm 6). Although monitors and queues are called interface modules and signals in Modula the concepts are essentially the same.

Now, process queues were originally proposed by me as an engineering tool to reduce the overhead of process scheduling on a single-processor computer (Brinch Hansen 1972). Each queue is used to delay a process until the monitor variables satisfy a particular condition, such as

not full   or   full

When a process delays itself in a queue until a condition holds it depends

```
interface module buffer;
  define get, put;

  var slot: char; full: boolean;
    nonempty, nonfull: signal;

  procedure put(c: char);
  begin if full then wait(nonfull);
    slot := c; full := true;
    send(nonempty)
  end put;

  procedure get(var c: char);
  begin if not full then wait(nonempty);
    c := slot; full := false;
    send(nonfull)
  end get;

begin full := false end buffer
```

Algorithm 6

on another process to continue its execution when the condition is satisfied.

In 1972, Tony Hoare published a much more elegant mechanism for process scheduling in the form of the *conditional critical region*

with v **when** B **do** S

which delays a process until a variable v satisfies a condition B and then executes a statement S. The execution of conditional regions on a given variable v will take place strictly one at a time in some order (Hoare 1972).

This beautiful concept requires a process to reevaluate a boolean expression B periodically until it yields the value true. The fear that this reevaluation would be too costly on a single processor motivated the introduction of queues (also called signals or conditions) as an engineering compromise between elegance of expression and efficiency of execution.

With the new inexpensive microprocessor technology now available, I feel that the much simpler concept of conditional critical region should be preferred. Occasional inefficiency is of minor importance on a microprocessor.

Hoare's original proposal made it possible for operations on different shared variables, such as

$$\textbf{with } v_1 \textbf{ when } B_1 \textbf{ do } S_1$$

and

$$\textbf{with } v_2 \textbf{ when } B_2 \textbf{ do } S_2$$

to take place simultaneously. For Edison I decided to use the simplest form of the conditional critical region

$$\textbf{when } B \textbf{ do } SL \textbf{ end}$$

where SL is a statement list of the form $S_1; S_2; \ldots; S_n$. The execution of all *when statements* will take place strictly one at a time. If several processes need to evaluate (or reevaluate) scheduling conditions simultaneously they will be able to do so one at a time in some fair order (for example cyclically).

Measurements of concurrent systems have shown that in a well-designed system each process spends most of its time operating on local data and only a small fraction of its time exchanging data with other processes. The additional overhead of expression evaluation will therefore most likely be quite acceptable. This performance issue can, of course, only be settled by measurements of running Edison programs. But it is an intellectual gamble that I feel quite comfortable about.

A monitor in Edison is simply a module in which the procedure bodies consist of single when statements as illustrated by the buffer example (Algorithm 7).

Notice that Edison does not include the monitor concept. A monitor is constructed by using a programming style that combines the simpler concepts of modules, variables, procedures, and when statements. In addition, processes are no longer required to manipulate scheduling queues, since the when statements implement the necessary delays of processes. This form of a monitor is very close to the original proposal which I called a "shared class" (Brinch Hansen 1973).

Once this module has been programmed correctly, the compiler will ensure that the buffer only is accessed by the synchronized get and put operations. The module is now as secure as any monitor.

But the programmer is no longer tied to the monitor concept, but can use simpler concepts, such as semaphores (Algorithm 8).

```
module "buffer"
  var slot: char; full: bool

* proc put(c: char)
  begin
    when not full do
      slot := c; full := true
    end
  end

* proc get(var c: char)
  begin
    when full do
      c := slot; full := false
    end
  end

begin full := false end
```

Algorithm 7

Semaphores can then be used to implement a multislot buffer in which sending and receiving can take place simultaneously from different slots (Algorithm 9).

If the mutually exclusive operations are as simple as wait and signal (rather than entire monitor procedures) then the conditional critical regions may well be more efficient in some cases than conventional monitors with scheduling queues.

4 Processes

In the RC 4000 system I dealt with the complexities of processes that may appear and disappear at any time during program execution. In Concurrent Pascal, I tried the opposite approach of processes that exist forever after their creation. This works quite well for operating systems and real-time programs which perform the same tasks over and over. In addition, it simplifies store allocation dramatically.

For Edison I selected a compromise between these two extremes. Pro-

```
module
* record semaphore(value: int)

* proc wait(var s: semaphore)
  begin
    when s.value > 0 do
      s.value := s.value − 1
    end
  end

* proc signal(var s: semaphore)
  begin
    when true do
      s.value := s.value + 1
    end
  end

* proc newsem(var s: semaphore; n: int)
  begin s.value := n end

begin skip end
```

Algorithm 8

cesses described by a *concurrent statement* of the form

$$
\begin{aligned}
&\textbf{cobegin } 1 \textbf{ do } SL_1 \\
&\textbf{also } 2 \textbf{ do } SL_2 \\
&\quad \cdots \\
&\textbf{also } n \textbf{ do } SL_n \textbf{ end}
\end{aligned}
$$

can appear and disappear dynamically—but only at the same time!

The concurrent statement was published with the following syntax by Dijkstra in 1968

$$\textbf{parbegin } S_1; S_2; \ldots; S_n \textbf{ parend}$$

I merely replaced the semicolon (which normally denotes sequential execution) with the word *also* (to indicate simultaneity).

The process constants 1, 2, ..., n were introduced to make it possible to select a particular processor in a multiprocessor system (usually because the

```
module
  const n = 10 "slots"
  array table [1:n] (char)
  var ring: table; head, tail: int;
    full, empty: semaphore

* proc put(c: char)
  begin wait(empty); ring[tail] := c;
    tail := tail mod n + 1; signal(full)
  end

* proc get(var c: char)
  begin wait(full); c := ring[head];
    head := head mod n + 1; signal(empty)
  end

begin head := 1; tail := 1;
  newsem(full, 0); newsem(empty, n)
end
```

Algorithm 9

given processor is the only one that is connected to a particular peripheral device). On a single-processor computer the process constants can either be ignored or used to define the storage requirements of processes. (If they are ignored the simplest implementation strategy is to divide the available storage space evenly among the processes.)

Consider now two processes that exchange a sequence of characters terminated by a period through a buffer. In Concurrent Pascal the producer can be declared as follows

```
type producer =
process (buf: buffer);
var x: char;
begin read(x);
  while x <> '.' do
  begin buf.put(x); read(x) end;
  buf.put(x)
end
```

To vary the theme a bit the consumer will be programmed in Modula

```
process consumer;
var y: char;
begin get(buf, y);
   while y <> '.' do
      write(y); get(buf, y)
   end;
   write(y)
end consumer
```

In both cases, a process is described by a special kind of module. These syntactic forms enable compilers to check that one process does not refer to the variables of another process—an extremely dangerous kind of programming error.

In Edison, the same operational security can be achieved by adopting a programming style in which processes are described by procedures which are called by concurrent statements (Algorithm 10). Since each procedure call creates fresh instances of the local variables of the given procedure, and since these variables are only accessible to the calling process, this solution is as secure as any.

On the other hand, the programmer can also write concurrent programs, such as the following in Edison

```
var x, y: char
begin read(x);
   while x <> '.' do
      y := x;
      cobegin 1 do write(y)
      also 2 do read(x) end
   end;
   write(x)
end
```

Since the compiler provides no assistance in checking whether these processes refer simultaneously to the same variables without proper synchronization, such programs must be written with extreme care.

The added flexibility (and insecurity) of Edison compared to Concurrent Pascal will be viewed by some as a step backwards and by others as a challenge. To me it is simply an experiment that will either confirm or contradict my current feeling that programming languages cannot be expected to support complex abstractions, but should instead make it reasonably convenient to adopt programming styles which use simpler concepts to construct

```
proc producer
var x: char
begin read(x);
   while x <> '.' do
      put(x); read(x)
   end;
   put(x)
end

proc consumer
var y: char
begin get(y);
   while y <> '.' do
      write(y); get(y)
   end;
   write(y)
end

cobegin 1 do producer
also 2 do consumer end
```

Algorithm 10

the more complex ones. Needless to say this makes the design of a programming language a delicate balance between the anarchy of assembler language and the straightjacket of highly specialized languages.

5   Scope Rules

Although Pascal is block structured it is not clear from the report whether this means that the scope of a named entity is the entire block in which the entity is declared or whether the entity is known from the point of its declaration to the end of the given block (Jensen 1974).

The former interpretation is used in the Algol 60 report from which the block concept originates (Naur 1962). The latter meaning is implemented by most Pascal compilers and is the one described in the Edison report.

The requirement that a named entity must be declared before it is used makes it possible for a compiler to build a name table and verify that the names are used correctly during a single scan of the program text. In most cases this convention is quite natural since we are used to reading text in the order in which it is written. Occasionally, however, programmers are mystified by the compiler's refusal to accept an Edison program with the following structure

array line [1:80] (char)
   · · ·

proc program(
  proc writetext(text: line))
array line [1:80] (char)
var x: line
   · · ·

begin · · · writetext(x) · · · **end**

The compiler insists that the statement

writetext(x)

contains a type error. The problem is an inadvertant use of two declarations of the type called line in nested blocks that are separated by more than a hundred lines of text and therefore do not appear on the same page of text.

To the compiler these declarations introduce two different data types with the same name. The scope of the first line type extends from its declaration in the outer block up to the declaration of the second line type in the inner block. The second line type is valid in the rest of the program. This makes the parameter of the procedure writetext of the first type while the argument of the procedure call is of the second type.

The record fields in Pascal do not follow the normal scope rules. If two variables are declared as follows

var x: **record** y, z: char **end**; y: boolean

then the name y denotes a boolean variable when it stands alone but refers to a character field when it occurs in the variable symbol $x.y$. Although this convention seems natural enough when it is illustrated by example, it is nevertheless an exception that adds to the complexity of an already quite subtle set of naming rules.

In looking at the first Edison compiler I found that its most complicated part, the semantic analysis, introduced about 400 distinct names of which less than 40 were field names of records. I decided that anyone who can invent 360 different names can surely invent another 40. Consequently, in Edison the scope of a field name (like any other name) extends from its declaration to the end of the block which contains the declaration. Although a field name y can only be used in a field variable symbol of the form $x.y$ it cannot be redeclared with another meaning in the same block.

The reasons for including modules which restrict the scope rules further in the language have already been discussed in previous sections. Later I will discuss the difficulties of explaining scope rules precisely in prose.

6   Data Types

The most significant advance made by Pascal ten years ago was the introduction of a set of data types which for the first time made systems programming in an abstract programming language practical. The influence of Pascal on Edison in the choice of data types is considerable. Nevertheless, it must be admitted that the finer conceptual details of the data types are somewhat complicated and are imprecisely described in the Pascal report.

In Edison I have tried to simplify and clarify some of the issues concerning data types. A type is a named set of values. Every value is of one and only one type, so the data types are disjoint.

The *subrange types* of Pascal can be used to introduce types that are either disjoint, contained in other types, or even overlapping, as illustrated by these examples

$$\textbf{var } x1: 1..10; \ x2: 11..20;$$
$$x3: 5..9; \ x4: 0..15$$

This raises complicated issues, such as: Is the expression $x1 + x2$ valid, and if so, what is its type (1..10, 11..20, 1..20, or perhaps 12..30)? Is a value of type 1..10 also of type 0..15? Are some of the values of type 0..15 also of type 1..10 while others are also of type 11..20? Are the values of these subrange types in general compatible with the integer values or are they distinct types?

The elimination of subrange types from Edison makes these issues irrelevant.

Subrange types may originally have been introduced in Pascal to define the possible values of array indices. In Edison the concept of *range* serves the same purpose. A range is not a type. It is a finite set of successive, elementary values of the same type from a lower bound to an upper bound (both included). An array type declaration, such as

$$\textbf{array} \text{ table } [1{:}100] \text{ (int)}$$

describes a range of possible indices from 1 to 100. The indices of the array elements are of type integer.

The syntactic rules of Pascal and Modula make type definitions of the form

$$\textbf{type} \text{ temperature} = \text{integer;}$$
$$\text{speed} = \text{integer}$$

legal but do not define the meaning of this. Are temperature and speed just different names for the standard type integer? In that case, the use of type synonyms serves no purpose since the addition of temperatures to speeds is now a valid operation (because they are just integers). If, on the other hand, temperature and speed are distinct types then we have conceptual confusion in the language. For although the types are now incompatible, we would presumably expect the arithmetic operations and the ordering relations to apply to both of them. But the set of values to which these operations apply is per definition the set of integers. And, to introduce several different kinds of incompatible "integers" nullifies in one stroke one of mankind's most important concepts.

Since the syntax of Edison does not include the rule

$$\text{Type name} = \text{Type name}$$

the problem never arises.

The conceptual clarity of operational security that is gained from the use of types is considerable. But, as all abstractions, types derive their power from an oversimplified view of the security problem: all integer values are considered compatible irrespective of the physical or conceptual properties they represent. One cannot hope to use the type concept to capture the subtle distinctions between temperatures and speed any more than it can describe the constraints among related values of the same type, such as the requirement that the sum of free and used pages on a disk must equal the total number of available pages.

In Pascal and Modula type declarations begin with a name as in

$$\text{T1} = \textbf{record} \text{ x: char; y: integer } \textbf{end;}$$
$$\text{T2} = \textbf{array} \text{ [1..10] } \textbf{of} \text{ char}$$

The compiler must therefore scan three symbols before it can determine whether the type is a record or an array. This is an ugly exception in a recursive descent compiler that otherwise only needs to look at a single symbol to determine which syntactic form it is the beginning of.

Error recovery is also complicated by the above syntax. After a syntax error, such as

> T1 = **record** x: char; y: integer ned;
> T2 = **array** [1..10] **of** char

the transcribed keyword *end* will now be interpreted as a misplaced field name *ned*, and so will the type name T_2 that follows the semicolon. The result is a burst of misleading error messages referring to all uses of variables of type T_2.

In Edison each type declaration begins with a word symbol (instead of a name), for example

> **record** T1 (x: char; y: int)
> **array** T2 [1:10] (char)

After a syntax error, such as

> **record** T1 (x: char; y: int]
> **array** T2 [1:10] (char)

the compiler will skip the right bracket and correctly recognize the word *array* as the beginning of a new type declaration.

It is true that assignments and procedure calls suffer from the same problem of error recovery since they both begin with names and also may contain names as operands. But the accidental erasure of a statement during compilation is not as serious as the erasure of a declaration since other statements cannot refer to the missing one by name.

It is characteristic of a superior tool like Pascal that its notation is felt to be so natural that there seems to be no reason for the programmer to look for a better one. So it was without much thought that I originally used Pascal's notation for type declarations in Edison. As I was testing an Edison compiler written in Pascal the problems of error recovery became apparent. But even then it took a while before I was mentally prepared to propose an alternative syntactic notation.

With one exception (strings) the fixed length of array types in Pascal has never bothered me in the design of operating systems and compilers. But *character strings* pose special problems that are cleverly hidden by the use of *ad hoc* means in Pascal and Concurrent Pascal. (The Modula report is too vague on this point for me to understand it.)

By their nature character strings are of different lengths, for example

'tape'   'emono'

How then does one write a procedure that outputs a string to some device (or file) one character at a time? In Pascal you can try the following

```
procedure writetext(text: phrase);
var i: integer; c: char;
begin i := 0;
  while i < n do
  begin i := i + 1;
    write(text[i])
  end
end
```

where

type phrase = **array** [1..n] **of** char

Now, if $n = 4$ the call

writetext('tape')

is valid, but the call

writetext('emono')

is not since the string argument is now of length 5.

Why then is it not felt as an intolerable problem in Pascal? Because Pascal includes a standard procedure named write which is cleverly designed to accept strings of any length as shown below

write('tape')   write('emono')

But this procedure cannot be written in the language itself.

Since Concurrent Pascal is a language for operating system design, a standard procedure such as write cannot be built into the language. For one of the purposes of Concurrent Pascal is to design a filing system that includes a write procedure.

This difficulty is circumvented by the following *ad hoc* rule in the Concurrent Pascal report: "An argument in a procedure call corresponding to a string parameter may be a string of any length." This rule makes it possible to write a procedure that outputs a string of any length terminated by a given delimiter, say #

```
procedure writetext(text: phrase);
var i: integer; c: char;
begin c := text[1]; i := 1;
   while c <> '#' do
   begin write(c); i := i + 1;
      c := text[i]
   end
end
```

This procedure can print any string of at most n characters as illustrated by the calls

writetext('tape#')   writetext('emono#')

In both cases, however, the actual parameter value will be a string of n characters consisting of the given character string followed by some characters of unknown value (an implementation detail that programmers fortunately seldom discover).

In designing the array constructors of Edison these problems were carefully considered. An array constructor, such as

phrase('t', 'a', 'p', 'e', '#', ' ', ' ')

denotes an array value of type phrase (assuming that $n = 7$). The elements of the array value are given by a list of characters.

In Edison a character string, such as

'tape#   '

can be used as an abbreviation for a character list

't', 'a', 'p', 'e', '#', ' ', ' '

that contains the same sequence of characters separated by commas. The previous array constructor can therefore also be written as follows

phrase('tape#   ')

In general, an array constructor must contain an expression for each element of the array type (unless it is a string type). In the latter case, the above constructor may be written simply as

phrase('tape#')

This is an abbreviation for an array value consisting of the given character values followed by spaces to make the string of length n.

A graphic character, such as #, is denoted '#' in Edison. A *control character* is given by its ordinal value in the character set. In the ASCII character set, the control character new line is character number 10. In Concurrent Pascal, Modula, and Edison the new line character is denoted

'(:10:)'   10C   char(10)

respectively. In Concurrent Pascal the control characters may be given names, such as

const nl = '(:10:)'

But the name nl cannot be used within a character string

'tapenl#'

because it is indistinguishable from the graphic letters n and l. This leads to the following awkward notation

'tape(:10:)#'

in Concurrent Pascal. Whether the string

'tape10C#'

has the intended meaning in Modula I cannot tell from the report. In Edison, the inclusion of character names in string constructors is straightforward

$$\textbf{const } nl = char(10)$$

$$phrase('tape', nl, '\#')$$

In Pascal and Modula the absence of constructors makes the use of constant tables so awkward that one soon adopts a programming style in which decisions are made by case statements rather than table lookup. The ability to initialize tables by a single assignment statement in Edison should once again make table-driven decision-logic an attractive alternative.

The Concurrent Pascal compiler, which is written in Sequential Pascal, makes extensive use of the *variant records* and *pointers* of Pascal (Hartmann 1977). Since these concepts are both complicated and insecure to use I decided to write an Edison compiler without using them. The resulting compiler was much easier to understand. Evidently these tools were only used previously because they were there.

Only in one part of the compiler did I feel the need for variant records. During semantic analysis a name index is used to retrieve the attributes of a named entity from a table. Since the attributes depend on the kind of entity the name refers to, the name table is best described as an array of variant records of the following Pascal type

```
nameattr =
  record link: integer;
    case kind: namekind of
      constant:
        (consttype, constvalue: integer);
          . . .
      procparam, procedur:
        (proclevel, procaddr, proctype,
          param: integer)
  end
```

In Edison the name table is described as an array of elements of the type

```
record nameattr (kind: namekind; link: int;
  none1, none2, none3, none4, none5: int)
```

The variants of the type are described by separate record types

```
record constattr (constkind: namekind;
    constlink, consttype, constvalue,
    none6, none7, none8: int)
    ...
record procattr (prockind: namekind;
    proclink, proclevel, procaddr, proctype,
    param, none11)
```

The above records are padded with fields to make them all of the same length.

The compiler first uses a name index x to select a general name description of type nameattr. If the kind field is equal to constant, the name description is then retyped to be of type constattr as illustrated by the following program piece

```
var x, value: int

if names[x].kind = constant do
    value := names[x]:constattr.constvalue
    ...
```

If v denotes a variable of some type T_1 then $v{:}T_2$ denotes the same variable considered to be of another type T_2 of the same length. The retyped variable $v{:}T_2$ has a value of type T_2 with the same stored value as the value of v. A selection of a field f of the retyped variable is denoted $v{:}T_2.f$.

I cannot recall any other system program that requires the use of variant records. If they are that rare in practice then dynamic retyping seems preferable to introducing a very complicated data type in Edison with a matching set of constructors and control statements. But, if the use of variant records is more frequent than I thought, then their elimination from Edison must be regarded as a mistake. Until the experimental data are available from a wide range of applications, the elimination of variant records seems a worthwhile experiment.

The pointers of Pascal have been omitted from Edison for the same reason that variant records were eliminated. It is a complicated concept that appears to be a concession to the current practice of programming even though its full implications are not well understood. The need to define cyclical data structures in terms of different record types that can point to one another breaks the general rule that a type must be declared before it can be used as a subtype of another type. Furthermore, like the tag fields of variant records, pointer variables must be initialized to nil automatically to enable a processor to detect the use of a meaningless pointer. Otherwise, the effect of an assignment can even change the code of a program (just as in assembler language). No other kind of variable poses this serious problem.

The dynamic allocation of storage accessed through pointers is quite complicated particularly when it is combined with the storage allocation of concurrent processes. And there is no secure way to release the storage again and make sure that it can no longer be accessed through existing pointer values. Since the aim of Edison is utter simplicity rather than a compromise dictated by tradition the pointer types of Pascal could only be excluded from the language.

Most operations on a pair of data values are valid only if the values are of the same type. Unfortunately, the precise meaning of *type equivalence* is not defined in the Pascal and Modula reports. The Concurrent Pascal report states that two types are compatible if one of the following conditions is satisfied:

1. Both types are defined by the same type or variable declaration, or

2. Both types are subranges of a single enumeration type, or

3. Both types are strings of the same length, or

4. Both types are sets of compatible base types. The empty set is compatible with any set.

Although this clarifies the matter, it is not particularly simple to remember or implement.

Every data type used in an Edison program has a name—either a standard name (int, char, bool) or a name introduced by a type declaration.

The nameless data types of Pascal and Modula, as in

var x: **array** [1..100] **of** integer

do not exist in Edison and nor do subrange types.

In Edison each set constructor includes the name of its type and so does a string constructor. Even the empty set has a type name!

Consequently, the issue of type equivalence is settled by the simple rule that two types are the same only if they are denoted by the same name and have the same scope.

7   Statements

Where Pascal and Modula use 11 and 9 different sequential statements, respectively, Edison supports only 5 (including the empty statement)

> skip
> assignment
> procedure call
> if statement
> while statement

Inspired by Dijkstra's guarded commands (1975) the syntactic forms of the *if* and *while* statements have been generalized and made more uniform

$$\begin{array}{ll}
\textbf{if } B_1 \textbf{ do } SL_1 & \textbf{while } B_1 \textbf{ do } SL_1 \\
\textbf{else } B_2 \textbf{ do } SL_2 & \textbf{else } B_2 \textbf{ do } SL_2 \\
\quad \cdots & \quad \cdots \\
\textbf{else } B_n \textbf{ do } SL_n \textbf{ end} & \textbf{else } B_n \textbf{ do } SL_n \textbf{ end}
\end{array}$$

where the $B's$ and $SL's$ denote boolean expressions and statement lists. But, in contrast to guarded commands, the if and while statements of Edison are deterministic since the boolean expressions are evaluated in the order written (and not in unpredictable order).

Programs, such as compilers, that accept both correct and incorrect input often describe a choice among several different actions on valid inputs followed by a single action to be taken on invalid input. For example

```
if mode = constant do
    constant_factor(typ, endfactor)
else mode in typékinds do
    constructor(typ, endfactor)
else mode in varkinds do
    variable_factor(typ, endfactor)
else mode in prockinds do
    function_call(typ, endfactor)
else true do
    kinderror2(x, typ); nextsym
end
```

If the order in which the expressions are evaluated is unknown (as it is for guarded commands) then the final expression in this example must be changed from *true* to the following monstrosity

```
(mode <> constant) and
not (mode in typekinds) and
not (mode in varkinds) and
not (mode in prockinds)
```

In Edison the execution of an if statement has no effect if all the boolean expressions yield the value false. For guarded commands, Dijkstra assumed that this would cause a program failure. If a programmer wishes to provoke such a failure it can be done by ending an if statement as follows

$$\cdots \textbf{ else } \text{true } \textbf{do} \text{ halt } \textbf{end}$$

where halt is a procedure that causes program failure when executed. (The language Edison-11 for the PDP 11 computers includes a standard procedure halt.)

Dijkstra has convincingly demonstrated the use of the while statement that describes a repeated choice among several conditional statements. A beautiful example of its use is found in the Edison compiler in a procedure that recognizes the syntax of a variable symbol consisting of a variable name possibly followed by one or more field names, index expressions, or type names (indicating a temporary retyping of the variable). When the variable name has been recognized the compilation proceeds as follows

```
while sym = period1 do
    field_selector(endvar)
else sym = lbracket1 do
    indexed_selector(endvar)
else sym = colon1 do
    type_transfer(endvar)
end
```

The if statements of Pascal are special cases of the ones in Edison and can be expressed as follows

$$\textbf{if } B \textbf{ do } S \textbf{ end}$$

$$\textbf{if } B_1 \textbf{ do } S_1$$
$$\textbf{else } \text{true } \textbf{do } S_2 \textbf{ end}$$

In an attempt to eliminate empty options, I have resisted the temptation to introduce an abbreviation for the clause

$$\textbf{else } \text{true } \textbf{do}$$

Needless to say, the compiler does not emit any code for this clause.

The while statements of Pascal and Modula are also special cases of the one used in Edison and can be expressed as follows

while B **do** SL **end**

The conditional critical region proposed by Hoare

when B **do** SL **end**

is a special case of the more general *when statement* of Edison which has the same syntactic structure as the if and while statements

when B_1 **do** SL_1
else B_2 **do** SL_2
$\ldots$
else B_n **do** SL_n **end**

In an earlier paper, Staunstrup and I introduced this language concept, which we called a guarded region, and illustrated it by examples (Brinch Hansen 1978). The following example describes a process that continuously polls three boolean variables and sounds an alarm if any one of them yields the value true.

```
proc poll(var on1, on2, on3: bool)
begin on1 := false; on2 := false; on3 := false;
  while true do
    when on1 do alarm(1); on1 := false
    else on2 do alarm(2); on2 := false
    else on3 do alarm(3); on3 := false end
  end
end
```

As Wirth has pointed out what is omitted from a programming language is as important as what is included.

The *repeat statement* of Pascal and Modula

repeat SL **until** B

can be represented in Edison either by the statements

SL; **while not** B **do** SL **end**

or by the following program piece

```
var again: bool
begin again := true;
   while again do
      SL; again := not B
   end
end
```

The *for statement* of Pascal

for $i := 1$ **to** n **do** S

can be written either as

$i := 0$;
while $i < n$ **do** $i := i + 1; S$ **end**

or as

$i := 1$;
while $i <= n$ **do** $S; i := i + 1$ **end**

in Edison. It may seem that the two representations of the for statement are not equivalent since the final value of the control variable i will be n in the first version and $n + 1$ in the second. Although the Pascal report is silent on this issue the more informal user report states that "the final value of the control variable is left undefined upon normal exit from the for statement." This rule is introduced precisely to give the language implementor the freedom to choose the most efficient implementation for a given machine.

The decreasing variant of the for statement in Pascal

for $i := n$ **downto** 1 **do** S

can be represented similarly in Edison.

The *case statement* of Pascal and Modula

```
case expression of
   constant₁: S₁;
   constant₂: S₂;
      · · ·
   constantₙ: Sₙ
end
```

was originally part of Edison as well, but was later removed. The experience
of writing the Edison compiler showed that a case statement often is used
to describe actions on symbols that are grouped together as in

```
case ch of
  'a', 'b', ..., 'z': name;
  '0', '1', ..., '9': numeral;
    ...
end
```

The same clarity and efficiency can be achieved by using a combination of
if statements and sets representing the necessary symbol classes, for example

```
if ch in letters do name
else ch in digits do numeral
  ...
end
```

This grouping of symbols reduces the number of conditional statements
to eight in the lexical analysis of the compiler.

The syntactic and semantic analysis of the Edison compiler use recursive
descent and include one procedure for each syntactic form of the language.
Since a given procedure only is prepared to recognize a small number of
symbols (corresponding to the syntactic form it represents), an if statement
combined with sets is again quite efficient. Several examples described earlier
illustrate this point.

The code generator is the only part of the compiler that inputs one
symbol at a time and immediately uses it to branch to one of about sixty
procedures. In that one case, I had to resort to an awkward construct of the
form

```
if op <= construct2 do
  if op = add2 do add
  else op = also2 do alsox(a, b)
  else op = and2 do andx
  else op = assign2 do assign(a)
  else op = blank2 do blank(a)
  else op = cobegin2 do cobeginx(a, b, c)
  else op = constant2 do constant(a)
  else op = construct2 do construct(a) end
else op <= endproc2 do
  if op = difference2 do difference
    ...
```

to obtain fast compilation. But that was only 64 lines out of a compiler of 4300 lines and hardly worth the addition of another kind of statement to the language.

The *with statement* of Pascal and Modula appears to be used mostly to assign values to all the fields of a record variable as in the following statement

```
with names[nameno] do
begin
  kind := mode;
  minlevel := scope;
  maxlevel := origin;
  originalname := x
end
```

In Edison this is expressed more concisely by means of an assignment statement and a record constructor

names[nameno] := nameattr(mode, scope, origin, x)

The *goto statement* of Pascal was already eliminated in Concurrent Pascal and was never missed during the five years of experience with this language.

Finally, I agree with Dijkstra that the *empty action* (like the number zero) should be denoted by a distinct symbol

skip

and not be implied by the absence of one.

Although the use of distinct terminators, such as *endif, endwhile, endwhen, coend, endproc,* and *endmodule* would have made error recovery more successful in the compiler, I have used the symbol *end* in all these cases to make the typographical image of correct programs more pleasing (for they are the only ones I publish). This is obviously a matter of personal preference.

8   Input/Output

In Concurrent Pascal, all input/output is handled by standard procedure calls of the form

io(data, operation, device)

The calling process is delayed until the operation is completed. In the meantime, other processes can continue to use the rest of the computer. The advantage of this approach is that a data transfer is just another sequential operation that takes a finite time and produces a reproducible result. Another benefit of making input/output an indivisible operation for a single process is that peripheral interrupts become irrelevant to the programmer. They are handled completely at the machine level as part of the implementation of the io operations.

The disadvantage of using a single standard procedure for low-level input/output is that the system kernel for the language must contain a separate piece of code for each kind of peripheral device. This means that industrial programmers must be prepared to extend the kernel (which is a non-trivial task since peripheral interrupts interact with the processor multiplexing).

In Modula, Niklaus Wirth offered a more practical solution in the form of *device modules* combined with device processes and device registers. The whole concept was tailored to the PDP 11 computers to enable programmers to write device procedures in the language itself. Algorithm 11 shows a device module that outputs one character at a time on a screen. The module consists of a device process, named driver, which is connected to an exported procedure, named display, through a set of variables used as a character buffer.

The standard procedure *doio* delays the device process until the screen produces an interrupt with the octal number 64B. Since the doio operation only can be performed by a device process and since a device process must be hidden within a device module the above appears to be the simplest possible way of displaying a character on the screen. It does not seem to be possible to eliminate a device process and let a user process control the peripheral directly. This example shows that Modula (like Concurrent Pascal) attempts to support and enforce a particular programming style by means of very specialized language constructs.

The Edison language implemented for the PDP 11 computers is called Edison-11. Since the language is designed to support inexpensive microprocessors I decided to anticipate this use and ignore interrupts completely on the PDP 11 (even at the machine level).

In Edison-11, input/output is controlled by standard procedure calls of the form

```
place(device address, value)
obtain(device address, variable)
sense(device address, value)
```

```
device module screen [4];
  define display;
  var slot: char; full: boolean;
    nonempty, nonfull: signal;

  procedure display(c: char);
  begin
    if full do wait(nonfull) end;
    slot := c; full := true;
    send(nonempty)
  end put;

  process driver [64B];
  var status [177564B]: bits;
    buffer [177566B]: char;
  begin
    loop
      if not full do wait(nonempty) end;
      buffer := slot; full := false;
      status[6] := true; doio; status[6] := false;
      send(nonfull)
    end
  end driver;

begin full := false; driver end screen
```

Algorithm 11

The operation *place(x,y)* assigns the integer value y to the device register with the byte address x. The operation *obtain(x,y)* assigns the value of the device register with the byte address x to the integer variable y. The operation *sense(x,y)* compares the integer value y to the value of the device register with the byte address x. If some of the corresponding bits of the two values both are equal to one then the operation yields the value true; otherwise, it yields the value false.

Edison-11 also includes octal numerals of the form

$$\#177564$$

to denote device addresses. This option is necessary because the computer manufacturer does not use the decimal system in the computer manuals.

Why I do not know.

A process described by a concurrent statement in Edison-11 can output a character directly on the screen by calling the following procedure

```
proc display(c: char)
const status = #177564; buffer = #177566;
   ready = #200
begin
   when sense(status, ready) do
      place(buffer, int(c))
   end
end
```

The effect of executing the when statement is to delay the output until the status register shows that the device is ready.

A PDP 11 computer executes one process at a time. This continues until the process either terminates or attempts to execute a when statement in which the boolean expressions yield the value false. The waiting processes are executed in cyclical order in Edison-11. The simplicity of process scheduling makes the overhead of process switching five times shorter than in Concurrent Pascal (which is interrupt driven). The Edison-11 implementation ignores all interrupts.

The input or output of non-elementary data types requires the use of a standard function call

$$addr(y)$$

which yields the byte address of a variable y of any type. The operation $place(x, addr(y))$ assigns the address of the variable y to the device register with the address x. This operation is necessary to transfer data between the variable y and a block-oriented device, such as a disk or magnetic tape.

9   Language Description

In 1967 the designer of the programming language Pascal, Niklaus Wirth, wrote that "the definition of a language, comprising its syntax specifying the set of well-formed sentences, and its semantics defining the meaning of these sentences, should not extend over more than 50 pages." The Edison report is comparable in size to the reports which define its predecessors: Algol 60 (43 pages), Pascal (38 pages), Concurrent Pascal (34 pages), and Modula

(29 pages). The Edison report is 34 pages long. (The sizes of these reports are measured in pages of 50 lines each.)

The shortness of a language report is, of course, of no help unless it is written with complete clarity. As Wirth put it: "In programming, we are dealing with complicated issues, and the more complicated the issue is, the simpler the language must be to describe it. Sloppy use of language—be it English, German, Fortran or PL/1—is an unmistakable symptom of inadequacy."

The only language report that has been widely recognized as a model of clarity is the Algol 60 report written by Peter Naur. In 1967 Donald Knuth wrote that "the most notable feature of the Algol 60 report was the new standard it set for language definition." Unfortunately, as Tony Hoare said, the Algol 60 report was a considerable improvement over its successors.

Even though the Pascal language was far more successful than Algol 60, Nico Habermann severely criticized Wirth for the imprecision of the Pascal report and pointed out that it was hiding some conceptual inconsistencies in the definition of data types (Habermann 1973). Peter Naur pointed out that the Concurrent Pascal report, which I wrote, suffered from similar problems.

The task of writing a language report that explains a programming language with complete clarity to its implementors and users may look deceptively easy to someone who hasn't done it before. But in reality it is one of the most difficult intellectual tasks in the field of programming.

In writing the Edison report I have benefited greatly from the constructive criticism of Peter Naur. Naur made almost no comments about my choice and design of language features. His main concern was the clarity of the report. I would write a complete draft of the language report and Naur would then point out what the weaknesses were and suggest broadly how they might be removed in my next draft. The following describes the stages of development which the Edison report went through over a period of two years.

The first Edison report of January 1979 used *syntax graphs* of the form shown below with an explanation such as the following:

"Each parameter declaration introduces a name to represent the parameter and specifies its type or procedure heading."

"A value parameter is a local variable which is assigned the value of an expression before the procedure is executed.

A variable parameter denotes a variable which is bound to the procedure before it is executed. The symbol *var* distinguishes a variable parameter param:

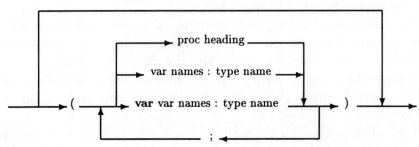

from a value parameter.

A procedure parameter denotes another procedure which is bound to the given procedure before the latter is executed."

About this report, Naur wrote the following:

"The weaknesses that will be described in most cases are such that may cause only little difficulty to a reader who is familiar with, for example, reports on the language Pascal, and who is generous in his willingness to rely on his own ability to fill in open holes by guesses and to remove inconsistencies. With the view taken all such holes and inconsistencies are unacceptable and should be removed, as far as possible."

"There is a poor connection between the formal syntactic description and the prose explanation."

I had used syntax graphs because they enable a programmer to see quite complex structures at a glance. Unfortunately, when a complicated concept is presented under a single name, the substructures of the graph have no names and cannot easily be referred to in the text. So, although the text refers to the concept of a "parameter declaration," the graph does not reveal what it is. The reader must also guess what the syntax of value, variable, and procedure parameters looks like. Note also that rather than explaining the meaning of certain concepts (such as variable parameters) the first report would use suggestive (but undefined) terms such as "binding."

In the second Edison report of July 1979 a parameter list was defined as follows (now using an extended *Backus-Naur form* instead of syntax graphs)

Parameter list:
   Parameter group [';' Parameter group]∗
Parameter group:

    Value parameter group # Variable parameter group
Value parameter group:
    Parameter name [',' Parameter name]* ':' Type name
Variable parameter group:
    'var' Parameter name [',' Parameter name]* ':' Type name
Parameter name:
    Name

(In this version of the language I had tentatively excluded the use of procedures as parameters of other procedures.)

These syntactic forms were now explained as follows:

"A parameter list consists of a sequence of parameter groups. Each
parameter group is either a value parameter group or a variable parameter
group.

A value parameter group introduces one or more names, called parameter
names, to denote value parameters. Each value parameter is a local variable
that is assigned the value of an argument before the procedure block is
executed.

A variable parameter group introduces one or more names to denote
variable parameters. Each variable parameter denotes a variable argument
which is selected before the procedure block is executed. During the execution of the procedure block all operations performed on the variable parameter stand for the same operations performed on the variable argument.
The variable parameter is said to be bound to the variable argument during
the execution of the procedure block."

The concept of a parameter list is now presented as the composition of
four simpler concepts. Each concept is described by a syntactic form that
introduces a name for the concept and defines its syntax. The prose explanation carefully follows the syntactic structures and explains their meaning
using the same terminology. As a minor detail the meaning of variable binding is now explained.

The idea of using an abundance of simple syntactic forms to introduce
names for most concepts, so that the text can refer directly to these definitions, had not occurred to me previously. But, once you realize that syntactic
forms can be used to define terminology (and not just syntax), the job of
writing a language report becomes far more well-defined. When the syntactic forms become very trivial the syntax graphs lose their visual appeal and
appear bulky and clumsy. So I returned to the BNF notation, which has the
great advantage that it can be included in program texts as comments.

Later, when I wrote the Edison compiler, I found that the syntactic
forms used in the report were so short that each of them conveniently could
be represented by a single procedure with the same name as the syntactic
form. Each procedure is now preceded by the corresponding syntactic form
written as a comment in BNF notation.

About the second report, Naur wrote this:

"The report is a vast improvement over the previous version in clarity,
consistency, and completeness. The remaining weaknesses, described below in detail, are to a large extent concerned merely with finer matters of
conceptual clarity."

After this pleasant introduction, Naur goes on to enumerate 79 conceptual problems. The first of these is that "a number of weaknesses of the
description can be traced to a general disinclination to accept abstract notions, not uniquely associated with syntactic entities of the language, as
well-defined useful constituents of the language and its description."

The conceptual difficulties of trying to describe all concepts purely in
terms of their notation are both philosophical and practical. If, for example,
the notion of a data value is purely notational then it is quite difficult to
explain why the relation

$$\text{'A'} = \text{char}(65)$$

is true for the ASCII character set. But the matter becomes quite simple if both symbols are viewed as different notations for the same abstract
concept—the first capital letter of the alphabet.

In the third report of January 1980 the distinction between fixed values
and the notations used to represent them in the language was made as follows: "A constant is a fixed value of a fixed type," and "A constant symbol
denotes a constant."

The distinction between an *abstract concept* and the *symbol* that denotes
the concept is immediately obscured when a syntactic form is given the same
name as the abstract concept. In the second Edison report, a variable used
as an operand was described by a syntactic form named variable

Variable:
  Whole variable # Subvariable

The report explained that "a variable denotes either a whole variable or
a subvariable." For a purist this is already unsatisfactory. Does the term
"variable" in that sentence refer to the abstract concept of a variable that

exists during program execution, or does it refer to one of the symbols in the program text described by the syntactic form named variable? For the writer of the language report it becomes downright awkward to describe what action a processor takes when a variable is used as an operand in a program. If we stick strictly to the rule of using the name introduced by the syntactic form, the result is the following cryptic sentence: "The evaluation of a variable causes the processor to locate the variable in the current context."

In the third report, the matter was settled by making a distinction between a variable (which is a named entity that may assume any of the values of a known type) and a variable symbol (which denotes a variable used as an operand). It was now easy to explain that "the evaluation of a variable symbol involves locating the corresponding variable in the current context."

The failure to make this conceptual distinction pervades most language reports. In the Pascal, Concurrent Pascal, and Modula reports one finds syntactic forms named constant, number, type, and variable instead of the more appropriate terms constant symbol, numeral, type description, and variable symbol (or similar ones).

After reading both the first and second drafts of the Edison report, Naur felt that "the central concept of types is not properly introduced, while the many different aspects of it are scattered around in an unsystematic and confusing manner." In the third version of the report I tried to clarify the *type concept* and its relation to the abstract notions of *value* and *operation*. I did not, however, succeed in organizing the report into chapters each describing all the aspects of a single type in one place.

The problem is that the type concept pervades the whole language. To explain even a simple type, such as boolean, in all its aspects, one must discuss constants, ranges, variables, expressions, functions, and statements as they relate to boolean values. Now that is practically the whole language right there. So, even to begin this chapter, one has to assume that the reader already understands all these concepts in general. And then one has to do it all over again for integers, characters, enumerations, arrays, records, and sets. It ends up being a very repetitive report in which the same story is told seven times. And that is, of course, because the language is designed in such a way that all the types have very similar properties which are described by very similar syntax.

After spending about 25 full working days trying to write a report along these lines I gave up and wrote another one instead (the third version). As a compromise, I now described several facets of each kind of type in the same chapter, namely the introduction of a new data type by means of a type declaration, the representation of values of the type by constants or constructors, and the meaning of the operators that apply to these values. The chapters on data types were followed by chapters describing the general properties of variables, expressions, statements, and procedures.

The concept of *scope* is explained quite concisely in the Algol 60 report:

"Every block automatically introduces a new level of nomenclature. This is realized as follows: Any identifier occurring within the block may through a suitable declaration be specified to be local to the block in question. This means (a) that the entity represented by this identifier inside the block has no existence outside it and (b) that any entity represented by this identifier outside the block is completely inaccessible inside the block.

Identifiers occuring within a block and not being declared to this block will be non-local to it, i.e. will represent the same entity inside the block and in the level immediately outside it."

"Since a statement of a block may itself be a block the concepts local and non-local must be understood recursively."

"No identifier may be declared more than once in any one block head."

One may complain about the complexity of block structure but not, I think, about the precision with which it is explained in the Algol 60 report. In the Pascal report written ten years later the explanation of the same concept is much more incomplete:

"All identifiers introduced in the formal parameter part, the constant definition part, the type definition part, the variable, procedure or function declaration parts are *local* to the procedure declaration which is called the *scope* of these identifiers. They are not known outside their scope."

This explanation fails to distinguish between a name and the entity it denotes. Since a name can be used with different meanings in different blocks, it is not the name itself that is unknown outside a given block but the use of the name to denote a given entity declared inside the block. In short, it is named entities (rather than names) which have scopes. I too failed to make that distinction in the earlier Edison reports.

More importantly, the above explanation from the Pascal report does not explain which entity a name denotes when it is declared with different meanings in nested blocks. To paraphrase an earlier remark, such weaknesses of the Pascal report have (fortunately) caused little difficulty for readers who are already familiar with the Algol 60 report.

The Concurrent Pascal and Modula reports also do not succeed in explaining scope rules precisely. This is much more unfortunate since these languages introduce new forms of modularity which primarily serve to change the traditional scope rules of block structured languages. My present attempts to explain these rules are contained in the chapter on Named Entities in the Edison report.

Having deprived myself of the opportunity to gloss over ill-understood issues in the Edison report it was quite embarrassing to explain the effect of executing processes described by *concurrent statements*. Although a programmer may have no difficulty understanding a particular concurrent statement, the language designer faces the much harder task of explaining in a few paragraphs the meaning of every conceivable use of this idea.

Unfortunately, one can only make a simple statement about the most trivial (and uninteresting) use of concurrent processes, which is the following: "If concurrent processes only operate on private variables and disjoint, common variables then the effect of executing a concurrent statement is the same as the effect of executing the process statements one at a time in any order."

As soon as processes begin to communicate, one needs the whole apparatus of the Gries–Owicki theory to reason about the effects of using semaphores, buffers, monitors, and so on (Owicki 1976). And, even so, processes must satisfy very rigid assumptions for the theory to apply. Although one can design language features (such as monitors) which enable a compiler to check that some of these assumptions are satisfied one cannot expect a programming language to capture all aspects of well-behaved concurrent programs. And, even if one could, it would not be very helpful to repeat the entire theory behind these concepts in a language report.

The difficulty of explaining what concurrent processes really do will, of course, arise in any report that describes a concurrent programming language. In yet another appeal to the generous reader the Concurrent Pascal and Modula reports evade the issue by suggestive use of undefined phrases to the effect that "all processes are executed concurrently." In writing the Edison report I decided to make the difficulty explicit by the following statement:

"If concurrent processes operate on intersecting, common variables then the effect of executing a concurrent statement is generally unpredictable since nothing is known about the order in which the processes operate on these variables. However by restricting the operations on intersecting variables to well-defined disciplines under the control of modules, procedures, and when statements it is possible to formulate concurrent statements that make predictable use of such variables. The theories used to reason about concurrent statements, when statements, and common variables are beyond the scope of this report."

In effect, the report says that one can write meaningless Edison programs that will produce unpredictable results. But it does not prescribe how to avoid doing this. This is surely a startling property of a programming tool. The report does, however, say that when this happens even the most basic programming concepts can lose their meaning:

"The meaning of variable retrieval and assignment defined earlier is valid only if these operations are performed one at a time on a given variable. Concurrent processes can ensure that this assumption is satisfied by performing all operations on intersecting, common variables within when statements."

The execution of recursive procedures and concurrent statements will generally create multiple instances of named entities, such as variables. Furthermore, procedures used as parameters of other procedures can have side-effects on some of these variable instances (and not necessarily the most recent ones!). In such cases, the language report must make it possible to decide which variable instance a process refers to at any given time.

In the fourth version of the Edison report (September 1980) the dynamic meaning of names is explained in terms of the so-called context of a process. This concept is introduced at the beginning of the report as follows:

"When a process executes a statement it operates on known entities selected from a set of entities called the current context of a process."

(A language implementor might say more loosely that a context is an abstract description of that part of a stack that is currently accessible to a process by following the chain of static links.)

Subsequent sections of the report then explain how the initial context of an executed program is established and how it is changed by the execution of procedure calls and concurrent statements.

A key idea is to associate contexts with procedures as well as processes. When a procedure body is executed by a process the current context of the process is attached as an attribute to all the local procedures declared in the body. If one of these procedures is called directly by the process its execution will take place in the context associated with the procedure. And if the procedure and its current context are bound to a parameter of another procedure the above rule still applies: when a procedure parameter is called it is executed in the context currently associated with the procedure parameter.

So the effect of any procedure call is now explained by a single rule.

This concludes the discussion of the linguistic dificulties which a language designer is faced with during the writing of a language report. The writing of the Edison report was far more difficult and time-consuming than the selection of the language features and the design of the first compiler.

References

Brinch Hansen, P. 1970. The nucleus of a multiprogramming system. *Communications of the ACM 13*, 4 (April), 238–250. *Article 2.*

Brinch Hansen, P. 1972. Structured multiprogramming. *Communications of the ACM 15*, 7 (July), 574–578. *Article 4.*

Brinch Hansen, P. 1973. *Operating System Principles.* Prentice-Hall, Englewood Cliffs, NJ (July).

Brinch Hansen, P. 1975. The programming language Concurrent Pascal. *IEEE Transactions on Software Engineering 1*, 2 (June), 199–207. *Article 7.*

Brinch Hansen, P. 1977. *The Architecture of Concurrent Programs.* Prentice-Hall, Englewood Cliffs, NJ, (July).

Brinch Hansen, P., and Staunstrup, J. 1978. Specification and implementation of mutual exclusion. *IEEE Transactions on Software Engineering 4*, 5 (September), 365–370.

Brinch Hansen, P. 1981. Edison—A multiprocessor language. *Software—Practice and Experience 11*, 4 (April), 325–361.

Dahl, O.-J., Dijkstra, E.W., and Hoare, C.A.R. 1972. *Structured Programming.* Academic Press, New York.

Dijkstra, E.W. 1968. Cooperating sequential processes. In *Programming Languages*, F. Genyus, Ed. Academic Press, New York.

Dijkstra, E.W. 1975. Guarded commands, nondeterminacy and formal derivation. *Communications of the ACM 18*, 8 (August), 453–457.

Habermann, A.N. 1973. Critical comments on the programming language Pascal. *Acta Informatica 3*, 47–57.

Hartmann, A.C. 1977. A Concurrent Pascal compiler for minicomputers. *Lecture Notes in Computer Science 50*, Springer-Verlag, New York.

Hoare, C.A.R. 1972. Towards a theory of parallel programming. In *Operating Systems Techniques*, C.A.R. Hoare and R.H. Perrott, Eds. Academic Press, New York, 61–71.

Hoare, C.A.R. 1974. Monitors: An operating system structuring concept. *Communications of the ACM 17*, 10 (October), 549–557.

Jensen, K., and Wirth, N. 1974. Pascal—User manual and report. *Lecture Notes in Computer Science 18*, New York.

Knuth, D.E. 1967. The remaining trouble spots in Algol 60. *Communications of the ACM 10*, 10 (October), 611–618.

Naur, P., Ed. 1962. *Revised Report on the Algorithmic Language Algol 60.* Regnecentralen, Copenhagen, Denmark.

Owicki, S., and Gries, D. 1976. An axiomatic proof technique for parallel programs. *Acta Informatica 6*, 319–340.

Welsh, J., and McKeag, M. 1980. *Structured System Programming*. Prentice-Hall, Englewood Cliffs, NJ.

Welsh, J., Sneeringer, W.J., and Hoare, C.A.R. 1977. Ambiguities and insecurities in Pascal. *Software—Practice and Experience 7*, (November–December), 685–696.

Wirth, N. 1971. The programming language Pascal. *Acta Informatica 1*, 35–63.

Wirth, N. 1977. Modula: A language for modular multiprogramming. *Software—Practice and Experience 7*, 1 (January–February), 3–35.

Joyce—A Programming Language for Distributed Systems[*]

(1987)

This paper describes a secure programming language called Joyce based on CSP and Pascal. Joyce permits unbounded (recursive) activation of communicating agents. The agents exchange messages through synchronous channels. A channel can transfer messages of different types between two or more agents. A compiler can check message types and ensure that agents use disjoint sets of variables only. The use of Joyce is illustrated by a variety of examples.

1 Introduction

Two years after the invention of the monitor concept (Brinch Hansen 1973; Hoare 1974), Concurrent Pascal had been developed (Brinch Hansen 1975) and used for operating system design (Brinch Hansen 1976). Within ten years, half a dozen production-quality languages were monitor-based, among them Modula (Wirth 1977), Pascal-Plus (Welsh 1979), Mesa (Lampson 1980) and Concurrent Euclid (Holt 1982).

Eight years after the CSP proposal (Hoare 1978), several CSP-based languages have been developed: these include CSP80 (Jazayeri 1980), RBCSP (Roper 1981), ECSP (Baiardi 1984), Planet (Crookes 1984) and the low-level language occam (Inmos 1984). But no experience has been reported on the use of these languages for non-trivial system implementation. Although CSP has been highly successful as a notation for theoretical work (Hoare 1985), it has probably been too far removed from the requirements of a secure programming language.

[*]P. Brinch Hansen, Joyce—A programming language for distributed systems. *Software—Practice and Experience 17* , 1 (January 1987), 29–50. Copyright © 1987, Per Brinch Hansen. Reprinted by permission.

This paper describes a secure programming language called Joyce for the design and implementation of distributed systems. Joyce is based on CSP and Pascal (Wirth 1971).

A Joyce program consists of nested procedures which define communicating agents. Joyce permits unbounded (recursive) activation of agents. The execution of a program activates an initial agent. Agents may dynamically activate subagents which run concurrently with their creators. The variables of an agent are inaccessible to other agents.

Agents communicate by means of symbols transmitted through channels. Every channel has an alphabet—a fixed set of symbols that can be transmitted through the channel. A symbol has a name and may carry a message of a fixed type.

Two agents match when one of them is ready to output a symbol to a channel and the other is ready to input the same symbol from the same channel. When this happens, a communication takes place in which a message from the sending agent is assigned to a variable of the receiving agent.

The communications on a channel take place one at a time. A channel can transfer symbols in both directions between two agents.

A channel may be used by two or more agents. If more than two agents are ready to communicate on the same channel, it may be possible to match them in several different ways. The channel arbitrarily selects two matching agents at a time and lets them communicate.

A polling statement enables an agent to examine one or more channels until it finds a matching agent. Both sending and receiving agents may be polled.

Agents create channels dynamically and access them through local port variables. When an agent creates a channel, a channel pointer is assigned to a port variable. The agent may pass the pointer as a parameter to subagents.

When an agent reaches the end of its defining procedure, it waits until all its subagents have terminated before terminating itself. At this point, the local variables and any channels created by the agent cease to exist.

This paper defines the concepts of Joyce and illustrates the use of the language to implement a variety of well-known programming concepts and algorithms.

2   Language Concepts

Joyce is based on a minimal Pascal subset: type integer, boolean, char and real; enumerated, array and record types; constants, variables and expressions; assignment, if, while, compound and empty statements.

This subset is extended with concurrent programming concepts called agent procedures, port types and channels, agent, port, input/output and polling statements.

The Joyce grammar is defined in extended BNF notation: $[E]$ denotes an E sentence (or none). $\{E\}$ denotes a finite (possibly empty) sequence of E sentences. Tokens are enclosed in quotation marks, e.g. "**begin**".

This paper concentrates on the concurrent aspects of Joyce.

Port types

    TypeDefinition = TypeName "=" NewType ";" .
    NewType = PascalType | PortType .
    PortType = "[" Alphabet "]" .
    Alphabet = SymbolClass { "," SymbolClass } .
    SymbolClass = SymbolName ["(" MessageType ")"] .
    MessageType = TypeName .

A Joyce program defines abstract concurrent machines called agents. The agents communicate by means of values called symbols transmitted through entities called channels. The set of possible symbols that can be transmitted through a channel is called its alphabet.

Agents create channels dynamically and access them through variables known as port variables. The types of these variables are called port types.

A type definition

$$T = [s_1(T_1), s_2(T_2), \ldots, s_n(T_n)];$$

defines a port type named T. The port value *nil* T is of type T and denotes a non-existing channel. All other port values of type T denote distinct channels with the given alphabet. The port values (also known as channel pointers) are unordered.

The alphabet is the union of a fixed number of disjoint symbol classes named $s_1, s_2, \ldots, s_n$.

A symbol class $s_i(T_i)$ consists of every possible value of type T_i prefixed with the name s_i. The T_i values are called messages.

A symbol class s_j consists of a single symbol named s_j without a message. The symbol is called a signal.

The symbol names $s_1, s_2, \ldots, s_n$ must be distinct, and $T_1, T_2, \ldots, T_n$ must be names of known types. (Every type has a name and is said to be known within its scope.) The message types cannot be (or include) port types.

Examples:

1. A port type named *stream* with two symbol classes named *int* and *eos*. Every *int* symbol includes a message of type integer. The *eos* symbol is a signal:

$$\text{stream} = [\text{int(integer)}, \text{eos}];$$

2. A port type named PV with two signals P and V:

$$PV = [P, V];$$

Note. Symbols of the same alphabet must have distinct names. Symbols of different alphabets may have the same names. Different symbols of the same alphabet may carry messages of the same type.

Port variables

PortAccess = VariableAccess .

A variable $v : T$ of a port type T holds a port value. If the value of v is *nil* T, a port access v denotes a non-existing channel; otherwise, it denotes a channel with the alphabet given by T. (The channel itself is not a variable, but a communication device shared by agents.)

Examples:

1. Access a port variable named *inp*:

$$\text{inp}$$

2. Access the ith element of an array of port variables named *ring*:

$$\text{ring[i]}$$

Port statements

> Statement = PascalStatement | PortStatement |
>   InputOutputStatement | PollingStatement |
>   AgentStatement .
> PortStatement = "+" PortAccess .

The creation of a new channel is called the activation of the channel. A port statement $+c$ denotes activation of a new channel. The variable access c must be of a known port type T.

When an agent executes the port statement, a new channel with the alphabet given by T is created and a pointer to the channel is assigned to the port variable c. The agent is called the creator of the channel. The channel itself is known as an internal channel of the agent. The channel ceases to exist when its creator terminates.

Examples:

1. Create a new channel and assign the pointer to the port variable *inp*:

$$+\text{inp}$$

2. Create a new channel and assign the pointer to the port variable *ring[i]*:

$$+\text{ring[i]}$$

Input/output statements

> InputOutputCommand = OutputCommand | InputCommand .
> OutputCommand = PortAccess "!" OutputSymbol .
> OutputSymbol = SymbolName ["(" OutputExpression ")"] .
> OutputExpression = Expression .
> InputCommand = PortAccess "?" InputSymbol .
> InputSymbol = SymbolName ["(" InputVariable ")"] .
> InputVariable = VariableAccess .
> InputOutputStatement = InputOutputCommand .

A communication is the transfer of a symbol from one agent to another through a channel. The sending agent is said to output the symbol, and the receiving agent is said to input the symbol. The agents access the channel through local port variables.

Consider an agent p which accesses a channel through a port variable b, and another agent q which accesses the same channel through a different port variable c. The port variables must be of the same type:

$$T = [s_1(T_1), s_2(T_2), \ldots, s_n(T_n)];$$

An output command $b!s_i(e_i)$ denotes output of a symbol $s_i(e_i)$ through the channel denoted by the port variable b. s_i must be the name of one of the symbol classes of T, and the expression e_i must be of the corresponding message type T_i.

An input command $c?s_i(v_i)$ denotes input of a symbol $s_i(v_i)$ through the channel denoted by the port variable c. s_i must be the name of one of the symbol classes of T, and the variable access v_i must be of the corresponding message type T_i.

When an agent p is ready to output the symbol s_i on a channel, and another agent q is ready to input the same symbol from the same channel, the two agents are said to match and a communication between them is said to be feasible. If and when this happens, the two agents execute the output and input commands simultaneously. The combined effect is defined by the following sequence of actions:

1. p obtains a value by evaluating the output expression e_i.

2. q assigns the value to its input variable v_i.

(If the symbol s_i is a signal, steps 1 and 2 denote empty actions.)

After a communication, the agents proceed concurrently.

When an agent reaches an input/output command which denotes a communication that is not feasible, the behavior of the agent depends on whether the command is used as an input/output statement or as a polling command (defined in the next section).

The effect of an input/output statement is to delay an agent until the communication denoted by the statement has taken place.

The communications on a channel take place one at a time. A channel can transfer symbols in both directions between two agents.

A channel may be used by two or more agents. If more than two agents are ready to communicate on the same channel, it may be possible to match them in several different ways. The channel arbitrarily selects two matching agents at a time and lets them communicate.

Examples:

1. Use the port variable *out* to output an *int* symbol with the message $x + 1$:

$$out!int(x + 1)$$

2. Use the port variable *inp* to input an *int* symbol and assign the message to *y*:

$$inp?int(y)$$

3. Use the port variable *out* to output an *eos* signal:

$$out!eos$$

4. Use the port variable *inp* to input an *eos* signal:

$$inp?eos$$

5. Use the port variable *ring[i]* to output a *token* signal:

$$ring[i]!token$$

Polling statements

```
PollingStatement =
  "poll" GuardedStatementList "end" .
GuardedStatementList =
  GuardedStatement { "|" GuardedStatement } .
GuardedStatement = Guard "->" StatementList .
Guard = PollingCommand [ "&" PollingExpression ] .
PollingCommand = InputOutputCommand .
PollingExpression = BooleanExpression .
```

A polling statement

```
poll
    C₁ & B₁ -> SL₁ |
    C₂ & B₂ -> SL₂ |
        ...
    Cₙ & Bₙ -> SLₙ
end
```

denotes execution of exactly one of the guarded statements

$$C_i \ \& \ B_i \ -> \ SL_i$$

An agent executes a polling statement in two phases, known as the polling and completion phases:

1. Polling: the agent examines the guards $C_1\&B_1$, $C_2\&B_2$, ..., $C_n\&B_n$ cyclically until finds one with a polling command C_i that denotes a feasible communication and a polling expression B_i that denotes true (or is omitted).

2. Completion: the agent executes the selected polling command C_i followed by the corresponding statement list SL_i.

While an agent is polling, it can be matched only by another agent that is ready to execute an input/output statement. Two agents polling at the same time do not match.

Example:

Use a port variable named *user* to either (1) input a P signal (provided an integer $x > 0$) and decrement x, or (2) input a V signal and increment x:

```
poll
    user?P & x > 0 -> x := x − 1 |
    user?V -> x := x + 1
end
```

Note. Polling has no side-effects, but may cause program failure if the expression evaluation causes a range error (or overflow).

Agent statements

AgentStatement =
  AgentName ["(" ActualParameterList ")"] .
ActualParameterList =
  ActualParameter { "," ActualParameter } .
ActualParameter = Expression .

An agent procedure P defines a class of agents. The creation and start of an agent is called its activation. The activation of a P agent creates a new instance of every variable defined in procedure P. These variable instances are called the own variables of the new agent. When the agent refers to a variable x in P, it refers to its own instance of x. The own variables of an agent are inaccessible to other agents.

An agent is always activated by another agent (called its creator). The new agent is called a subagent of its creator. After the creation, the subagent and its creator run concurrently.

An agent statement

$$P(e_1, e_2, \ldots, e_m)$$

denotes activation of a new agent. P must be the name of a known agent procedure (defined in the next section). The actual parameter list must contain an actual parameter e_i for every formal parameter a_i defined by P. e_i must be an expression of the same type as a_i.

When an agent executes an agent statement, a subagent is created in two steps:

1. The own variables of the subagent are created as follows:

   (a) The formal parameters of P are created one at a time in the order listed. Every formal parameter a_i is assigned the value denoted by the corresponding actual parameter e_i.

   (b) The variables defined in the procedure body of P are created with unpredictable initial values.

2. The subagent is started.

A port operand used as an actual parameter denotes a channel which is accessible to both the subagent and its creator. It is known as an external channel of the subagent.

An agent defined by a procedure P may activate P recursively. Every activation creates a new P agent with its own variables.

Example:

Activate a semaphore agent with two actual parameters: the integer 1 and a port value named *user*:

semaphore(1, user)

Agent procedures

AgentProcedure = **"agent"** AgentName ProcedureBlock ";" .
ProcedureBlock =
  ["(" FormalParameterList ")"] ";" ProcedureBlock .
FormalParameterList =
  ParameterDefinition { ";" ParameterDefinition } .
ParameterDefinition =
  VariableName { "," VariableName } ":" TypeName .
ProcedureBlock =
  [ConstantDefinitionPart][TypeDefinitionPart]
  { AgentProcedure } [VariableDefinitionPart]
  CompoundStatement .

An agent procedure P defines a class of agents. Every formal parameter is a local variable that is assigned the value of an expression when a P agent is activated.

After its activation, a P agent executes the corresponding procedure body in two steps:

1. The agent executes the compound statement of P.

2. The agent waits until all its subagents (if any) have terminated. At this point, the own variables and internal channels of the agent cease to exist, and the agent terminates.

Example: semaphore

An agent procedure that defines a semaphore which accepts P and V signals:

```
agent semaphore(x: integer; user: PV);
begin
  while true do
    poll
      user?P & x > 0 -> x := x - 1|
      user?V -> x := x + 1
    end
end;
```

Programs

```
Program =
  [ ConstantDefinitionPart ][ TypeDefinitionPart ]
  AgentProcedure .
```

A program defines an agent procedure P. The program is executed by activating and executing a single P agent (the initial agent). The activation of the initial agent is the result of executing an agent statement in another program (an operating system). A program communicates with its operating system through the external channels of the initial agent (the system channels).

3   Program Examples

The following examples illustrate the use of Joyce to implement stream processing, functions, data representations, monitors and ring nets. The examples have been compiled and run on an IBM PC using a Joyce compiler and interpreter written in Pascal.

Stream processing

First, we look at agents that input and output bounded data streams. Every stream is a (possibly empty) sequence of integers ending with an *eos* signal:

$$\textbf{type stream} = [\text{int(integer)}, \text{eos}];$$

Example: generate

An agent that generates an arithmetic progression $a_0, a_1, \ldots, a_{n-1}$, where $a_i = a + i \times b$:

```
agent generate(out: stream;
   a, b, n: integer);
var i: integer;
begin
  i := 0;
  while i < n do
    begin
      out!int(a + i*b); i := i + 1
    end;
  out!eos
end;
```

Example: copy

An agent that copies a stream:

```
agent copy(inp, out: stream);
var more: boolean; x: integer;
begin
  more := true;
  while more do
    poll
      inp?int(x) -> out!int(x)|
      inp?eos -> more := false
    end;
  out!eos
end;
```

Example: merge

An agent that outputs an arbitrary interleaving of two input streams:

```
agent merge(inp1, inp2, out: stream);
var n, x: integer;
begin
  n := 0;
  while n < 2 do
    poll
      inp1?int(x) -> out!int(x)|
      inp1?eos -> n := n + 1|
```

```
        inp2?int(x) -> out!int(x)|
        inp2?eos -> n := n + 1
      end;
    out!eos
  end;
```

A value input from one of the streams inp_1 and inp_2 is immediately output. The agent terminates when both input streams have been exhausted ($n = 2$).

Example: suppress duplicates

An agent that outputs a stream derived from an ordered input stream by suppressing duplicates:

```
agent suppress(inp, out: stream);
var more: boolean; x, y: integer;
begin
  poll
    inp?int(x) -> more := true|
    inp?eos -> more := false
  end;
  while more do
    poll
      inp?int(y) ->
        if x <> y then
          begin out!int(x); x := y end|
      inp?eos -> out!int(x); more := false
    end;
  out!eos
end;
```

Example: iterative buffer

A buffer implemented as a pipeline of 10 copy agents:

```
agent buffer(inp, out: stream);
const n = 9;
type net = array [1..n] of stream;
use copy;
var a: net; i: integer;
```

```
begin
  +a[1]; copy(inp, a[1]); i := 2;
  while i <= n do
    begin
      +a[i]; copy(a[i−1], a[i]); i := i + 1
    end;
  copy(a[n], out)
end;
```

The buffer agent is a composite agent which activates an array of copy agents and channels by iteration. The length $n + 1$ of the iterative array is specified by a constant n. During compilation, the *use* sentence is replaced by the text of the copy agent.

This algorithm is an example of "information hiding". A user agent may regard the copy and buffer agents as different implementations of the same mechanism: a copying agent with an input and an output channel. The subagents and internal channels of the buffer agent are therefore made invisible to its environment.

Example: recursive buffer

A recursive version of the previous buffer:

```
agent buffer(n: integer; inp, out: stream);
use copy;
var succ: stream;
begin
  if n = 1 then copy(inp, out)
  else
    begin
      +succ; copy(inp, succ);
      buffer(n − 1, succ, out)
    end
end;
```

The length n of the recursive array is specified when it is activated. If $n = 1$, the buffer consists of a single copy agent only; otherwise, it consists of a copy agent followed by a buffer of length $n − 1$.

The next two examples illustrate the use of a programming paradigm known as a dynamic accumulator. This is a pipeline which uses an input stream to compute another stream. The pipeline accumulates the new stream while it is being computed and outputs it as a whole when it is complete. Every agent (except the last one) in the pipeline holds one element of the new stream. The last agent is empty. Each time the pipeline has computed another element, the last agent receives an element and extends the pipeline with a new empty agent. Since the length of the computed stream is not known *a priori*, the pipeline begins as a single empty agent. At the end of the input stream, the pipeline outputs the elements of the computed stream one at a time and terminates.

Example: recursive sorting

A dynamic accumulator that inputs a (possibly empty) stream and outputs the elements in non-decreasing order:

```
agent sort(inp, out);
var more: boolean; x, y: integer;
    succ: stream;
begin
  poll
    inp?int(x) -> +succ;
      sort(succ, out); more := true;|
    inp?eos -> out!eos; more := false
  end;
  while more do
    poll
      inp?int(y) ->
        if x > y then
          begin succ!int(x); x := y end
        else succ!int(y)|
      inp?eos -> out!int(x);
        succ!eos; more := false
    end
end;
```

The sorting agents share a common output channel. Initially, an agent is the last one in the chain and is empty. After receiving the first value from its predecessor, the agent creates a successor and becomes non-empty. The agent now inputs the rest of the stream from its predecessor and keeps the smallest value *x* received so far. The rest it sends to its successor. When the agent inputs an *eos* signal it terminates as follows: if it is empty, the agent sends *eos* through the common channel; otherwise it outputs x on the common channel and sends *eos* to its successor.

As an example, while sorting the sequence

$$3, 1, 2, \ eos$$

the accumulator s starts as a single empty agent denoted by $< \phi >$ and is extended by a new agent for every value input:

Initially:	$s = < \phi >$
After inputting 3:	$s = < 3 >, < \phi >$
After inputting 1:	$s = < 1 >, < 3 >, < \phi >$
After inputting 2:	$s = < 1 >, < 2 >, < 3 >, < \phi >$

The sorting accumulator may be tested by means of a pipeline with three agents:

```
agent pipeline1;
use generate, sort, print;
var a, b: stream;
begin
   +a; +b; generate(a, 10, −1, 10);
   sort(a, b); print(b)
end;
```

The print agent accepts a stream and prints it.

The next pipeline merges two unordered streams, sorts the results, suppresses duplicates and prints the rest:

```
agent pipeline2;
use generate, merge, sort, suppress, print;
var a, b, c, d, e: stream;
begin
   +a; +b; +c; +d; +e;
   generate(a, 1, 1, 10);
   generate(b, 10, −1, 10);
   merge(a, b, c); sort(c, d);
   suppress(d, e); print(e)
end;
```

Example: prime sieve

A dynamic accumulator that inputs a finite sequence of natural numbers 1, 2, 3, ..., n and outputs those that are primes:

```
agent sieve(inp, out: stream);
var more: boolean; x, y: integer;
  succ: stream;
begin
  poll
    inp?int(x) -> +succ;
      sieve(succ, out); more := true|
    inp?eos -> out!eos; more := false
  end;
  while more do
    poll
      inp?int(y) ->
        if y mod x <> 0 then succ!int(y)|
      inp?eos -> out!int(x);
        succ!eos; more := false
    end;
end;
```

Initially, a sieve agent inputs a prime x from its predecessor and activates a successor. The agent then skips all further input which is divisible by x and sends the rest to its successor. At the end, the agent sends x through the common channel and sends *eos* either to its successor (if any) or through the output channel.

The sieve can be optimized somewhat by letting every agent output its prime as soon as it has been input. The present form of the algorithm was chosen to show that the sort and sieve agents are almost identical variants of the same programming paradigm. (They differ in one statement only!)

Since 2 is the only even prime, we may as well feed the sieve with odd numbers 3, 5, 7, ... only. The following pipeline prints all primes between 3 and 9999:

```
agent primes;
use generate, sieve, print;
var a, b: stream;
begin
  +a; +b; generate(a, 3, 2, 4999);
```

```
        sieve(a, b); print(b)
    end;
```

Function evaluation

A function $f(x)$ can be evaluated by activating an agent with two parameters denoting the argument x and a channel. The agent evaluates $f(x)$, outputs the result on the channel and terminates.

A procedure can be implemented similarly.

Example: recursive Fibonacci

An agent that computes a Fibonacci number recursively by means of a tree of subagents:

```
    type func = [val(integer)];

    agent fibonacci(f: func; x: integer);
    var g, h: func; y, z: integer;
    begin
      if x <= 1 then f!val(x)
      else
        begin
          +g; fibonacci(g, x − 1);
          +h; fibonacci(h, x − 2);
          g?val(y); h?val(z); f!val(y + z)
        end
    end;
```

3.1   Data representation

An agent can also implement a set of operations on a data representation.

Example: recursive set

Problem. Represent a set of integers as an agent with an input and an output channel. Initially, the set is empty. The set agent accepts three kinds of commands from a single user agent only:

1. Insert an integer n in the set:

$$\text{inp!insert(n)}$$

2. Return a boolean b indicating if n is in the set:

$$\text{inp!has(n); out?return(b)}$$

3. Delete the set:

$$\text{inp!delete}$$

Solution.

```
type
   setinp = [insert(integer), has(integer), delete];
   setout = [return(boolean)];

agent intset(inp: setinp; out: setout);
type state = (empty, nonempty, deleted);
var s: state; x, y: integer; succ: setinp;
begin
   s := empty;
   while s = empty do
      poll
         inp?insert(x) -> +succ;
            intset(succ, out); s := nonempty|
         inp?has(x) -> out!return(false)|
         inp?delete -> s := deleted
      end;
   while s = nonempty do
      poll
         inp?insert(y) ->
            if x > y then
               begin succ!insert(x); x := y end
            else if x < y then succ!insert(y)|
         inp?has(y) ->
            if x >= y then out!return(x = y)
               else succ!has(y)|
         inp?delete -> succ!delete; s := deleted
```

```
        end
    end;
```

The set agent is very similar to the sort and sieve agents. It contains either one member of the set or none. Initially, the agent is empty and answers false to all membership queries. After the first insertion, it activates an empty successor to which it passes any command it cannot handle. To speed up processing, the set is ordered. Many insertions can proceed simultaneously in the pipeline. Insertion of an already existing member has no effect. A delete signal propagates through all the set agents and makes them terminate.

Monitors

A monitor is a scheduling agent that enables two or more user agents to share a resource. The user agents can invoke operations on the resource one at a time only. A monitor may use boolean expressions to delay operations until they are feasible.

Example: ring buffer

A monitor that implements a non-terminating ring buffer which can hold up to ten messages:

```
agent buffer(inp, out: stream);
const n = 10;
type contents = array [1..n] of integer;
var head, tail, length: integer;
    ring: contents;
begin
    head := 1; tail := 1; length := 0;
    while true do
        poll
            inp?int(ring[tail]) & length < n ->
                tail := tail mod n + 1;
                length := length + 1|
            out!int(ring[head]) & length > 0 ->
                head := head mod n + 1;
                length := length - 1
        end
    end;
```

An empty buffer may input a message only. A full buffer may output only. When the buffer contains at least one and at most nine values, it is ready either to input or to output a message.

Example: scheduled printer

A monitor that gives one user agent at a time exclusive access to a printer during a sequence of write operations. The user agent must open the printer before writing and close it afterwards:

```
type printsym = [open, write(char), close];

agent printer(user: printsym);
var more: boolean; x: char;
begin
  while true do
    begin
      user?open; more := true;
      while more do
        poll
          user?write(x) -> print(x)|
          user?close -> more := false
        end
    end
end;
```

When the printer has received an open symbol from a user agent, it accepts only a (possibly empty) sequence of write symbols followed by a close symbol. This protocol prevents other agents from opening the printer and using it simultaneously. (The details of printing are ignored.)

Ring nets

So far, we have only considered agents connected by acyclic nets of channels. In the final example, the agents are connected by a cyclic net of channels.

Example: nim players

From a pile of 20 coins, three players take turns picking one, two or three coins from the pile. The player forced to pick the last coin loses the game.

The game is simulated by three agents connected by a ring of three channels. When the game begins, one of the agents receives all the coins:

```
agent nim;
use player;
var a, b, c: stream;
begin
  +a; +b; +c; player(20, a, b);
  player(0, b, c); player(0, c, a);
end;
```

The players behave as follows:

```
agent player(pile: integer;
  pred, succ: stream);
var more: boolean;
begin
  if pile > 0 then succ!int(pile − 1);
  more := true;
  while more do
    poll
      pred?int(pile) −>
        if pile > 1 then succ!int(pile − 1)
        else { loser }
          begin
            succ!eos; pred?eos; more := false
          end|
      pred!eos −> succ!eos; more := false
    end
end;
```

When an agent receives the pile from its predecessor, it reduces it and sends the rest (if any) to its successor. (To simplify the algorithm slightly, an agent always removes a single coin). The agent that picks the last coin sends *eos* to its successor and waits until the signal has passed through the other two agents and comes back from its predecessor. At that point, the loser terminates. When a non-losing agent receives *eos* instead of a pile, it passes the signal to its successor and terminates.

The dining philosophers problem (Hoare 1978) is another example of a ring net. It is left as an exercise to the reader.

4   Design Issues

The following motivates some of the design decisions of Joyce.

Terminology and notation

In the literature, the word "process" often denotes a sequential process. Since a composite agent is not sequential, I prefer to use another word for communicating machines (namely, "agents").

It was tempting to use the notation of CSP (Hoare 1978) or one of the successors of Pascal, for example Modula-2 (Wirth 1982). However, in spite of its limitations, Pascal has a readable notation which is familiar to everyone. Chosing a pure Pascal subset has enabled me to concentrate on the concurrent aspects of Joyce.

Indirect naming

One of the major advantages of monitors is their ability to communicate with processes and schedule them without being aware of process names. Joyce agents also refer indirectly to one another by means of port variables.

In CSP, an input/output command must name the source or destination process directly. The text of a process must therefore be modified when it is used in different contexts. This complicates the examples in (Hoare 1978): the user of a process array $S(1..n)$ is itself named $S(0)$! And the prime sieve is composed of three different kinds of processes to satisfy the naming rules.

Direct process naming also makes it awkward to write a server with multiple clients of different kinds (such as the scheduled printer). If the clients are not known *a priori*, it is in fact impossible.

ECSP and RBCSP use process variables for indirect naming. CSP80, occam, Planet and a theoretical variant of CSP, which I shall call TCSP (Hoare 1985), use ports or channels.

Message declarations

So far, the most common errors in Joyce programs have been type errors in input/output commands. I am therefore convinced that any CSP language must include message declarations which permit complete type checking during compilation. In this respect, CSP and occam are insecure languages.

Although ECSP does not include message declarations, the compiler performs type checking of messages after recognizing (undeclared) channels by statement analysis.

The simplest idea is to declare channels which can transfer messages of a single type only (as in CSP80 or Planet). But this does not even work well for a simple agent that copies a bounded stream. Such an agent needs two channels, both capable of transferring two different kinds of symbols. Otherwise, four channels are required: two for stream values and two for *eos* signals.

As a modest increase in complexity, I considered a channel which can transfer messages of a finite number of distinct types $T_1, T_2, \ldots, T_n$. But this proposal is also problematic since (1) it is necessary to treat signals as distinct data types, and (2) an agent still needs multiple channels to distinguish between different kinds of messages of the same type (such as the *has* and *insert* symbols in the *intset* example).

To avoid a confusing proliferation of channels, the ability to define channel alphabets with named symbols seems essential. The symbol names play the same role as the (undeclared) "constructors" of CSP or the procedure names of monitors: they describe the nature of an event in which a process participates.

Channel sharing

The *intset* pipeline is made simpler and more efficient by the use of a single output channel shared by all the agents. A set agent which receives a query about the member it holds can immediately output the answer through the common channel instead of sending it through all its successors. This improvement was suggested in (Dijkstra 1982).

Channel sharing also simplifies the scheduled printer. If every channel can be used by two processes only, it is necessary to connect a resource process to multiple users by means of a quantifier called a "replicator."

I expect channel sharing to work well for lightly used resources. But, if a shared resource is used heavily, some user agents may be bypassed by others and thus prevented from using the resource. In such cases, it may be necessary to introduce separate user channels to achieve fairness.

Output polling

In CSP, ECSP, RBCSP and occam, polling is done by input commands only. This restriction prevents a sender and receiver from polling the same channel simultaneously. Unfortunately, it also makes the input and output of a ring buffer asymmetric (Hoare 1978).

Like CSP80 and TCSP, Joyce permits both input and output polling. It is the programmer's responsibility to ensure that a polling agent is always matched by an agent that executes an input/output statement. This property is automatically satisfied in a hierarchical system in which every agent polls its masters only (Silberschatz 1979).

Polling loops

CSP includes a polling loop that terminates when all the processes polled have terminated. Hoare (1985) remarks: "The trouble with this convention is that it is complicated to define and implement."

In RBCSP, a process waiting for input from a terminated process is terminated only when all processes are waiting or terminated.

A Joyce agent terminates when it reaches the end of its procedure. This is a much more flexible mechanism which enables an agent to send a termination signal to another agent without terminating itself.

I resisted the temptation to include polling loops, such as

do inp?int(x) −> out!int(x)
until inp?eos −> out!eos **end**

Although this simplifies the copy and printer agents, it cannot be used directly in the other examples. It may even complicate programs, if it is used where it is inappropriate.

Unbounded activation

In CSP one can activate only a fixed number of processes simultaneously. If these processes terminate, they do it simultaneously. A process cannot activate itself recursively. It is, however, possible to activate a fixed-length array of indexed processes which can imitate the behavior (but not quite the elegance) of a recursive process.

Joyce supports unbounded (recursive) agent activation. The beauty of the recursive algorithms is sufficient justification for this feature. The ability to activate identical agents by iteration and recursion removes the need for indexed agents (as in CSP, RBCSP, Planet and occam). The rule that an agent terminates only when all its subagents have terminated was inspired by the task concept of Ada (Roubine 1980).

Procedures and functions

To force myself to make agents as general as possible, I excluded ordinary procedures and functions from Joyce. As a result, I felt obliged to design an agent concept which includes the best features of Pascal procedures: value parameters, recursion and efficient implementation. Although agent procedures may be recursive, every agent has one instance only of its own variables. Consequently, a compiler can determine the lengths of agent activation records. This simplifies storage allocation considerably.

Security

A programming language is secure if its compiler and run-time support can detect all violations of the language rules (Hoare 1973). Programs written in an insecure language may cause obscure system-dependent errors which are inexplicable in terms of the language report. Such errors can be extremely difficult to locate and correct.

Joyce is a far more secure language than Pascal (Welsh 1977). A compiler can check message types and ensure that agents use disjoint sets of variables only. (The disjointness is automatically guaranteed by the syntax and scope rules.)

When an agent is activated, every word of its activation record may be set to nil. Afterwards a simple run-time check can detect unitialized port variables.

There are no dangling references, either, to channels that have ceased to exist. Every port variable of an agent is either nil or points to an internal or external channel of the agent. Now, an internal channel exists as long as the agent and its port variables exist. And an external channel exists as long as the ancestor that created it. This ancestor, in turn, exists at least as long as the given agent. So, a port variable is either nil or points to an existing channel.

Implementability

The first Joyce compiler is a Pascal program of 3300 lines which generates P-code. The code is currently interpreted by a Pascal program of 1000 lines. (Reals are not implemented yet.) The surprisingly simple implementation of agents and channels will be described in a future paper.

Proof rules

The problems of finding proof rules for Joyce are currently being studied and are not discussed here. However, the algorithms shown have a convincing simplicity that makes me optimistic in this respect.

Language comparison

Table 1 summarizes the key features of the CSP languages (except TCSP).

Table 1

	CSP	occam	ECSP	Planet	RBCSP	CSP80	Joyce
Indirect naming	−	+	+	+	+	+	+
Message declaration	−	−	−	+	+	+	+
Input polling	+	+	+	−	+	+	+
Output polling	−	−	−	−	−	+	+
Recursion	−	−	−	−	−	−	+

Hoare (1978) emphasized that CSP should not be regarded as suitable for use as a programming language but only as a partial solution to the problems tackled. However, all that remained to be done was to modify these concepts. CSP is still the foundation for the new generation of concurrent programming languages discussed here.

5 Final Remarks

This paper has presented a secure programming language which removes several restrictions of the original CSP proposal by introducing:

1. port variables

2. channel alphabets

3. output polling

4. channel sharing

5. recursive agents

The language has been implemented on a personal computer.

More work remains to be done on verification rules and implementation of the language on a parallel computer. The language needs to be used extensively for the design of parallel algorithms before a final evaluation can be made.

Acknowledgements

It is a pleasure to acknowledge the helpful comments of Birger Andersen, Peter T. Andersen, Lotte Bangsborg, Peter Brinch, Niels Christian Juul and Bo Salomon.

References

Baiardi, F., Ricci, L., and Vanneschi, M. 1984. Static checking of interprocess communication in ECSP. *ACM SIGPLAN Notices 19*, 6 (June), 290–299.

Brinch Hansen, P. 1973. *Operating System Principles*. Prentice-Hall, Englewood Cliffs, NJ.

Brinch Hansen, P. 1975. The programming language Concurrent Pascal. *IEEE Transactions on Software Engineering 1*, 2 (June), 199–205. *Article 7.*

Brinch Hansen, P. 1976. The Solo operating system. *Software—Practice and Experience 6*, 2 (April–June), 141–205. *Articles 8–9.*

Crookes, D., and Elder, J.W.G. 1984. An experiment in language design for distributed systems. *Software–Practice and Experience 14*, 10 (October), 957–971.

Dijkstra, E.W. 1982. *Selected Writings on Computing: A Personal Perspective.* Springer-Verlag, New York, 147–160.

Hoare, C.A.R. 1973. Hints on programming language design. Computer Science Department, Stanford University, Stanford, CA, (December).

Hoare, C.A.R. 1974. Monitors: An operating system structuring concept. *Communications of the ACM 17*, 10 (October), 549–557.

Hoare, C.A.R. 1978. Communicating sequential processes. *Communications of the ACM 21*, 8 (August), 666–677.

Hoare, C.A.R. 1985. *Communicating Sequential Processes*. Prentice-Hall, Englewood Cliffs, NJ.

Holt, R.C. 1982. A short introduction to Concurrent Euclid. *ACM SIGPLAN Notices 17*, (May), 60–79.

Inmos, Ltd. 1984. *occam Programming Manual.* Prentice-Hall, Englewood Cliffs, NJ.

Jazayeri, M., Ghezzi, C., Hoffman, D., Middleton, D., and Smotherman, M. 1980. CSP/80: A language for communicating sequential processes. *IEEE Compcon Fall,* (September), 736–740.

Lampson, B.W., and Redell, D.D. 1980. Experience with processes and monitors in Mesa. *Communications of the ACM 23,* 2 (February), 105–117.

Roper, T.J., and Barter, C.J. 1981. A communicating sequential process language and implementation. *Software—Practice and Experience 11,* 11 (November), 1215–1234.

Roubine, O., and Heliar, J.-C. 1980. Parallel processing in Ada. In *On the Construction of Programs,* R.M. McKeag, and A.M. Macnaghten, Eds. Cambridge University Press, Cambridge, 193–212.

Silberschatz, A. 1979. Communication and synchronization in distributed systems. *IEEE Transactions on Software Engineering 5,* 6 (November), 542–546.

Welsh, J., Sneeringer, W.J., and Hoare, C.A.R. 1977. Ambiguities and insecurities in Pascal. *Software—Practice and Experience 7,* 6 (November–December), 685–696.

Welsh, J., and Bustard, D.W. 1979. Pascal-Plus—Another language for modular multiprogramming. *Software—Practice and Experience 9,* 11 (November), 947–957.

Wirth, N. 1971. The programming language Pascal. *Acta Informatica 1,* 35–63.

Wirth, N. 1977. Modula—A language for modular multiprogramming. *Software—Practice and Experience 7,* 1 (January–February), 3–35.

Wirth, N. 1982. *Programming in Modula-2.* Springer-Verlag, New York.

19

A Multiprocessor Implementation
of Joyce[*]

(1989)

Joyce is a programming language for parallel computers based on CSP and Pascal. A Joyce program defines concurrent agents which communicate through unbuffered channels. This paper describes a multiprocessor implementation of Joyce.

1   Introduction

Joyce is a programming language for parallel computers based on CSP and Pascal (Wirth 1971; Hoare 1978; Brinch Hansen 1987a). A Joyce program defines concurrent agents which communicate through unbuffered channels. The Joyce compiler is a Pascal program that generates portable code. A small kernel written in assembly language interprets the Joyce code.

The first Joyce kernel was written for a single processor, the IBM PC (Brinch Hansen 1987b). This paper describes the Joyce kernel for a multiprocessor, the Encore Multimax (Encore Corp. 1987). The main difference between the two kernels is the addition of load balancing and locks in the multiprocessor version. This paper is a completely revised version of Brinch Hansen (1987b). The multiprocessor implementation was guided by performance experiments described in Brinch Hansen (1988).

2   Language Concepts

The following is a brief summary of the concurrent programming concepts of Joyce.

---
[*]P. Brinch Hansen, A multiprocessor implementation of Joyce. *Software—Practice and Experience 19*, 6 (June 1989), 579–592. Copyright © 1989, Per Brinch Hansen. Reprinted by permission.

Agents

A Joyce program consists of nested procedures which define concurrent processes known as agents. When the execution of a program begins, a single, initial agent is automatically activated. Any agent p may activate other agents which are known as the subagents of p.

An agent procedure

> **agent** Q(formal parameters);
> **var** uninitialized variables;
> **begin** SL **end**;

defines a class of identical agents called Q agents. The formal parameters are value parameters only.

When an agent p executes an agent statement

> Q(actual parameters)

it activates a new subagent q defined by the procedure Q. The activation creates a new instance of every variable defined in Q. These variable instances are called the own variables of the new agent and are inaccessible to other agents. The formal parameters of q are assigned the values obtained by evaluating the corresponding actual parameters. The other variables of q are uninitialized.

The agent q executes the statement SL defined by its procedure and waits until all its subagents (if any) have terminated. At this point, the own variables of the agent (and all channels created by the agent) cease to exist, and the agent terminates.

An agent procedure Q may be recursive. Every activation of Q creates a new agent with its own variables.

Channels and ports

Agents exchange symbols through unbuffered channels. Every symbol has a name and may carry a message. A channel can transfer a finite set of symbols only known as the channel alphabet.

The type definition

> **type** $T = [s_1(T_1),\ s_2(T_2),\ \ldots,\ s_n(T_n)]$;

defines a channel alphabet consisting of symbols named $s_1, s_2, \ldots, s_n$. These symbols carry messages of types $T_1, T_2, \ldots, T_n$, respectively.

An agent accesses a channel through a local variable

$$c\colon T$$

which points to the channel. The variable c is known as a port variable and its type T is called a port type. (The channel itself is not a variable, but a communication device.)

The creation of a new channel is called the activation of the channel. When an agent p executes a port statement

$$+c$$

a new channel with the alphabet given by type T is created and a pointer to the channel is assigned to the port variable c. The channel is known as an internal channel of p.

If an agent p activates a subagent q using a port variable c as an actual parameter, c denotes a channel which is accessible to both p and q. The channel is known as an external channel of q.

Input/output

A communication between two agents takes place when one of them is ready to execute an output statement

$$b!s_i(e)$$

and the other one is ready to execute an input statement

$$c?s_i(v)$$

where

1. b and c are port variables of the same type T which point to the same channel.

2. s_i is the name of a symbol in the alphabet of T. The symbol carries a message of type T_i.

3. e is an expression and v is a variable of type T_i.

When two agents are ready to execute the above statements, the agents are said to match and a communication between them is said to be feasible. The communication consists of assigning the value of e to v.

An input/output statement delays an agent until the corresponding communication has taken place.

Two or more agents may share the same channel, but the channel handles only one communication at a time. If agents waiting to communicate can be matched in several different ways, the channel will arbitrarily select two matching agents at a time and let them communicate.

Polling

An agent may poll one or more channels until it finds that a communication is feasible on one of them. A polling statement

$$\textbf{poll } G_1 \mid G_2 \mid \ldots \mid G_n \textbf{ end}$$

delays an agent until exactly one of the guarded statements $G_1, G_2, \ldots, G_n$ has been executed. Every guarded statement is either a guarded output statement or a guarded input statement.

A guarded output statement

$$c!s_i(e) \ \& \ B \ -> \ SL$$

consists of an output statement $c!s_i(e)$, a boolean expression B and a statement SL. The guarded statement is executed only if the output is feasible and B denotes true. The execution consists of performing the output followed by execution of SL.

Similarly, a guarded input statement

$$c?s_i(v) \ \& \ B \ -> \ SL$$

is executed only if the input $c?s_i(v)$ is feasible and B denotes true. The execution consists of performing the input and then executing SL.

An agent delayed by a polling statement can be matched only by another agent that executes an input/output statement. It cannot be matched by another agent waiting to execute a polling statement.

3   Multiprocessor

The Encore Multimax 320 at Syracuse University is a multiprocessor with 18 NS32332 processors. A shared bus connects the processors to a shared memory of 128 Mbytes.

Each processor has a local cache of 64 Kbytes. The cache reduces the load on the shared bus by maintaining local copies of memory locations accessed by the processor.

When a processor needs the value of a memory location, it attempts to fetch the value from its cache. If the cache does not contain a copy of the location, its value is read from the memory and stored in the cache.

When a processor writes a value into a memory location, the value is stored in both the local cache and the memory. If other caches contain previous copies of the same location, these copies are removed.

Any memory location can be used as a spinlock to ensure that processors do not access shared data structures simultaneously. When waiting on a closed lock, a processor first reads the value of the lock into its cache, and then fetches it repeatedly from the cache until another processor changes the lock by opening it.

4   Agent Implementation

The multiprocessor system uses the same memory allocation scheme as the single-processor system. Data structures representing agents and channels are kept in memory where they can be accessed by every processor. The most challenging problem of the multiprocessor implementation is to distribute the workload evenly among the processors.

Program stack

The memory allocation is inspired by the well-known method for implementing recursive, sequential procedures: it uses dynamic allocation of fixed-length segments which are not relocated during their existence.

When an agent (or channel) is activated, it is assigned a fixed segment of memory known as an activation record. An activation record is either an agent record or a channel record. The length of an activation record is determined during compilation.

The creator–subagent relation between agents defines a tree structure in which every agent (and channel) is placed immediately below its creator.

The initial agent is the root of the tree. Since every agent exists at least as long as its subagents (and internal channels), the tree shrinks from the top towards the bottom. More precisely, in every directed branch from a leaf to the root, the agents (and channels) are activated and terminated in LIFO order. Consequently, the activation records form a tree-structured stack. The problem is to allocate this tree-structured stack in a linear memory.

We use a surprisingly simple method for doing this. The method works very well for a large class of interesting programs (but not for all programs). The memory is organized as a single stack of activation records called the program stack.

When an agent (or channel) is activated, its activation record is pushed on top of the program stack and the agent (or channel) is now said to be active. Every agent is linked to its creator and keeps track of how many active subagents it currently has. An agent also keeps a linked list of its internal channels.

When an agent terminates, it becomes passive and all its internal channels are marked as being dead. When all its subagents are dead, a passive agent is also marked as dead. A processor removes a dead activation record only when it is at the top of the program stack.

The program stack has a single lock that prevents processors from removing activation records simultaneously. The processors do not lock the stack during the execution of agents.

Agent records

An agent record represents an agent p and consists of four parts:

1. An agent state (defined below).

2. The own variables of p (formal parameters and uninitialized variables).

3. The expression stack of p.

4. The length of the agent record.

The agent state is defined by the following fields:

1. Phase: an agent is either active, passive or dead.

2. Creator: a pointer to the agent record (if any) which represents the creator of p. (The initial agent is the only agent that has no creator.)

3. Subagents: the number of active subagents of p.

4. Channel list: a pointer to a channel record (if any) created by p. This is the beginning of a linked list of all channel records created by p.

5. Queue links: if p is waiting in a queue, the queue links point to the two agents which precede and follow p in the queue.

6. Register values: if p is waiting in a queue, this field holds the current values of the instruction counter and the expression stack pointer of p.

During its lifetime, an agent goes through three phases:

1. Active: the agent has not yet reached the end of its procedure.

2. Passive: the agent is waiting for the termination of its subagents.

3. Dead: the agent and its subagents have terminated. The activation record of the agent (and its internal channels) may be removed from the program stack. These records are not removed until they are at the top of the stack. This may occur immediately after the termination of a given agent, or later, when another agent terminates.

Ready queues

The agent currently being executed by a processor P is called the running agent of P and is represented by a pointer to the corresponding agent record.

Agents that are ready to run wait in FIFO queues called ready queues. Every processor has its own ready queue. The use of multiple ready queues is essential for the performance of parallel programs (Brinch Hansen 1988).

The ready queue of a processor P consists of three parts:

1. An agent queue (described below).

2. The queue length defines the number of agents currently served by P. This is the number of agents waiting in the ready queue plus the running agent of P (if any).

3. A lock associated with the queue enables other processors to enter agents in the queue in order to distribute a parallel computation evenly among the processors.

The agent records in a queue form a doubly-linked list. The queue is represented by a single pointer to the agent record (if any) at the head of the queue.

Processor scheduling

At the beginning of a program execution, one of the processors creates the initial agent and starts executing it. The other processors are initially idle.

An idle processor inspects its own ready queue continuously until the program execution is stopped by another processor or the queue is non-empty. At this point, the processor either selects a running agent from the queue or terminates.

An empty queue becomes non-empty only if another processor enters an agent in the queue in order to balance the computational load of the multiprocessor.

A shared stop signal indicates whether the multiprocessor should stop or continue its execution of agents. When a processor detects termination (or failure) of the program execution, it sets the stop signal.

The scheduling algorithm of an idle processor is called

Select a running agent (if any)

and is defined as follows

1. LOCK own ready queue;
2. **while not** stop **and** the ready queue is empty **do**
      begin
         UNLOCK ready queue;
         Delay;
         LOCK ready queue
      end;
3. **if not** stop **then**
      begin
         Remove an agent from the ready queue
         and make it the running agent;
         UNLOCK the ready queue
      end
   else
      begin
         UNLOCK the ready queue;

Terminate the processor
>   **end**

The temporary unlocking of the ready queue in step 2 enables another processor to lock the same queue and enter an agent in the queue. To avoid locking conflicts, an idle processor delays itself by executing the following loop without locking its ready queue:

Delay:
>   **while not** stop **and** the ready queue is empty **do**
>   {skip}

When a processor enters an agent q in the ready queue, it executes a scheduling algorithm called

>   Resume the agent q

which is defined below:

1. Find the shortest ready queue;
2. LOCK the ready queue;
3. Enter the agent q in the ready queue;
4. UNLOCK the ready queue.

The processors attempt to distribute the workload evenly among themselves by keeping all ready queues of the same length. The abstract algorithms shown here do not include the obvious updating of the ready queue lengths.

While a processor examines all ready queues to find the shortest one, it does not lock and unlock each queue. This prevents unnecessary delays of idle processors that are ready to lock their own queues and select running agents. Occasionally two processors may select the same queue mistakenly, but this will only make the queue slightly longer than it should have been for a short period.

A processor executes a running agent until one of the following events occurs:

1. The agent reaches the end of its procedure.

2. The agent reaches an input/output statement that cannot be completed at the moment.

3. The agent reaches a polling statement that cannot be completed yet.

The scheduling actions taken after each of these events will be explained in the following.

Agent activation

A running agent p executes an agent statement

$$Q(\text{actual parameters})$$

in seven steps:

1. Evaluate the actual parameters in the expression stack of p;
2. LOCK the program stack;
3. Push a new agent record q on the program stack and initialize the state fields of q;
4. Pop the actual parameter values from the expression stack of p and assign the values to the formal parameter part of q;
5. Resume the agent q;
6. Increment the number of subagents of p by 1;
7. UNLOCK the program stack.

During the activation of an agent, the "uninitialized" variables are set to zero, which represents a nil pointer. This enables the kernel to detect any attempt by the agent to communicate through a non-existing channel.

Agent termination

When a running agent reaches the end of its procedure, its processor executes the following algorithm:

1. LOCK the program stack;
2. Let p initially be the running agent and mark p as passive;
3. **while** p is a passive agent with no subagents **do**
   begin
      for each internal channel of p **do**
        begin
          LOCK the channel;
          Mark the channel as dead;
          UNLOCK the channel

          end;
        Mark p as dead;
        if p has a creator **then**
           begin {p is not the initial agent}
             $p :=$ creator of p;
             Decrement the subagents of p by 1
           end
        end;
4. **while** there is a dead activation record
     at the top of the program stack **do**
       Pop the record;
5. **if** the program stack is empty **then** stop := true;
6. UNLOCK the program stack;
7. Select a running agent (if any).

Every channel has its own lock. The first and last fields of any activation record define the phase and length of an agent (or channel). This convention simplifies the popping of dead records from the program stack.

5   Channel Implementation

The implementation of channels also attempts to combine simplicity with efficiency:

1. A message is always copied directly from the activation record of the output agent to the activation record of the input agent without the use of an intermediate buffer.

2. A communication between two matching agents requires only that one of the processors executing the two agents perform a single context switch from one of the agents to another agent. (If one of the agents is polling, several context switches may be necessary.)

These objectives are achieved by allocating a separate queue for each symbol in the alphabet of a channel x. When an agent p is ready to output (or input) a symbol s_i through x, it examines the corresponding symbol queue to determine if a matching agent q is waiting to participate in the communication. In that case, p obtains the address of the input variable v and the output value e from the expression stacks of p and q, assigns e to v, and resumes q by moving it to the shortest ready queue. However, if p

does not find a matching agent, p enters the symbol queue and waits until a matching agent completes the communication and resumes p.

Since a channel may be used by more than two agents, an agent must be able to determine whether the agents in a symbol queue are waiting to input or output the corresponding symbol. Notice that a symbol queue cannot hold both input and output agents simultaneously. It is therefore sufficient to supplement every queue with a boolean indicating whether the queue holds input or output agents when it is non-empty. The solution we have used is to associate both an input and an output queue with every symbol. The amount of memory is the same in both cases: a single word.

Communicating agents circulate between ready queues and channel queues until they terminate. Since agents are resumed in the shortest ready queues, they tend to migrate from one processor to another as the load changes. The migration is trivial to implement because each processor can access any activation record and queue in memory.

Channel records

A channel record represents a channel x created by an agent p. The record consists of five parts:

1. A channel phase indicating whether x is active or dead.

2. A lock associated with the channel.

3. A channel pointer which links the channel record to another channel record (if any) created by p. The agent record of p contains the beginning of this chain of internal channels.

4. The channel queues consist of a pair of queues for every symbol s_i in the channel alphabet: a queue of agents waiting to input s_i through x and a queue of agents waiting to output s_i through x. The agents waiting in a queue form a doubly linked list. Each queue is represented by a single pointer to the agent (if any) at the head of the queue.

5. The length of the channel record.

Channel activation

A running agent p executes a port statement

$$+c$$

in six steps:

1. Push the address of the port variable c on the expression stack of p;
2. LOCK the program stack;
3. Push a new channel record on the program stack, mark it as active with an open lock, and make the channel queues empty;
4. Link the channel record to the agent record of p;
5. UNLOCK the program stack;
6. Assign the channel pointer to the variable c and pop the address of c from the stack of p;

Input/output

When a running agent p reaches an output statement

$$c!s_i(e)$$

its processor does the following:

1. Push the channel pointer c and the output value e on the expression stack of p;
2. LOCK the channel denoted by c;
3. **with** the channel queues of symbol s_i **do**
    if the input queue of s_i is non-empty **then**
      begin
        Remove an agent q from the input queue;
        UNLOCK the channel;
        Pop the address of the input variable v
        and c from the stack of q;
        Pop the output value e and c from the
        stack of p and assign e to v;
        Resume the agent q
      end
    else
      begin
        Enter p in the output queue;

UNLOCK the channel;
Select a running agent (if any)
end

A processor executes an input statement

$$c?s_i(v)$$

of the running agent p as follows:

1. Push the channel pointer c and the address of
   the input variable v on the expression stack
   of p;
2. LOCK the channel denoted by c;
3. **with** the channel queues of symbol s_i **do**
   if the output queue of s_i is non-empty **then**
   begin
   Remove an agent q from the output queue;
   UNLOCK the channel;
   Pop the address of v and c from the stack
   of p;
   Pop the output value e and c from the
   stack of q and assign e to v;
   Resume the agent q
   end
   else
   begin
   Enter p in the input queue;
   UNLOCK the channel;
   Select a running agent (if any)
   end

Polling

Polling may involve repeated examination of channel queues until a matching
agent is found. It is therefore particularly important to reduce the overhead
of context switching and channel examination as much as possible.

We use the following method: when an agent p has examined all guarded
statements in a polling statement without success, p re-enters the ready
queue of its current processor in the hope that a matching agent will enter

an appropriate symbol queue before p gets another chance to examine the same guarded statements.

More precisely, when a running agent p reaches a guarded output statement

$$c!s_i(e) \mathbin{\&} B \mathbin{->} SL$$

its processor performs the following actions:

1. Push c, e and B on the expression stack of p;
2. LOCK the channel denoted by c;
3. **with** the channel queues of symbol s_i **do**
       if the input queue of s_i is non-empty **and** B **then**
         begin
           Remove an agent q from the input queue;
           UNLOCK the channel;
           Pop the address of the input variable v
           and c from the stack of q;
           Pop B, e and c from the stack of p and
           assign e to v;
           Resume the agent q;
           SL;
           Go to the end of the polling statement
         end
       else
         begin
           UNLOCK the channel;
           Pop B, e and c from the stack of p;
           Go to another guarded statement
         end

where

             Go to another guarded statement

stands for one of the following actions:

1. If a guarded statement G_i is followed by another guarded statement G_{i+1} in the same polling statement, then go to G_{i+1}.

2. Otherwise, set the instruction counter of p at the beginning of the first guarded statement G_1 in the polling statement, re-enter p in the ready queue of its current processor, and select a running agent from the ready queue. When the execution of p is resumed, it will repeat the examination of the same guarded statements beginning with G_1.

Notice that the examination of a guarded statement has no effect if it cannot be executed.

The execution of a guarded input statement is very similar.

System channel

A Joyce program communicates with the computer peripherals through a predefined channel known as the system channel. The initial agent has access to this channel through an actual parameter initialized by the kernel. A communication through this channel is implemented by a system procedure which performs the corresponding peripheral operation. The system channel has its own lock.

6   Locks

When a processor needs simultaneous access to several shared data structures, it locks them one at a time in fixed order to prevent deadlock (Brinch Hansen 1973):

1. The program stack.

2. A channel activated by an agent.

3. A ready queue.

4. The system channel.

As an example, during the activation of a new agent, a processor locks the program stack before locking the ready queue in which the agent is entered. Similarly, during the termination of an agent, a processor locks the program stack before locking any channel created by the agent.

Since the system channel has the lowest priority, a processor can lock it during any kernel operation and display a trace of a significant event, such as the activation or termination of an agent or channel or the completion of a communication.

The numbers of ready queues and locks used are based on performance experiments described in Brinch Hansen (1988).

7   Unix Interface

The Joyce kernel runs under Umax 4.2, a Multimax version of the Berkeley Unix system (Encore Corp. 1987).

Initially a user communicates with a single Unix process called the master process. When the user decides to run a Joyce program on p processors, the master process creates p additional Unix processes known as the Joyce processors. The Joyce processors share two memory segments which contain the kernel, the Joyce program, the program stack and p ready queues. In addition, every Joyce processor has a local memory segment for its own temporaries.

Every Joyce processor has a unique index which identifies its ready queue. To begin with, one of the processors creates the initial agent and starts executing it. The other processors remain idle until agents arrive in their queues (or the program execution is stopped).

A Joyce processor stops the program execution by setting the stop signal and performing an exit operation. This wakes up the master process, which then kills every Joyce processor and terminates itself.

A Joyce program has access to two text files: an input file and an output file. The program accesses these files through the system channel. Communication through the system channel is performed by means of Unix procedures.

8   Execution Times

Table 1 illustrates the performance that can be achieved by a portable implementation of a parallel programming language. The execution times of Joyce programs running on an Encore Multimax 320 are expressed in terms of

c: the number of channels activated by an agent.
m: the number of simple components in a structured operand.
n: the number of iterations.
p: the number of processors used.
s: the number of symbols in a channel alphabet.

Table 1 Execution times (μs).

	Simple operands (1 word)	Real operands (2 words)	Structured operands (m words)
Constant	4.1	7	$15 + 2.8m$
Variable address	4.8	5	5
Variable value	4.8	8	$14 + 1.2m$
$v[i]$ address	23	23	23
$v[i]$ value	27	30	$32 + 1.2m$
:=	4.7	7	$9 + 1.2m$
$< = > <= <> >=$	4.7	9	$11 + 2.7m$
$-$ sign	5.1	8	
$+ -$	5.5	9	
$*$	9.0	9	
/ div mod	12	13	
and or	4.2		
not	3.8		
real(i)	13		
integer(i)		15	
$v!s(i)\ v?s(i)$	$93 + 5.2p$	$95 + 5.2p$	$96 + 1.7m + 5.2p$

The input/output times increase with the message length m and the number of processors p. When a processor resumes a communicating agent it examines all ready queues to find the shortest one and changes the length of that queue. Since all processors examine the ready queues, any change will eventually force all of them to refetch the updated queue length from memory. So the search and refetching both introduce communication overhead proportional to the number of processors. This overhead effectively limits the speedup of Joyce programs when the number of processors is increased.

Other execution times are:

Port statement $+v$	$44 + 7.6s$
Agent statement $P(e)$	$160 + e$
Agent termination	$110 + 42c$
if B then S_1	$8.5 + B + S_1$ or
else S_2	$5.3 + B + S_2$
while B do S	$5.3 + B + (8.5 + B + S)n$
Empty program	$10000 + 60000p$

The execution time of an agent statement is the activation time of an agent with a small number of own variables, such as the sorting agent defined in Brinch Hansen (1987a).

The execution time of an empty program is mainly the overhead required to activate and terminate p Unix processes.

9   Final Remarks

We have moved the parallel programming language Joyce from a single processor to a multiprocessor. We now plan to use the multiprocessor implementation for scientific and engineering computations.

Acknowledgements

Anand Rangachari reprogrammed the Joyce kernel for the Encore Multimax. It is a pleasure to acknowledge the constructive comments of Birger Andersen, Gideon Frieder and Anand Rangachari. This work was conducted using the computational resources of the Northeast Parallel Architectures Center (NPAC) at Syracuse University, which is funded by DARPA, under contract to Rome Air Development Center (RADC), Griffis AFB, NY.

References

Brinch Hansen, P. 1973. *Operating System Principles*. Prentice-Hall, Englewood Cliffs, NJ.

Brinch Hansen, P. 1987a. Joyce—A programming language for distributed systems. *Software—Practice and Experience 17*, 1 (January), 29–50. *Article 18*.

Brinch Hansen, P. 1987b. A Joyce implementation. *Software—Practice and Experience 17*, 4 (April), 267–276.

Brinch Hansen, P., and Rangachari, A. 1988. Joyce performance on a multiprocessor. School of Computer and Information Science, Syracuse University, Syracuse, NY.

Encore Corp. 1987. *Multimax Technical Summary*. Encore Computer Corporation, Marlboro, MA.

Hoare, C.A.R. 1978. Communicating sequential processes. *Communications of the ACM 21*, 8 (August), 666–677.

Wirth, N. 1971. The programming language Pascal. *Acta Informatica 1*, 35–63.

The Nature of Parallel Programming[*]

(1989)

Parallel programming is the art of writing programs for computers that perform many operations simultaneously. This essay discusses the nature of parallel programming without going into technical details. It uses a sorting problem
to illustrate what it means to solve a problem in parallel, how we write parallel programs, how parallel computers execute them, and how fast they run.
The author expects that scientific users of parallel computers may find ease of
programming more important than maximum performance. He suggests ways
of making this possible.

Asking the right questions

As a computer scientist I have been fascinated by parallel programming since
I first encountered it twenty-five years ago. I welcome this opportunity to
explain the essence of my field to scientists and engineers.

Parallel programming is the art of writing programs for computers that
perform many operations simultaneously. Parallel computers with tens and
hundreds of processors are already commercially available. Researchers are
now working on computers with thousands of processors. Programming
these machines sounds like an exciting idea until you try it. It is often too
complicated, but for the wrong reason: Most of our programming languages
and computer architectures do not really support parallelism as well as they
could.

In this essay I will discuss the nature of parallel programming without
going into technical details. It seems natural to begin by asking some fundamental questions:

[*]P. Brinch Hansen, The nature of parallel programming. Inaugural Symposium at Syracuse University, Syracuse, NY, March 1989. In *Natural and Artificial Parallel Computation*, M.A. Arbib and J.A. Robinson, Eds. The MIT Press, Cambridge, MA, (1990), 31–46.
Copyright © 1990, Massachusetts Institute of Technology. Reprinted by permission.

- What does it mean to solve problems in parallel?

- How do we write parallel programs?

- How do parallel computers execute such programs?

- How fast can parallel programs run?

- Can we make parallel programming easier?

I will try to answer these questions by stripping away the inessentials and penetrating to the core of the problem.

One step at a time

A well-chosen example is often an important source of insight. I will use a sorting problem to illustrate the ideas of parallel programming. Once you understand these ideas, the example becomes merely a detail in the great scheme of things.

Bridge players often sort their hands by picking up one card at a time and inserting it where it belongs. This is the simplest way to sort a small number of cards. But, if you are sorting thousands of cards, there are much faster methods.

One of them is called *merge sorting*. As early as 1945 John von Neumann wrote computer programs for merge sorting. Let me describe how you would use this method to sort eight numbers manually:

Write each number on a separate card and place the cards in front of you in any order

Pick up two cards at a time and put them down as an ordered pair of cards. You now have four ordered pairs

Take the first two pairs

and merge them into a single, ordered sequence of four cards

Then combine the last two pairs into an ordered sequence

Finally merge the two ordered sequences of four cards each into a single, ordered sequence of eight cards

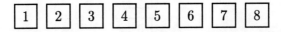

This completes the sorting.

Let me explain the merging more carefully. The first card in the merged sequence is the smallest of the eight cards. Since the two original sequences are ordered, the smallest card is the first card of one of these sequences. Take this card and place it below the two sequences as the first card of the merged sequence

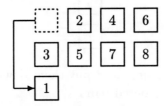

Continue to remove the smallest remaining card and add it to the merged sequence until one of the original sequences is empty

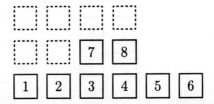

Then add the rest of other sequence to the merged one.

The mergesort works by repeatedly merging shorter, ordered sequences into longer ones. Eight sequences of length 1 are merged into four sequences of length 2, which, in turn, are merged into two sequences of length 4, and finally into one sequence of length 8. You can picture the sorting process as a tree of merging steps

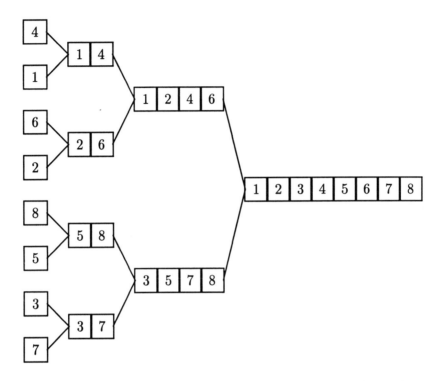

I have described merge sorting as a *sequential process* performed one step at a time. This is indeed how it would be done on a traditional computer. Merge sorting can, however, be speeded up by performing the merging steps simultaneously on a parallel computer.

Running in parallel

The mergesort solves a problem by dividing it into smaller instances of the same problem. The subproblems can be solved independently of one another. This property makes the algorithm well-suited for parallel execution.

We can build a parallel computer that sorts eight numbers. This machine is organized as a *tree*. It consists of 15 processors connected by 16 communication channels. The processors and channels are drawn as circles and arrows

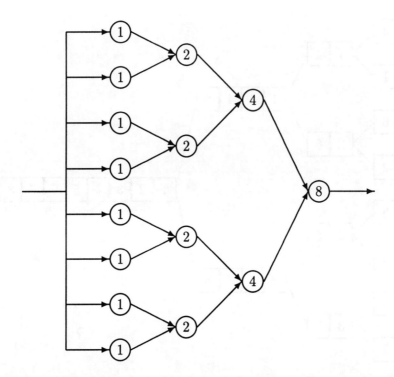

The eight processors on the left are the *leaves* of the tree. The single processor on the right is the *root* of the whole tree. Each processor in the middle is the root of a smaller tree within the larger one.

The eight numbers move from left to right in the tree. Each leaf receives a single number from a shared channel and sends it to its successor in the tree. Each root receives two sequences of numbers from its predecessors and sends them as a merged sequence to its successor. The main root sends the eight numbers through a channel is ascending order. Each processor merges either 1, 2, 4 or 8 numbers as shown in the circles.

The processors operate in parallel. Processors which are at the same vertical *level* in the tree communicate simultaneously with their neighbors. Each root holds only two numbers at a time. When a root has sent a number to the right, it immediately receives another one from the left. Meanwhile its successors can process the previous number.

In general when a tree machine sorts N numbers, we will simplify the discussion a bit by assuming that N is a power of two. In other words, N is a number in the series

$$1, 2, 4, 8, \ldots, 1024, \ldots$$

Since the number of processors doubles from one level to the next, the total number of processors in the tree machine is $1 + 2 + 4 + \cdots + N$. This adds up to $2N-1$. So the tree machine needs 2047 processors to sort 1024 numbers. If N is large the number of processors is almost 2N.

In practice we do not always have two separate processors and channels for each of the sorted numbers. We often have a parallel computer with a much smaller number of processors and channels. We use these processors and channels to *simulate* a large number of slower processors and channels. This simulation is a crucial part of the implementation of a programming language for parallel programming.

Getting down to fundamentals

A parallel computation may involve millions of small steps. The mind obviously cannot comprehend such a multitude of simultaneous events in detail. We must impose order on the complexity by describing it in terms of a small number of general concepts. The most important *abstractions* in parallel programming are processes and communication.

A *process* is an abstract model of a computation. A sequential process is a sequence of steps which take place one at a time. A parallel process is a set of processes performed simultaneously. And a *communication* is a transfer of data from one process to another. These concepts are the essence of parallel programming. The rest is detail.

From now on we will view the parallel mergesort as a tree of processes. Whether these processes run on real or simulated processors is a technical detail.

When you have discovered powerful thinking tools, it becomes essential to express them in a *concise notation*. For parallel computations we need a programming language which can describe individual processes and combinations of processes precisely. I will not discuss the merits of particular programming languages. Instead I have invented a simple notation which will give you the flavor of a parallel language.

The simplest processes in a parallel merge tree are the sequential leaves. A leaf is connected to two channels.

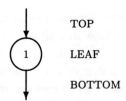

All leaves behave in the same way. We can therefore write a single procedure that describes the behavior of these identical processes. In a programming language this procedure might look as follows

$$\text{LEAF(top, bottom)} =$$
1. receive(x, top);
2. send(x, bottom).

The notational details are unimportant. The procedure consists of two numbered steps. Each step describes an action performed by a leaf:

1. Receive a number x through the top channel.

2. Send the same number through the bottom channel.

When a leaf has done this, it terminates and ceases to exist.

From a user's point of view a sorting tree is a single process that receives N numbers through one channel and sends them in ascending order through another channel.

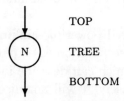

A closer look reveals that a sorting process takes one of two forms. A tree that "sorts" one number only is just a single leaf. A tree that sorts more than one number consists of a root process and two smaller trees connected by a left and a right channel.

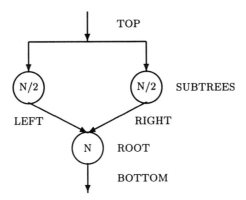

In this picture each subtree is viewed as a single process. Internally it may be composed of other processes, but right now we choose to ignore these details.

The following procedure defines the behavior of a tree that sorts N numbers:

TREE(N, top, bottom) =
  if N = 1 **run** LEAF(top, bottom)
  if N > 1 **run**
          TREE(N/2, top, left),
          TREE(N/2, top, right),
          ROOT(N, left, right, bottom)
       in parallel

Again the programming symbols are not important. Here is what they mean:

1. If N = 1 a tree is just a single leaf. The effect of the command

    run LEAF(top, bottom)

    is to activate a leaf process with access to the top and bottom channels of the tree. When the leaf terminates, the tree ceases to exist.

2. If N > 1 a tree splits into two subtrees and a root process running in parallel. When all three processes have terminated, the whole tree disappears.

The above procedure defines a tree in terms of smaller trees. A parallel process which is defined in terms of other processes of the same kind is called a *recursive process*.

A root is a sequential process that receives two ordered sequences from a left and a right channel and sends a merged sequence through a bottom channel. I will omit the programming details of this process and describe it in English.

ROOT(N, left, right, bottom) =
1. Receive the first left and right numbers.
2. Send the smaller of the two through the bottom channel and replace it by the next number (if any) from the same left or right sequence;
3. Repeat step 2 until the left or right sequence is empty;
4. Copy the rest (if any) of the other left or right sequence.

Parallelism is a mechanism for splitting larger computations into smaller ones which can be performed simultaneously. A notation for recursive processes is essential in a parallel programming language. The reason is simple. In a highly parallel program it is impractical to formulate thousands of processes with different behaviors. We must instead rely on repeated use of a small number of behaviors. The simplest problems that satisfy this requirement are those that can be reduced to smaller problems of the same kind and solved by combining the partial results. Recursion is the natural programming tool for expressing these *divide and conquer* algorithms.

A good programming language has an air of economy and an element of surprise. The economy comes from using a small number of concepts: processes, channels and communication. The surprise is the elegance and utility of recursive, parallel processes. This wonderful concept can be used not only for sorting, but also for fast Fourier transforms, N-body simulation, computational geometry and matrix multiplication on parallel computers.

Hidden complexity

A programming language should hide irrelevant details of computer hardware and support more abstract models of computation efficiently. You will immediately appreciate the significance of this requirement if you catch a glimpse of what really happens when a parallel computer executes a program.

In a parallel computation the number of processes often exceeds the number of physical processors. This is only too obvious when you run thousands of processes on a parallel computer with ten processors only. Programs that are more parallel than the computer itself are executed by switching the processors rapidly between processes to give the illusion that they are executed simultaneously on a slower, parallel computer.

The simplest kind of parallel computer is a *multiprocessor* which consists of tens of processors connected to a common memory. A language implementer views a multiprocessor as a *queueing system* with a finite population of customers (the processes) and multiple servers (the processors).

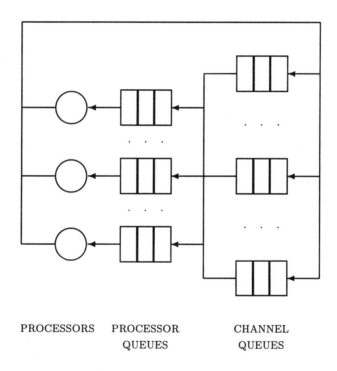

PROCESSORS   PROCESSOR   CHANNEL
              QUEUES   QUEUES

In the common memory each process is represented by a small block of memory called a *process record*. This record holds the parameters and local variables of the process. Each processor has a separate queue of processes that are ready to run. The queue is a list of process records chained together.

An idle processor removes a process from its queue and executes it until the process, for example, is ready to send a message through a channel. The processor then puts the process in a queue associated with the channel. Immediately afterwards the processor resumes the execution of another process from its own queue.

When a process is ready to receive from the same channel, a message is copied from the record of the sending process to the record of the receiving process. The delayed process is then moved from the channel queue to one of the processor queues. Sooner or later the corresponding processor resumes the execution of the process.

To achieve the highest performance of a parallel computer it is important to divide a computation evenly among the processors, so that all of them can work at full speed whenever possible. This is called *load balancing*.

On a multiprocessor it is easy to balance the load, if the processors share a table defining the lengths of all processor queues. When a processor removes a process from a channel queue, it scans the table and puts that process in the shortest processor queue. Load balancing is in effect achieved by letting communicating processes *migrate* from processor to processor.

If several processors simultaneously attempt to manipulate the same queue, they must be forced to do it one at a time in unpredictable order. So parallelism introduces an element of chance in computation. The study of machines with *nondeterministic* behavior is still a fertile area of research in computer science.

A well-designed programming language enables the programmer to ignore these implementation details of processes and communications. However, the programmer cannot ignore the efficiency of the language implementation.

Limits to parallelism

The parallel mergesort is not particularly efficient. To understand why, we need a theoretical model of its performance.

The most critical performance figures for a highly parallel program are the execution times of process activation, communication and termination. We will assume that each of these steps takes exactly one unit of time. This is a reasonable approximation for the parallel mergesort written in the programming language Joyce and executed on a multiprocessor (the Encore Multimax).

It is customary to compare the running time T_1 of a parallel program on a single processor with its running time T_p on p processors.

For large N the *serial running time* is approximately

$$T_1 = N(L + 5) \text{ units}$$

where L is the number of process *levels* in the tree. T_1 includes the activation and termination of 2N processes and the communication of N numbers through all levels in the tree. I cannot go into further details here. You will find them in Brinch Hansen (1989b). For mathematically inclined readers: It turns out that $L = \log N + 1$, where $\log N$ is the binary logarithm of N.

A tree that sorts 1024 numbers has 11 process levels. It takes 16384 time units to run the sorting on a single processor.

The *parallel running time* is approximately

$$T_p = N(3 + (L + 2)/p) \text{ units}$$

Most of the steps are now executed p times faster. But there are 3N steps which cannot be speeded up by the use of multiple processors. These serial steps can be attributed to the initial creation of the process tree and the sequential communications of the root. (See the paper cited above.)

The following figure shows the predicted and measured running times (in time units) for sorting 1024 numbers on 1 to 10 processors. The run times were measured on the Multimax.

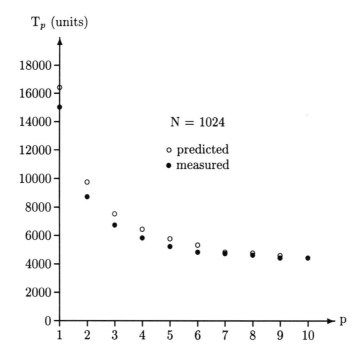

The *speedup* $S_p = T_1/T_p$ defines how much faster a program runs on p processors compared to a single processor. Ideally p processors should make a parallel program run p times faster. If the speedup is less than p, it means that some processors are idle part of the time.

The next figure shows the predicted and measured speedup of the parallel sorting of 1024 numbers. The approximate model is fairly accurate.

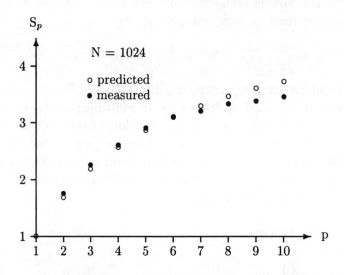

No matter how many processors you use, parallel merge sorting cannot be speeded up by more than

$$S_{max} = (L + 5)/3$$

For N = 1024 the maximum speedup is five only. The limiting factor is the number of serial steps in the parallel algorithm. This is known as *Amdahl's law*. Many other parallel algorithms have similar limitations.

As you add more processors, the algorithm runs slightly faster, but wastes more and more processor time. In practice one should probably stop adding more processors when

$$S_p = p/2$$

since more than half of the processing capacity will be wasted beyond this point. Consequently the speedup of the parallel mergesort is limited to

$$S_p = (L + 8)/6 \qquad \text{for } p = (L + 8)/3$$

For N = 1024 the sorting program runs only three times faster on six processors. And it does not pay to use more processors. This modest speedup is acceptable for parallel computers with tens of processors, but not for thousands of processors.

After this brief discussion of the nature of parallel programming it is time to draw conclusions.

Looking ahead

As we move from tens to thousands of processors, our parallel algorithms will often be unable to run that much faster. There is only one way out of this problem: We must perform numerous experiments with new algorithms until we know how to use highly parallel computers well.

Scientific computer users, who are primarily interested in getting numerical results fast, will constantly have to reprogram new parallel architectures and may become increasingly frustrated at the difficulty of doing this.

Parallel programs are often written in the conventional languages Fortran and C extended with subroutines for parallelism. To my taste these programs are difficult to read and lack the beauty which scientists expect of their own research. This state of affairs puts a scientist in an unreasonable dilemma: should you study the unnecessary complexity of existing programs or reinvent similar ones?

I am convinced that *the most important task in computational science is to make the programming of parallel computers easier.* This is even more important than increasing computational power, and we should be prepared to sacrifice some performance to solve the programming problem. With this important goal in mind, I propose three requirements for the next generation of parallel hardware and software.

- *Requirement 1:* Parallel programs must be written in abstract notations that hide irrelevant hardware detail and express parallelism concisely.

The essence of parallel computing is process creation and communication. These basic operations are implemented in software on most parallel computers. Consequently they are an order of magnitude slower than subroutine calls in Fortran. Due to the lack of hardware support for the process concept, the parallel mergesort is only slightly faster than the best sequential method for sorting (quicksort)!

- *Requirement 2*: Process creation and communication must be hardware operations which are only an order of magnitude slower than memory references.

In the future we can expect to see highly parallel programs which use a mixture of process structures simultaneously. Sorting trees and image meshes may, for example, coexist. A computation may also change its process structures from one phase to another. When a parallel program spawns numerous processes with changing topologies it is not meaningful to ask the programmer to specify on which processor each process should run. This leads me to the last requirement.

- *Requirement 3*: Most parallel computers must be able to distribute the computational load automatically with reasonable efficiency.

The driving force

I will end on a personal note. Parallel programming is not just about computation. It is about beautiful ideas that happen to be useful. The study of parallelism is driven by the same powerful ideas as the rest of science and mathematics. They are the concepts of *number*, *form*, *arrangement*, *movement* and *chance*. In mathematics, these notions led to arithmetic, geometry, combinatorics, calculus and probability. In parallel programming, they reappear as data, processes, networks, communication and nondeterminism.

The most enjoyable thing about computer programming is the insight it provides into the deep similarities of all creative endeavors.

Acknowledgements

This essay has been improved by valuable advice from Gideon Frider, Milena Hansen, Carlos Hartmann, Erik Hemmingsen, Anand Rangachari and Ernest Sibert.

This work was conducted using the computational resources of the Northeast Parallel Architectures Center (NPAC) at Syracuse University, which is funded by DARPA, under contract to Rome Air Development Center (RADC), Griffiss AFP, NY.

Digging deeper

Athas, W.C., and Seitz, C.L. 1988. Multicomputers: Message-passing concurrent computers. *IEEE Computer 21*, (August), 9–24. (A status report on a research project.)

Barnes, J., and Hut, P. 1986. A hierarchical O(NlogN) force calculation algorithm. *Nature 324*, (December), 446–449. (A parallel divide and conquer algorithm for the N-body problem.)

Bitton, D., DeWitt, D.J., Hsiao, D.K., and Menon, J. 1984. A taxonomy of parallel sorting. *ACM Computing Surveys 16*, (September), 287–318. (Includes sorting algorithms that are much faster than the parallel mergesort.)

Brinch Hansen, P. 1987. Joyce—A programming language for distributed systems. *Software—Practice and Experience 17*, 1 (January), 29–50. (Explains Joyce by examples.) *Article 18.*

Brinch Hansen, P. 1989a. A multiprocessor implementation of Joyce. *Software—Practice and Experience 19*, 6 (June), 579–592. (A detailed explanation of how parallel processes and communication channels are implemented.) *Article 19.*

Brinch Hansen, P. 1989b. Analysis of a parallel mergesort. School of Computer and Information Science, Syracuse University, Syracuse, NY. (An exact performance model of the parallel mergesort.)

Dally, W.J. 1987. *A VLSI Architecture for Concurrent Data Structures.* Kluwer Academic Publishers, Norwell, MA. (Proposes a programming language and a parallel computer based on message passing.)

Fox, G., Johnson, M., Lyzenga, G., Otto, S., Salmon, J., and Walker, D. 1988. *Solving Problems on Concurrent Processors*, Vol. 1. Prentice-Hall, Englewood Cliffs, NJ. (Explains how many scientific problems can be solved on hypercube architectures. Chapter 11 outlines a parallel divide and conquer algorithm for the fast Fourier transform.)

Gehani, N., and McGettrick, A.D. 1988. *Concurrent Programming.* Addison-Wesley, Reading, MA. (A collection of classical papers on parallel programming languages.)

Gustafson, J.L. 1988, The scaled-size model: A revision of Amdahl's law. *Supercomputing 88*, International Supercomputing Institute, St. Petersburg, FL, 130–133. (Reports impressive performance of parallel computations by redefining the meaning of speedup. The problem size is scaled up in proportion to the number of processors to finesse the limitations of Amdahl's law.)

Hillis, W.D. 1985. *The Connection Machine.* The MIT Press, Cambridge, MA. (A clear description of a revolutionary idea: A parallel architecture with 64,000 synchronous processors executing identical processes in lock step.)

Hoare, C.A.R. 1985. *Communication Sequential Processes.* Prentice-Hall, Englewood Cliffs, NJ. (A mathematical theory of communicating processes.)

Jenkins, R.A. 1989. New approaches in parallel computing. *Computers in Physics 3*, (January–February), 24–32. (A recent survey of parallel architectures.)

Kahn, G., and MacQueen, D.B. 1977. Coroutines and networks for parallel processes. In *Information Processing 77*, B. Gilchrist, Ed. North Holland Publishing, Amsterdam, The Netherlands, 993–998. (Presents an elegant parallel language with recursive processes.)

May, D. 1988. The influence of VLSI technology on computer architecture. *Supercomputing 88*, International Supercomputing Institute, St. Petersburg, FL, 247–256. (Includes a short overview of the nonrecursive language occam and the Transputer processor which has machine instructions for process creation, communication and termination.)

Preparata, F.P., and Shamos, M.I. 1985. *Computational Geometry: An Introduction.* Springer-Verlag, New York. (Chapter 3 describes a parallel divide and conquer algorithm for finding the convex hull of a finite set of points in the plane.)

Quinn, M.J. 1987. *Designing Efficient Algorithms for Parallel Computers.* McGraw-Hill, New York. (A short introduction to parallel sorting and searching, matrix multiplication, and graph algorithms.)

Whiddett, D. 1987. *Concurrent Programming for Software Engineers.* Halstead Press, New York. (Explains the three major paradigms for parallel programming: Monitors, message passing and remote procedures.)

21

Monitors and Concurrent Pascal:
A Personal History*

(1993)

This is a personal history of the early development of the monitor concept
and its implementation in the programming language Concurrent Pascal. The
paper explains how monitors evolved from the ideas of Dahl, Dijkstra, Hoare,
and the author (1971–73). At Caltech the author and his students developed
and implemented Concurrent Pascal and used it to write several model operating systems (1974–75). A portable implementation of Concurrent Pascal
was widely distributed and used for system design (1976–90). The monitor
paradigm was also disseminated in survey papers and text books. The author ends the story by expressing his own mixed feelings about monitors and
Concurrent Pascal.

1 A Programming Revolution

In the 1970s new programming languages were developed to express asynchronous, concurrent processes. These languages support the now familiar
paradigms for process communication known as *monitors, remote procedure
calls*, and *synchronous communication*. The most influential early idea was
the monitor concept and its implementation in the programming language
Concurrent Pascal.

   This is a personal history of how monitors and Concurrent Pascal were
invented. I have tried to write the history of an *idea*—how it arose and
spread through the scientific community. I have also described the struggles
of the creative process, how you grope your way through obscurities and
blind alleys until you find an elegant way of expressing an idea.

---

*P. Brinch Hansen, Monitors and Concurrent Pascal: A personal history. *2nd ACM
Conference on the History of Programming Languages*, Cambridge, MA, April 1993. In
SIGPLAN Notices 28, 3 (March 1993), 1–35. Copyright © 1993, Association for Comput-
ing Machinery, Inc. Reprinted by permission.

The story of Concurrent Pascal frequently refers to my own work. However, I have let other researchers assess the merits and flaws of the language through quotations from the published literature. At the end of the paper I express my own reservations about the monitor concept and Concurrent Pascal. The appendix includes the personal comments of computer scientists who reviewed earlier drafts of this paper.

As someone who participated in these discoveries, I cannot claim to have written a complete and unbiased history of these events. In many cases my knowledge of related work is derived solely from the literature. I hope that historians will take care of these flaws by comparing my story with other sources.

From my perspective there are three distinct phases in the early history of monitors:

1971–73. Monitors evolved from the ideas of Ole-Johan Dahl, Edsger Dijkstra, Tony Hoare, and me. In 1973 Hoare and I independently published programming notations for monitors.

1974–75. Working with a few students and a professional programmer at Caltech, I developed and implemented the first programming language with monitors. My ambition was to do for operating systems what Pascal (and other programming languages) had done for compilers: to reduce the programming effort by an order of magnitude compared to assembly language. This was indeed achieved for small operating systems (but not for larger ones).

1976–90. A portable implementation of Concurrent Pascal was widely distributed and used for system design. The monitor paradigm was now disseminated throughout the computer science community in survey papers and textbooks on operating systems, concurrent programming, and programming languages.

Each phase will be described in a separate section of the paper.

After 1975 the monitor concept inspired other researchers to develop verification rules, monitor variants, and more programming languages (Andrews 1983). Originally I intended to include a broad review of these later developments, which I know only from the literature. However, after writing several earlier drafts of this paper, I realized that I can only provide meaningful historical remarks on ideas and events that I have first-hand knowledge about. The reviewers' comments confirmed this impression.

I will therefore limit the scope of this personal history to the discovery of the monitor concept and the development and use of the first monitor language Concurrent Pascal. Since I can only speak for myself, I have not imposed the same restriction on the reviewers' comments quoted in the appendix.

2 Monitors

On the road toward monitors several alternatives were considered. It may be easier to appreciate the piecemeal discovery if I briefly summarize the final idea. Monitors enable concurrent processes to share data and resources in an orderly manner. A monitor is a combination of shared variables and procedures. Processes must call these procedures to operate on the shared variables. The monitor procedures, which are executed one at a time, may delay the calling processes until resources or data become available.

Beginner's luck

I started out in industry as a systems programmer for the Danish computer manufacturer Regnecentralen in Copenhagen. In 1967 I became responsible for the development of the RC 4000 multiprogramming system.

In the 1960s most operating systems were huge, unreliable programs that were extremely difficult to understand and modify. The RC 4000 system was a radical departure from this state of affairs. It was not a complete operating system, but a small kernel upon which operating systems for different purposes could be built in an orderly manner. The kernel provided the basic mechanisms for creating a hierarchy of parallel processes that communicated by messages. The idea of designing a general kernel for operating system design was due to Jørn Jensen, Søren Lauesen, and me (Brinch Hansen 1969).

I consider myself lucky to have started in industry. The RC 4000 project convinced me that a fundamental understanding of operating systems would change computer programming radically. I was so certain of this that I decided to leave industry and become a researcher.

In November 1970 I became a Research Associate in the Department of Computer Science at Carnegie-Mellon University. My goal was to write the first comprehensive textbook on operating system principles (Brinch Hansen 1973b).

As soon as I started writing, it became clear that I needed an algorithmic language to express operating system functions concisely without unneces-

sary trivia. In an outline of the book I explained my choice of description
language (Brinch Hansen 1971a):

> So far nearly all operating systems have been written partly
> or completely in machine language. This makes them unneces-
> sarily difficult to understand, test and modify. I believe it is
> desirable and possible to write efficient operating systems almost
> entirely in a *high-level language*. This language must permit *hier-*
> *archal structuring* of data and program, extensive *error checking*
> at compile time, and production of *efficient machine code*.
>
> To support this belief, I have used the programming language
> *Pascal* throughout the text to define operating system concepts
> concisely by algorithms. Pascal combines the clarity needed for
> teaching with the efficiency required for design. It is easily un-
> derstood by programmers familiar with Algol 60 or Fortran, but
> is a far more natural tool than these for the description of oper-
> ating systems because of the presence of data structures of type
> record ... and pointer.
>
> At the moment, Pascal is designed for sequential program-
> ming only, but I extend it with a suitable notation for multipro-
> gramming and resource sharing.

Bold words indeed from a programmer who had never designed a programming language before, who did not have access to a Pascal compiler,
and who had no way of knowing whether Pascal would ever be used for
teaching! Niklaus Wirth (1971) had just published the first paper on Pascal,
and there were, of course, no textbooks based on this new language.

A beautiful idea

The key problem in concurrent programming was to invent language concepts
for asynchronous processes that share data in a common memory.

Dijkstra (1965) had argued that it is essential to treat operations on
shared variables as *critical regions* that must be performed strictly one at a
time in arbitrary order. He had also shown how to implement critical regions
using semaphores. But he had not suggested a notation for this idea.

Hoare (1971b) proposed a notation that identifies a variable as a *resource*
shared by concurrent processes. A good example is a ring buffer represented
by an array with input/output indices and a message counter:

```
        B: record inpointer, outpointer, count: integer;
               buffer: array 0..N−1 of T end;
        {resource B; Producer//Consumer}
```

The buffer is shared by two concurrent processes which produce and consume messages, respectively. (In most examples, including this one, I have used the programming notation of the original papers.)

In his paper Hoare also introduced the elegant concept of a *conditional critical region* that is delayed until a resource satisfies a particular condition (defined by a Boolean expression).

The send operation on the ring buffer is a conditional critical region that is executed when the buffer is not full:

```
        with B when count < N do
            begin buffer[inpointer] := next value;
                  inpointer := (inpointer + 1) mod N;
                  count := count + 1
            end
```

The receive operation is similar:

```
        with B when count > 0 do
            begin this value := buffer[outpointer];
                  outpointer := (outpointer + 1) mod N;
                  count := count − 1
            end
```

A compiler must check that the resource is accessed only within critical regions. A computer must guarantee that these regions are executed one at a time without overlapping.

In retrospect, the limitations of conditional critical regions are perhaps obvious:

• The resource concept is unreliable.

The same variable may be treated as a scheduled resource in some contexts and as an ordinary variable in other contexts. This may enable one process to refer directly to a variable while another process is within a "critical" region on the same variable.

• The scheduling mechanism is too restrictive.

When a process is delayed by a Boolean expression without side effects, it cannot indicate the urgency of its request to other processes. This complicates the programming of priority scheduling.

- The context switching is inefficient.

It did not seem possible to implement conditional critical regions efficiently. The problem was to limit the repeated reevaluation of Boolean expressions until they became true.

- There is no precise idea of data abstraction.

The declaration of a resource and the operations associated with it are not combined into a single, syntactical form, but are distributed throughout the program text.

Attempts to remove these problems eventually led to the discovery of monitors.

Readers and writers

During the International Summer School in Marktoberdorf, Germany, July 1971, I removed the first two limitations of conditional critical regions by solving an interesting problem (Brinch Hansen 1972a).

Two kinds of processes, called *readers* and *writers*, share a single resource. Readers can use it simultaneously, but a writer can use the resource only when nobody else is using it. When a writer is ready to use the resource, it should be enabled to do so as soon as possible (Courtois 1971). This is, of course, a priority scheduling problem.

First, I solved a slightly simpler problem which permits several writers to use the resource simultaneously. A *shared variable* was now introduced by a single declaration:

var v: **shared record** readers, writers: integer **end**

This notation makes it clear that a shared variable may be accessed *only* within critical regions.

A reader waits until writers are neither using the resource nor waiting for it:

```
region v when writers = 0 do
   readers := readers + 1;
read;
region v do readers := readers − 1
```

A writer immediately announces itself and waits until no readers are using the resource:

```
region v do writers := writers + 1
   await readers = 0;
write;
region v do writers := writers − 1
```

The scheduling condition may appear at the beginning or at the end of a critical region. The latter permits *scheduling with side effects*. It was an obvious extension to permit a scheduling condition to appear anywhere within a critical region (Brinch Hansen 1972b).

Courtois (1972) and others had strong reservations about conditional critical regions and my solution to the readers and writers problem (Brinch Hansen 1973a).

A new paradigm

The idea of *monitors* evolved through discussions and communications between E.W. Dijkstra, C.A.R. Hoare, and me during the summer and fall of 1971. My own ideas were particularly influenced by our discussions at the International Summer School in Marktoberdorf, Germany, July 19–30, 1971. Hoare and I continued the exchange of ideas at the Symposium on Operating Systems Techniques in Belfast, August 30–September 3, 1971.

At Marktoberdorf, Dijkstra (1971) briefly outlined a paradigm of *secretaries* and *directors*:

> Instead of N sequential processes cooperating in critical sections via common variables, we take out the critical sections and combine them into a $N + 1^{st}$ process, called a "secretary"; the remaining N processes are called "directors."

> A secretary presents itself primarily as a bunch of non-reentrant routines with a common state space.

> When a director calls a secretary ... the secretary may decide to keep him asleep, a decision that implies that she should

wake him up in one of her later activities. As a result the identity
of the calling program cannot remain anonymous as in the case
of the normal subroutine. The secretaries must have variables of
type "process identity." Whenever she is called the identity of
the calling process is handed over in an implicit input parameter; when she signals a release—analogous to the return of the
normal subroutine—she will supply the identity of the process to
be woken up.

In Belfast I presented an outline of a course on operating system principles which included the following remarks (Brinch Hansen 1971a):

> The conceptual simplicity of simple and conditional critical
> regions is achieved by ignoring the sequence in which waiting
> processes enter these regions. This abstraction is unrealistic for
> heavily used resources. In such cases, the operating system must
> be able to identify competing processes and control the schedul-
> ing of resources among them. This can be done by means of a
> *monitor*—a set of shared procedures which can delay and activate
> individual processes and perform operations on shared data.

During a discussion on monitors I added (Discussion 1971):

> You can imagine the (monitor) calls as a queue of messages
> being served one at a time. The monitor will receive a message
> and try to carry out the request as defined by the procedure and
> its input parameters. If the request can immediately be granted
> the monitor will return parameters ... and allow the calling pro-
> cess to continue. However, if the request cannot be granted, the
> monitor will prevent the calling process from continuing, and en-
> ter a reference to this transaction in a queue local to itself. This
> enables the monitor, at a later time when it is called by another
> process, to inspect the queue and decide which interaction should
> be completed now. From the point of view of a process a mon-
> itor call will look like a procedure call. The calling process will
> be delayed until the monitor consults its request. The monitor
> then has a set of scheduling queues which are completely local
> to it, and therefore protected against user processes. The latter
> can only access the shared variables maintained by the monitor

through a set of well defined operations ... the monitor procedures.

At the Belfast Symposium, Hoare expressed his own reservations about conditional critical regions (Discussion 1971):

> As a result of discussions with Brinch Hansen and Dijkstra, I feel that this proposal is not suitable for operating system implementation.
>
> My proposed method encourages the programmer to ignore the question of which of several outstanding requests for a resource should be granted.
>
> The scheduling decision cannot always be expressed by means of a single Boolean expression without side effects. You sometimes need the power of a general procedural program with storage in order to make scheduling decisions. So it seems reasonable to take all these protected critical regions out, and put them together and call it a secretary or monitor.

In the 1960s the resident part of an operating system was often known as a *monitor*. The kernel of the RC 4000 multiprogramming system was called the monitor and was defined as a program that "can execute a sequence of instructions as an indivisible entity" (Brinch Hansen 1969).

At Belfast we discussed the disadvantages of the classical monitor written in assembly language (Discussion 1971):

> Brinch Hansen: The difficulty with the classical "monolithic" monitor is not the fact that while you are performing an operation of type A you cannot perform another operation of type A, but that if you implement them by a single critical section which inhibits further monitor calls then the fact that you are executing an operation A on one data set prevents all other operations on completely unrelated data sets. That is why I think the ability to have several monitors, each in charge of a single set of shared data, is quite important.
>
> Hoare: A monitor is a high-level language construction which has two properties which are not possessed by most monitors as actually implemented in machine code. Firstly, like all good

programming ideas it can be called in at several levels: monitors
can call other monitors declared in outer blocks. Secondly, the
use of the high-level language feature enables you to associate
with each monitor the particular variables and tables which are
relevant for that monitor in controlling the relative progress of
the processes under its care. The protection, which prevents
processes from corrupting this information and prevents monitors
from gaining access to information which has no relevance, is
established by Algol-like scope rules.

These quotations show that Dijkstra, Hoare, and I had reached an informal understanding of monitors. But it was still no more than a verbal
outline of the idea. The discovery of a queueing mechanism, a notation, and
an implementation was left as an exercise for the reader.

Abandoned attempts

When a programming concept is understood informally, it would seem to be
a trivial matter to invent a language notation for it. But in practice this is
hard to do. The main problem is to replace an intuitive, vague idea with a
precise, unambigious definition of its meaning and restrictions.

In the search for a suitable monitor notation many ideas were considered
and rejected. I will describe two proposals that were abandoned. You may
find them hard to understand. In retrospect, so do I!

At the Belfast Symposium, Hoare (1971a) distributed an unpublished
draft of a monitor proposal which included a single-buffer characterized as
follows:

$$
\begin{aligned}
&\text{status} = -1 && \text{buffer empty (consumer waiting)} \\
&\text{status} = 0 && \text{buffer empty (consumer not waiting)} \\
&\text{status} = 1 && \text{buffer full (producer not waiting)} \\
&\text{status} = 2 && \text{buffer full (producer waiting)}
\end{aligned}
$$

The send operation is defined by a monitor entry named p:

```
p(prod) entry
begin
  if status ≤ 0 then input (prod)p(buffer);
  if status = −1 then output (cons)c(buffer);
  status := status + 1
end
```

This entry is not a procedure in the usual sense; p is the name of a communication between a producer and the buffer. The entry defines the protocol for this communication.

A producer outputs a message e to the buffer by executing the statement

$$\textbf{output } p(e)$$

The following takes place:

1. The producer is automatically delayed and its identity is assigned to a variable named *prod*.

2. If the buffer is empty, it immediately inputs the message from the producer and assigns it to a variable named *buffer* by executing the statement

$$\textbf{input } (prod)p(buffer)$$

The input automatically enables the producer to continue its execution.

3. If a consumer is waiting to input a message, the buffer immediately outputs the last message by executing the statement

$$\textbf{output } (cons)c(buffer)$$

The details of this statement will be explained shortly.

4. If the buffer is full it cannot input the message yet. In that case, the producer will remain delayed until a consumer empties the buffer as explained below.

5. Finally the buffer status is updated.

The receive operation is defined by a similar monitor entry named c:

```
c(cons) entry
begin
   if status ≥ 1 then output (cons)c(buffer);
   if status = 2 then input (prod)p(buffer);
   status := status − 1
end
```

A consumer inputs a message and assigns it to a variable x by executing the statement

$$\textbf{input } c(x)$$

This has the following effect:

1. The consumer is automatically delayed and its identity is assigned to a variable named *cons*.

2. If the buffer is full, it immediately outputs the last message to the consumer by executing the statement

$$\textbf{output } (\text{cons})c(\text{buffer})$$

3. If a producer is waiting to output a message to the buffer, the buffer now accepts that message by executing the statement

$$\textbf{input } (\text{prod})p(\text{buffer})$$

4. If the buffer is empty, it cannot output a message yet. In that case, the consumer will remain delayed until a producer fills the buffer as explained earlier.

5. Finally the buffer status is updated.

The proposal offers an efficient mechanism for process scheduling. The basic idea is that one monitor entry can complete a communication that was postponed by another monitor entry. This is the programming style one naturally adopts in a monolithic monitor written in assembly language.

The description of parameter transfers as unbuffered input/output later became the basis for the concept of *communicating sequential processes* (Hoare 1978).

This early monitor proposal did not combine monitor entries and shared variables into a modular unit and did not specify parameter types. In an attempt to remedy these problems, I sent Hoare an unpublished draft of "a monitor concept which closely mirrors the way in which the RC 4000 monitor was programmed" (Brinch Hansen 1971c). Algorithm 1 illustrates the use of this notation to implement a single-buffer.

```
monitor
var send2: ref send; receive2: ref receive;
   ready: Boolean;

entry send(const x: message)
call send1;
begin
  if ready then
    complete send1, receive2 do
    begin y := x; ready := false end
  else
    begin send2 := send1; ready := true end
end

entry receive(var y: message)
call receive1;
begin
  if ready then
    complete receive1, send2 do
    begin y := x; ready := false end
  else
    begin receive2 := receive1; ready := true end
end

begin ready := false end
```

Algorithm 1 An abandoned proposal.

A monitor is now a module that combines shared variables, procedures and an initial statement. The latter must be executed before the monitor can be called.

When the producer calls the *send* procedure, the following happens:

1. A reference to the call is stored in a local variable named *send1*. This is called a send reference.

2. If the consumer has called the *receive* procedure and is ready to receive a message, the monitor completes the send and receive calls simultaneously by assigning the value parameter x in the send call to the variable parameter y in the receive call. The completion statement extends the

scope of the send entry with the parameters of the corresponding receive entry. It also has the side effect of resuming the two processes
associated with the procedure calls.

3. If the consumer is not ready, the monitor stores the identity of the send
   call in a global variable named *send2* and indicates that the producer
   is ready to communicate.

The *receive* procedure is similar.

The use of *call references* enables a compiler to check parameter declarations in completion statements.

The most serious flaw of both proposals is the unreliable nature of process
scheduling. As Hoare put it: "It would be a grave error for a monitor
to specify an interaction with a process which was not waiting for that
interaction to take place." I concluded that it is generally "impossible ...
to check the validity of process references."

In a collection of papers by Hoare (1989), C.B. Jones introduces Hoare's
1974 paper on monitor and writes: "The first draft of this paper was distributed to the participants of the 1971 Belfast Symposium."

However, there is very little resemblance between these two papers. The
reason is quite simple. In 1971 we had some understanding of abstract data
types. But a key ingredient of monitors was still missing: a secure, efficient
method of context switching. We now turn to this problem.

The waiting game

On February 16, 1972, I presented a completely different solution to the problem of process scheduling at the California Institute of Technology (Brinch
Hansen 1972b).

I will illustrate the idea by an exercise from Brinch Hansen (1973b).
Processes $P_1, P_2, \ldots, P_n$ share a single resource. A process requests exclusive
access to the resource before using it and releases it afterwards. If the
resource is free, a process may use it immediately; otherwise the process
waits until another process releases the resource. If several processes are
waiting for the resource, it is granted to the waiting process P_i with the
lowest index i.

Algorithm 2 shows a priority scheduler for this problem. The resource
is represented by a *shared record r*. The key idea is to associate *scheduling
queues* with the shared variable. The queues are declared as variables of

```
var r: shared record
              free: Boolean;
              waiting: array [1..n] of Boolean;
              grant: array [1..n] of event r
           end

procedure request(i: 1..n);
region r do
begin
  if free then free := false
  else
     begin
       waiting[i] := true;
       await(grant[i]);
       waiting[i] := false
     end
end

procedure release;
var i, m: 1..n;
region r do
begin
  i := 1; m := n;
  while i < m do
    if waiting[i] then m := i
    else i := i + 1;
  if waiting[i] then cause(grant[i])
  else free := true
end
```

Algorithm 2 Context switching queues.

type *event r*. The resource scheduler can delay processes in these queues and resume them later by means of two standard procedures named *await* and *cause*.

If a process P_i calls the request procedure when the resource is not free, the Boolean *waiting[i]* is set to true and the process is entered in the event queue *grant[i]*. The await operation makes the process leave its critical region temporarily.

When a process P_j calls the *release* procedure while other processes are waiting, the most urgent process P_i is selected and enabled to resume as soon as P_j leaves its own region. At that moment P_i reenters its previous region and continues execution after the await statement.

Instead of letting one critical region complete the execution of another region, we simply switch back to the context of the previous region. Consequently, a scheduling decision can be viewed merely as a delay during the execution of a critical region.

This queueing mechanism enables the programmer to ignore the identity of a process and think of it only as "the calling process" or "the process waiting in this queue." There is no need for variables of type process reference.

The only possible operations on a queue are *cause* and *await*, performed within critical regions. The problem of dangling process references is solved by making the queues empty to begin with and preventing assignments to them.

My proposal included a feature that was never used. Suppose several processes are waiting in the same queue until a Boolean expression B is true. In that case, a *cause* operation on the queue enables *all* of them to resume their critical regions one at a time. Mutual exclusion is still maintained, and processes waiting to resume critical regions have priority over processes that are waiting to enter the beginning of critical regions. In this situation, a resumed process may find that another process has made the scheduling condition B false again. Consequently, processes must use waiting loops of the form

while not B do await(q)

My 1972 paper, which introduced scheduling queues, was an invited paper written under great time pressure. When someone later mentioned that multiple resumption might be inconvenient, I looked at the paper again and saw that it presented one example only of the use of scheduling queues. And that example used a separate queue for each process! The programming examples in my operating systems book (Brinch Hansen 1973b) did the same. In Concurrent Pascal I turned this programming style into a programming language rule (Brinch Hansen 1974d).

In spite of the unintended generality, my 1972 process queues were *not* the same as the classical event queues of the 1960s, which caused the programmer to lose control over scheduling. The crucial difference was that the new queues were associated with a shared variable, so that all scheduling operations were mutually exclusive operations. The programmer could control the scheduling of processes to any degree desired by associating each queue with a *group* of processes or an *individual* process.

The idea of associating scheduling queues with a shared variable to enable processes to resume critical regions was the basis of all subsequent monitor proposals. Context switching queues have been called *events* (Brinch Hansen 1972b), *queues* (Brinch Hansen 1973b), and *conditions* (Hoare 1973a). Some are single-process queues; others are multiprocess queues. The details vary, but they all combine process scheduling with context switching and mutual exclusion.

We now had all the pieces of the monitor puzzle. And I had adopted a programming style which combined shared variables, queues, critical regions, and procedures in a manner that closely resembled monitors (Algorithm 2).

A moment of truth

In the spring of 1972 I read two papers by Dahl (1972b) and Hoare (1972b) on the *class* concept of the programming language *Simula 67*. Although Simula is not a concurrent programming language, it inspired me in the following way: So far I had thought of a monitor as a program module that defines all operations on a *single* instance of a data structure. From Simula I learned to regard a program module as the definition of a *class* of data structures accessed by the same procedures.

This was a moment of truth for me. Within a few days I wrote a chapter on resource protection for my operating systems book. I proposed to represent monitors by *shared classes* and pointed out that resource protection and type checking are part of the same problem: to verify automatically that all operations on data structures maintain certain properties (called *invariants*).

My book includes the buffer monitor defined by Algorithm 3. The shared class defines a data structure of type B, two procedures which can operate on the data structure, and a statement that defines its initial state.

```
shared class B =
  buffer: array 0..max−1 of T;
  p, c: 0..max−1;
  full: 0..max;

  procedure send(m: T);
  begin
    await full < max;
    buffer[p] := m;
    p := (p + 1) mod max;
    full := full + 1;
  end

  procedure receive(var m: T);
  begin
    await full > 0;
    m := buffer[c];
    c := (c + 1) mod max;
    full := full − 1;
  end

begin p := 0; c := 0; full := 0 end
```

Algorithm 3 A monitor with conditional waiting.

The class notation permits multiple instances of the same monitor type. A buffer variable b is declared as follows:

var b: B

Upon entry to the block in which the buffer variable is declared, storage is allocated for its data components, and the buffer is initialized by executing the statement at the end of the class definition.

Send and *receive* operations on the buffer b are denoted

b.send(x)   b.receive(y)

A shared class is a notation that explicitly restricts the operations on a data type and enables a compiler to check that these restrictions are obeyed.

It also indicates that all operations on a particular instance must be executed as critical regions.

In May 1972 I submitted the manuscript of my book to Prentice-Hall and sent copies to Dijkstra and Hoare. On November 3, 1972, I gave a seminar on shared classes at the University of California at Santa Barbara.

In July 1973 *Operating System Principles* was published with my monitor proposal based on Simula classes (Brinch Hansen 1973b). My decision to use conditional waiting in this proposal was a matter of taste. I might just as well have used queues, which I had introduced in another chapter.

I also included the monitor notation in the first draft of a survey paper on concurrent programming (Brinch Hansen 1973d). A referee, who felt that it was inappropriate to include a recent idea in a survey paper, suggested that I remove it, which I did.

I discussed monitors with queues in the first report on Concurrent Pascal, April 1974, and at the IFIP Congress in Stockholm, August 1974 (Brinch Hansen 1974a, 1974c).

Parallel discovery

Two influential papers concluded the early development of monitors. In the first paper Hoare (1973b) used a monitor in the design of a paging system. He begins the paper by acknowledging that "The notations used ... are based on those of Pascal ... and Simula 67." In the second paper Hoare (1974a) illustrated the monitor concept by several examples, including a ring buffer (Algorithm 4). Communicating processes are delayed and resumed by means of *wait* and *signal* operations on first-in, first-out queues called *condition* variables.

In an unpublished draft of his condition proposal Hoare (1973a) correctly pointed out that

> The synchronization primitives proposed here are very similar to Brinch Hansen's "await" and "cause", but they involve less retesting inside waiting operations, and may be slightly more efficient to implement.

According to Hoare (1989), his first monitor paper was submitted in October 1972; his second paper was submitted in February 1973 and the material presented at IRIA, Paris, France, on May 11, 1973. I received them shortly before they were published in August 1973 and October 1974, respectively.

```
bounded buffer: monitor
  begin buffer: array 0..N−1 of portion;
    lastpointer: 0..N−1;
    count: 0..N;
    nonempty, nonfull: condition;
    procedure append(x: portion);
      begin if count = N then nonfull.wait;
        note 0 ≤ count < N;
        buffer[lastpointer] := x;
        lastpointer := lastpointer ⊕ 1;
        count := count + 1;
        nonempty.signal
      end append;
    procedure remove(result x: portion);
      begin if count = 0 then nonempty.wait;
        note 0 < count ≤ N;
        x := buffer[lastpoint ⊖ count];
        count := count − 1;
        nonfull.signal
      end remove;
    count := 0; lastpointer := 0
  end bounded buffer;
```

Algorithm 4 A monitor with queues.

While writing this history I discovered a working paper by McKeag (1973) submitted to an ACM meeting in Savannah, Georgia, April 9–12, 1973. This early paper includes a single example of Hoare's monitor notation.

Milestones

The classical monitor of the 1960s was not a precisely defined programming concept based on rules enforced by a compiler. It was just a vague term for the resident part of an operating system, which was programmed in assembly language. The monitor concept that emerged in the 1970s should not be regarded as a refinement of an operating systems technique. It was a new programming language concept for concurrent programs running on shared-memory computers. Operating systems were just a challenging application area for this synchronization concept.

This brings us to the end of the phase where the monitor concept was discovered. The milestones were:

> 1971 Conditional critical regions
> Scheduling with side effects
> Monitor idea
> 1972 Context switching queues
> Class concept papers
> Monitor notation
> 1973 *Operating System Principles*
> Monitor papers

The next task was to develop a programming language with monitors.

3 Concurrent Pascal

Concurrent Pascal extended the sequential programming language Pascal with concurrent processes, monitors, and classes. The polished presentations of the language in professional journals and text books fail to show the long arduous road we had to travel to understand what undergraduates now take for granted.

A matter of philosophy

In designing Concurrent Pascal I followed a consistent set of principles for programming languages. These principles carried structured programming into the new realm of modular, concurrent programming. Let me summarize these principles and show *when* and *how* I first expressed them in writing.

- Concurrent programs can be written exclusively in high-level languages.

In the fall of 1971 I expressed this belief, which seems commonplace today, but was novel at the time (see the earlier quotation in "Beginner's luck"). Later I will explain why I did not consider Burroughs Algol and PL/I as high-level programming languages for operating system design.

In Brinch Hansen (1974c) I repeated the same idea:

> I am convinced that in most cases operating system design-
> ers do not need to control low-level machine features (such as
> registers, addresses, and interrupts) directly, but can leave these

problems to a compiler and its run-time environment. A consistent use of abstract programming concepts in operating system design should enable a compiler to check the access rights of concurrent processes and make enforcement of resource protection rules at run time largely unnecessary.

Hoare (1971b) and Brinch Hansen (1971b) introduced a fundamental requirement of any concurrent programming language:

- Time-dependent programming errors must be detected during compilation.

In the spring of 1972 I explained this requirement as follows (Brinch Hansen 1973b):

> The main dificulty of multiprogramming is that concurrent activities can interact in a time-dependent manner which makes it practically impossible to locate programming errors by systematic testing. Perhaps, more than anything else, this explains the difficulty of making operating systems reliable.
>
> *If we wish to succeed in designing large, reliable multiprogramming systems, we must use programming tools which are so well-structured that most time-dependent errors can be caught at compile time.* It seems hopeless to try to solve this problem at the machine level of programming, nor can we expect to improve the situation by means of so-called "implementation languages," which retain the traditional "right" of systems programmers to manipulate addresses freely.

In 1976 I put it this way (Brinch Hansen 1977b):

> One of the primary goals of Concurrent Pascal is to push the role of *compilation checks* to the limit and reduce the use of *execution checks* as much as possible. This is not done just to make compiled programs more efficient by reducing the overhead of execution checks. In program engineering, compilation and execution checks play the same role as preventive maintenance and flight recorders do in aviation. The latter only tell you why a system crashed; the former prevents it. This distinction seems

essential to me in the design of real-time systems that will control vital functions in society. Such systems must be highly reliable *before* they are put into operation.

Time-dependent errors occur when processes refer to the same variables without proper synchronization. The key to preventing these *race conditions* turned out to be the requirement that

- A concurrent programming language should support a programming discipline that combines data and procedures into modules.

I realized this even *before* discovering a monitor notation. The following quotation refers to my earlier proposal of associating shared variables with critical regions and scheduling queues (Brinch Hansen 1972b):

> The basic idea is to associate data shared by concurrent processes explicitly with operations defined on them. This clarifies the meaning of programs and permits a large class of time-dependent errors to be caught at compile-time.

In the spring of 1972 I described my own monitor notation as a natural extension of the module concept of Simula 67 (Brinch Hansen 1973b):

> In Simula 67, the definition of a structured data type and the meaningful operations on it form a single syntactical unit called a *class*.

> An obvious idea is to represent critical regions by the concept *shared class*, implying that the operations ... on a given variable v of type T exclude one another in time.

> My main purpose here is to show a notation which explicitly restricts operations on data and enables a compiler to check that these restrictions are obeyed. Although such restrictions are not enforced by Simula 67, this would seem to be essential for effective protection.

Concurrent Pascal was the first realization of *modular, concurrent programming*. During the 1970s researchers also introduced modularity in sequential programming languages. However, these languages were completed and implemented *after* Concurrent Pascal (Popek 1977; Liskov 1981; Shaw 1981).

In the spring of 1975, after implementing Concurrent Pascal and writing the first operating system in the language, I wrote the following (Brinch Hansen 1975c):

> The combination of a data structure and the operations used to access it is called an *abstract data type*. It is abstract because the rest of the system only needs to know what operations one can perform on it but can ignore the details of how they are carried out. A Concurrent Pascal program is constructed from three kinds of abstract data types: processes, monitors, and classes.

Race conditions are prevented by a simple scope rule that permits a process, monitor, or class to access its own variables only. In a suitably restricted language this rule can easily be checked by a compiler. However, in a language with pointers and address arithmetic, no such guarantee can be offered.

The principles discussed so far were largely derived from my perception of concurrent programming in 1972. Intuitively I also followed a more general principle of language design, which I only formulated four years later:

- A programming language should be abstract and secure.

In the spring of 1976 I explained this requirement as follows (Brinch Hansen 1977b):

> The main contribution of a good programming language to simplicity is to provide an abstract *readable notation* that makes the parts and structures of programs obvious to a reader. An abstract programming language *suppresses machine detail* (such as addresses, registers, bit patterns, interrupts, and sometimes even the number of processors available). Instead the language relies on *abstract concepts* (such as variables, data types, synchronizing operations, and concurrent processes). As a result, program texts written in abstract languages are often an order of magnitude shorter than those written in machine language. This *textual reduction* simplifies program engineering considerably.

We shall also follow the crucial principle of language design suggested by Hoare: *The behavior of a program written in an abstract language should always be explainable in terms of the concepts of that language and should never require insight into the details of compilers and computers.* Otherwise, an abstract notation has no significant value in reducing complexity.

A programming language that satisfies this requirement is said to be *secure* (Hoare 1974b).

A programming language that permits unrestricted use of assembly language features, such as jumps, typeless machine words, and addresses is insecure. A program written in such a language may have unpredictable effects that force the programmer to go beyond the abstract concepts, which the programming language pretends to support. In order to locate obscure programming errors, the programmer may now have to consider machine-dependent details, which vary from one computer to another (or even from one execution to another on the same computer).

The Burroughs B6700 and Multics operating systems were written in programming languages that permit unrestricted address manipulation (extended Algol 60 and PL/I). These insecure programming languages and operating systems had no influence on Concurrent Pascal and the model operating systems written in the language. The Unix system, written in the insecure language C, had not yet been described when Concurrent Pascal was being developed.

The controversy over whether a programming language should give you unrestricted access to hardware features or impose restrictions that simplify programs and facilitate error detection has continued to this day.

Facing complexity

On July 1, 1972, I became Associate Professor of Computer Science at the California Institute of Technology. During my first academic year I prepared three new courses and introduced Pascal on campus. These tasks kept me busy for a while.

I also started thinking about designing a programming language with concurrent processes and monitors. To reduce the effort, I decided to include these concepts in an existing sequential language. Pascal was an obvious choice for me, since I had used the language in my operating systems book. I liked Pascal because of its similarity to Algol 60, which I had used extensively at Regnecentralen. I named the new language *Concurrent Pascal* and did not consider any other base language. Apart from that, nothing else was obvious.

With a notation for monitors now in hand, you would think it would be easy to include it in Pascal. I had no idea of how to do this. I remember sitting in my garden in Pasadena, day after day, staring at a blank piece of paper and feeling like a complete failure.

Let me just mention some of the complicated issues I faced for the first time:

How can a programming language support

- The different scope rules of Pascal blocks and Simula classes?

- Hierarchical composition of processes and monitors?

- Multiple instances of the same process or monitor type?

- Dynamic activation and termination of processes and monitors?

- Elementary input/output from arbitrary peripherals?

How can a compiler check that

- Processes communicate by monitor procedures only?

- Monitors do not deadlock by calling themselves recursively (either directly or indirectly)?

How can a minicomputer with inadequate facilities for dynamic memory allocation

- Execute concurrent programs efficiently?

It took me almost two years to find reasonable solutions to most of these problems and make compromises which enabled me to ignore the most thorny issues.

A new language

In September 1973 and April 1974 I distributed the first descriptions of Concurrent Pascal. A final paper and a language report were both published in June 1975 (Brinch Hansen 1973c, 1974a, 1974d, 1975a).

I now understood what I was doing. One day the Caltech president, Harold Brown, came to my office and asked me to explain my research. After listening for half an hour, he said, "That sounds easy." I agreed because that was how I felt at the time.

A Concurrent Pascal program defines a fixed number of concurrent processes which communicate by monitors only. One of the first programs I wrote in Concurrent Pascal implements a pipeline that reads and prints an endless sequence of punched cards. Figure 1 shows the hierarchical structure of the pipeline. It consists of three processes connected by two line buffer monitors. An arrow from a process to a monitor indicates that the process can call that monitor. I named this kind of representation an *access graph*. It became our main tool for "programming in the large."

CARD READER   LINE BUFFERS   LINE PRINTER

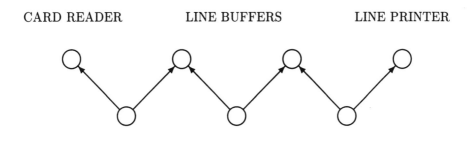

CARD PROCESS   COPY PROCESS   PRINTER PROCESS

Figure 1 An access graph.

I will use the pipeline in Fig. 1 to illustrate the *syntax* and *semantics* of Concurrent Pascal.

Both *line buffers* in this pipeline are defined by the same *monitor type* (Algorithm 5). Each buffer can hold a single line at a time. A Boolean variable defines whether or not a buffer is full. Two variables of type *queue* are used to delay and continue the sender and receiver, respectively.

The pipeline program uses two line buffers, which are declared and ini-

```
type linebuffer =
monitor
var contents: line; full: Boolean;
     sender, receiver: queue;

procedure entry receive(var text: line);
begin
  if not full then delay(receiver);
  text := contents; full := false;
  continue(sender)
end;

procedure entry send(text: line);
begin
  if full then delay(sender);
  contents := text; full := true;
  continue(receiver)
end;

begin full := false end
```

Algorithm 5 A monitor type.

tialized as follows:

```
var inbuffer, outbuffer: linebuffer;

init inbuffer, outbuffer
```

For each buffer, the *init* statement allocates memory space for fresh instances of the shared variables declared at the beginning of the monitor type. The initialization also causes the statement at the end of the monitor to be executed, which makes a buffer empty to begin with. Each buffer is now ready to be shared by a sender and a receiver as shown in Fig. 1.

The Concurrent Pascal compiler checks that processes only access a line buffer by calling the monitor procedures *send* and *receive*. This restriction is guaranteed by a scope rule that makes the shared variables inaccessible from outside the monitor.

A sender outputs a line of text through a particular buffer by calling the *send* procedure as follows:

var text: line;

outbuffer.send(text)

If the buffer is full, the send procedure *delays* the calling process in the sender queue. The delay lasts until another process calls the *receive* procedure, which performs a *continue* operation on the sender queue. In any case, the sender cannot complete the *if* statement until the buffer is empty. At that point, the sender puts a message in the queue, performs a continue operation on the receiver queue and returns from the send procedure.

The *receive* procedure is similar.

While a process executes a monitor procedure, it has exclusive access to the shared variables. If another process attempts to call the same monitor while a process has exclusive access to that monitor, the latter call will automatically be delayed until the former process has released its exclusive access.

A process releases its exclusive access to a monitor in one of three ways:

1. By reaching the end of a monitor procedure.

2. By delaying itself temporarily in a queue declared within the monitor. The process regains its exclusive access when another process performs a continue operation on the same queue.

3. By performing a continue operation on a queue. The process performing the continue operation automatically returns from its monitor procedure. If another process is waiting in the queue, that process will immediately resume the execution of the monitor procedure in which it was delayed.

A monitor queue is either empty or holds a single process. A multiprocess queue can be implemented as an array of single-process queues.

In October 1973 Ole-Johan Dahl suggested to Tony Hoare that a continue operation should terminate a monitor call (Hoare 1974a; McKeag 1991). Hoare may have told me about this idea during his visit to Caltech in January 1974.

In the pipeline example a *printer process* is defined by a *process type* (Algorithm 6). A process parameter defines the only monitor (a line buffer) that is accessible to the process.

The pipeline program initializes a printer process as follows:

```
type printerprocess =
process(buffer: linebuffer);
var param: ioparam; text: line;
begin
  param.operation := output;
  cycle
    buffer.receive(text);
    repeat io(text, param, printdevice)
    until param.status = complete
  end
end
```

Algorithm 6 A process type.

```
var outbuffer: linebuffer; writer: printerprocess;

init writer(outbuffer)
```

The *init* statement allocates memory for fresh instances of the local variables declared at the beginning of the process type and starts execution of the process.

The Concurrent Pascal compiler ensures that the local variables of a process are inaccessible to other processes (and monitors). It also checks that a printer process uses its own line buffer only.

A printer process repeats the same *cycle* of operations endlessly. In each cycle the process receives a line from the buffer and prints it. The standard procedure *io* delays the process until the line has been output (or the printing has failed). In this simple example, the printing is repeated until it has been successfully completed.

All input/output are indivisible operations that hide peripheral interrupts. Consequently a process and a peripheral device cannot access the same variable simultaneously.

The complete *pipeline program* defines a parameterless process known as the *initial process*. This process includes definitions of all the monitor and process types used by the pipeline (Algorithm 7).

The execution of the program activates a single initial process, which then initializes two buffer monitors and activates three concurrent processes (by means of an *init* statement).

In addition to processes and monitors, Concurrent Pascal also includes

```
type linebuffer =
monitor
  . . .
end;

type cardprocess =
process(buffer: linebuffer);
  . . .
end;

type copyprocess =
process(inbuffer, outbuffer: linebuffer);
  . . .
end;

type printerprocess =
process(buffer: linebuffer);
  . . .
end;

var inbuffer, outbuffer: linebuffer;
    reader: cardprocess;
    copier: copyprocess;
    writer: printerprocess;
begin
  init inbuffer, outbuffer,
       reader(inbuffer),
       copier(inbuffer, outbuffer),
       writer(outbuffer)
end.
```

Algorithm 7 A program.

classes. A class is a module that cannot be called simultaneously by processes. It must be local to a single process, monitor or class.

Algorithm 8 shows a *class type*. A module of this type has access to a single line buffer. The class procedure extends a line with a left margin of 26 spaces and terminates it with a newline character before sending the line through the buffer.

```
type linemaker =
class(buffer: linebuffer);
var image: line; charno: integer;

procedure entry write(text: line);
begin
  for charno := 27 to 106 do
    image[charno] := text[charno−26];
  buffer.send(image)
end;

begin
  for charno := 1 to 26 do
    image[charno] := space;
  image[107] := newline
end
```

Algorithm 8 A class type.

A Simula program can bypass the procedures of a class and change the class variables in ways that are incompatible with the function of the class. This loophole was removed in Concurrent Pascal. A variable declared within a class can be read (but not changed) outside the class, provided the variable is prefixed with the word *entry*. Entry variables are not permitted in monitors.

Table 1 shows how Concurrent Pascal differs from Pascal. It lists the features that were added to Pascal as well as those that were excluded.

I have already illustrated the major concepts of Concurrent Pascal: processes, monitors, classes, and queues, as well as init and cycle statements (Algorithms 5–8).

The programming of terminal and printer drivers is supported by a notation for *control characters*. The following example

Table 1 Concurrent Pascal versus Pascal.

Added features	Excluded features
process types	file types
monitor types	pointer types
class types	packed arrays
queues	variant records
init statements	goto statements
cycle statements	recursion
control characters	
universal parameters	
program declarations	

const formfeed = '(:12:)'

defines *form feed* as ASCII character number 12.

When you program a procedure that reads a disk page, you cannot anticipate all the possible data types that users will assign to this page in the future. This is one of the few cases in which one cannot hide machine detail.

Concurrent Pascal uses *universal parameters* to relax type checking in device procedures. In the following procedure declaration

type diskpage = **array** [1..256] **of** integer;

procedure readdisk(pageno: integer;
  var page: **univ** diskpage);
begin ... **end**

the key word *univ* indicates that the procedure may be called with any argument that has the same length as an array of 256 integers. The type checking is relaxed only at the point where the procedure is called. No variable is treated as a typeless bit pattern throughout a program (Brinch Hansen 1975d).

A *program declaration* enables a Concurrent Pascal program to call a sequential user (or system) program written in a subset of Pascal. The program declaration includes a list of procedures that the Pascal program may call. The details of this *ad hoc* mechanism are described in the Concurrent Pascal report (Brinch Hansen 1975a).

Since an operating system written in Concurrent Pascal must implement its own filing system, *file types* cannot be built into the language.

Pointer types were excluded to prevent a process from obtaining unsynchronized access to a variable of another process through a pointer transmitted through a monitor. In the absence of pointers, processes can access shared variables through monitor procedures only.

Packed arrays, variant records, and *goto statements* were eliminated to simplify the language.

Later I will explain my reasons for eliminating *recursive procedures and functions.*

The complete syntax and semantics of Concurrent Pascal are defined in the language report (Brinch Hansen 1975a).

Concurrent Pascal was designed according to the principles discussed earlier. It is a programming language that supports modular programming with processes, monitors, and classes. The syntax clearly shows that each module consists of a set of variables, a set of procedures, and an initial statement. Each module defines the representation and possible transformations of a data structure. A module cannot access the variables of another module. This simple scope rule enables a compiler to detect race conditions before a program is executed. The automatic synchronization of monitor calls prevents other race conditions at run time.

The programming tricks of assembly language are impossible in Concurrent Pascal: there are no typeless memory words, registers, and addresses in the language. The programmer is not even aware of the existence of physical processors and interrupts. The language is so secure that concurrent processes run without any form of memory protection!

My working habits unfortunately make it impossible for me to remember the alternative forms of syntax, scope, and type rules that I must have considered while designing the language. I evaluate language concepts by using them for program design. I develop a program by writing numerous drafts of the program text. A draft is immediately rejected if it is not in some way simpler and more elegant than the previous one. An improved draft immediately replaces the previous one, which is thrown in the waste basket. Otherwise I would drown in paper and half-baked ideas. As I jump from one draft to another without slowing myself down, a beautiful design eventually emerges. When that happens, I write a simple description of the program and rewrite it one more time using the same terminology as in the description. By then I have already forgotten most of the alternatives. And, twenty years later, I don't remember any of them.

The translation problem

An early six-pass compiler was never released. Although it worked perfectly, I found it too complicated. Each pass was written by a different student who had difficulty understanding the rest of the compiler.

From June through September 1974 my student, Al Hartmann, wrote another Concurrent Pascal compiler. His goal was to be able to compile small operating systems on a PDP 11/45 minicomputer with at least 32 k bytes of memory and a slow, removable disk. The compiler was divided into seven passes to fit into a small memory. It consisted of 8300 lines written in Pascal and could be completely understood by one person. Systematic testing of the compiler took three months, from October through December 1974.

The Concurrent Pascal compiler was used from January 1975 without problems. It was described in the Ph.D. thesis (Hartmann 1975), later published as a monograph.

In another month Al Hartmann derived a compiler for a Pascal subset known as *Sequential Pascal* (Brinch Hansen 1975b). It compiled the largest pass of the Concurrent Pascal compiler in 3 min. The compilation speed was limited mostly by the disk.

When we say that a program is concurrent, we are really talking about its behavior at run time. During compilation a program written in any language is just a piece of text, which is checked for correct syntax, scope of declarations, and types of operands. Consequently, the compilation of processes, monitors, and classes in Concurrent Pascal is very similar to the compilation of data types and procedures in Sequential Pascal.

The art of compromise

The Concurrent Pascal compiler generated code for a simple machine tailored to the language. I borrowed this idea from a portable Pascal compiler (Nori 1974). My main concern was to simplify code generation. The portability of Concurrent Pascal was just a useful by-product of this decision.

The Concurrent Pascal machine was simulated by a kernel of 8 k bytes written in assembly language. The kernel multiplexed a PDP 11/45 processor among concurrent processes and executed them using a technique known as *threaded code* (Bell 1973). It also performed basic input/output from a fixed set of peripherals (terminal, disk, magnetic tape, line printer, and card reader).

I wrote the kernel in Pascal extended with classes. Robert Deverill and Tom Zepko translated the kernel into assembly language. It was completed in January 1975 and described in a report (Brinch Hansen 1975e).

I made major compromises to make program execution as efficient as possible:

- All procedures must be non-recursive. This rule imposes a strict hierarchical structure on processes and monitors that prevents monitor deadlocks.

- All processes, monitors, and classes exist forever. This is acceptable in operating systems and real-time systems that perform a fixed number of tasks forever.

- All processes and monitors must be activated by the initial process.

These compromises made memory allocation trivivial. The first rule enabled the compiler to determine the memory requirements of each module. The first two rules made static memory allocation possible. The third rule made it possible to combine the kernel, the program code, and all monitor variables into a single memory segment that was included in the address space of every process. This prevented fragmentation of a limited address space and made monitor calls almost as fast as simple procedure calls.

By putting simplicity and efficiency first we undoubtedly lost generality. But the psychological effect of these compromises was phenomenal. Suddenly an overwhelming task seemed manageable.

Fifteen years later, I realized that the severe restrictions of Concurrent Pascal had made it impossible for me to discover and appreciate the powerful concept of recursive processes (Brinch Hansen 1989a, 1989b).

Learning to program again

After defining Concurrent Pascal, I wrote a series of model operating systems to evaluate the language. The new language had a dramatic (and unexpected) impact on my style of programming.

It was the first time I had programmed in a language that enabled me to divide programs into modules that could be programmed and tested separately. The creative part was clearly the initial selection of modules and the combination of modules into hierarchical structures. The programming of each module was often trivial. I soon adopted the rule that each module should consist of no more than one page of text. This discipline made programs far more readable and reliable than traditional programs that operate on global data structures.

The first operating system written in Concurrent Pascal (called *Deamy*) was used only to evaluate the expressive power of the language and was never built (Brinch Hansen 1974b). The second one (called *Pilot*) was used for several months but was too slow.

In May 1975 I finished the *Solo* system, a single-user operating system for the development of Concurrent and Sequential Pascal programs on a PDP 11/45. The operating system was written in Concurrent Pascal. All other programs, including the Concurrent and Sequential Pascal compilers, were written in Sequential Pascal. The heart of Solo was a job process that compiled and ran programs stored on a disk. Two additional processes performed input and output simultaneously. System commands enabled the user to replace Solo with any other Concurrent Pascal program stored on disk, or to restart Solo again. Al Hartmann had already written the compilers. I wrote the operating system and its utility programs in three months. Wolfgang Franzen measured and improved the performance of the disk allocation algorithm.

Solo was the first major example of a concurrent program consisting of processes, monitors, and classes (Brinch Hansen 1975c).

At Regnecentralen I had been involved in the design of process control programs for a chemical plant, a power plant, and a weather bureau. These real-time applications had one thing in common: each was unique in its software requirements. Consequently the programs were expensive to develop.

When the cost of a large program cannot be shared by many users, the only practical way of reducing cost is to give process control engineers a high-level language for concurrent programming. I illustrated this point by means of a real-time scheduler, which had been programmed in assembly language at Regnecentralen. I now reprogrammed the same scheduler in Concurrent Pascal.

The *real-time scheduler* executed a fixed number of task processes with frequencies chosen by an operator. I wrote it in three days. It took 3 hours of machine time to test it systematically. Writing a description took another couple of days. So the whole program was developed in less than a week (Brinch Hansen 1975f).

At the end of 1975 I wrote a *job-stream system* that compiled and executed short Pascal programs input from a card reader and output on a line printer. Input, execution, and output took place simultaneously using buffers stored on a disk. A user job was preempted if its compilation and execution time exceeded 1 minute. I designed, programmed, and tested the system in 10 days. When the system was finished, it ran short jobs continuously at the speed of the line printer (Brinch Hansen 1976a).

It was a pleasant surprise to discover that 14 modules from Solo could be used unchanged in the job stream system. This is the earliest example I know of different operating systems using the same modules.

Each model operating system was a Concurrent Pascal program of about 1000 lines of text divided into 15–25 modules. A module was roughly one page of text (50–60 lines) with about 5 procedures of 10–15 lines each (Table 2).

Table 2 Model operating systems.

	Solo	Job stream	Real time
Lines	1300	1400	600
Modules	23	24	13
Lines/module	57	58	46
Procedures/module	5	4	4
Lines/procedure	11	15	12

These examples showed that it was possible to build nontrivial concurrent programs from very simple modules that could be studied page by page (Brinch Hansen 1977a).

Compared to assembly language, Concurrent Pascal reduced my programming effort by an order of magnitude and made concurrent programs so simple that a journal could publish the entire text of a 1300 line program (Brinch Hansen 1975c).

The modules of a concurrent program were tested one at a time starting with those that did not depend on other modules. In each test run, the initial process was replaced by a short test process that called the top module and made it execute all its statements at least once. When a module worked, another one was tested on top of it. Detailed examples of how this was done are described in Brinch Hansen (1977b, 1978d).

Dijkstra (1967) had used a similar procedure to test the T.H.E. multiprogramming system, which was written in assembly language. Concurrent

Pascal made bottom-up testing secure. The compilation checks of access rights ensured that new (untested) modules did not make old (tested) modules fail. My experience was that a well-designed concurrent program of one thousand lines required a couple of compilations followed by one test run per module. And then it worked (Brinch Hansen 1977a).

The end of the beginning

In July 1976 I joined the University of Southern California as Professor and Chairman of Computer Science. I also finished a book on the new programming methodology entitled *The Architecture of Concurrent Programs* (Brinch Hansen 1977b).

My research on Concurrent Pascal was now entering its final phase. I wrote my last Concurrent Pascal program: a message router for a *ring network* of PDP 11/45 computers. I proved that it was deadlock-free and would deliver all messages within a finite time. The ideas of this program were developed in discussions with B. Heidebrecht, D. Heimbigner, F. Stepczyk, and R. Vossler at TRW Systems (Brinch Hansen 1977c).

My Ph.D. student, Jørgen Staunstrup, and I introduced *transition commands*—a formal notation for specifying process synchronization as state transitions (Brinch Hansen 1978a). In his Ph.D. thesis, Staunstrup (1978) used this tool to specify major parts of the Solo system.

Another of my Ph.D. students, Jon Fellows, wrote one more operating system in Concurrent Pascal: the *Trio* system, which enabled users to simultaneously develop and execute programs on a PDP 11/55 minicomputer with three terminals and a memory of 160 k bytes. Jon Fellows was assisted in a few cases by Habib Maghami (Brinch Hansen 1980; Fellows 1980).

I now moved into another area that was little understood at the time: the programming of processes on a multicomputer without shared memory. I introduced the idea of a synchronized procedure that can be called by one process and executed by another process (Brinch Hansen 1978b). This proposal combined processes and monitors into a single concept, called *distributed processes*.

This communication paradigm is also known as *remote procedure calls*. I recently discovered that it was first proposed by Jim White (1976). However, White did not explain how to prevent race conditions between unsynchronized remote calls and local processes, which are being executed by the same processor. This flaw potentially made remote procedure calls as unsafe as interrupts that cannot be disabled! Disaster was avoided by a programming convention: a process that handled a remote call immediately made a similar call to a local monitor (Lynch 1991). In other words, insecure remote procedure calls were used only as an implementation technique for secure remote monitor calls.

My Ph.D. student, Charles Hayden (1979), implemented an experimental language with distributed processes on an LSI 11 and evaluated the new paradigm by writing small simulation programs.

According to Roubine (1980), my proposal was "a source of inspiration in the design of the Ada tasking facilities." The Ada *rendezvous* combines the remote procedure call of distributed processes with the selection of alternative interactions in communicating sequential processes (Hoare 1978).

My keynote address on concurrent programming at the IEEE Computer Software and Applications Conference in Chicago, November 1978, concluded five years of experience with the first abstract programming language for operating system development (Brinch Hansen 1978c).

The *milestones* of the project were:

1974	Concurrent Pascal defined
	Concurrent Pascal implemented
1975	Concurrent Pascal paper
	Solo operating system
	Real-time scheduler
	Job-stream system
1976	Solo papers
	System distribution
1977	*The Architecture of Concurrent Programs*
	Ring network
1978	Trio operating system
	Distributed processes

In Brinch Hansen (1980), Jon Fellows and I concluded that

> The underlying concepts of processes, monitors and classes can now be regarded as proven tools for software engineering. So it is time to do something else.

Feedback

Concurrent Pascal and Solo have been assessed by a number of computer scientists.

In a paper on programming languages for real-time control, C.A.R. Hoare (1976) summarized Concurrent Pascal:

> This is one of the few successful extensions of Pascal, and includes well structured capabilities for parallel processing, for exclusion and for synchronization. It was tested before publication in the construction of a small operating system, which promises well for its suitability for real-time programming. Although it does not claim to offer a final solution of the problem it tackles, it is an outstanding example of the best of academic research in this area.

In a detailed assessment of Concurrent Pascal, D. Coleman (1980) wrote:

> The process, monitor and class concepts work equally well for application and system programs. Therefore in that respect the language works admirably. However, because the language is meant for operating systems, all programs run on the bare Pascal machine and every application program must contain modules to provide facilities normally provided by the operating system, e.g. to access the file store.

P.W. Abrahams (1978) found that the modularity of the model operating systems definitely contributed to their readability. However,

> Since the programs are always referring to entities defined earlier, and since these entities are often quite similar, I found that a good deal of page flipping was in fact necessary.

In a review of *The Architecture of Concurrent Programs*, R.A. Maddux and H. Mills (1979) wrote: "This is, as far as we know, the first book published on concurrent programming." They were particularly pleased with the Solo system:

> Here, an entire operating system is visible, with every line of program open to scrutiny. There is no hidden mystery, and after studying such extensive examples, the reader feels that he could tackle similar jobs and that he could change the system at will. Never before have we seen an operating system shown in such detail and in a manner so amenable to modification.

In a survey paper on Concurrent Programming, R.E. Bryant and J.B. Dennis (1979) found that

> The ability to write an operating system in a high level language, including the communication and synchronization between processes, is an important advance in concurrent programming.

A final remark by D. Coleman (1980):

> Concurrent Pascal's main achievement is that it shows how much can be achieved by a simple language that utilises compile time checking to the maximum. It will be a great pity if future language designers do not adhere to these same two principles.

The limitations of the language will be discussed below.

4   Further Development

Since 1975 many other researchers have explored the use of Concurrent Pascal on a variety of computers.

Moving a language

At Caltech we prepared a distribution tape with the source text and portable code of the Solo system, including the Concurrent and Sequential Pascal compilers. The system reports were supplemented by implementation notes (Brinch Hansen 1976b).

By the spring of 1976 we had distributed the system to 75 companies and 100 universities in 21 countries: Australia, Austria, Belgium, Canada, Denmark, Finland, France, Germany, Great Britain, Holland, India, Ireland, Italy, Japan, Norway, South Africa, the Soviet Union, Spain, Sweden, Switzerland, and the United States.

D. Neal and V. Wallentine (1978) moved Concurrent Pascal and Solo to an Interdata 8/32 minicomputer in four months and to an NCR 8250 in another two months. The biggest stumbling block was the addressing scheme of the PDP 11. They wrote:

> It is clear that a system requiring so little effort to be moved between vastly differing architectures must have been well designed from the outset. In addition, with a single exception (sets

and variants), all of the problem points were mentioned by the implementation notes accompanying the distributed system.

M.S. Powell (1979) and two students moved Concurrent Pascal to a Modular 1 in six months. Architectural differences between the source and target computers caused some portability problems. According to Powell,

> Brinch Hansen makes no claims about the portability of Solo, yet our experience shows that a system designed and documented this way can be moved fairly easily even when the target machine has a totally different architecture to that of the source machine.

> Since the system has been in use we have found it easy to use and simple to modify at both high and low levels.

S.E. Mattson (1980) moved Concurrent Pascal (without Solo) to an LSI 11 in four months. He found four errors in the compiler. He felt that

> The kernel is a rather complex program and although the assembly code was commented in a language that resembles Concurrent Pascal it was hard to understand in detail.

> The implementation is a tool of significant value for teaching, research, and engineering. It has been used with success in an undergraduate course.

J.M. Kerridge (1982) moved Concurrent Pascal to an IBM 370/145 in nine months part-time by rewriting the kernel in Fortran. He then moved it to a Honeywell system in one day! In his view

> The original software was extremely well documented and commented but there was still a large amount of 'hacking' which had to be undertaken before the system could be transported.

Concurrent Pascal was moved to many other computers (Löhr 1977; Bochmann 1979; Dunman 1982; Ravn 1982).

The limits of design

Several researchers described the experience of using Concurrent Pascal for
system design.

A research group at TRW Systems used Concurrent Pascal for signal and
image processing on a network of PDP 11/70s. Initially, the group had to
extend the kernel with complicated device drivers written in assembly language. Later, D. Heimbigner (1978) redefined the *io* procedure and was able
to program arbitrary device drivers in Concurrent Pascal (without extending
the kernel).

N. Graef (1979) and others designed a small time-sharing system based
on Solo with swapping of job processes. They described the performance as
unsatisfactory compared to Unix.

After designing a multiterminal version of Solo, D. Coleman (1979) and
others concluded that

> *writing minicomputer operating systems by using Concurrent Pas-
> cal to provide the framework of concurrency for Sequential Pascal
> utilities is only really suited to single user systems.*

G.V. Bochmann and T. Joachim (1979) implemented the X.25 communication protocol in Concurrent Pascal on a Xerox Sigma 6.

H.S.M. Kruijer (1982b) described a multiterminal system for transaction
processing implemented by a Concurrent Pascal program of 2200 lines for a
PDP 11/34. He wrote:

> The work described in this paper shows that Concurrent Pas-
> cal is suitable for the construction of medium-sized multi-user
> systems. It has been found that the application of techniques
> which aim at enhancing portability, namely the exclusion of low-
> level features from the language and their implementation in the
> form of a kernel simulating a virtual machine, does not prevent
> systems written in Concurrent Pascal from being efficient. More-
> over, both the properties of the language (its simplicity, high
> level, dependence on syntax rules) and its facilities (especially
> those for modularization) greatly contribute to obtaining reli-
> able and adaptable system software. To illustrate this point it is
> relevant to mention that for the Multi operating system, a num-
> ber of modules of Solo have been used which together amount to
> about 700 lines of Concurrent Pascal. The use of these modules

in a different context was accomplished without interfacing problems and revealed only one error in one of the modules. These
observations are in sharp contrast to our experience with commercially available operating systems.

Kruijer (1982a) also discovered a single (but subtle) error in the Concurrent
Pascal kernel.

P. Møller-Nielsen and J. Staunstrup (1984) summarized four years of experience with a multiprocessor programmed in Concurrent Pascal. They discussed parallel algorithms for quicksort, mergesort, root finding, and branch-
and-bound optimization.

The static memory allocation of the Concurrent Pascal implementation
made the language impractical for the design of larger operating systems. In
Brinch Hansen (1977b) I pointed out that the language was never intended
for that purpose:

> This book describes a range of small operating systems. Each
> of them provides a special service in the most efficient and simple
> manner. They show that Concurrent Pascal is a useful program-
> ming language for minicomputer operating systems and dedi-
> cated real-time applications. I expect that the language will be
> useful (but not sufficient) for writing large, general-purpose op-
> erating systems. But that still remains to be seen. I have tried
> to make a programming tool that is very convenient for many
> applications rather than one which is tolerable for all purposes.

Evolution of an idea

Concurrent Pascal was followed by more than a dozen *monitor languages*
(Table 3). Some were inspired by Concurrent Pascal; others were developed
independently, inspired by the monitor concept.

I will not attempt to discuss monitor languages that were developed after
Concurrent Pascal. I hope that the designers of these languages will write
personal histories of their own contributions. However, since I have not
programmed in their languages, I cannot evaluate them or compare them
with Concurrent Pascal.

Table 3 Monitor languages.

Language	Reference
Concurrent Pascal	Brinch Hansen (1974d)
Simone	Kaubisch (1976)
Modula	Wirth (1977)
CSP/k	Holt (1978)
CCNPascal	Narayana (1979)
PLY	Nehmer (1979)
Pascal Plus	Welsh (1979)
Mesa	Lampson (1980)
SB-Mod	Bernstein (1981)
Concurrent Euclid	Holt (1982)
Pascalc	Whiddett (1983)
Concurrent C	Tsujino (1984)
Emerald	Black (1986)
Real-time Euclid	Kligerman (1986)
Pascal-FC	Burns (1988)
Turing Plus	Holt (1988)
Predula	Ringström (1990)

Spreading the word

Monitors and monitor languages have been discussed in many survey papers and textbooks. The following list of publication dates gives an idea of how rapidly the monitor paradigm spread through the computer science community.

- *Survey papers*

  Brinch Hansen (1973d), Andrews (1977), Bryant (1979), Stotts (1982), Andrews (1983), Appelbe (1985), Bal (1989).

- *Operating systems texts*

  Brinch Hansen (1973b), Tsichritzis (1974), Peterson (1983), Deitel (1984), Janson (1985), Krakowiak (1988), Pinkert (1989), Nutt (1992), Tanenbaum (1992).

- *Concurrent programming texts*

  Brinch Hansen (1977b), Holt (1978), Welsh (1980), Ben-Ari (1982), Holt (1983), Andre (1985), Boyle (1987), Perrott (1987), Whiddett

(1987), Bustard (1988), Gehani (1988), Krishnamurthy (1989), Raynal (1990), Williams (1990), Andrews (1991).

- *Programming language texts*

  Turski (1978), Tennent (1981), Ghezzi (1982), Young (1982), Horowitz (1983a), Schneider (1984), Bishop (1986), Wilson (1988), Sebesta (1989).

- *Annotated bibliography*

  Bell (1983).

5 In Retrospect

It seems natural to end the story by expressing my own mixed feelings about monitors and Concurrent Pascal.

The neglected problems

Today I have strong reservations about the monitor concept. It is a very clever combination of shared variables, procedures, process scheduling, and modularity. It enabled us to solve problems that we would not have undertaken without a commitment to this paradigm. But, like most of our programming tools, it is somewhat baroque and lacks the elegance that comes from utter simplicity only.

The monitor concept has often been criticized on two grounds: the complex details of process scheduling and the issue of nested monitor calls.

As a language designer, I have always felt that one should experiment with the simplest possible ideas before adopting more complicated ones. This led me to use single-process queues and combine process continuation with monitor exit. I felt that the merits of a signaling scheme could be established only by designing real operating systems (but not by looking at small programming exercises). Since Concurrent Pascal was the first monitor language, I was unable to benefit from the practical experience of others. After designing small operating systems, I concluded that first-in, first-out queues are indeed more convenient to use.

In 1974, when I designed the language, the papers by Howard (1976a, 1976b) and Kessels (1977) on monitor signaling had not yet been published. In any case, the virtues of different signaling mechanisms still strike me as being only mildly interesting. In most cases, any one of them will do, and all of them (including my own) are somewhat complicated. Fortunately, monitors have the marvelous property of *hiding* the details of scheduling from concurrent processes.

In my first monitor paper (Brinch Hansen 1974c) I characterized *nested monitor calls* as a natural and desirable programming feature:

> A monitor can call shared procedures implemented within other monitors. This makes it possible to build an operating system as a *hierarchy of processes and monitors*.

If a process delays itself within a nested sequence of monitor calls, it releases access to the last monitor only, but leaves the previous monitors temporarily inaccessible to other processes. Lister (1977) felt that this situation might degrade performance or cause deadlock:

> The only implementation known to the author in which the nested call problem is tackled head-on, rather than being merely avoided, is that by Brinch Hansen (1975e). In this [Concurrent Pascal] implementation a local exclusion mechanism is used for each monitor, and a [delay] operation causes release of exclusion on only the most recently called monitor. It is not clear what measures, if any, are taken to avoid the degradation of performance and potential for deadlock mentioned earlier.

Lister (1977) offered no performance figures or program examples to prove the existence of such a problem. The hypothetical "problem" of nested monitor calls was discussed further by Haddon (1977), Keedy (1978), Wettstein (1978), and Kotulski (1987)—still without experimental evidence. In a paper on "The non-problem of nested monitor calls" Parnas (1978) finally declared that the problem was too vaguely formulated to be solvable.

Two years before this discussion started I had written three model operating systems in Concurrent Pascal. I used nested monitor calls in every one of them without any problems. These calls were a natural and inevitable consequence of the hierarchical program structures.

The discomfort of complexity

The monitor was undoubtedly a paradigm that for a time provided model problems and solutions to the computer science community. It may be argued that its proper role is to define a useful programming style, and that it is a mistake to include it in a programming language. To an engineer, this viewpoint has merits. To a scientist, it is less convincing.

When an idea is seen just as a programming style, programmers seldom define it precisely. They constantly bend the (unstated) rules of the game and mix it with other imprecise paradigms. This lack of rigor makes it rather difficult to explore the limits of a new idea.

I never considered Concurrent Pascal to be a final solution to anything. It was an experimental tool that imposed an intellectual discipline on me. By embedding monitors in a programming language I committed myself to defining the concept and its relationship to processes concisely. I deliberately made monitors the only communication mechanism in the language to ensure that we would discover the limitations of the concept.

Concurrent Pascal was the first programming language I designed. From my present perspective, it has all the flaws that are inevitable in a first venture.

In a later essay on language description (Brinch Hansen 1981), I wrote:

> The task of writing a language report that explains a programming language with complete clarity to its implementors and users may look deceptively easy to someone who hasn't done it before. But in reality it is one the most difficult intellectual tasks in the field of programming.

Well, I was someone who hadn't done it before, and the Concurrent Pascal report suffered from all the problems I mentioned in the essay.

I am particularly uncomfortable with the many *ad hoc* restrictions in the language. For example,

- Module types cannot be defined within procedures.

- Procedures cannot be defined within procedures.

- Module instances cannot be declared within procedures.

- Queues can only be declared as global variables of monitor types.

- Queues cannot be parameters of procedure entries.

- Process instances can only be declared in the initial process.

- A module type cannot refer to the variables of another module type.

- A module type cannot call its own procedure entries.

- A procedure cannot call itself.

- A continue operation can only be performed within a monitor procedure entry.

- Assignments cannot be performed on variables of type module or queue.

These rules were carefully chosen to make the language secure and enforce the compromises discussed earlier. But they all *restrict* the *generality* of the language concepts and the ways in which they may be combined.

There are about twenty rules of this kind in Concurrent Pascal (Brinch Hansen 1975a). I will spare you the rest. They are an unmistakable symptom of complexity.

After Concurrent Pascal I developed two smaller languages. Each of them was again designed to explore a single programming concept: conditional critical regions in *Edison*, and synchronous communication in *Joyce* (Brinch Hansen 1981, 1989a).

There are exactly three *ad hoc* restrictions in Joyce:

- A process cannot access global variables.

- A message cannot include a channel reference.

- Two processes cannot communicate by polling the same channel(s).

I think only the first one is really necessary.

Inventing the future

What am I most proud of? The answer is simple: We did something that had not been done before! We demonstrated that it is possible to write nontrivial concurrent programs exclusively in a secure programming language.

The particular paradigm we chose (monitors) was a detail only. The important thing was to discover if it was possible to add a new dimension to programming languages: *modular concurrency.*

Every revolution in programming language technology introduces abstract programming concepts for a new application domain. Fortran and Algol 60 were the first abstract languages for numerical computation. Pascal was used to implement its own compiler. Simula 67 introduced the class concept for simulation.

Before Concurrent Pascal it was not known whether operating systems could be written in secure programming languages without machine-dependent features. The discovery that this was indeed possible for small operating systems and real-time systems was far more important (I think) than the introduction of monitors.

Monitors made process communication abstract and secure. That was, of course, a breakthrough in the art of concurrent programming. However, the monitor concept was a detail in the sense that it was only one possible solution to the problem of making communication secure. Today we have three major communication paradigms: monitors, remote procedures, and message passing.

The development of secure language concepts for concurrent programming started in 1971. Fifteen years later Judy Bishop (1986) concluded:

> It is evident that the realm of concurrency is now firmly within the ambit of reliable languages and that future designs will provide for concurrent processing as a matter of course.

In the first survey paper on concurrent programming I cited 11 papers only, written by four researchers. None of them described a concurrent programming language (Brinch Hansen 1973d). The development of monitors and Concurrent Pascal started a wave of research in concurrent programming languages that still continues. A recent survey of the field lists over 200 references to nearly 100 languages (Bal 1989).

I don't think we have found the right programming concepts for parallel computers yet. When we do, they will almost certainly be very different from anything we know today.

Acknowledgements

This paper is dedicated to my former students who contributed to the Concurrent Pascal project:

Jon Fellows	Charles Hayden	Jørgen Staunstrup
Wolfgang Franzen	Habib Maghami	Tom Zepko
Al Hartmann		

I thank the following 60 colleagues for their helpful comments on earlier drafts of this paper:

Birger Andersen	Tony Hoare	Harlan Mills
Greg Andrews	Ric Holt	Peter O'Hearn
Bill Atwood	Jim Horning	Ross Overbeek
Art Bernstein	Giorgio Ingargiola	Niels Pedersen
Jean Bezivin	David Jefferson	Ron Perrott
Judy Bishop	Mathai Joseph	Malcolm Powell
Coen Bron	Eric Jul	Brian Randell
Dave Bustard	Jon Kerridge	Anders Ravn
Mani Chandy	Don Knuth	Charles Reynolds
Derek Coleman	Henk Kruijer	Johan Ringström
Ole-Johan Dahl	Andrew Lister	Bob Rosin
Peter Denning	Bart Locanthi	Fred Schneider
Jerry Feldman	Ewing Lusk	Avi Silberschatz
Jon Fellows	Bill Lynch	Jørgen Staunstrup
Narain Gehani	Rich McBride	Wlad Turski
Jonathan Greenfield	Mike McKeag	Virgil Wallentine
Al Hartmann	Jan Madey	Peter Wegner
Charles Hayden	Roy Maddux	Dick Whiddett
Dennis Heimbigner	Mike Mahoney	Niklaus Wirth
John Hennessy	Skip Mattson	Tom Zepko

I also thank the anonymous referees for their careful reviews of earlier drafts.

The Concurrent Pascal project was supported by the National Science Foundation under grant numbers DCR74-17331 and MCS77-05696, the design of Trio by the Army Research Office under contract number DAAG29-77-G-0192, and the development of Distributed Processes by the Office of Naval Research under contract numbers NR048-647 and NR049-415.

Appendix: Reviewers' Comments

In 1991 I sent earlier drafts of this paper to a number of computer scientists with a letter asking for their comments "with the understanding that I may quote your letter in the final paper." Many of their suggestions are incorporated in the revised paper. Here are some of their remaining remarks.

G. Andrews:

You claim that the particular paradigm you chose (monitors) was a ... detail. The most important aspect of monitors is their role as a data encapsulation mechanism.

. . .

The contribution of Concurrent Pascal was indeed that it added a new dimension to programming languages: modular concurrency. Monitors (and classes) were essential to this contribution. And the modularization they introduced has greatly influenced most subsequent concurrent language proposals.

What is debateable about monitors are the details of synchronization, especially the signaling discipline.

. . .

I have not seen any radical new programming ideas emerge for several years now. Thus, I suspect that in the future the programming concepts we use for parallel computers will merely be refinements of things we know today.

D.W. Bustard:

The statement ... "Today I have strong reservations about the monitor concept" tends to suggest that the *concept* is flawed. I don't agree. The basic concept of a data structure allowing processes exclusive access to its data still seems very important. What has never been handled satisfactorily, however, is the explicit queuing mechanism for process suspension and activation. I tinkered with several possibilities over a period of years but now (like Parnas) I feel that it would be better to give access to lower level facilities that allow users to implement a policy of their own liking. It is a mistake for language designers to treat potential users like children!

O.-J. Dahl:

I am grateful for your recognition of the role of the Simula 67 class concept; however, in the reference to it the name of my colleague Kristen Nygaard should occur along with mine ... [Our] own historic paper, given at the ACM Conference on the "History of Programming Languages" ... shows the extent to which either of us was dependent on the other in the discovery of the class concept.

. . .

I take issue with some of your reservations about Concurrent Pascal. Of course a language built around a small number of mechanisms used orthogonally is an ideal worth striving for. Still, when I read your 1977 book my reaction was that the art of imposing the right restrictions may be as important from an engineering point of view. So, here for once was a language, beautiful by its orthogonal design, which at the same time was the product of a competent engineer by the restrictions imposed in order to achieve implementation and execution efficiency. The adequacy of the language as a practical tool has been amply demonstrated.

P.J. Denning:

I had a love-hate relationship with monitors since first meeting them as "critical regions" in your 1973 book and then in Hoare's 1974 paper in the ACM Communications. What I loved about them was the way they brought together data abstraction (as we now call it) and synchronization. Suddenly we had a simple notation that allowed the expression of correct programs for the hard problems we faced constantly in operating systems design. What I hated about them was the need to understand the details of the queuing mechanism in order to understand how to use them. My students had to study carefully Hoare's notes on using semaphores to do the queueing. In this sense monitors had not broken away from the fine-grain mechanisms of semaphores.

I was therefore much interested in the next stages that you and Hoare reached, expressed in your 1978 papers in the ACM Communications. You had continued the line of development of monitors into distributed processes; Hoare had proposed communicating sequential processes, an approach motivated by the constraints of microprocessor design. I was more attracted to Hoare's proposal because of my own biases in thinking about how operating systems and parallel computers are actually built and how they manage work.

. . .

Even though in the end I found the monitor concept less to my liking than communicating processes, I still think that the monitor is a good idea, and that the observer it makes one of how operating systems work is a worthy observer to learn to be.

J.A. Feldman:

I was not personally involved with the [Concurrent Pascal] effort, but admired it and now find somewhat to my surprise that my current parallel Sather project relies on a version of monitors.

...

[It is] now clear that any large, scalable parallel machine will have physically distributed memory. There is a great deal of current research on hardware and software for uniform memory abstractions, but this seems to me unlikely to work. The structure of the programming language and code can provide crucial information on locality requirements so that the system doesn't need to do it all mindlessly. And that is where monitors come in.

Sather is an object-oriented language ... The parallel constructs ... are based on a primitive monitor type ... [It] is remarkable that 20 years later the monitor concept is central to language developments well beyond the original conception.

J. Fellows:

Looking back at my studies at USC from 1978 to 1981, I can separate my thoughts into three areas: the concepts that underly monitors and classes, the language constructs that implement these concepts, and the quality of the demonstration programs that you (PBH) wrote. You have already addressed the first two in your paper. As for the third, I believe that the beauty of the structures you created using Concurrent Pascal created an aura of magical simplicity. While working with my own programs and those of other graduate students, I soon learned that ordinary, even ugly, programs could also be written in Concurrent Pascal ... My current feeling is that the level of intellectual effort required to create a beautiful program structure cannot be reduced by programming language features, but that these features can more easily reveal a program's beauty to others who need to understand it.

...

The topic I chose to explore [in the Trio system] was the use of Concurrent Pascal's access restrictions to explicitly create a program access graph (or "uses" hierarchy between type instances) that achieved least privilege visibility between program components, meaning that no component has access to another component unless it is needed. For this purpose, I still believe that Concurrent Pascal's initialization-time binding of components is an improvement over the scope-based facilities of Modula, Edison, and Ada.

...

It is interesting to note that one of the most common complaints I heard (and made myself) was that classes should have been left in [Sequential

Pascal]. This would have extended many of the benefits available to system programmers to application programmers.

...

As I discovered when moving the compilers from Solo to Trio, there was a point at which the Operating System/Sequential Pascal interface was unsafe. As I recall, there was no type checking across the program invocation interface, which depended on correct hand-tailoring and consistent usage of the prefix for Sequential Pascal programs. In general, program invocation was the one operating system area that was not made transparently simple in Solo and Trio.

A.C. Hartmann:

There are really two histories interwoven in this paper—the history of the development of concurrent modular programming, and the history of one man's ruthless quest for simplicity in design and programming. The former topic is indifferent to whether one chooses to develop concurrency mechanisms for greater expressive power and more complex functionality, or, as you have chosen, to radically shorten and simplify the design of common concurrent systems. The Solo operating system is downright primitive in the sparseness of its features, representing a counter-cultural current against ever-increasing operating system complexity. Your style and taste in programming run almost counter to the second law of thermodynamics, that all closed systems tend towards increasing entropy and disorder.

In a world of Brinch Hansens (which may exist in some parallel dimension to ours), all systems tend towards reduced entropy over time and toward a blissful state of ultimate simplicity. Each new release of the operating system for one's personal workstation is smaller than the previous release, consumes fewer system resources, runs faster on simpler hardware, provides a reduced set of easier to use features than the last release, and carries a lower price tag. Hardware designers espousing the same philosophy produce successive single-chip microprocessors with exponentially declining transistor counts from generation to generation, dramatically shrinking die sizes, and reducing process steps by resorting to fewer, simpler device types. No one would need to "invent" RISC computing in this world, since reduced feature sets would be an inexorable law of nature.

...

Ironically the Concurrent Pascal compiler that I wrote was written in the language of its sister Sequential Pascal compiler, which had neither classes nor monitors. It was fifteen years later when I finally had access to a C++ system on a personal computer that I wrote my first modular program using abstract typing. To this day I have not written a concurrent program.

C.C. Hayden:

What was remarkable about [Concurrent Pascal] is that one could write experimental operating systems on a virtual machine without having to resort to machine registers, assembly language, etc. The development environment provided a way to do operating systems in a controlled way, on the "bare hardware" of a much nicer machine than any real computer...

I think the significance of the system was ... that one could provide a protected environment for concurrent programming—a high-level language environment which could maintain the illusion that there was no "machine" level. It was remarkable that through compile time restrictions and virtual machine error checking, that you could understand the program behavior by looking at the Pascal, not at the machine's registers and memory. It was remarkable that the machine could retain its integrity while programs were being developed, without hardware memory protection.

. . .

How has the monitor concept evolved? From my perspective, the concept of message passing between processes in disjoint address spaces was around before monitors, and has continued to dominate the monitor concept. The operating systems in most common use today have message passing paradigms. The Macintosh, Microsoft Windows, Unix running X windows: all force applications to be organized around an event loop, which receives an event message, unpacks it and dispatches to a handler, and carries out an action. These are just the "real time" system architecture of the 1960s. The monitor concept was an advance over the earlier message passing systems because it eliminated the event loop, message packing and unpacking, dispatching, etc. Concurrent Pascal hid all that mess, and made it possible to do it more efficiently by absorbing it into machine code or microcode, and eliminated the possibility of making errors. Why did it not become better accepted?

. . .

Maybe the problem monitors were meant to solve (concurrency in shared memory systems) was never really that important after all. The conventional wisdom is that concurrent systems cannot scale up if they share memory.

. . .

I have a deep respect for the monitor concept: in my opinion it is better than message passing, which is what we are stuck with. It is particularly powerful if used in the form of conditional critical regions. And I think the language Concurrent Pascal made a real advance in permitting easy experimentation with operating systems concepts and implementations. It allowed me to further my own education by building programs that I would not otherwise have been able to build. This taught me valuable lessons about programming styles and paradigms, about how important it is to be able to reason about programs when they cannot be reliably tested. Concurrent Pascal had to deal with such restrictive and peculiar hardware, almost unthinkably limiting by today's standards.

As your thinking evolved, the systems you built seemed to get smaller and more elegant, trying to achieve more generality and less complexity. This is a laudable goal for research languages, but I could never come to believe in it as applied to programming tools such as editors, formatters, etc. I know of few people who would want to adopt simpler tools ... Perhaps there is no longer any call for this kind of programming ... I am glad that I was able to educate myself before it was too late. The Concurrent Pascal system made that possible.

D. Heimbigner:

Concurrent Pascal is one of those languages that is very much under-appreciated. It was one of the first widely available languages to introduce both object-oriented concepts and concurrency (in the form of processes and monitors).

Concurrent Pascal is perhaps best known as one of the first languages to provide monitors as a synchronization device. Initially, I was a very strong believer in the monitor construct. After using the construct for a while, I recognized its flaws and was rather disenchanted with them. Since then, I have had some experience with Ada and its tasking model, and I am beginning to think that perhaps monitors were not such a bad concept after all.

I should also note that I am continually surprised at how long it is taking for concurrency constructs to become a standard part of every programmer's toolkit. The C and C++ communities, for example, are still arguing over a standard threads package. Most Unix kernels (except Mach) have no special provisions for handling threads, most Unix libraries are still not capable of working correctly in a parallel environment, and most Unix machines are still single processor. This seems to me to be a disgrace.

The concurrency elements of Concurrent Pascal were important, but I would also like to comment on its object-orientation. It was my first introduction to an object-oriented language. At the same time, (1976–1978), Smalltalk was mostly a rumor; it would be several years before it became available. Simula-67 was not widely available on any machine to which I had access.

So, when I encountered Concurrent Pascal, I spent a fair amount of time experimenting with its object-oriented constructs. As a result, I became a firm believer in that approach for programming and have continued to use the paradigm to this day.

It is interesting to compare Concurrent Pascal with, for example, Modula-2 and Ada. At one time, there was a discussion in the language community about the merits of objects (as represented in Smalltalk and Concurrent Pascal and Euclid) versus the merits of packages (as represented in Modula-2 and Ada). In retrospect, it seems amusing that these two concepts were considered comparable, rather than complementary. It also clear that the object point of view has prevailed (witness Modula-3 and Ada 9x).

J. Hennessy:

I had one interesting insight that I wanted to communicate to you. We have been experimenting with an object-oriented language (called Cool and based on C++) for programming parallel machines. The idea is to use the object structure as a basis for synchronization, dealing with data locality, and for implementing load balancing. Initially, we anticipated using a variety of synchronization primitives, including things such as futures, in addition to monitor-based constructs. Surprisingly, we found that the synchronization mechanisms based on monitors were adequate for most cases, and were much easier to implement (more efficient), and easier to understand. My advice is not to undersell monitors. I suspect that we will find that there are many more instances where this basic concept is useful!

C.A.R. Hoare:

I read your personal history with great enjoyment: it brings back with sharp clarity the excitement of our discussions at Marktoberdorf and Belfast in 1971. Even more valuably, it describes the whole history of a remarkably successful research engineering project, conducted with utmost regard for scientific integrity, and principles, which has enlarged the understanding of a whole generation of computing scientists and software engineers. That a subsequent generation has lost the understanding could be explained in another, much sadder, paper.

My only serious debate with your account is with the very last sentence. I do not believe that there is any "right" collection of programming concepts for parallel (or even sequential) computers. The design of a language is always a compromise, in which the good designer must take into account the desired level of abstraction, the target machine architecture, and the proposed range of applications. I therefore believe that the monitor concept will continue to be highly appropriate for implementation of operating systems on shared-store multi-processors. Of course, it will improve and adapt; its successful evolution is now the responsibility of those who follow your footsteps. Your full account of the original voyage of exploration will continue to inform, guide, and inspire them.

G. Ingargiola:

Your paper is faithful to what I remember.

You had this tremendous clarity about what you were doing in concurrency and languages; you made restrictive choices usually on the basis of efficiency (you list a number of such choices in your paper). You stated something like "start with as few and simple mechanisms as possible; add later only if it becomes necessary."

At least in your discussions and lectures, you built programs from english statements, making explicit the invariants and refining these statements, usually not modifying them, until the program was done.

I was amazed at how slowly you developed code when lecturing, and, by contrast, how fast you got debugged running code for the Concurrent Pascal compiler, and for various concurrent programs and the Solo OS.

You had very little interest in computer science topics outside of the area in which you were doing research. You made polite noises, you indicated interest, but your span of attention was minimal ...

The personnel involved in the Concurrent Pascal implementation is as small as you say ... Deverill contributed with his knowledge of the PDP 11 architecture and of its assembly language. Hartmann and you did the work. ...

I remember your excitement with the notion of "threaded code;" if I remember correctly, you thought it was your own invention and found out only later that others found it before.

In 1977, on the phone, you told me that you were working on a model of distributed computing where processes could make synchronous calls across processors. When later I heard about remote procedure calls, I assumed it was a variation on what you had said.

M. Joseph:

[Your paper] made very interesting reading and it took me back to the exciting days of early 1975 when you lectured on Concurrent Pascal in Bombay!

We spent quite a lot of 1975 studying Concurrent Pascal and deciding whether and how it could be used for our multiprocessor operating system project ...

Our version of the language (which we called CCNPascal, both because of its antecedents in Concurrent Pascal and because it was the language for the Close-Coupled Network project) ... was implemented on a DEC-10 and generated code for the DEC-10, PDP-11 and TDC-16 (and later a group produced a code generator for the Intel 8086). So perhaps it is fair to say that Concurrent Pascal had close 'cousins' on all of these machines!

I think there has been some general confusion about the role of Concurrent Pascal. On the one hand, it was used very successfully in the version that you supplied, by many people and for a variety of applications. On the other hand, the design of Concurrent Pascal also provided the springboard for people (like us) to make use of its concepts for designing larger languages which were applied to fairly ambitious tasks. So the monitor concept was fairly rugged and stood up well to the test of being used for large applications, and this is something that is not widely known.

Moreover, it was a language for which high quality code could be generated (something that implementors of Ada still aspire to). We had multi-pass cross-compiling versions of our compiler which generated extremely tight code and I later produced a one-pass version of the compiler which did a lot of on-the-fly optimization and produced PDP-11 code ...

With interest returning to shared memory multiprocessors, it seems quite appropriate that people should be reminded of the achievements of Concurrent Pascal.

J.M. Kerridge:

One of the reasons that I acquired Concurrent Pascal was to enable access to a Pascal system which at the time (1978) was the only way it could be made accessible on our IBM 370. It had the added benefit of introducing me to concurrent programming. This has lead me to continue working in the area of parallel systems allowing me to build highly parallel database machines based around the transputer and occam.

In this respect I find your comments ... concerning the compromises that were made to effect efficient processing surprising. In the transputer/occam combination the same limitations have, to a large extent, also been imposed. This enables compile time checking of memory allocation and process inter-action, which is vital for real-time embedded control systems. It is inter-esting that this too was the application environment from which you came originally.

If we consider the use of Ada for such safety-critical real-time systems then we have to use Safe Ada, which has exactly the same limitations. The full capability of Ada is only available with a large run-time support system about which it is impossible to reason!

Given the above points I believe that you have been somewhat hard in criticising Concurrent Pascal ... Hindsight is a valuable tool especially after nearly 20 years! Many of the restrictions were reasonable given that you were experimenting with concurrency and not constructing a sequential language. Keeping things simple is a good axiom and though it is useful to have nested procedure declarations, as an example, it was not fundamental to the needs of concurrency experimentation. If many of these restrictions had been relaxed then Concurrent Pascal may never have seen the light of day.

H.S.M. Kruijer:

I (continue to) regard the specification and implementation of Concurrent Pascal as an impressive piece of work, combining the best results of Com-puter Science and making them available in the area of Software Engineering. More specifically, I regard this work and the publications on it as large-scale examples of the application of sound (computer) science resulting into high-quality "real-life" (software) engineering products, which still serve as a yardstick and a source of inspiration not only for (computer) scientists but also (more importantly) for practicising (software) engineers ...

The use of Concurrent Pascal has played a major organising and professionalising role in the Computer science & Software engineering section of our Mathematics and Systems Engineering department.   My paper in "Software—Practice and Experience" (1982) described a project carried out in the period 1976–1980, but other work has been done that has not been published:

—We have extended, during 1981–1983, the prototype application system referred to in my paper (namely a multi-user system for order taking and stock updating suited to Shell's Marketing (Sales) business) so as to run on a number of PDP 11 computers coupled via one common, shared communication channel (eventually an Ethernet). Therefore the Multi operating system described was transformed systematically into a distributed version, using remote procedure calls and client-server mechanisms and using Concurrent Pascal for the implementation of the data communication software needed.

. . .

—A prototype data acquisition system (for Shell's process control system in refineries and chemical plants) has been developed during 1981–1985, using Concurrent Pascal as implementation language.

—A data acquisition system for our Materials Research department has been developed during 1986–1989, using Concurrent Pascal for specification and design and using DEC hardware and software for implementation.

E.L. Lusk:

Our group's adoption of monitors as a central theme in our parallel programming work did not arise from an interest in elegant operating systems; it was absolutely forced on us by the task of writing application programs for real parallel processors. In 1983 Los Alamos obtained a Denelcor HEP, in many respects the first commercially available multiprocessor. Several different groups at Argonne tried it out, in 1984 Argonne got one too, and that facility evolved into Argonne's Advanced Computing Research Facility.

The HEP was programmed in a dialect of Fortran that allowed direct access to the full/empty bits in memory as a way of allowing ordinary program variables to be used for a kind of dataflow synchronization. The mechanism was efficient but dangerous. Ross Overbeek and I chose as our first project the parallel implementation of the unification algorithm from theorem proving. We found this a humbling experience, to say the least. While our colleagues proceeded smoothly with parallel versions of regular numerical algorithms, we suffered every type of bug associated with parallel algorithms. Finally we realized that we would have to retreat to intellectually higher ground. For the shared-memory computational model, monitors represented an abstraction that could be understood, reasoned about, and efficiently implemented. We used the HEP constructs to implement locks, used the locks to construct the basic monitor-building primitives, used these to build (portable, now, at this level) a library of useful monitors, and our problems disappeared for good. The macro package for the HEP has evolved through several generations, and its descendants are widely used for programming nearly all current shared-memory machines in C and Fortran.

. . .

I believe that the simple domain-composition algorithms that pay the freight for the current generation of massively-parallel machines are distracting many current users from realizing the long-term validity of the shared-memory model. Fast communication speeds do not make the shared memory irrelevant; it is the programming model that is important. Although the programming model for message passing is now relatively stable . . ., no such consensus has arisen for the shared memory model . . . In the long run monitors will be seen as the most useful paradigm for expressing algorithms for the shared-memory model. The shared-memory model, in turn, will return to greater prominence as more complex algorithms are moved to parallel computers.

Monitors shall arise again!

W.C. Lynch:

I think that monitors may have achieved more contemporary success than you might believe. In one sense I think of your description as one of the birth pains of an idea that has matured and stood the test of time.

. . .

In 1977 Xerox PARC/SDD [had] to construct a real time . . . operating system (subsequently called "Pilot"). A large part of the problem was the specification of facilities for concurrent operation. The input experiences were . . . 1) my experience in the design and implementation 1970–71 of Chios utilizing light-weight processes and Dijkstra PV operators . . ., 2) Butler Lampson's proposal to incorporate Monitors and Condition variables, as described by Hoare, into Mesa and hence into Pilot . . ., 3) the pre-disposition of management to leverage their experience with message passing paradyms in the SDS-XDS operating systems.

I was the convenor of this task force. Among others, Butler Lampson, Dave Redell, and Hugh Lauer were participants. Roger Needham was an occasional consultant.

Inputs 1) and 2) quickly converged, supported by the reality of your previous experience with Concurrent Pascal, but 3) led to a contentious stalemate, with each party claiming some inherent superiority over the other. This was finally resolved by the arguement presented in (Lauer 1978) which demonstrated that the views were equivalent in the sense that each could be executed in terms of the other. Since the intention was to combine support for concurrent processing with the benefits of Mesa, it was clear that the procedural view of Monitors was most compatible with the procedural language Mesa.

The design that resulted, smoothly incorporating threads (nee light weight processes), monitors, and condition variables into Mesa as built-in types, was eventually described in (Lampson 1980).

Lampson, Redell, and others moved on to DEC SRC and continued their work there. With the work on and introduction of the object oriented Modula-3, it was realized that a class structure allows the above threads related types to be implemented as a library without being implemented in the language ...

Today threads libraries, a direct linear descendent of monitors, are de rigeur in the Unix world. I would say that the ideas created in the process that you describe are still a major force today.

...

I don't know what more one could ask in the way of ultimate triumph for an idea.

R.A. Overbeek:

In the early 1980's, E. Lusk and I were offered the opportunity of developing applications for a new parallel processor, the Denelcor HEP. Our application area was automated deduction, and our background in parallel computation was quite limited. In our first experiments, we worked with the programming constructs offered by Denelcor Fortran, which were low-level synchronization constructs. It became immediately apparent that we needed to develop higher-level, portable constructs. Our central source of both ideas and implementation guidelines during that period was Concurrent Pascal and your work that gave detailed implementation information. We developed a rather primitive set of tools and began work on several applications.

A year later, we were faced with moving our applications to several other machines. To our delight, we were able to port a 50,000 line implementation of a parallel logic programming engine from the HEP to a new Sequent Balance in just 4 hours. We went on to port the code to a variety of other shared-memory multiprocessors, and the benefits of portable constructs were quite apparent. Indeed, the ability to develop programs on machines in which the environment was relatively stable and for which adequate performance monitoring and debugging tools existed (most notably, the Sequent machines) and then move them to a number of "production" environments was extremely useful.

Later, we shifted our programming paradigm to include message-passing constructs. It is a tenable position that there are relatively few applications that benefit substantially from parallel processing, and that a majority of these can be formulated in ways that allow effective use of parallelism with message-passing constructs; that is, they do not require the capabilities we built into our earlier tools based on monitors. Furthermore, the ability to port applications based on message-passing to platforms like multicomputers or clusters of workstations is really quite attractive. I consider this a far from settled issue, but I have tentatively adopted this position.

Our work based on developing portable tools for exploring the potential exploitation of parallelism on the wide variety of machines that appeared in the 1980s benefited directly from the pioneering work on monitors. While we were never fortunate enough to be directly involved with the individuals that drove that effort, we did gradually come to grasp some of the issues that they had clarified.

N. Holm Pedersen:

It is with a feeling of nostalgia that we, at Brüel & Kjœr, read about the emerging of the ideas on which we have based most of the programming of our instruments for the last decade. We are still using the Concurrent Pascal (CP) language in full scale i.e. just finishing 2 instruments, each with programs of more than 1 Mbyte code written in Concurrent Pascal.

It is remarkable that the ideas of Concurrent Pascal is having a major effect on modern blockstructured languages such as Ada and C++. Excluding the monitor concept, Ada has inherited the structures of CP, and C++ has reinvented the Class-type. It caused some confusion in our company to hear C++ being named "the invention of the century" as we have created objects since 1980 in the form of Monitors and Classes. We are in the process of discovering that the freedom (nonhierarchical nature) of C++ is very nice but dangerous ...

M.S. Powell:

I read the first draft of your paper "Monitors and Concurrent Pascal: A Personal History" with great interest. The work I did with Concurrent Pascal and the Solo system took place near the beginning of my academic career and much of my subsequent work has been strongly influenced by it. Your paper fills in many gaps in my knowledge of the history of the development of the underlying ideas. A number of things I did with Concurrent Pascal and Solo which may be of interest, but have never been published, are described below.

The characteristics of Solo which made it easy to port to a machine with a very different architecture to the PDP-11, also made it very easy to change and extend for practical and experimental purposes. The final configuration supported on Modular 1 hardware at UMIST ran across three processors with the file store distributed across two 28M byte exchangeable disk drives shared between the three processors. In this form the system supported many final year project students and research projects. Many compiler and language extensions were introduced, e.g. the Concurrent Pascal compiler was modified to support generic classes and the compiler and virtual machine were modified to support message passing through inter-process channels. A system which ran up to two passes of the compiler pipelined concurrently by two processors was also implemented.

...

After the Modular 1 system (around 1982) we moved onto a network of DEC LSI-11s connected together by a Cambridge ring. A distributed Concurrent Pascal implementation was constructed for this environment. During execution of the initial process, extensions to the virtual machine allowed processes and monitors to be assigned interactively to selected processors on the network. Monitor entry routine calls were implemented by remote procedure calls, and distribution was transparent to the concurrent program, i.e. we were able to run programs produced on the Modular 1 without recompilation.

...

A spin-off of my research work has been a system called Paradox which has been used to support teaching in the Computation Department for the last four years.

. . .

Inside the implementation of Paradox, unseen by most, Concurrent Pascal is alive and well at UMIST, and helping to support nearly 250 users every year.

A.P. Ravn:

I really enjoyed reading your paper on the history of Monitors and Concurrent Pascal. I shall refrain from commenting on who got the ideas for the monitor first; but I am sure that Concurrent Pascal was central for the dissemination of these ideas in software enginering.

. . .

The Concurrent Pascal system and its literature made it possible to combine theoretical concepts with experimental work. Probably the only way engineering can be taught.

It was a pleasure teaching courses based on Concurrent Pascal, and the students, who are now software developers, received a thorough knowledge of good system programming concepts. In some ways too good; when I meet them now, they find it hard to break away from these paradigms, even in distributed systems.

C.W. Reynolds:

There seem to me to be two central issues treated during the early period 1971–1973. First was the issue of medium term scheduling. How does a process wait for some condition to be true? . . .

It seems to me that the critical insight occurred in realizing that the responsibility for determining an awaited event has occurred must lie with the application programmer and not with the underlying run-time support. The awakening of processes awaiting events is part of the application algorithm and must be indicated by explicit announcement of the events by means of "signal" or "cause" commands present in the application algorithm.

This idea is clearly present as early as Brinch Hansen (1972b). Of less importance, but necessary to mention, is that there and in Concurrent Pascal, at most one process can be suspended in a single queue. Although this can be efficiently implemented and although it is possible to use it to simulate a queue containing multiple processes, the history of the last twenty years has shown the multiple process condition queue of Hoare (1974a) to be more popular.

The second central issue in this early period is the class notion from Simula. And there are two aspects to this. First is the encapsulation of procedures together with their shared variables and the prohibition of access to these shared variables by any procedures other than those encapsulated procedures. This notion of encapsulation appears in the unpublished draft Brinch Hansen (1971c) and it definitely appears in the textbook Brinch Hansen (1973b).

The second important aspect of the class concept is that a class is a mechanism for type definition so that multiple distinct variables of a class can be declared ... But, in the context of monitors, there is an important difference that appears in short-term scheduling of exclusive access to the monitor. Is this exclusion enforced for each class instance or is it enforced for the whole class at once? ... Mutual exclusion on individual instances of a class is possible in languages such as Concurrent Pascal and Mesa which adopted the Simula class style, whereas it is not possible in languages such as Pascal Plus, SP/k, Concurrent Euclid, Modula-2 and Ada which did not.

The treatment of monitors as Simula classes appears in the textbook Brinch Hansen (1973b) and is notably absent in Hoare (1974a).

I believe that another central issue treated but never resolved in this early period was the relationship between short-term scheduling in monitor access and medium term scheduling for awaited events. Evidence of this issue is found in the variety of signaling semantics proposed during this period. These included the Signal/Return semantics of Concurrent Pascal, the Signal/Unconditional-Wait semantics of Hoare (1974a) and the more prevalent Signal/Wait semantics of languages like SP/k and others. Multiple not-quite-satisfactory solutions to the problem indicate that it has not been resolved.

V. Wallentine:

Your comments on our experience porting Concurrent Pascal were completely accurate.

However, many things cannot be included in journal articles. The thrill of porting a useful language with such a small investment of time made it possible to use Concurrent Pascal in the academic environment. Many, many students were able to learn the concepts of concurrent programming and encapsulation using Concurrent Pascal. Having a concrete language to experiment with is essential to understanding the monitor concept. Using the concept of monitors as implemented in Concurrent C as a concrete example, they were able to better understand additional scheduling (and signaling) techniques.

I remember spending many hours with my research group discussing different signaling paradigms and hierarchical monitors. We also spent a significant amount of time implementing a distributed operating system (on top of Unix). This was a good test for the strength of the monitor concept.

T. Zepko:

Part of the history you describe is an important part of my own history.

At the time I was involved with Concurrent Pascal, I was an undergraduate and not so much concerned with the conceptual significance of the language as with learning how to build a language system from the ground up. I got the practical experience I wanted by working on the Concurrent Pascal compiler, the threaded code interpreter, and the operating system kernel. I have continued to do this same kind of work for the last fifteen years.

The concepts behind the Concurrent Pascal, the evolution of the ideas as you describe them, are clearer to me now than they were as a student. The needs you were addressing do require some years of experience to appreciate. But even as a student, some things left a lasting impression. What I learned from you, beyond specific programming techniques, is what I can only describe as a passion for clear thinking. This was obvious in the way you approached program design, and it was obviously the driving force behind the design of the Concurrent Pascal language.

...

Some of the ideas embodied in Concurrent Pascal were radical at the time. That they seem less so now is a tribute to the trailblazing nature of your work. Your approach to programming and to language design now has many advocates. Structured programming, modular design, strong typing, data encapsulation, and so on, are all considered essential elements of modern programming and have found their way into a wide variety of languages. I'm thankful to have played a part in this work.

References

Abrahams, P.W. 1978. Review of the Architecture of Concurrent Programs. *Computing Reviews 19*, (September).

Andre, F., Herman, D., and Verjus, J.-P. 1985. *Synchronization of Parallel Programs*, MIT Press, Cambridge, MA.

Andrews, G.R., and McGraw, J.R. 1977. Language features for process interaction. *SIGPLAN Notices 12*, (March), 114–127.

Andrews, G.R., and Schneider, F.B. 1983. Concepts and notations for concurrent programming. *ACM Computing Surveys 15*, 1 (January), 3–43. Reprinted in Gehani (1988), 3–69.

Andrews, G.R. 1991. *Concurrent Programming: Principles and Practice*. Benjamin/Cummings, Redwood City, CA.

Appelbe, W.F., and Hansen, K. 1985. A survey of systems programming languages: concepts and facilities. *Software—Practice and Experience 15*, 2 (February), 169–190.

Bal, H.E., Steiner, J.G., and Tanenbaum, A.S. 1989. Programming languages for distributed computing systems. *ACM Computing Surveys 21*, (September), 261–322.

Bauer, F.L., and Samelson, K. 1976. Language hierarchies and interfaces. Proceedings of an International Summer School at Marktoberdorf, Germany, July 23–August 2, 1975. *Lecture Notes in Computer Science 46*, Springer-Verlag, New York.

Bell, D.H., Kerridge, J.M., Simpson, D., and Willis, N. 1983. *Parallel Programming—A Bibliography*. Wiley Heyden, New York.

Bell, J.R. 1973. Threaded code. *Communications of the ACM 16*, 6 (June), 370–372.

Ben-Ari, M. 1982. *Principles of Concurrent Programming*. Prentice-Hall, Englewood Cliffs, NJ.

Bergland, G.D., and Gordon, R.D., Eds. 1981. *Software Design Strategies*. IEEE Computer Society, Los Angeles, CA.

Bernstein, A.J., and Ensor, J.R. 1981. A Modula based language supporting hierarchical development and verification. *Software—Practice and Experience 11*, 3 (March), 237–255.

Bishop, J. 1986. *Data Abstraction in Programming Languages*. Addison-Wesley, Reading, MA.

Black, A., Hutchinson, N., Jul, E., and Levy, H. 1986. Object structure in the Emerald system. *SIGPLAN Notices 21*, (November), 78–86.

Bochmann, G.V., and Joachim, T. 1979. The development and structure of an X.25 implementation. *IEEE Transactions on Software Engineering 5*, 5 (May), 429–439.

Boyle, J., Butler, R., Disz, T., Glickfeld, B., Lusk, E., Overbeek, R., Patterson, J., and Stevens, R. 1987. *Portable Programs for Parallel Processors*. Holt, Rinehart and Winston, New York.

Brinch Hansen, P. 1969. *RC 4000 Software: Multiprogramming System*. Regnecentralen, Copenhagen, Denmark, (April). Revised version in Brinch Hansen (1973b), 237–286.

Brinch Hansen, P. 1971a. An outline of a course on operating system principles. *Seminar on Operating Systems Techniques*, Belfast, Northern Ireland, (August). In Hoare (1972a), 29–36. Review: *Computing Reviews*, 26738, (1973). *Article 3*.

Brinch Hansen, P. 1971b. Short-term scheduling in multiprogramming systems. *ACM Symposium on Operating Systems Principles*, Palo, Alto, CA, (October), 101–105. Review: Bibliography 27, *Computing Reviews*, (1972).

Brinch Hansen, P. 1971c. Multiprogramming with monitors. Carnegie-Mellon University, Pittsburgh, PA, (November). Privately circulated.

Brinch Hansen, P. 1972a. A comparison of two synchronizing concepts. *Acta Informatica 1*, 190–199. Submitted November 1971. Review: *Computing Reviews*, 26837, (1974).

Brinch Hansen, P. 1972b. Structured multiprogramming. Invited paper, *Communications of the ACM 15*, 7 (July), 574–578. Also in Gries (1978), 215–223. Review: *Computing Reviews*, 24238, (1972). *Article 4*.

Brinch Hansen, P. 1973a. A reply to comments on "A comparison of two synchronizing concepts." *Acta Informatica 2*, 189–190.

Brinch Hansen, P. 1973b. *Operating System Principles*, Prentice-Hall. Englewood Cliffs, NJ, (July). Submitted May 1972. Translations: Kindai Kagaku Sha, Tokyo, Japan, 1976; Carl Hanser Verlag, Munich, Germany, 1977; SNTL, Prague, Czechoslovakia, 1979; Wydawnictwa Naukowo-Techniczne, Warsaw, Poland, 1979; Naučna Knjiga, Belgrade, Yugoslavia, 1982. Reviews: *Computing Reviews*, 26104, (1973), and 29801, (1976); *American Scientist, Computer, BIT*, (1975); *Embedded Systems Programming*, (1990).

Brinch Hansen, P. 1973c. On September 6, 1973, I sent Mike McKeag "a copy of a preliminary document that describes my suggestion for an extension of Pascal with concurrent processes and monitors" (McKeag 1991). No longer available.

Brinch Hansen, P. 1973d. Concurrent programming concepts. Invited paper, *ACM Computing Surveys 5*, 4 (December), 223–245. Review: *Computing Reviews*, 26927, (1974).

Brinch Hansen, P. 1974a. Concurrent Pascal: a programming language for operating system design. Information Science, California Institute of Technology, Pasadena, CA, (April). Referenced in Silberschatz (1977). No longer available.

Brinch Hansen, P. 1974b. Deamy—a structured operating system. Information Science, California Institute of Technology, Pasadena, CA, (May). Referenced in Brinch Hansen (1975c).

Brinch Hansen, P. 1974c. A programming methodology for operating system design. Invited paper, *Proceedings of the IFIP Congress 74*, (August), 394–397, North-Holland, Amsterdam, The Netherlands. Review: *Computing Reviews*, 27985, (1975).

Brinch Hansen, P. 1974d. The programming language Concurrent Pascal, (Part I. The purpose of Concurrent Pascal; Part II. The use of Concurrent Pascal). Information Science, California Institute of Technology, Pasadena, CA, (November). Revised February 1975. Also in Proceedings of the International Conference on Reliable Software, Los Angeles, CA, April 1975, *SIGPLAN Notices 10*, 6 (June), 305–309 (Part I only); Invited paper, *IEEE Transactions on Software Engineering 1*, 2 (June 1975), 199–207; Bauer (1976), 82–110; Gries (1978), 224–261; Wasserman (1980), 465–473; Kuhn (1981), 313–321; Horowitz (1983b), 262–272; Gehani (1988), 73–92. Review: *Computing Reviews*, 29418, (1976). *Article 7*.

Brinch Hansen, P. 1975a. Concurrent Pascal report. Information Science, California Institute of Technology, Pasadena, CA, (June). Also in Brinch Hansen (1977b), 231–270.

Brinch Hansen, P., and Hartmann, A.C. 1975b. Sequential Pascal report. Information Science, California Institute of Technology, Pasadena, CA, (July).

Brinch Hansen, P. 1975c. The Solo operating system. Information Science, California Institute of Technology, Pasadena, CA, (June–July). Also in *Software—Practice and Experience 6*, 2 (April–June 1976), 141–200; Brinch Hansen (1977b), 69–142. Review: *Computing Reviews*, 31363, (1977). *Articles 8–9*.

Brinch Hansen, P. 1975d. Universal types in Concurrent Pascal. *Information Processing Letters 3*, (July), 165–166.

Brinch Hansen, P. 1975e. Concurrent Pascal machine. Information Science, California Institute of Technology, Pasadena, CA, (October). Also in Brinch Hansen (1977b), 271–297.

Brinch Hansen, P. 1975f. A real-time scheduler. Information Science, California Institute of Technology, Pasadena, CA, (November). Also in Brinch Hansen (1977b), 189–227.

Brinch Hansen, P. 1976a. The job stream system. Information Science, California Institute of Technology, Pasadena, CA, (January). Also in Brinch Hansen (1977b), 148–188.

Brinch Hansen, P. 1976b. Concurrent Pascal implementation notes. Information Science, California Institute of Technology, Pasadena, CA. Referenced in Powell (1979). No longer available.

Brinch Hansen, P. 1977a. Experience with modular concurrent programming. *IEEE Transactions on Software Engineering 3*, 2 (March), 156–159. *Article 11.*

Brinch Hansen, P. 1977b. *The Architecture of Concurrent Programs.* Prentice-Hall, Englewood Cliffs, NJ, (July). Submitted July 1976. Translations: Kagaku-Gijyutsu, Tokyo, Japan, 1980; Oldenbourg, Munich, Germany, 1981. Reviews: *Choice, Ingeniøren*, (1978); *Computing Reviews*, 33358, *Computer*, (1979); *Embedded Systems Programming*, (1990).

Brinch Hansen, P. 1977c. Network—a multiprocessor program. *IEEE Computer and Software Applications Conference*, Chicago, IL, (November), 336–340. Also in *IEEE Transactions on Software Engineering 4*, 3 (May 1978), 194–199. Review: *Computing Reviews*, 33840, (1978). *Article 13.*

Brinch Hansen, P., and Staunstrup, J. 1978a. Specification and implementation of mutual exclusion. *IEEE Transactions on Software Engineering 4*, 5 (September), 365–370.

Brinch Hansen, P. 1978b. Distributed Processes: a concurrent programming concept. *Communications of the ACM 21*, 11 (November), 934–941. Submitted September 1977, revised December 1977. Also in Bergland (1981), 289–296; Saib (1983), 500–507; Gehani (1988), 216–233. *Article 14.*

Brinch Hansen, P. 1978c. A keynote address on concurrent programming. *IEEE Computer Software and Applications Conference*, Chicago, IL, (November), 1–6. Also in *Computer 12*, (May 1979), 50–56; *Selected Reprints in Software*, M.V. Zelkowitz, Ed., IEEE Computer Society, Los Angeles, CA, (1982), 42–48. Review: *Computing Reviews*, 35247, (1979). *Article 16.*

Brinch Hansen, P. 1978d. Reproducible testing of monitors. *Software—Practice and Experience 8*, 6 (November–December), 721–729. *Article 15.*

Brinch Hansen, P., and Fellows, J.A. 1980. The Trio operating system. Computer Science Department, University of Southern California, Los Angeles, CA, (June). Also in *Software—Practice and Experience 10*, 11 (November 1980), 943–948. Review: *Computing Reviews*, 37637, (1981).

Brinch Hansen, P. 1981. The design of Edison. *Software—Practice and Experience 11*, 4 (April), 363–396. *Article 17.*

Brinch Hansen, P. 1989a. The Joyce language report. *Software—Practice and Experience 19*, 6 (June), 553–578.

Brinch Hansen, P. 1989b. A multiprocessor implementation of Joyce. *Software—Practice and Experience 19*, 6 (June), 579–592. *Article 19.*

Bryant, R.E., and Dennis, J.B. 1979. Concurrent programming. In Wegner (1979), 584–610.

Burns, A., and Davies, G. 1988. Pascal-FC: a language for teaching concurrent programming. *SIGPLAN Notices 23*, (January), 58–66.

Bustard, D.W., Elder, J., and Welsh, J. 1988. *Concurrent Program Structures*. Prentice-Hall, Englewood Cliffs, NJ.

Coleman, D., Gallimore, R.M., Hughes, J.W., and Powell, M.S. 1979. An assessment of Concurrent Pascal. *Software—Practice and Experience 9*, 10 (October), 827–837. Also in Gehani (1988), 351–364.

Coleman, D. 1980. Concurrent Pascal—an appraisal. In McKeag (1980), 213–227.

Courtois, P.J., Heymans, F., and Parnas, D.L. 1971. Concurrent control with "readers" and "writers." *Communications of the ACM 14*, 10 (October), 667–668.

Courtois, P.J., Heymans, F., and Parnas, D.L. 1972. Comments on "A comparison of two synchronizing concepts." *Acta Informatica 1*, 375–376.

Dahl, O.-J., Dijkstra, E.W., and Hoare, C.A.R. 1972a. *Structured Programming*. Academic Press, New York.

Dahl, O.-J., and Hoare, C.A.R. 1972b. Hierarchical program structures. In Dahl (1972a), 175–220.

Deitel, H.M. 1984. *An Introduction to Operating Systems*. Revised first edition, Addison-Wesley, Reading, MA.

Dijkstra, E.W. 1965. Cooperating sequential processes. Mathematical Department, Technological University, Eindhoven, The Netherlands, (September). Also in Genuys (1968), 43–112.

Dijkstra, E.W. 1967. The structure of the "THE"-multiprogramming system. *ACM Symposium on Operating System Principles*, Gatlinburg, TN. Also in *Communications of the ACM 11*, 5 (May 1968), 341–346, and *26*, (January 1983), 49–52.

Dijkstra, E.W. 1971. Hierarchical ordering of sequential processes. *Acta Informatica 1*, 115–138. Also in Hoare (1972a), 72–93.

Discussion. 1971. Discussion of conditional critical regions and monitors. *Seminar on Operating Systems Techniques*, Belfast, Northern Ireland, (August). In Hoare (1972a), 110–113.

Dunman, B.R., Schack, S.R., and Wood, P.T. 1982. A mainframe implementation of Concurrent Pascal. *Software—Practice and Experience 12*, 1 (January), 85–90.

Fellows, J.A. 1980. Applications of abstract data types: The Trio operating system. Ph.D. thesis, Computer Science Department, University of Southern California, Los Angeles, CA.

Gehani, N., and McGettrick, A.D., Eds. 1988. *Concurrent Programming*. Addison-Wesley, Reading, MA.

Genuys, F., Ed. 1968. *Programming Languages*. Academic Press, New York.

Ghezzi, C., and Jazayeri, M. 1982. *Programming Language Concepts*. John Wiley, New York.

Graef, N., Kretschmer, H., Löhr, K.-P., and Morawetz, B. 1979. How to design and implement small time-sharing systems using Concurrent Pascal. *Software—Practice and Experience 9*, 1 (January), 17–24.

Gries, D., Ed. 1978. *Programming Methodology—A Collection of Articles by Members of IFIP WG2.3*. Springer-Verlag, New York.

Haddon, B.K. 1977. Nested monitor calls. *Operating Systems Review 11*, (October), 18–23.

Hartmann, A.C. 1975. A Concurrent Pascal compiler for minicomputers. Ph.D. thesis, Information Science, California Institute of Technology, Pasadena, CA, (September). Also published as *Lecture Notes in Computer Science 50*, (1977), Springer-Verlag, New York.

Hayden, C. 1979. Distributed processes: experience and architectures. Ph.D. thesis, Computer Science Department, University of Southern California, Los Angeles, CA.

Heimbigner, D. 1978. Writing device drivers in Concurrent Pascal. *Operating Systems Review 12*, 4 (April), 16–33.

Hoare, C.A.R. 1971a. Towards a theory of parallel programming. Queen's University, Belfast, Northern Ireland, (August). Privately circulated. Not to be confused with Hoare (1971b) of the same title.

Hoare, C.A.R. 1971b. Towards a theory of parallel programming. *Seminar on Operating Systems Techniques*, Belfast, Northern Ireland, (August). In Hoare (1972a), 61–71. Also in Gries (1978), 202–214. Not to be confused with Hoare (1971a) of the same title.

Hoare, C.A.R., and Perrott, R.H., Eds. 1972a. *Operating Systems Techniques*, Proceedings of a seminar at Queen's University, Belfast, August 30–September 3, 1971. Academic Press, New York.

Hoare, C.A.R. 1972b. Proof of correctness of data representations. *Acta Informatica 1*, 271–281. Submitted February 1972. Also in Bauer (1976), 183–193; Gries (1978), 269–281; Hoare (1989), 103–115.

Hoare, C.A.R. 1973a. A pair of synchronising primitives. On January 11, 1973, Hoare gave Jim Horning a copy of this undated, unpublished draft (Horning 1991).

Hoare, C.A.R. 1973b. A structured paging system. *Computer Journal 16*, (August), 209–214. Submitted October 1972. Also in Hoare (1989), 133–151.

Hoare, C.A.R. 1974a. Monitors: an operating system structuring concept. *Communications of the ACM 17*, (October), 549–557. Submitted February 1973, revised April 1974. Also in Gries (1978), 224–243; Wasserman (1980), 156–164; Gehani (1988), 256–277; Hoare (1989), 171–191.

Hoare, C.A.R. 1974b. Hints on programming language design. In *Computer Systems Reliability*, C. Bunyan, Ed., Infotech International, Berkshire, England, 505–534. Also in Wasserman (1980), 43–52; Hoare (1989), 193–216.

Hoare, C.A.R. 1976. Hints on the design of a programming language for real-time command and control. In *Real-time Software: International State of the Art Report*, J.P. Spencer, Ed., Infotech International, Berkshire, England, 685–699.

Hoare, C.A.R. 1978. Communicating sequential processes. *Communications of the ACM 21*, (August), 666–677. Submitted March 1977, revised August 1977. Also in Wasserman (1980), 170–181; Bergland (1981), 277–288; Kuhn (1981), 323–334; *Communications of the ACM 26*, (January 1983), 100–106; Horowitz (1983b), 306–317; Saib (1983), 508–519; Gehani (1988), 278–308; Hoare (1989), 259–288.

Hoare, C.A.R., and Jones, C.B., Ed., 1989. *Essays in Computing Science*. Prentice-Hall, Englewood Cliffs, NJ.

Holt, R.C., Graham, G.S., Lazowska, E.D., and Scott, M.A. 1978. *Structured Concurrent Programming with Operating Systems Applications*. Addison-Wesley, Reading, MA.

Holt, R.C. 1982. A short introduction to Concurrent Euclid. *SIGPLAN Notices 17*, (May), 60–79.

Holt, R.C. 1983. *Concurrent Euclid, the Unix System and Tunis.* Addison-Wesley, Reading, MA.

Holt, R.C. 1988. Device management in Turing Plus. *Operating System Review 22*, 1 (January), 33–41.

Horning, J.J. 1991. Personal communication, (May).

Horowitz, E. 1983a. *Fundamentals of Programming Languages.* Computer Science Press, Rockville, MD.

Horowitz, E., Ed. 1983b. *Programming Languages: A Grand Tour.* Computer Science Press, Rockville, MD.

Howard, J.H. 1976a. Proving monitors. *Communications of the ACM 19*, 5 (May), 273–279.

Howard, J.H. 1976b. Signalling in monitors. *IEEE Conference on Software Engineering,* San Francisco, CA, (October), 47–52.

Janson, P.A. 1985. *Operating Systems: Structures and Mechanisms.* Academic Press, New York.

Kaubisch, W.H., Perrott, R.H., and Hoare, C.A.R. 1976. Quasiparallel programming. *Software—Practice and Experience 6*, (July–September), 341–356.

Keedy, J.L. 1978. On structuring operating systems with monitors. *Australian Computer Journal 10*, 1 (February), 23–27.

Kerridge, J.M. 1982. A Fortran implementation of Concurrent Pascal. *Software—Practice and Experience 12*, 1 (January), 45–56.

Kessels, J.L.W. 1977. An alternative to event queues for synchronization in monitors. *Communications of the ACM 20*, 7 (July), 500–503.

Kligerman, E., and Stoyenko, A.D. 1986. Real time Euclid: a language for reliable real time systems. *IEEE Transactions on Software Engineering 12*, 9 (September), 941–949.

Kotulski, L. 1987. About the semantic nested monitor calls. *SIGPLAN Notices 22*, 4 (April), 80–82.

Krakowiak, S. 1988. *Principles of Operating Systems.* MIT Press, Cambridge, MA.

Krishnamurthy, E.V. 1989. *Parallel Processing: Principles and Practice.* Addison-Wesley, Reading, MA.

Kruijer, H.S.M. 1982a. Processor management in a Concurrent Pascal kernel. *Operating Systems Review 16*, (April), 7–17.

Kruijer, H.S.M. 1982b. A multi-user operating system for transaction processing written in Concurrent Pascal. *Software—Practice and Experience 12*, 5 (May), 445–454.

Kuhn, R.H., and Padua, D.A., Eds. 1981. *Parallel Processing.* IEEE Computer Society, Los Angeles, CA, (August).

Lampson, B.W., and Redell, D.D. 1980. Experience with processes and monitors in Mesa. *Communications of the ACM 23*, 2 (February), 105–117. Also in Gehani (1988), 392–418.

Lauer, H.C., and Needham, R.M. 1978. On the duality of operating system structures. *International Symposium on Operating Systems,* IRIA, France (October). Also in *Operating Systems Review 13*, 2 (April 1979), 3–19.

Liskov, B., Atkinson, R., Bloom, T., Moss, E., Schaffert, J.C., Scheifler, R., and Snyder, A. 1981. CLU reference manual. *Lecture Notes in Computer Science 114*. Quote: "By the summer of 1975, the first version of the language had been completed. Over the next two years, the entire language design was reviewed and two implementations were produced ... A preliminary version of this manual appeared in July 1978" (p. III).

Lister, A.M. 1977. The problem of nested monitor calls. *Operating Systems Review 11*, (July), 5–7.

Löhr, K.-P. 1977. Beyond Concurrent Pascal. *SIGPLAN Notices 12*, (November), 128–137.

Lynch, W.C. 1991. Personal communication, (October).

McKeag, R.M. 1973. Programming languages for operating systems. *ACM SIG-PLAN/SIGOPS Interface Meeting*, Savannah, GA, (April). In *SIGPLAN Notices 8*, 9 (September 1973), 109–111.

McKeag, R.M., and Macnaghten, A.M., Eds. 1980. *On the Construction of Programs*. Cambridge University Press, New York.

McKeag, R.M. 1991. Personal communication, (August).

Maddux, R.A., and Mills, H.D. 1979. Review of The Architecture of Concurrent Programs. *IEEE Computer 12*, (May), 102–103.

Mattson, S.E. 1980. Implementation of Concurrent Pascal on LSI-11. *Software—Practice and Experience 10*, 3 (March), 205–218.

Møller-Nielsen, P., and Staunstrup, J. 1984. Experiments with a multiprocessor. Computer Science Department, Aarhus University, Aarhus, Denmark (November).

Narayana, K.T., Prasad, V.R., and Joseph, M. 1979. Some aspects of concurrent programming in CCNPascal. *Software—Practice and Experience 9*, 9 (September), 749–770.

Neal, D., and Wallentine, V. 1978. Experiences with the portability of Concurrent Pascal. *Software—Practice and Experience 8*, 3 (May–June), 341–354.

Nehmer, J. 1979. The implementation of concurrency for a PL/I-like language. *Software—Practice and Experience 9*, 12 (December), 1043–1057.

Nori, K.V., Ammann, U., Jensen, K., and Naegeli, H.H. 1974. The Pascal P compiler: implementation notes. Institut für Informatik, ETH, Zurich, Switzerland, (December).

Nutt, G.J. 1992. *Centralized and Distributed Operating Systems*. Prentice-Hall, Englewood Cliffs, NJ.

Parnas, D.L. 1978. The non-problem of nested monitor calls. *Operating Systems Review 12*, (January), 12–14.

Perrott, R.H. 1987. *Parallel Programming*. Addison-Wesley, Reading, MA.

Peterson, J.L., and Silberschatz, A. 1983. *Operating Systems Concepts*. Addison-Wesley, Reading, MA.

Pinkert, J.R., and Wear, L.L. 1989. *Operating Systems: Concepts, Policies and Mechanisms*. Prentice-Hall, Englewood Cliffs, NJ.

Popek, G.J., Horning, J.J., Lampson, B.W., Mitchell, J.G., and London, R.L. 1977. Notes on the design of Euclid. *SIGPLAN Notices 12*, 11–12. Quote: "The System Development Corporation is currently implementing Euclid" (p. 12).

Powell, M.S. 1979. Experience of transporting and using the Solo operating system. *Software—Practice and Experience 9*, 7 (July), 561–570.

Ravn, A.P. 1982. Use of Concurrent Pascal in systems programming teaching. *Micropro-cessing and Microprogramming 10*, 33–35.

Raynal, M., and Helary, J.-M. 1990. *Synchronization and Control of Distributed Systems and Programs*. John Wiley, New York.

Ringstöm, J. 1990. Predula: a multi-paradigm parallel programming environment. Department of Computer and Information Science, Linköping University, Linköping, Sweden, (November).

Roubine, O., and Heliard, J.-C. 1980. Parallel processing in Ada. In McKeag (1980), 193–212. Also in Gehani (1988), 142–159.

Saib, S.H., and Fritz, R.E., Eds. 1983. *The Ada Programming Language*. IEEE Computer Society, Los Angeles, CA.

Schneider, H.J. 1984. *Problem Oriented Programming Languages*. John Wiley, New York.

Sebesta, R.W. 1989. *Concepts of Programming Languages*. Benjamin/Cummings, Redwood City, CA.

Shaw, M., Ed. 1981. *Alphard: Form and Content*. Springer-Verlag, New York. Quotes: "The preliminary language report appeared as a ... technical report [in February 1978]. No final report was issued;" ... "We curtailed development of the compiler in 1979 when it became clear that another iteration on the language design was necessary" (pp. 191 and 315).

Silberschatz, A., Kieburtz, R.B., and Bernstein, A.J. 1977. Extending Concurrent Pascal to allow dynamic resource management. *IEEE Transactions on Software Engineering 3*, (May), 210–217.

Staunstrup, J. 1978. Specification, verification, and implementation of concurrent programs. Ph.D. thesis, Computer Science Department, University of Southern California, Los Angeles, CA, (May).

Stotts, P.D. 1982. A comparative survey of concurrent programming languages. *SIGPLAN Notices 17*, 10 (October), 76–87. Also in Gehani (1988), 419–435.

Tanenbaum, A.S. 1992. *Modern Operating Systems*. Prentice-Hall, Englewood Cliffs, NJ.

Tennent, R.D. 1981. *Principles of Programming Languages*. Prentice-Hall, Englewood Cliffs, NJ.

Tsichritzis, D.C., and Bernstein, P.A. 1974. *Operating Systems*. Academic Press, New York.

Tsujino, Y., Ando, M., Araki, T., and Tohura, N. 1984. Concurrent C: a programming language for distributed multiprocessor systems. *Software—Practice and Experience 14*, 11 (November), 1061–1078.

Turski, W.M. 1978. *Computer Programming Methodology*. Heyden, Philadelphia, PA.

Wasserman, A.I., Ed. 1980. *Programming Language Design*. IEEE Computer Society, Los Angeles, CA, (October).

Wegner, P., Ed. 1979. *Research Directions in Software Technology*. MIT Press, Cambridge, MA.

Welsh, J., and Bustard, D.W. 1979. Pascal-Plus—another language for modular multiprogramming. *Software—Practice and Experience 9*, 11 (November), 947–957.

Welsh, J., and McKeag, R.M. 1980. *Structured System Programming*. Prentice-Hall, Englewood Cliffs, NJ.

Wettstein, H. 1978. The problem of nested monitor calls revisited. *Operating Systems Review 12*, (January), 19–23.

Whiddett, R.J. 1983. Dynamic distributed systems. *Software—Practice and Experience 13*, 4 (April), 355–371.

Whiddett, R.J. 1987. *Concurrent Programming for Software Engineers*. Halstead Press, New York.

White, J.E. 1976. A high-level framework for network-based resource sharing. *National Computer Conference*, AFIPS Press, Montvale, NJ, (June), 561–570.

Williams, S.A. 1990. *Programming Models for Parallel Systems*. John Wiley, New York.

Wilson, L.B., and Clark, R.G. 1988. *Comparative Programming Languages*. Addison-Wesley, Reading, MA.

Wirth, N. 1971. The programming language Pascal. *Acta Informatica 1*, 35–63.

Wirth, N. 1977. Modula: a programming language for modular multiprogramming. *Software—Practice and Experience 7*, 1 (January–February), 3–35. Also in Horowitz (1983b), 273–305.

Young, S.J. 1982. *Real Time Languages: Design and Development*. Halstead Press, New York.

Model Programs for Computational Science: A Programming Methodology for Multicomputers*

(1993)

We describe a programming methodology for computational science based on programming paradigms for multicomputers. Each paradigm is a class of algorithms that have the same control structure. For every paradigm, a general parallel program is developed. The general program is then used to derive two or more model programs, which solve specific problems in science and engineering. These programs have been tested on a Computing Surface and published with every detail open to scrutiny. We explain the steps involved in developing model programs and conclude that the study of programming paradigms provides an architectural vision of parallel scientific computing.

1 Introduction

For the past three years I have studied *computational science* from the point of view of a computer scientist (Brinch Hansen 1990b–1992f). I have followed the advice of Geoffrey Fox (1990) to "use real hardware to solve real problems with real software." But, where the Caltech group concentrated on scientific applications for their own sake, I have used them as realistic case studies to illustrate the use of *structured programming* in computational science.

My research explores the role of *programming paradigms* in parallel computing. In programming the word *paradigm* is often used with a general (but vague) connotation, such as "the high level methodologies that we recognize as common to many of our effective algorithms" (Nelson 1987). I will use

---

*P. Brinch Hansen, Model programs for computational science: A programming methodology for multicomputers. *Concurrency—Practice and Experience* 5, 5 (August 1993), 407–423. Copyright © 1993, John Wiley & Sons, Ltd. Reprinted by permission.

the term in a more narrow (but precise) sense: A *programming paradigm* is a class of algorithms that solve different problems but have the same control structure.

I have studied paradigms for all-pairs computations, tuple multiplication, divide-and-conquer, Monte Carlo trials and cellular automata (Brinch Hansen 1990c, 1991a, 1991d, 1992d, 1992f). For each paradigm I have written a general program that defines the common control structure. Such a program is sometimes called an *algorithmic skeleton*, a *generic program*, or a *program template* (Cole 1989; Brinch Hansen 1991b).

From a general parallel program I derive two or more *model programs* that illustrate the use of the paradigm to solve specific problems. A general program includes a few unspecified data types and procedures that vary from one application to another. A model program is obtained by replacing these data types and procedures with the corresponding data types and procedures from a sequential program that solves a specific problem. The essence of the programming methodology is that a model program has a parallel component that implements a paradigm and a sequential component for a specific application. The clear separation of the issues of parallelism and the details of application is essential for writing model programs that are easy to understand.

My own model programs solve typical problems in science and engineering: linear equations, n-body simulation, matrix multiplication, shortest paths in graphs, sorting, fast Fourier transforms, simulated annealing, primality testing, Laplace's equation, and forest fire simulation.

I have run these parallel programs on a *Computing Surface* configured as a pipeline, a tree, a cube or a matrix of *transputers*.

It has been fun to enter an interdisciplinary field, refresh my memory of mathematics and physics I learned as an undergraduate, study numerical analysis, and teach myself the art of *multicomputer programming*.

My one serious criticism of computational science is that it largely has ignored the issue of *precision* and *clarity* in parallel programming that is essential for the education of future scientists. A written explanation is not an algorithm. A graph of computational steps is not an algorithm. A picture of a systolic array is not an algorithm. A mathematical formula is not an algorithm. A program outline written in non-executable "pseudocode" is not an algorithm. And, a complicated "code" that is difficult to understand will not do either.

Subtle algorithms must be presented in their entirety as well-structured programs written in readable, executable programming languages (Forsythe 1966; Ignizio 1973; Wirth 1976; Brinch Hansen 1977; Dunham 1982; Press 1989). This has been my main reason for publishing model programs for parallel scientific computing.

In the following, I will describe parallel programming paradigms and explain why I use different programming languages and computers for publication and implementation of model programs. I will also outline the steps involved in developing model programs based on paradigms. Finally, I will argue that the study of programming paradigms provides an architectural vision of parallel scientific computing.

2 The Computing Surface

When I started this research, I knew that my programs would soon become obsolete unless I wrote them for parallel architectures of the future. So I had to make an educated guess about the direction in which hardware and software technology would move parallel architectures during the 1990s.

By 1989 I had tentatively formulated the following requirements for a general-purpose parallel computer of the future (May 1988, 1990; Valiant 1989; Brinch Hansen 1990a):

1. A parallel architecture must be expandable from tens to thousands of processors.

2. A parallel computer must consist of general-purpose processors.

3. A parallel computer must support different process structures (pipelines, trees, matrices, and so on) in a transparent manner.

4. Process creation, communication, and termination must be hardware operations that are only an order of magnitude slower than memory references.

5. A parallel computer should automatically distribute the computational load and route messages between the processors.

The first three requirements eliminated multiprocessors, SIMD machines, and hypercubes, respectively. The only architecture that satisfied the first four requirements was the *Computing Surface* (Meiko 1987; McDonald 1991). No parallel computer satisfied the fifth condition.

In the summer of 1989 a Computing Surface was installed at Syracuse University. It is a *multicomputer* with 48 processors that can be extended to 1000 processors. Every processor is a T800 *transputer* with one or more megabytes of memory. The transputers are connected by a communication network that can be reconfigured before program execution. Direct communication is possible only among connected transputers, but is very fast (a few microseconds only). Process creation and termination are also hardware operations.

The programming tool is the parallel programming language *occam 2* (Inmos 1988; Cok 1991). This language makes it possible to define parallel processes that communicate by messages.

3   The All-Pairs Pipeline

Although I knew nothing about numerical analysis, I thought that parallel solution of *linear equations* would be a useful programming exercise for a beginner. I chose the problem for the following reason: When a pipeline with p processors solves n linear equations in parallel, the numerical computation requires $O(n^3/p)$ time, while the input/output takes $O(n^2)$ time. If the problem size n is large compared to the machine size p, the overhead of processor communication is negligible. The high ratio of computation to communication makes the problem ideal for efficient parallel computing.

A colleague recommended *Householder reduction* as an attractive method for solving linear equations on a parallel computer. The main strength of the method is its unconditional numerical stability (Householder 1958). The familiar Gaussian elimination is faster but requires a dynamic rearrangement of the equations, known as *pivoting*, which complicates a parallel program somewhat (Fox 1988).

Unfortunately, I could not find a well-written, understandable explanation of Householder's method. Most textbooks on numerical analysis produce Householder's matrix like a rabbit from a magician's top hat without explaining why it is defined the way it is. At this point I stopped writing parallel programs and concentrated on sequential Householder reduction. After several frustrating weeks I was able to write a *tutorial* on Householder reduction (Brinch Hansen 1990b). Two pages were sufficient to explain the purpose and derive the equation of Householder's matrix. I then explained the computational rules for Householder reduction and illustrated the method by a numerical example and a Pascal program.

I was beginning to think that others might have the same difficulty understanding this fundamental computation. So I submitted the tutorial to
a journal that published it. One of the reviewers wrote that he "found the
presentation far superior to the several descriptions I have seen in numerical
analysis books." I quote this review not just because I like it, but because
it was my first lesson about computational science: In order to understand
a computation, I must first explain it to myself by writing a tutorial that
includes a complete sequential program.

After studying parallel programming for 25 years it was not too difficult for me to program a *Householder pipeline* (Brinch Hansen 1990c). The
parallel program was written in occam for the Computing Surface. I used
a coarse-grain pipeline to reduce communication overhead. To achieve approximate *load-balancing*, the pipeline was folded three times across an array
of p transputers (Brinch Hansen 1990d). Figure 1 shows the *folded pipeline*.
The squares and lines represent pipeline nodes and communication channels,
respectively. Each column represents a single transputer that executes four
parallel nodes.

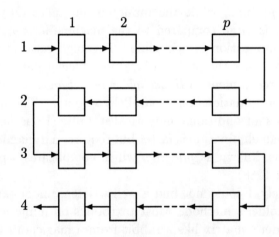

Figure 1 A folded pipeline.

My next exercise was to compute the trajectories of n particles that interact by gravitation only. I considered the *n-body problem* to be particularly
challenging on a parallel computer since it involves interactions among all
the particles in each computational step. This means that every proces-

sor must communicate, directly or indirectly, with every other processor. My description of an *n-body pipeline* included a brief summary of Newton's laws of gravitation and a Pascal program for sequential *n*-body simulation (Brinch Hansen 1991a). Others have solved the same problem using a ring of processors (Ellingworth 1988; Fox 1988).

It was a complete surprise for me to discover that the sequential Pascal programs for Householder reduction and *n*-body simulation had practically identical control structures. I suddenly understood that both of them are instances of the same *programming paradigm*: Each algorithm solves an *all-pairs problem*—a computation on every possible subset consisting of two elements chosen from a set of *n* elements. I have not found this insight mentioned in any textbook on numerical analysis or computational physics.

I now discarded both parallel algorithms and started all over. This time I programmed a general pipeline algorithm for all-pairs computations (Brinch Hansen 1990c). This program is a parallel implementation of the common control structure. It provides a mechanism for performing the same operation on every pair of elements chosen from an array of *n* elements without specifying what the elements represent and how they "interact" pairwise.

I then turned the *all-pairs pipeline* into a Householder pipeline by using a few data types and procedures from the sequential Householder program. This transformation of the parallel program was completely mechanical and required no understanding of Householder's method. A similar transformation turned the all-pairs pipeline into an *n*-body pipeline.

Later I discovered that all-pairs pipelines were described informally by Shih (1987), and Cosnard (1988), but without concise algorithms.

I had now found my *research theme*: the use of parallel programming paradigms in computational science.

4   The Multiplication Pipeline

After programming a subtle parallel program, I looked for the simplest problem that would illustrate the benefits of developing generic algorithms for parallel programming paradigms that can be adapted to different applications.

This time I chose *matrix multiplication*, which can be pipelined in a straightforward way as shown in Fig. 2 (Kung 1989).

First, the rows of a matrix *a* are distributed evenly among the nodes of the pipeline. Then the columns of a matrix *b* pass through the pipeline

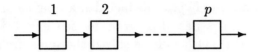

Figure 2 A simple pipeline.

while each node computes a portion of the matrix product $a \times b$. Finally, the pipeline outputs the product matrix.

For sequential algorithms it is well-known that matrix multiplication is similar to the problem of finding the *shortest paths* between every pair of nodes in a directed graph with n nodes (Cormen 1990).

After studying both algorithms, the unifying concept seemed to me to be an operation that I called *tuple multiplication*: the product of two n-tuples a and b is an $n \times n$ matrix c. The matrix elements are obtained by applying the same function f to every ordered pair consisting of an element of a and an element of b, that is $c_{ij} = f(a_i, b_j)$.

In the case of matrix multiplication, the tuple elements are rows and columns, respectively, and every function value is the dot product of a row and a column. The input to the shortest paths problem is the adjacency matrix of a graph. The output is a distance matrix computed by a sequence of tuple multiplications. In every multiplication, tuple a consists of the n rows of the adjacency matrix, while tuple b consists of the n columns of the distance matrix. The function value $f(a_i, b_j)$ defines the shortest path length found so far between nodes i and j of the graph.

The task was now obvious. I wrote a paper that defined a pipeline algorithm for tuple multiplication. I briefly explained matrix multiplication and the all-pairs shortest-path problem by means of Pascal algorithms. I then transformed the parallel program into pipeline algorithms for the two applications by defining the data types of the tuples and the corresponding variants of the function f. After rewriting the parallel programs in occam, I analyzed and measured their performance on the Computing Surface (Brinch Hansen 1991b).

5   The Divide and Conquer Tree

My third paradigm was a parallel *divide-and-conquer* algorithm for a binary tree of processor nodes (Browning 1980; Brinch Hansen 1991d). Figure 3 shows the *tree machine*.

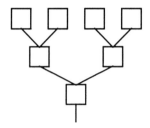

Figure 3 A tree machine.

The root node of the tree inputs a complete problem, splits it into two parts, and sends one part to its left child node and the other part to its right child node. The splitting process is repeated at higher levels in the tree. Eventually, every leaf node inputs a problem from its parent node, solves it, and outputs the solution to its parent. Every parent node in the tree inputs two partial solutions from its children and combines them into a single solution, which is output to its parent. Finally, the root node outputs the solution to the complete problem.

A problem and its solution are both defined by an array of n elements of the same type. The element type and the procedures for splitting problems and combining solutions are the only parts of the parallel algorithm that depend on the nature of a specific problem. Consequently, it was easy to transform the general algorithm into parallel versions of *quicksort* (Hoare 1961) and the *fast Fourier transform* (Cooley 1965; Brigham 1974; Brinch Hansen 1991c).

The emphasis on the common paradigm enabled me to discover an unexpected similarity between these well-known algorithms. After programming an iterative version of the fast Fourier transform, I suddenly realized that it must also be possible to write a *quicksort without a stack!* In standard quicksort, the *partition* procedure divides an array into two slices of unpredictable sizes. Why not replace this algorithm with the *find* procedure (Hoare 1971) and use it to split an array into two halves? Then you don't need a stack to remember where you split the array.

On the average, *find* is twice as slow as *partition*. That is probably the reason why a balanced quicksort is seldom used for sequential computers. However, on a multicomputer, the unpredictable nature of standard quicksort causes severe *load imbalance* (Fox 1988). If the two halves of a tree machine sort sequences of very different lengths, half of the processors are doing most of the work, while the other half are idle most of the time. As a compromise, I used *find* in the parent nodes and *partition* in the leaf nodes. Measurements show that the *balanced parallel quicksort* consistently runs faster than the unbalanced algorithm.

I selected the divide-and-conquer paradigm to demonstrate that some parallel computations are inherently *inefficient*. The average sorting time of n elements is $O(n\log n)$ on a sequential computer. A tree machine cannot reduce the sorting time below the $O(n)$ time required to input and output the n elements through the root node. So, for problems of size n, the *parallel speed-up* cannot exceed $O(\log n)$. No matter how many processors you use to sort, say, a million numbers, they can do it only an order of magnitude faster than a single processor. This modest speed-up makes divide-and-conquer algorithms unsatisfactory for multicomputers with hundreds or thousands of processors.

6   The Divide and Conquer Cube

I have never been enamored of *hypercube* architectures (Seitz 1985). I felt that hypercube algorithms would be dominated by the problem of mapping problem-oriented process configurations onto a hypercube. This prediction turned out to be true, I think (Fox 1988). Hypercubes can probably be made reasonably easy to use if they are supported by a library of programming paradigms that hide the mapping problem from scientific users. But I pity the professional programmers, who will have to cope with the awkward details of paradigm implementation.

In the future, most parallel architectures will almost certainly support automatic routing of messages between any pair of nodes. Although the hardware architecture may be a hypercube, this structure will be transparent to the programmer, who will define abstract configurations of nodes connected by virtual channels (May 1988; Valiant 1989). In the meantime, reconfigurable multicomputers are a reasonable compromise.

On a general-purpose multicomputer, a programmer may, of course, choose the hypercube as a programming paradigm in its own right. So, I was curious to find out if a hypercube sorts faster than a tree machine. Figure 4 shows a *cube* with eight processor nodes.

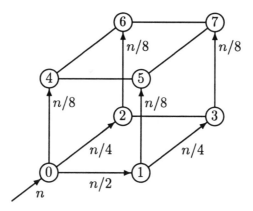

Figure 4 Data distribution in a cube.

First, node 0 inputs n numbers, splits them into two halves, sends one half to node 1, and keeps the other half. Then nodes 0 and 1 each split their halves into quarters. Finally, nodes 0, 1, 2, and 3 each keep an eighth of the numbers and sends the other eighths to nodes 4, 5, 6, and 7. All the nodes now work in parallel while each of them sorts one eighth of the numbers. Afterwards, nodes 0, 1, 2, and 3 each input a sorted sequence of size $n/8$ from their "children" and combine them with their own numbers to form sorted sequences of size $n/4$. Nodes 0 and 1 repeat the combination process and form sorted sequences of size $n/2$. At the end, node 0 outputs n sorted numbers to its environment.

A larger hypercube follows the same general pattern of splitting a sorting problem into smaller problems, solving them in parallel and combining the results. Needless to say, the sorting algorithm can easily be replaced by a fast Fourier transform.

On a hypercube, every node sorts a portion of the numbers. However, on a tree machine, sorting is done by the leaf nodes only. In spite of this, I found that a hypercube with 32 or more nodes sorts only marginally faster than a tree machine of the same size. This conclusion was based on a performance model verified by experiments (Brinch Hansen 1991e). The reason is simple. On a large tree machine, the sorting time of the leaf nodes is small compared to the data distribution time of the remaining nodes. So there is is not much gained by reducing the sorting time further.

7 Parallel Monte Carlo Trials

Monte Carlo methods are algorithms that use random number generators to simulate stochastic processes. Probabilistic algorithms have been applied successfully to combinatorial problems, which cannot be solved exactly because they have a vast number of possible solutions.

The most famous example is the problem of the *traveling salesperson* who must visit n cities (Lawler 1985). No computer will ever be able to find the shortest possible tour through 100 cities by examining all the 5×10^{150} possible tours. For practical purposes, the problem can be effectively solved by *simulated annealing* (Kirkpatrick 1983; Aarts 1989). This Monte Carlo method has a high probability of finding a near-optimal tour of 100 cities after examining a random sample of one million tours.

Fox *et al.* (1988) have shown that a hypercube can solve the traveling salesperson problem by simulated annealing. Allwright and Carpenter (1989) have solved the same problem on an array of transputers. These algorithms use parallelism to speed up the annealing process.

After a while I noticed that papers on simulated annealing often included remarks such as the following: "Our results [are] averaged over 20 initial random tours" (Moscato 1989). When you think about it, it makes sense: Due to the probabilistic nature of Monte Carlo methods, the best results are obtained by performing the same computation many times with different random numbers.

The advantage of using a multicomputer for *parallel Monte Carlo trials* is obvious. When the same problem has been broadcast to every processor, the trials can be performed simultaneously without any communication between the processors. Consequently, the processor efficiency is very close to 1 for non-trivial problems.

A straightforward implementation of the Monte Carlo paradigm requires a *master* processor that communicates directly with p *servers*. Each processor performs m/p trials. The master then collects the m solutions from the servers. Unfortunately, most multicomputers permit each processor to communicate with only a few neighboring processors. For p larger than, say, 4, the data must be transmitted through a chain of processors. The simplest way to do this is to use a *pipeline* with p processors controlled by a master processor (Brinch Hansen 1992d).

I used this paradigm to compute ten different tours of 2500 cities simultaneously and select the shortest tour obtained (Brinch Hansen 1992a).

My second application of the paradigm was *primality testing* of a large integer, which is of considerable interest in *cryptography* (Rivest 1978). It is not feasible to determine whether or not a 150-digit integer is a prime by examining all the 10^{75} possible divisors. The *Miller–Rabin algorithm* tests the same integer many times using different random numbers (Rabin 1980). If any one of the trials shows that a number is composite, then this is the correct answer. However, if all trials fail to prove that a number is composite, then it is almost certainly prime. The probability that the algorithm gives the wrong answer after, say, 40 trials is less than 10^{-24}.

I programmed the Miller–Rabin algorithm in occam and used the Monte Carlo paradigm to perform 40 tests of a 160-digit random number simultaneously on 40 transputers (Brinch Hansen 1992b).

For primality testing, I had to program multiple-length arithmetic. These serial operations imitate the familiar paper-and-pencil methods. I thought it would be easy to find a textbook that includes a simple algorithm for *multiple-length division* with a complete explanation. Much to my surprise, I was unable to find such a book. I ended up spending weeks on this "well-known" problem and finally wrote a tutorial that includes a complete Pascal algorithm (Brinch Hansen 1992c). I mention this unexpected difficulty to illustrate what happens when a standard algorithm is not published as a well-structured program in an executable language.

8   Parallel Cellular Automata

A *cellular automaton* is a discrete model of a system that varies in time and space. The discrete space is an array of identical cells, each representing a local state. As time advances in discrete steps, the system evolves according to universal laws. Every time the clock ticks, the cells update their states simultaneously. The next state of a cell depends only on the current states of the cell and its nearest neighbors.

John von Neumann (1966) and Stan Ulam (1986) introduced cellular automata to study self-reproducing systems. John Conway's game, *Life*, is undoubtedly the most widely known cellular automaton (Gardner 1970). Another well-known automaton simulates the life cycles of sharks and fish on the imaginary planet *Wa-Tor* (Dewdney 1984).

Cellular automata can simulate continuous physical systems described by *partial differential equations.* The numerical solution of, say, Laplace's equation by grid iteration is really a discrete simulation of heat flow performed by a cellular automaton.

Fox *et al.* (1988) described a Wa-Tor simulator for a hypercube. Numerical solution of Laplace's equation on multicomputers has been discussed by Barlow and Evans (1982), Evans (1984), Pritchard *et al.* (1987), Saltz *et al.* (1987), and Fox *et al.* (1988).

I developed and published a model program for parallel execution of a cellular automaton on a multicomputer configured as a *matrix* of processors (Fig. 5).

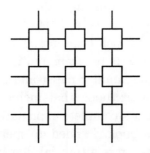

Figure 5 Processor matrix.

The combined state of a cellular automaton is represented by an $n \times n$ *grid.* The $q \times q$ processors hold *subgrids* of size $n/q \times n/q$. In each step, every node exchanges boundary values with its four nearest neighbors (if any). The nodes then update their subgrids simultaneously. At the end of a simulation, the nodes output their final values to a master processor that assembles a complete grid.

The shared boundary values raise the familiar concern about time-dependent errors in parallel programs. Race conditions are prevented by assigning a binary *parity* to every grid element. *Even* and *odd* elements are updated in two separate phases (Barlow 1982). Deadlock is prevented by letting every node communicate simultaneously with its four neighbors (Brinch Hansen 1992f).

The only parts of the parallel program that vary from one application to another are the possible *states* of the cells and the state *transition function.*

I have used a 6 × 6 matrix of transputers to simulate a *forest fire* on a

480 × 480 grid. Every element represents a tree that is either alive, burning, or dead. In each step, the next state of every tree is defined by probabilistic rules (Bak 1990).

I used the same paradigm to solve *Laplace's equation* for equilibrium temperatures in a square region with fixed temperatures at the boundaries. Every element represents the temperature at a single point in the region. In each step, the temperature of every interior element is replaced by a weighted sum of the previous temperature and the average of the surrounding temperatures (Brinch Hansen 1992e). In numerical analysis, this method is known as *successive overrelaxation* with *parity ordering* (Young 1971; Press 1989). The parallel program used 6 × 6 transputers to solve the heat equation on a 1500 × 1500 grid.

9   Program Characteristics

After studying the paradigms separately, it is instructive to consider what they have in common.

I was surprised by the *specialized* nature of some of the paradigms (Table 1). It may well be that some of them apply to only a small number of problems. To me that is a minor concern. The essence of the programming method is that you attempt to write two or more programs simultaneously. The intellectual discipline required to do this seems almost inevitably to produce well structured programs that are easy to understand.

The model programs illustrate programming methods for a variety of multicomputer *architectures* (Table 2). The reconfigurable Computing Surface was ideal for this purpose.

If a parallel architecture is not reconfigurable, it may be necessary to reprogram some of the paradigms. However, since all instances of a paradigm have the same sequential control structure, you know that if you can implement any one of them on a parallel architecture, the rest will turn out to be variations of the same theme.

Every program has a parallel component that implements a *paradigm* and a sequential component for a specific *application* (Table 3). The paradigm typically accounts for 60% of a program and is the most difficult part to write.

To make the programs *readable*, I divided them into short procedures of 10–20 lines each. No procedure exceeds one page of text (Table 4).

I have always found that a good *description* of a program is considerably

Table 1 Paradigms.

Program	Paradigm
Annealing	Monte Carlo trials
Primality	Monte Carlo trials
Multiply	Multiplication
Paths	Multiplication
Householder	All-pairs
N-body	All-pairs
FFT tree	Divide-and-conquer
Sorting tree	Divide-and-conquer
Sorting cube	Divide-and-conquer
Laplace	Cellular automata
Forest fire	Cellular automata

Table 2 Architectures.

Program	Architecture
Annealing	Pipeline
Primality	Pipeline
Multiply	Pipeline
Paths	Pipeline
Householder	Pipeline
N-body	Pipeline
FFT tree	Tree
Sorting tree	Tree
Sorting cube	Cube
Laplace	Matrix
Forest fire	Matrix

longer than the program text (Table 5). Fifteen years ago, I put it this way: "Programming is the art of writing essays in crystal clear prose and making them executable" (Brinch Hansen 1977).

Table 6 illustrates the *performance* of the model programs on a Computing Surface in terms of the size of the problems solved and the speedup S_p achieved by p processors running in parallel.

Table 3 Program lengths.

Program	Paradigm (lines)	Application (lines)
Annealing	150	200
Primality	150	520
Multiply	150	30
Paths	150	90
Householder	190	120
N-body	190	130
FFT tree	140	100
Sorting tree	140	80
Sorting cube	170	80
Laplace	280	30
Forest fire	280	60

Table 4 Procedure lengths.

Program	Lines/procedure		
	Min	Aver	Max
Annealing	1	12	34
Primality	3	15	43
Multiply	6	12	28
Paths	6	14	28
Householder	8	18	50
N-body	2	12	26
FFT tree	6	14	24
Sorting tree	6	13	24
Sorting cube	6	13	29
Laplace	3	12	31
Forest fire	3	13	31

Table 5 Program descriptions.

Program	Program (pages)	Report (pages)
Annealing	8	20
Multiply	5	10
Householder	7	40
FFT tree	6	30
Laplace	7	40

Table 6 Program performance.

Program	Problem size	p	S_p
Annealing	400	10	10
Primality	160	40	40
Multiply	1400×1400	35	31
Householder	1250×1250	25	20
N-body	9000	45	36
FFT tree	32768	31	4
Sorting tree	131072	31	3
Sorting cube	131072	8	2
Laplace	1500×1500	36	34

10   Programming Languages

As I was describing my first parallel paradigm, I became disenchanted with occam as a *publication language*. To my taste, occam looks clumsy compared to Pascal. (I hasten to add that I prefer occam to its competitors, Fortran, C, and Ada.)

At the time, no programming language was suitable for writing elegant, portable programs for multicomputers. As a compromise, I used *Pascal* extended with *parallel statements* and *communication channels* as a publication language.

To avoid dealing with the obscure behavior of incorrect programs on a multicomputer, I tested the parallel programs on a sequential computer. Since my publication language was not executable, I rewrote the model programs in an executable Pascal dialect that includes parallel statements and conditional critical regions. I used conditional critical regions to implement message passing and tested the programs on an IBM-PC with 64 Kbytes of memory.

When the parallel programs worked, I rewrote them in occam, changed a few constants, and used them to solve much larger problems on a Computing Surface with 48 transputers and 48 Mbytes of distributed memory. Sometimes I used *Joyce* to run the same computation on an Encore Multimax, a multiprocessor with 16 processors and 128 Mbytes of shared memory (Brinch Hansen 1987, 1989). The manual translation of correct readable programs into occam or Joyce was a trivial task.

The ease with which I could express the model programs in three different programming languages and run them on three different computer architectures prove that they are eminently portable.

The development of an executable publication language was a long-term goal of my research. One of my reasons for writing the model programs was to identify language features that are indispensable and some that are unnecessary for parallel scientific computing.

The published paradigm for the tree machine includes a recursive procedure that defines a tree of processes as a root process running in parallel with two subtrees. A notation for *recursive processes* is essential for expressing this idea concisely (Brinch Hansen 1990a). After using Joyce, I found the lack of recursion in occam unacceptable.

So far I have not found it necessary to use a statement that enables a process to poll several channels until a communication takes place on one of them. I have tentatively adopted the position that *non-deterministic communication* is necessary at the hardware level in a routing network, but is probably superfluous for scientific programming. It would be encouraging if this turns out to be true, since polling can be inefficient (Brinch Hansen 1989).

In practice, programmers will often be obligated to implement programs in complicated languages. However, wise programmers will prefer to develop and publish their ideas in the simplest possible languages, even if they are expected to use archaic or abstruse *implementation languages* for their final software products. Since it is no problem to rewrite a model program in another language, it is not particularly important to be able to use publication and implementation languages on the same machine.

Nevertheless, I must confess that the relentless efforts to adapt the world's oldest programming language for parallel computing strike me as futile. A quarter of a century ago, Alan Perlis boldly selected *Algol 60* as the publication language for algorithms in *Communications of the ACM*. In response to his critics, he said: "It is argued that more programmers now know Fortran than Algol. While this is true, it is not necessarily relevant since this does not increase the readability of algorithms in Fortran" (Perlis 1966).

Present multicomputers are difficult to program, because every program must be tailored to a particular architecture. It makes no sense to me to complicate hard intellectual work by poor notation. Nor am I swayed by the huge investment in existing Fortran programs. Every generation of scientists must reprogram these programs if they wish to understand them in depth and verify that they are correct. And the discovery of new architectures will continue to require reprogramming in unfamiliar notations that have not been invented yet.

11   Research Method

It took me a year to study numerical analysis, learn multicomputer programming, select a research theme, understand the development steps involved and complete the first paradigm. From then on, every paradigm took about one semester of research.

I followed the same steps for every paradigm:

1. Identify two computational problems with the same sequential control structure.

2. For each problem, write a tutorial that explains the theory of the computation and includes a complete Pascal program.

3. Write a parallel program for the programming paradigm in a readable publication language.

4. Test the parallel program on a sequential computer.

5. Derive a parallel program for each problem by trivial substitutions of a few data types, variables and procedures, and analyze the complexity of these programs.

6. Rewrite the parallel programs in an implementation language and measure their performance on a multicomputer.

7. Write clear descriptions of the parallel programs.

8. Rewrite the programs using the same terminology as in the descriptions.

9. Publish the programs and descriptions in their entirety with no hidden mysteries and every program line open to scrutiny.

The most difficult step is the *discovery* of paradigms and the *selection* of interesting instances of these paradigms. This creative process cannot be reduced to a simplistic recipe. Now that I know what I am looking for, I find it helpful to browse through books and journals on the computational aspects of biology, engineering, geology, mathematics and physics. When I see an interesting problem I ask myself: "Is there any way this computation can be regarded as similar to another one?" *Luck* clearly plays a role in the search for paradigms. However, as the French philosopher Bernard de Fontenelle (1657–1757) once observed: "These strokes of fortune are only for those who play well!" So I keep on trying.

12   Conclusions

I have described a collection of model programs for computational science. Every program is a realistic case study that illustrates the use of a paradigm for parallel programming. A programming paradigm is a class of algorithms that solve different problems but have the same control structure. The individual algorithms may be regarded as refinements of a general algorithm that defines the common control structure.

Parallel programming paradigms are elegant solutions to non-trivial problems:

1. Paradigms are *beautiful* programs that challenge your intellectual abilities and programming skills.

2. A programming paradigm is a *unifying* concept that reveals unexpected similarities between algorithms and raises new questions about familiar algorithms.

3. Viewing a parallel algorithm as an instance of a paradigm enables you to *separate* the issues of parallelism from the details of application. This sharp distinction contributes to program clarity.

4. Every paradigm defines an effective *programming style* that becomes part of your mental tool kit and enables you to apply previous insight to new problems (Nelson 1987).

5. Paradigms serve as case studies that illustrate the use of *structured programming* in scientific computing (Dijkstra 1972).

6. A commitment to *publish* paradigms as complete, executable programs imposes an intellectual discipline that leaves little room for vague statements and missing details. Such programs may serve as *models* for other scientists who wish to study them with the assurance that every detail has been considered, explained, and tested.

7. Model programs may also teach students the neglected art of program *reading* (Wirth 1976; Mills 1988).

8. Parallel paradigms capture the essence of *parallel architectures* such as pipelines, trees, hypercubes and matrices.

9. Parallel programs based on the same paradigm can be *moved* to different architectures with a reasonable effort by rewriting the general program that defines the common control structure. The individual programs can then be moved by making minor changes to the paradigm (Dongarra 1989).

10. Since a paradigm defines a whole class of useful algorithms, it is an excellent choice as a *benchmark* for parallel architectures.

11. A collection of paradigms can provide valuable guidance for *programming language design* (Floyd 1987). If the paradigms are rewritten in a proposed notation, the readability of the programs will reveal whether or not the language concepts are essential and concise.

After using this programming methodology for three years, the evidence strikes me as overwhelming: *The study of programming paradigms provides an architectural vision of parallel scientific computing!*

Acknowledgements

I am grateful to Coen Bron, Mani Chandi, Peter Denning, Jack Dongarra, Paul Dubois, Geoffrey Fox, Jonathan Greenfield, Tony Hey, Harlan Mills, Peter O'Hearn, Les Valiant and Virgil Wallentine for their constructive comments on earlier drafts of this paper.

References

Aarts, E. and Korst, J. 1989. *Simulated Annealing and Boltzmann Machines*. Wiley, New York.

Allwright, J.R.A. and Carpenter, D.B. 1989. A distributed implementation of simulated annealing. *Parallel Computing 10*, 335–338.

Bak, P. and Chen, K. 1990. A forest-fire model and some thoughts on turbulence. *Physics Letters A 147*, 5–6, 297–299.

Barlow, R.H., and Evans, D.J. 1982. Parallel algorithms for the iterative solution to linear systems. *Computer Journal 25*, 1, 56–60.

Brigham, E.O. 1974. *The Fast Fourier Transform*. Prentice Hall, Englewood Cliffs, NJ.

Brinch Hansen, P. 1977. *The Architecture of Concurrent Programs*. Prentice Hall, Englewood Cliffs, NJ.

Brinch Hansen, P. 1987. Joyce—A programming language for distributed systems. *Software—Practice and Experience 17*, 29–50. *Article 18*.

Brinch Hansen, P. 1989. A multiprocessor implementation of Joyce. *Software—Practice and Experience 19*, 579–592. *Article 19*.

Brinch Hansen, P. 1990a. The nature of parallel programming. In *Natural and Artificial Parallel Computation*, M.A. Arbib and J.A. Robinson, Eds. The MIT Press, Cambridge, MA, (1990), 31–46. *Article 20*.

Brinch Hansen, P. 1990b. Householder reduction of linear equations. School of Computer and Information Science, Syracuse University, Syracuse, NY. Revised version in *ACM Computing Surveys 24*, (June 1992), 185–194.

Brinch Hansen, P. 1990c. The all-pairs pipeline. School of Computer and Information Science, Syracuse University, Syracuse, NY.

Brinch Hansen, P. 1990d. Balancing a pipeline by folding. School of Computer and Information Science, Syracuse University, Syracuse, NY.

Brinch Hansen, P. 1991a. The n-body pipeline. School of Computer and Information Science, Syracuse University, Syracuse, NY.

Brinch Hansen, P. 1991b. A generic multiplication pipeline. School of Computer and Information Science, Syracuse University, Syracuse, NY.

Brinch Hansen, P. 1991c. The fast Fourier transform. School of Computer and Information Science, Syracuse University, Syracuse, NY.

Brinch Hansen, P. 1991d. Parallel divide and conquer. School of Computer and Information Science, Syracuse University, Syracuse, NY.

Brinch Hansen, P. 1991e. Do hypercubes sort faster than tree machines? School of Computer and Information Science, Syracuse University, Syracuse, NY.

Brinch Hansen, P. 1992a. Simulated annealing. School of Computer and Information Science, Syracuse University, Syracuse, NY.

Brinch Hansen, P. 1992b. Primality testing. School of Computer and Information Science, Syracuse University, Syracuse, NY.

Brinch Hansen, P. 1992c. Multiple-length division revisited: A tour of the minefield. School of Computer and Information Science, Syracuse University, Syracuse, NY.

Brinch Hansen, P. 1992d. Parallel Monte Carlo trials. School of Computer and Information Science, Syracuse University, Syracuse, NY.

Brinch Hansen, P. 1992e. Numerical solution of Laplace's equation. School of Computer and Information Science, Syracuse University, Syracuse, NY.

Brinch Hansen, P. 1992f. Parallel cellular automata: A model program for computational science. School of Computer and Information Science, Syracuse University, Syracuse, NY.

Browning, S.A. 1980. Algorithms for the tree machine. In *Introduction to VLSI Systems*, C. Mead and L. Conway, Eds. Addison-Wesley, Reading, MA, 295–313.

Cok, R.S. 1991. *Parallel Programs for the Transputer*. Prentice Hall, Englewood Cliffs, NJ.

Cole, M.I. 1989. *Algorithmic Skeletons: Structured Management of Parallel Computation*. MIT Press, Cambridge, MA.

Cooley, J.W. and Tukey, J.W. 1965. An algorithm for machine calculation of complex Fourier series. *Mathematics of Computation 19*, 297–301.

Cormen, T.H., Leiserson, C.E. and Rivest, R.L. 1990. *Introduction to Algorithms*, The MIT Press, Cambridge, MA.

Cosnard, M. and Tchuente, M. 1988. Designing systolic algorithms by top-down analysis. *The Third International Conference on Supercomputing*, Vol. 3, International Supercomputing Institute, St. Petersburg, FL, 9–18.

Dewdney, A.K. 1984. Sharks and fish wage an ecological war on the toroidal planet Wa-Tor. *Scientific American 251*, 6, 14–22.

Dijkstra, E.W. 1972. Notes on structured programming. In *Structured Programming*, O.-J. Dahl, E.W. Dijkstra, and C.A.R. Hoare, Eds. Academic Press, New York.

Dongarra, J.J. and Sorenson, D.C. 1989. Algorithmic design for different computer architectures. In *Opportunities and Constraints of Parallel Computing*, J.L.C. Sanz, Ed. Springer-Verlag, New York, 33–35.

Dunham, C.B. 1982. The necessity of publishing programs. *Computer Journal 25*, 61–62.

Ellingworth, H.R.P. 1988. Transputers and computational chemistry: an application. *The Third International Conference on Supercomputing*, Vol. 1, International Supercomputing Institute, St. Petersburg, FL, 269–274.

Evans, D.J. 1984. Parallel SOR iterative methods. *Parallel Computing 1*, 3–18.

Floyd, R.W. 1987. The paradigms of programming. In *ACM Turing Award Lectures: The First Twenty Years, 1966–1985*, R.L. Ashenhurst and S. Graham, Eds. ACM Press, New York, 131–142.

Forsythe, G.E. 1966. Algorithms for scientific computing. *Communications of the ACM 9*, 255–256.

Fox, G.C., Johnson, M.A., Lyzenga, G.A., Otto, S.W., Salmon, J.K. and Walker, D.W. 1988. *Solving Problems on Concurrent Processors*, Vol. I, Prentice-Hall, Englewood Cliffs, NJ.

Fox, G.C. 1990. Applications of parallel supercomputers: scientific results and computer science lessons. In *Natural and Artificial Parallel Computation*, M.A. Arbib and J.A. Robinson, Eds. The MIT Press, Cambridge, MA, 47–90.

Gardner, M. 1970. The fantastic combinations of John Conway's new solitaire game "Life." *Scientific American 223*, 10, 120–123.

Hoare, C.A.R. 1961. Algorithm 64: Quicksort. *Communications of the ACM 4*, 321.

Hoare, C.A.R. 1971. Proof of a program: Find. *Communications of the ACM 14*, 39–45.

Householder, A.S. 1958. Unitary triangularization of a nonsymmetric matrix. *Journal of the ACM 5*, 339–342.

Ignizio, J.P. 1973. Validating claims for algorithms proposed for publication. *Operations Research 21*, 852-854.

Inmos Ltd. 1988. *occam 2 Reference Manual*. Prentice Hall, Englewood Cliffs, NJ.

Kirkpatrick, S., Gelatt, C.D. and Vechi, M.P. 1983. Optimization by simulated annealing. *Science 220*, 671–680.

Kung, H.T. 1989. Computational models for parallel computers. In *Scientific Applications of Multiprocessors*, R. Elliott and C.A.R. Hoare, Eds. Prentice Hall, Englewood Cliffs, NJ, 1–15.

Lawler, E.L., Lenstra, J.K., Rinnooy Kan, A.H.G. and Shmoys, D.B., Eds. 1985. *The Traveling Salesman Problem: A Guided Tour of Combinatorial Optimization*. Wiley, Chichester, England.

McDonald, N. 1991. Meiko Scientific Ltd. In *Past, Present, Parallel: A Survey of Available Parallel Computing Systems*, A. Trew and G. Wilson, Eds. Springer-Verlag, New York, 165–175.

May, D. 1988. The influence of VLSI technology on computer architecture. *The Third International Conference on Supercomputing*, Vol. 2, International Supercomputing Institute, St. Petersburg, FL, 247–256.

May, D. 1990. Towards general-purpose parallel computers. In *Natural and Artificial Parallel Computation*, M.A. Arbib and J.A. Robinson, Eds. The MIT Press, Cambridge, MA, 91–121.

Meiko Ltd. 1987. *Computing Surface Technical Specifications*. Meiko Ltd., Bristol, England.

Mills, H.D. 1988. *Software Productivity*. Dorset House, New York, NY.

Moscato, P. and Fontanari, J.F. (1989) Stochastic vs. deterministic update in simulated annealing. California Institute of Technology, Pasadena, CA.

Nelson, P.A. and Snyder, L. 1987. Programming paradigms for nonshared memory parallel computers. In *The Characteristics of Parallel Algorithms*, L.H. Jamieson, D. Gannon, and R.J. Douglas, Eds. The MIT Press, Cambridge, MA, 3–20.

Perlis, A.J. 1966. A new policy for algorithms? *Communications of the ACM 9*, 255.

Press, W.H., Flannery, B.P., Teukolsky, S.A. and Vetterling, W.T. 1989. *Numerical Recipes in Pascal: The Art of Scientific Computing*. Cambridge University Press, Cambridge, MA.

Pritchard, D.J., Askew, C.R., Carpenter, D.D., Glendinning, I., Hey, A.J.G. and Nicole, D.A. 1987. Practical parallelism using transputer arrays. *Lecture Notes in Computer Science 258*, 278–294.

Rabin, M.O. 1980. Probabilistic algorithms for testing primality. *Journal of Number Theory 12*, 128–138.

Rivest, R.L., Shamir, A. and Adleman, L.M. 1978. A method for obtaining digital signatures and public-key cryptosystems. *Communications of the ACM 21*, 120–126.

Saltz, J.H., Naik, V.K. and Nicol, D.M. 1987. Reduction of the effects of the communication delays in scientific algorithms on message passing MIMD architectures. *SIAM Journal on Scientific and Statistical Computing 8*, 1, s118–s134.

Seitz, C.L. 1985. The Cosmic Cube. *Communications of the ACM 28*, 22–33.

Shih, Z., Chen, G. and Lee, R.T.C. 1987. Systolic algorithms to examine all pairs of elements. *Communications of the ACM 30*, 161–167.

Ulam, S. 1986. *Science, Computers, and People: From the Tree of Mathematics*, Birkhäuser, Boston, MA.

Valiant, L.G. 1989. Optimally universal parallel computers. In *Scientific Applications of Multiprocessors*, R. Elliott and C.A.R. Hoare, Eds. Prentice Hall, Englewood Cliffs, NJ, 17–20.

von Neumann, J. 1966. *Theory of Self-Reproducing Automata*. Edited and completed by A.W. Burks, University of Illinois Press, Urbana, IL.

Wirth, N. 1976. *Algorithms + Data Structures = Programs*. Prentice Hall, Englewood Cliffs, NJ.

Young, D.M. 1971. *Iterative Solution of Large Linear Systems*. Academic Press, New York.

Parallel Cellular Automata: A Model Program for Computational Science*

(1993)

We develop a generic program for parallel execution of cellular automata on a multicomputer. The generic program is then adapted for simulation of a forest fire and numerical solution of Laplace's equation for stationary heat flow. The performance of the parallel program is analyzed and measured on a Computing Surface configured as a matrix of transputers with distributed memory.

1 Introduction

This is one of several papers that explore the benefits of developing *model programs for computational science* (Brinch Hansen 1990, 1991a, 1991b, 1992a). The theme of this paper is *parallel cellular automata*.

A cellular automaton is a discrete model of a system that varies in space and time. The discrete space is an array of identical cells, each representing a local state. As time advances in discrete steps, the system evolves according to universal laws. Every time the clock ticks, the cells update their states simultaneously. The next state of a cell depends only on the current state of the cell and its nearest neighbors.

In 1950 John von Neuman and Stan Ulam introduced cellular automata to study self-reproducing systems (von Neumann 1966; Ulam 1986). John Conway's game of *Life* is undoubtedly the most widely known cellular automaton (Gardner 1970, 1971; Berlekamp 1982). Another well known automaton simulates the life cycles of sharks and fish on the imaginary planet

*P. Brinch Hansen, Parallel Cellular Automata: A model program for computational science. *Concurrency—Practice and Experience 5*, 5 (August 1993), 425–448. Copyright © 1993, John Wiley & Sons, Ltd. Revised version. Reprinted by permission.

Wa-Tor (Dewdney 1984). The numerous applications include forest infesta-
tion (Hoppensteadt 1978), fluid flow (Frisch 1986), earthquakes (Bak 1989),
forest fires (Bak 1990) and sandpile avalanches (Hwa 1989).

Cellular automata can simulate continuous physical systems described by
partial differential equations. The numerical solution of, say, Laplace's equation by grid relaxation is really a discrete simulation of heat flow performed
by a cellular automaton.

Cellular automata are ideally suited for parallel computing. My goal
is to explore *programming methodology for multicomputers.* I will illustrate
this theme by developing a generic program for parallel execution of cellular
automata on a multicomputer with a square matrix of processor nodes. I
will then show how easy it is to adapt the generic program for two different
applications: (1) simulation of a *forest fire,* and (2) numerical solution of
Laplace's equation for stationary heat flow. On a *Computing Surface* with
transputer nodes, the parallel efficiency of these model programs is close to
one.

2   Cellular Automata

A *cellular automaton* is an array of parallel processes, known as *cells.* Every
cell has a discrete *state.* At discrete moments in *time,* the cells update their
states *simultaneously.* The state *transition* of a cell depends only on its
previous state and the states of the *adjacent* cells.

I will program a *two-dimensional* cellular automaton with *fixed boundary
states* (Fig. 1). The automaton is a square matrix with three kinds of cells:

1. *Interior cells,* marked "?", may change their states dynamically.

2. *Boundary cells,* marked "+", have fixed states.

3. *Corner cells,* marked "−", are not used.

Figure 2 shows an interior cell and the four neighbors that may influence
its state. These five cells are labeled c (central), n (north), s (south), e (east),
and w (west).

The cellular automaton will be programmed in *SuperPascal* (Brinch Hansen 1994). The execution of k statements $S_1, S_2, \ldots, S_k$ as parallel processes
is denoted

$$\textbf{parallel } S_1|S_2|\cdots|S_k \textbf{ end}$$

−	+	+	+	+	+	+	−
+	?	?	?	?	?	?	+
+	?	?	?	?	?	?	+
+	?	?	?	?	?	?	+
+	?	?	?	?	?	?	+
+	?	?	?	?	?	?	+
+	?	?	?	?	?	?	+
−	+	+	+	+	+	+	−

Figure 1 A cellular automaton.

Figure 2 Adjacent cells.

The parallel execution continues until every one of the k processes has terminated.

The *forall* statement

$$\textbf{forall } i := 1 \textbf{ to } k \textbf{ do } S(i)$$

is equivalent to

$$\textbf{parallel } S(1)|S(2)|\cdots|S(k) \textbf{ end}$$

I assume that parallel processes communicate through *synchronous channels* only. The *creation* of a new channel c is denoted

$$\text{open}(c)$$

The *input* and *output* of a value x through a channel c are denoted

$$\text{receive}(c,x) \qquad \text{send}(c,x)$$

A cellular automaton is a set of parallel communicating cells. If you ignore boundary cells and communication details, a two-dimensional automaton is defined as follows:

> **forall** i := 1 **to** n **do**
> **forall** j := 1 **to** n **do**
> cell(i,j)

After initializing its own state, every interior cell goes through a fixed number of state transitions before outputting its final state:

> initialize own state;
> **for** k := 1 **to** steps **do**
> **begin**
> exchange states with
> adjacent cells;
> update own state
> **end**;
> output own state

The challenge is to transform this fine-grained parallel model into an efficient program for a *multicomputer* with distributed memory.

3   Initial States

Consider a cellular automaton with 36 interior cells and 24 boundary cells. In a sequential computer the combined state of the automaton can be represented by an 8×8 matrix, called a *grid* (Fig. 3). For reasons that will be explained later, the grid elements are indicated by 0's and 1's.

Figure 4 shows the *initial values* of the elements. The boundary elements have fixed values u_1, u_2, u_3 and u_4. Every interior element has the same initial value u_5.

In general, a grid u has $n \times n$ interior elements and $4n$ boundary elements:

> **const** n = ...;
> **type** state = (...);
>   row = **array** [0..n+1] **of** state;
>   grid = **array** [0..n+1] **of** row;
> **var** u: grid;

Since the possible *states* of every cell vary from one application to another, I deliberately leave them unspecified. The grid dimension n and the initial states u_1, u_2, u_3, u_4 and u_5 are also application dependent.

On a sequential computer, the grid is initialized as follows:

−	1	0	1	0	1	0	−
1	0	1	0	1	0	1	0
0	1	0	1	0	1	0	1
1	0	1	0	1	0	1	0
0	1	0	1	0	1	0	1
1	0	1	0	1	0	1	0
0	1	0	1	0	1	0	1
−	0	1	0	1	0	1	−

Figure 3 A square grid.

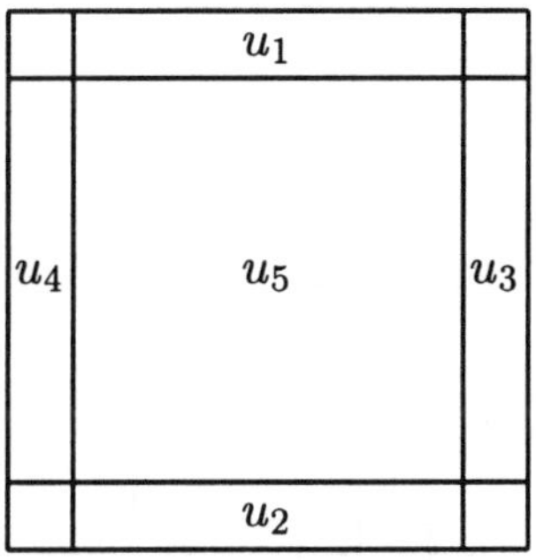

Figure 4 Initial values.

```
for i := 0 to n + 1 do
  for j := 0 to n + 1 do
    u[i,j] := initial(i,j)
```

Algorithm 1 defines the *initial* value of the element element $u[i, j]$. The values of the corner elements are arbitrary (and irrelevant).

4   Data Parallelism

For simulation of a cellular automaton, the ideal *multicomputer architecture* is a square matrix of identical processor *nodes* (Fig. 5). Every node is connected to its nearest neighbors (if any) by four communication *channels*.

```
function initial(i, j: integer): state;
begin
  if i = 0 then
    initial := u1
  else if i = n + 1 then
    initial := u2
  else if j = n + 1 then
    initial := u3
  else if j = 0 then
    initial := u4
  else
    initial := u5
end;
```

Algorithm 1

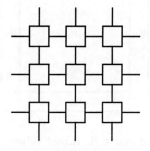

Figure 5 Processor matrix.

Figure 6 shows a grid with 36 interior elements divided into 9 subgrids. You now have a 3×3 matrix of nodes and a 3×3 matrix of subgrids. The two matrices define a one-to-one correspondence between subgrids and nodes. I will assign each subgrid to the corresponding node and let the nodes update the subgrids simultaneously. This form of distributed processing is called *data parallelism*.

Every processor holds a 4×4 *subgrid* with four interior elements and eight boundary elements (Fig. 7). Every boundary element holds either an interior element of a neighboring subgrid or a boundary element of the entire grid. (I will say more about this later.)

–	1	0	1	0	1	0	–
1	0	1	0	1	0	1	0
0	1	0	1	0	1	0	1
1	0	1	0	1	0	1	0
0	1	0	1	0	1	0	1
1	0	1	0	1	0	1	0
0	1	0	1	0	1	0	1
–	0	1	0	1	0	1	–

Figure 6 A subdivided grid.

–	1	0	–
1	0	1	0
0	1	0	1
–	0	1	–

Figure 7 A subgrid.

5   Processor Nodes

With this background, I am ready to program a cellular automaton that runs
on a $q \times q$ *processor matrix*. The *nodes* follow the same script (Algorithm 2).

A node is identified by its row and column numbers (q_i, q_j) in the processor matrix, where

$$1 \le q_i \le q \text{ and } 1 \le q_j \le q$$

Four communication channels, labeled *up*, *down*, *left*, and *right*, connect
a node to its nearest neighbors (if any).

Every node holds a subgrid with $m \times m$ interior elements and $4m$ boundary elements (Fig. 7):

```
const m = ...;
type
    subrow = array [0..m+1] of state;
    subgrid = array [0..m+1] of subrow;
```

```
procedure node(qi, qj, steps: integer;
   up, down, left, right: channel);
var u: subgrid; k: integer;
begin
   newgrid(qi, qj, u);
   for k := 1 to steps do
      relax(qi, qj, up, down,
         left, right, u);
   output(qi, qj, right, left, u)
end;
```

Algorithm 2

The grid dimension n is a multiple of the subgrid dimension m:

$$n = m * q$$

After initializing its subgrid, a node updates the subgrid a fixed number of times before outputting the final values. In numerical analysis, grid iteration is known as *relaxation*.

Node (q_i, q_j) holds the following subset

$$u[i_0..i_0 + m + 1, \; j_0..j_0 + m + 1]$$

of the complete grid $u[0..n + 1, \; 0..n + 1]$, where

$$i_0 = (q_i - 1)m \text{ and } j_0 = (q_j - 1)m$$

The initialization of a subgrid is straightforward (Algorithm 3).

6 Parallel Relaxation

In each time step, every node updates its own subgrid. The next value of an interior element is a function of its current value u_c and the values u_n, u_s, u_e and u_w of the four adjacent elements (Fig. 2). Every application of a cellular automaton requires a different set of *state transitions*. In some applications, *probabilistic* state transitions require the use of a random number generator that updates a global seed variable. Since functions cannot

```
procedure newgrid(qi, qj: integer;
    var u: subgrid);
var i, i0, j, j0: integer;
begin
    i0 := (qi − 1)∗m;
    j0 := (qj − 1)∗m;
    for i := 0 to m + 1 do
        for j := 0 to m + 1 do
            u[i,j] := initial(i0+i, j0+j)
end;
```

Algorithm 3

have side-effects in *SuperPascal*, the *next state* of a cell $u[i, j]$ is defined by a procedure (Algorithm 4).

Parallel relaxation is not quite as easy as it sounds. When a node updates row number 1 of its subgrid, it needs access to row number m of the subgrid of its northern neighbor (Fig. 6). To relax its subgrid, a node must share a single row or column with each of its four neighbors.

The solution to this problem is to let two neighboring grids *overlap* by one row or column vector. Before a node updates its interior elements, it exchanges a pair of vectors with each of the adjacent nodes. The overlapping vectors are kept in the boundary elements of the subgrids (Fig. 7). If a neighboring node does not exist, a local boundary vector holds the corresponding boundary elements of the entire grid (Figs. 4 and 6).

The northern neighbor of a node outputs row number m of its subgrid to the node, which inputs it in row number 0 of its own subgrid (Fig. 7). In return, the node outputs its row number 1 to its northern neighbor, which inputs it in row number $m + 1$ of its subgrid. Similarly, a node exchanges rows with its southern neighbor, and columns with its eastern and western neighbors (Fig. 5).

The *shared elements* raise the familiar concern about time-dependent errors in parallel programs. *Race conditions* are prevented by a rule of *mutual exclusion:* While a node updates an element, another node cannot access the same element. This rule is enforced by an ingenious method (Barlow 1982).

Every grid element $u[i, j]$ is assigned a *parity*

$$(i + j) \bmod 2$$

```
procedure nextstate(var u: subgrid;
  i, j: integer);
{ 1 <= i <= m, 1 <= j <= m }
begin u[i,j] := ... end;
```

Algorithm 4

```
procedure relax(qi, qj: integer;
  up, down, left, right: channel;
  var u: subgrid);
var b, i, j, k: integer;
begin
  for b := 0 to 1 do
    begin
      exchange(qi, qj, 1 - b,
        up, down, left, right, u);
      for i := 1 to m do
        begin
          k := (i + b) mod 2;
          j := 2 - k;
          while j <= m - k do
            begin
              nextstate(u, i, j);
              j := j + 2
            end
        end
    end
end;
```

Algorithm 5

which is either *even* (0) or *odd* (1) as shown in Figs. 3 and 6. To eliminate tedious (and unnecessary) programming details, I assume that the subgrid dimension m is *even*. This guarantees that every subgrid has the same *parity ordering* of the elements (Figs. 6 and 7).

Parity ordering reveals a simple property of grids: The next values of the even interior elements depend only on the current values of the odd elements, and vice versa. This observation suggests a reliable method for parallel relaxation.

In each relaxation step, the nodes scan their grids twice:

- *First scan:* The nodes exchange odd elements with their neighbors and update all even interior elements simultaneously.

- *Second scan:* The nodes exchange even elements and update all odd interior elements simultaneously.

The key point is this: In each scan, the simultaneous updating of local elements depends only on shared elements with constant values! In the terminology of parallel programming, the nodes are *disjoint processes* during a scan.

The *relaxation* procedure uses a local variable to update elements with the same *parity b* after exchanging elements of the opposite parity $1 - b$ with its neighbors (Algorithm 5).

7   Local Communication

The nodes communicate through *synchronous channels* with the following properties:

1. Every channel connects exactly two nodes.

2. The communications on a channel take place one at a time.

3. A communication takes place when a node is ready to output a value through a channel and another node is ready to input the value through the same channel.

4. A channel can transmit a value in either direction between two nodes.

5. The four channels of a node can transmit values simultaneously.

These requirements are satisfied by *transputer* nodes programmed in *occam* (Cok 1991).

The identical behavior of the nodes poses a subtle problem. Suppose the nodes simultaneously attempt to input from their northern neighbors. In that case, the nodes will *deadlock*, since none of them are ready to output through the corresponding channels. There are several solutions to this problem. I use a method that works well for transputers.

Before the nodes scan elements of the same parity, they communicate with their neighbors in two phases (Fig. 8).

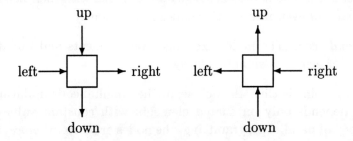

Figure 8 Communication phases.

In each phase, every node communicates simultaneously on its four channels as shown below. Phases 1 and 2 correspond to the left and right halves of Fig. 8.

Channel	Phase 1	Phase 2
up	input	output
down	output	input
left	input	output
right	output	input

Since every input operation on a channel is matched by a simultaneous output operation on the same channel, this *protocol* is *deadlock free*. It is also very *efficient*, since every node communicates simultaneously with its four neighbors.

Algorithm 6 defines the *exchange* of elements of parity b between a node and its four neighbors.

Phase 1 is defined by Algorithm 7. The *if* statements prevent boundary nodes from communicating with nonexisting neighbors (Fig. 5).

```
procedure exchange(qi, qj, b: integer;
    up, down, left, right: channel;
    var u: subgrid);
begin
    phase1(qi, qj, b,
        up, down, left, right, u);
    phase2(qi, qj, b,
        up, down, left, right, u)
end;
```

Algorithm 6

Phase 2 is similar (Algorithm 8).

I have used this protocol on a *Computing Surface* with transputer nodes. Since transputer links can communicate in both directions simultaneously, the two communication phases run in parallel. So every transputer inputs and outputs simultaneously through all four links!

If the available processors cannot communicate simultaneously with their neighbors, a sequential protocol must be used (Dijkstra 1982). This is also true if the overhead of parallelism and communication is substantial. However, the replacement of one protocol by another should only change Algorithms 6–8 and leave the rest of the program unchanged.

8   Global Output

At the end of a simulation, the nodes output their final values to a *master* processor that assembles a complete grid. The boundary channels of the processor matrix are not used for grid relaxation (Fig. 5). I use the horizontal boundary channels to connect the nodes and the master M into a *pipeline* for *global output* (Fig. 9).

The boundary elements of the entire grid have known fixed values (Fig. 4). These elements are needed only during relaxation. The final output is an $n \times n$ matrix of interior elements only. Every element defines the final state of a single cell.

So I redefine the full grid, omitting the boundary elements:

```
procedure phase1(qi, qj, b: integer;
    up, down, left, right: channel;
    var u: subgrid);
var k, last: integer;
begin
    k := 2 − b;
    last := m − b;
    while k <= last do
        begin
            { 1 <= k <= m }
            [sic] parallel
                if qi > 1 then
                    receive(up, u[0,k])|
                if qi < q then
                    send(down, u[m,k])|
                if qj > 1 then
                    receive(left, u[k,0])|
                if qj < q then
                    send(right, u[k,m])
            end;
            k := k + 2
        end
end;
```

Algorithm 7

```
type
    row = array [1..n] of state;
    grid = array [1..n] of row;
```

The *master* inputs the final grid row by row, one element at a time (Algorithm 9).

The nodes use a common procedure to *output* interior elements in row order (Algorithm 10). Every row of elements is distributed through a row of nodes (Figs. 5 and 6). For each of its subrows, node (q_i, q_j) outputs the m interior elements, and copies the remaining $(q - q_j)m$ elements of the same row from its eastern neighbor. This completes the output of the rows of elements, which are distributed through row q_i of the processor matrix. The node then copies the remaining $(q - q_i)m$ complete rows of n elements each.

A simple procedure is used to *copy* a fixed number of elements from

```
                procedure phase2(qi, qj, b: integer;
                   up, down, left, right: channel;
                   var u: subgrid);
                var k, last: integer;
                begin
                  k := b + 1;
                  last := m + b − 1;
                  while k <= last do
                    begin
                      { 1 <= k <= m }
                      [sic] parallel
                        if qi > 1 then
                          send(up, u[1,k])|
                        if qi < q then
                          receive(down, u[m+1,k])|
                        if qj > 1 then
                          send(left, u[k,1])|
                        if qj < q then
                          receive(right, u[k,m+1])
                      end;
                      k := k + 2
                    end
                end;
```

Algorithm 8

one channel to another (Algorithm 11). In my program for the Computing Surface, I extended the copy procedure with parallel input/output. I also modified Algorithms 2 and 9 slightly to enable the program to output intermediate grids at fixed intervals.

9 Processor Network

Figure 10 illustrates the *network* that ties the processors together. The network consists of a horizontal channel matrix h and a vertical channel matrix v.

The following examples illustrate the abbreviations used:

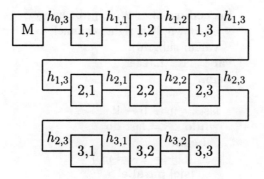

Figure 9 Output pipeline.

```
procedure master(right: channel;
    var u: grid);
var i, j: integer;
begin
  for i := 1 to n do
    for j := 1 to n do
        receive(right, u[i,j])
end;
```

Algorithm 9

M	master
3,2	node(3,2)
$v_{2,2}$	channel $v[2,2]$
$h_{3,1}$	channel $h[3,1]$

Algorithm 12 defines parallel *simulation* of a cellular automaton that computes a relaxed grid u. Execution of the parallel statement activates (1) the master, (2) the first column of nodes, and (3) the rest of the nodes.

This completes the development of the generic program. I will now demonstrate how easily the program can be adapted to different applications of cellular automata.

```
procedure output(qi, qj: integer;
   inp, out: channel; var u: subgrid);
var i, j: integer;
begin
  for i := 1 to m do
    begin
      for j := 1 to m do
        send(out, u[i,j]);
      copy((q − qj)*m, inp, out)
    end;
  copy((q − qi)*m*n, inp, out)
end;
```

Algorithm 10

10   Example: Forest Fire

A typical application of a cellular automaton is simulation of a *forest fire*. Every cell represents a *tree* that is either *alive, burning,* or *dead*. In each time-step, the next state of every tree is defined by *probabilistic rules* similar to the ones proposed by Bak (1990):

1. If a live tree is next to a burning tree, it burns; otherwise, it catches fire with probability p_b.

2. A burning tree dies.

3. A dead tree has probability p_a of being replaced by a live tree.

   Parallel simulation of a forest fire requires only minor changes of the generic program:

1. The possible *states* are:

$$\textbf{type } \text{state} = (\text{alive, burning, dead});$$

2. The *initial* states may, for example, be:

$$u_1 = u_2 = u_3 = u_4 = \text{dead}, u_5 = \text{alive}$$

3. Algorithm 4.1 defines state *transitions*.

4. A *random number* generator is added.

```
procedure copy(no: integer;
    inp, out: channel);
var k: integer; uk: state;
begin
  for k := 1 to no do
    begin
      receive(inp, uk);
      send(out, uk)
    end
end;
```

Algorithm 11

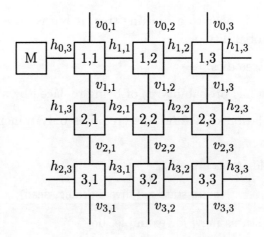

Figure 10 Processor network.

```
procedure simulate(
  steps: integer; var u: grid);
type
  line = array [1..q] of channel;
  matrix = array [0..q] of line;
var h, v: matrix; i, j: integer;
begin
  open(h[0,q]);
  for i := 1 to q do
    for j := 1 to q do
      open(h[i,j]);
  for i := 0 to q do
    for j := 1 to q do
      open(v[i,j]);
  parallel
    master(h[0,q], u)|
    forall j := 1 to q do
      node(j, 1, steps,
          v[j−1,1], v[j,1],
          h[j−1,q], h[j,1])|
    forall i := 1 to q do
      forall j := 2 to q do
        node(i, j, steps,
            v[i−1,j], v[i,j],
            h[i,j−1], h[i,j])
  end
end;
```

Algorithm 12

```
procedure nextstate(var u: subgrid;
  i, j: integer);
{ 1 <= i <= m, 1 <= j <= m }
const pa = 0.3; pb = 0.01;
var x: real;
begin
  case u[i,j] of
    alive:
      if
        (u[i−1,j] = burning) or
        (u[i+1,j] = burning) or
        (u[i,j+1] = burning) or
        (u[i,j−1] = burning)
      then u[i,j] := burning
      else
        begin
          random(x);
          if x <= pb then
            u[i,j] := burning
        end;
    burning:
      u[i,j] := dead;
    dead:
      begin
        random(x);
        if x <= pa then
          u[i,j] := alive
      end
  end
end;
```

Algorithm 4.1

11 Example: Laplace's Equation

A cellular automaton can also solve *Laplace's equation* for *equilibrium temperatures* in a square region with fixed temperatures at the boundaries. Every cell represents the temperature at a single point in the region. In each time-step, the next temperature of every cell is defined by a simple *deterministic rule.*

Parallel simulation of heat flow requires the following changes of the generic program:

1. The *states* are temperatures represented by reals.

2. A possible choice of *initial* temperatures is:

$$
\begin{aligned}
u_1 &= 0 \\
u_2 &= 100 \\
u_3 &= 100 \\
u_4 &= 0 \\
u_5 &= 50
\end{aligned}
$$

3. Algorithm 4.2 defines the *next* temperature of an interior cell $u[i,j]$. In steady-state, the temperature of every interior cell is the average of the neighboring temperatures:

$$ u_c = (u_n + u_s + u_e + u_w)/4.0 $$

This is the discrete form of Laplace's equation. The *residual res*, is a measure of how close a temperature is to satisfying this equation. The correction of a temperature u_c is proportional to its residual.

4. A *relaxation factor* f_{opt}, is added: For a large square grid relaxed in parity order, the relaxation factor

$$ f_{opt} = 2 - 2\pi/n $$

ensures the fastest possible convergence towards stationary temperatures. In numerical analysis, this method is called *successive overrelaxation* with *parity ordering.* The method requires n relaxation *steps* to achieve 3-figure accuracy of the final temperatures (Young 1954; Press 1989).

```
procedure nextstate(var u: subgrid;
  i, j: integer);
{ 1 <= i <= m, 1 <= j <= m }
var res: real;
begin
  res :=
    (u[i-1,j] + u[i+1,j] +
      u[i,j+1] + u[i,j-1])/4.0
      - u[i,j];
  u[i,j] := u[i,j] + fopt*res
end;
```

Algorithm 4.2

The complete algorithm for parallel simulation of steady-state heat flow is listed in the Appendix. The corresponding sequential program is explained in Brinch Hansen (1992b). Numerical solution of Laplace's equation on multicomputers is also discussed in Barlow (1982), Evans (1984), Pritchard (1987), Saltz (1987), and Fox (1988).

12   Complexity

In each time-step, every node exchanges overlapping elements with its neighbors in $O(m)$ time, and updates its own subgrid in $O(m^2)$ time. The final output takes $O(n^2)$ time. The *parallel run time* required to relax an $n \times n$ grid n times on p processors is

$$T(n,p) = n(am^2 + O(m)) + O(n^2)$$

where a is a system-dependent constant of relaxation and

$$n = m\sqrt{p} \tag{1}$$

The complexity of parallel simulation can be rewritten as follows:

$$T(n,p) = n^2(an/p + O(1) + O(1/\sqrt{p}))$$

For $1 \leq p \ll n$, the communication times are insignificant compared to the relaxation time, and you have approximately

$$T(n, p) \approx an^3/p \quad \text{for } n \gg p \qquad (2)$$

If the same simulation runs on a single processor, the *sequential run time* is obtained by setting $p = 1$ in (2):

$$T(n, 1) \approx an^3 \quad \text{for } n \gg 1 \qquad (3)$$

The *processor efficiency* of the parallel program is

$$E(n, p) = \frac{T(n, 1)}{p\, T(n, p)} \qquad (4)$$

The numerator is proportional to the number of processor cycles used in a sequential simulation. The denominator is a measure of the total number of cycles used by p processors performing the same computation in parallel.

By (2), (3) and (4) you find that the parallel efficiency is close to one, when the problem size n is large compared to the machine size p:

$$E(n, p) \approx 1 \quad \text{for } n \gg p$$

Since this analysis ignores the (insignificant) communication times, it cannot predict how close to one the efficiency is.

In theory, the efficiency can be computed from (4) by measuring the sequential and parallel run times for the same value of n. Unfortunately, this is not always feasible. When 36 nodes relax a 1500×1500 grid of 64-bit reals, every node holds a subgrid of $250 \times 250 \times 8 = 0.5$ Mbyte. However, on a single processor, the full grid occupies 18 Mbytes.

A more realistic approach is to make the $O(n^2)$ grid proportional to the machine size p. Then every node has an $O(m^2)$ subgrid of constant size independent of the number of nodes. And the nodes always perform the same amount of computation per time-step.

When a *scaled simulation* runs on a single processor, the run time is approximately

$$T(m, 1) \approx am^3 \quad \text{for } m \gg 1 \qquad (5)$$

since $p = 1$ and $n = m$.

From (1), (3) and (5) you obtain

$$T(n, 1) \approx p^{3/2}\, T(m, 1) \quad \text{for } m \gg 1 \qquad (6)$$

The computational formula you need follows from (4) and (6):

$$E(n,p) \approx \frac{\sqrt{p}\, T(m,1)}{T(n,p)} \qquad \text{for } m \gg 1 \tag{7}$$

This formula enables you to compute the efficiency of a parallel simulation by running a scaled-down version of the simulation on a single node.

13   Performance

I reprogrammed the model program in *occam2* and ran it on a *Computing Surface* with T800 transputers configured as a square matrix with a master node (Meiko 1987; Inmos 1988; McDonald 1991). The program was modified to solve *Laplace's equation* as explained in Sec. 11. The complete program is found in the Appendix.

Table 1 shows measured (and predicted) run times $T(n,p)$ in seconds for n relaxations of an $n \times n$ grid on p processors. In every run, the subgrid dimension $m = 250$.

Table 1 Run times.

p	n	$T(n,p)$ (s)		E_p
1	250	278	(281)	1.00
4	500	574	(563)	0.97
9	750	863	(844)	0.97
16	1000	1157	(1125)	0.96
25	1250	1462	(1406)	0.95
36	1500	1750	(1688)	0.95

The predicted run times shown in parentheses are defined by (2) using

$$a = 18 \ \mu s$$

The processor efficiency $E(n,p)$ was computed from (7) using the measured run times.

14   Final Remarks

I have developed a generic program for parallel execution of cellular automata on a multicomputer with a square matrix of processor nodes. I have adapted the generic program for simulation of a forest fire and numerical solution of Laplace's equation for stationary heat flow. On a Computing Surface with 36 transputers the program performs 1500 relaxations of a 1500 × 1500 grid of 64-bit reals in 29 minutes with an efficiency of 0.95.

15 Appendix: Complete Algorithm

The complete algorithm for parallel solution of *Laplace's equation* is composed of Algorithms 1–12.

```
const q = 6; m = 250 { even };
  n = 1500 { m*q };
type
  row = array [1..n] of real;
  grid = array [1..n] of row;

procedure laplace(var u: grid;
  u1, u2, u3, u4, u5: real;
  steps: integer);
type
  subrow = array [0..m+1] of real;
  subgrid = array [0..m+1] of subrow;
  channel = *(real);

  procedure node(qi, qj, steps: integer;
    up, down, left, right: channel);
  const pi = 3.14159265358979;
  var u: subgrid; k: integer; fopt: real;

    procedure copy(no: integer;
      inp, out: channel);
    var k: integer; uk: real;
    begin
      for k := 1 to no do
        begin
          receive(inp, uk);
          send(out, uk)
        end
    end;
```

```
procedure output(qi, qj: integer;
    inp, out: channel; var u: subgrid);
var i, j: integer;
begin
  for i := 1 to m do
    begin
      for j := 1 to m do
          send(out, u[i,j]);
      copy((q − qj)*m, inp, out)
    end;
  copy((q − qi)*m*n, inp, out)
end;


procedure phase1(qi, qj, b: integer;
    up, down, left, right: channel;
    var u: subgrid);
var k, last: integer;
begin
  k := 2 − b;
  last := m − b;
  while k <= last do
    begin
      { 1 <= k <= m }
      [sic] parallel
        if qi > 1 then
            receive(up, u[0,k])|
        if qi < q then
            send(down, u[m,k])|
        if qj > 1 then
            receive(left, u[k,0])|
        if qj < q then
            send(right, u[k,m])
      end;
      k := k + 2
    end
end;
```

```
procedure phase2(qi, qj, b: integer;
    up, down, left, right: channel;
    var u: subgrid);
var k, last: integer;
begin
  k := b + 1;
  last := m + b - 1;
  while k <= last do
    begin
      { 1 <= k <= m }
      [sic] parallel
        if qi > 1 then
          send(up, u[1,k])|
        if qi < q then
          receive(down, u[m+1,k])|
        if qj > 1 then
          send(left, u[k,1])|
        if qj < q then
          receive(right, u[k,m+1])
      end;
      k := k + 2
    end
end;

procedure exchange(qi, qj, b: integer;
    up, down, left, right: channel;
    var u: subgrid);
begin
  phase1(qi, qj, b,
    up, down, left, right, u);
  phase2(qi, qj, b,
    up, down, left, right, u)
end;

function initial(i, j: integer): real;
begin
  if i = 0 then
    initial := u1
```

```
    else if i = n + 1 then
      initial := u2
    else if j = n + 1 then
      initial := u3
    else if j = 0 then
      initial := u4
    else
      initial := u5
end;

procedure nextstate(var u: subgrid;
  i, j: integer);
{ 1 <= i <= m, 1 <= j <= m }
var res: real;
begin
  res :=
    (u[i−1,j] + u[i+1,j] +
      u[i,j+1] + u[i,j−1])/4.0
      − u[i,j];
  u[i,j] := u[i,j] + fopt*res
end;

procedure newgrid(qi, qj: integer;
  var u: subgrid);
var i, i0, j, j0: integer;
begin
  i0 := (qi − 1)*m;
  j0 := (qj − 1)*m;
  for i := 0 to m + 1 do
    for j := 0 to m + 1 do
      u[i,j] := initial(i0+i, j0+j)
end;

procedure relax(qi, qj: integer;
  up, down, left, right: channel;
  var u: subgrid);
var b, i, j, k: integer;
begin
```

```
        for b := 0 to 1 do
          begin
            exchange(qi, qj, 1 − b,
                up, down, left, right, u);
            for i := 1 to m do
              begin
                k := (i + b) mod 2;
                j := 2 − k;
                while j <= m − k do
                  begin
                    nextstate(u, i, j);
                    j := j + 2
                  end
              end
          end
      end;

  begin
    fopt := 2.0 − 2.0*pi/n;
    newgrid(qi, qj, u);
    for k := 1 to steps do
      relax(qi, qj, up, down,
          left, right, u);
    output(qi, qj, right, left, u)
  end { node };

  procedure master(right: channel;
    var u: grid);
  var i, j: integer;
  begin
    for i := 1 to n do
      for j := 1 to n do
        receive(right, u[i,j])
  end;

  procedure simulate(
    steps: integer; var u: grid);
  type
```

```
      line = array [1..q] of channel;
      matrix = array [0..q] of line;
  var h, v: matrix; i, j: integer;
  begin
    open(h[0,q]);
    for i := 1 to q do
      for j := 1 to q do
        open(h[i,j]);
    for i := 0 to q do
      for j := 1 to q do
        open(v[i,j]);
    parallel
      master(h[0,q], u)|
      forall j := 1 to q do
        node(j, 1, steps,
            v[j−1,1], v[j,1],
            h[j−1,q], h[j,1])|
      forall i := 1 to q do
        forall j := 2 to q do
          node(i, j, steps,
              v[i−1,j], v[i,j],
              h[i,j−1], h[i,j])
    end
  end;

begin
  simulate(steps, u)
end { laplace };
```

Acknowledgements

It is a pleasure to acknowledge the constructive comments of Jonathan Greenfield.

References

Bak, P., and Tang, C. 1989. Earthquakes as a self-organized critical phenomenon. *Journal of Geophysical Research 94*, B11, 15635–15637.

Bak, P., and Chen, K. 1990. A forest-fire model and some thoughts on turbulence. *Physics Letters A 147*, 5–6, 297–299.

Barlow, R.H., and Evans, D.J. 1982. Parallel algorithms for the iterative solution to linear systems. *Computer Journal 25*, 1, 56–60.

Berlekamp, E.R., Conway, J.H., and Guy, R.K. 1982. *Winning Ways for Your Mathematical Plays*. Vol. 2, Academic Press, New York, 817–850.

Brinch Hansen, P. 1990. The all-pairs pipeline. School of Computer and Information Science, Syracuse University, Syracuse, NY.

Brinch Hansen, P. 1991a. A generic multiplication pipeline. School of Computer and Information Science, Syracuse University, Syracuse, NY.

Brinch Hansen, P. 1991b. Parallel divide and conquer. School of Computer and Information Science, Syracuse University, Syracuse, NY.

Brinch Hansen, P. 1992a. Parallel Monte Carlo trials. School of Computer and Information Science, Syracuse University, Syracuse, NY.

Brinch Hansen, P. 1992b. Numerical solution of Laplace's equation. School of Computer and Information Science, Syracuse University, Syracuse, NY.

Brinch Hansen, P. 1994. SuperPascal—A publication language for parallel scientific computing. *Concurrency—Practice and Experience 6*, 5 (August), 461–483. *Article 24*.

Cok, R.S. 1991. *Parallel Programs for the Transputer*. Prentice Hall, Englewood Cliffs, NJ.

Dewdney, A.K. 1984. Sharks and fish wage an ecological war on the toroidal planet Wa-Tor. *Scientific American 251*, 6, 14–22.

Dijkstra, E.W. 1982. *Selected Writings on Computing: A Personal Perspective*. Springer-Verlag, New York, 334–337.

Evans, D.J. 1984. Parallel SOR iterative methods. *Parallel Computing 1*, 3–18.

Fox, G.C., Johnson, M.A., Lyzenga, G.A., Otto, S.W., Salmon, J.K., and Walker, D.W. 1988. *Solving Problems on Concurrent Processors*, Vol. I, Prentice-Hall, Englewood Cliffs, NJ.

Frisch, U., Hasslacher, B., and Pomeau, Y. 1986. Lattice-gas automata for the Navier-Stokes equation. *Physical Review Letters 56* 14, 1505–1508.

Gardner, M. 1970. The fantastic combinations of John Conway's new solitaire game "Life." *Scientific American 223*, 10, 120–123.

Gardner, M. 1971. On cellular automata, self-reproduction, the Garden of Eden and the game "Life." *Scientific American 224*, 2, 112–117.

Hoppensteadt, F.C. 1978. Mathematical aspects of population biology. In *Mathematics Today: Twelve Informal Essays*, L.A. Steen, Ed. Springer-Verlag, New York.

Hwa, T., and Kardar, M. 1989. Dissipative transport in open systems: An investigation of self-organized criticality. *Physical Review Letters 62*, 16, 1813–1816.

Inmos Ltd. 1988).*occam 2 Reference Manual*. Prentice Hall, Englewood Cliffs, NJ.

McDonald, N. 1991. Meiko Scientific Ltd. In *Past, Present, Parallel: A Survey of Available Parallel Computing Systems*, A. Trew and G. Wilson, Eds. Springer-Verlag, New York, 165–175.

Meiko Ltd. 1987. *Computing Surface Technical Specifications*. Meiko Ltd., Bristol, England.

Press, W.H., Flannery, B.P., Teukolsky, S.A., and Vetterling, W.T. 1989. *Numerical Recipes in Pascal: The Art of Scientific Computing*. Cambridge University Press, Cambridge, MA.

Pritchard, D.J., Askew, C.R., Carpenter, D.D., Glendinning, I., Hey, A.J.G., and Nicole, D.A. 1987. Practical parallelism using transputer arrays. *Lecture Notes in Computer Science 258*, 278–294.

Saltz, J.H., Naik, V.K., and Nicol, D.M. 1987. Reduction of the effects of the communication delays in scientific algorithms on message passing MIMD architectures. *SIAM Journal on Scientific and Statistical Computing 8*, 1, s118–s134.

Ulam, S. 1986. *Science, Computers, and People: From the Tree of Mathematics*, Birkhäuser, Boston, MA.

von Neumann, J. 1966. *Theory of Self-Reproducing Automata*. Edited and completed by A.W. Burks, University of Illinois Press, Urbana, IL.

Young, D.M. 1954. Iterative methods for solving partial difference equations of elliptic type. *Transactions of the American Mathematical Society 76*, 92–111.

SuperPascal—A Publication Language For Parallel Scientific Computing[*]

(1994)

Parallel computers will not become widely used until scientists and engineers adopt a common programming language for publication of parallel scientific algorithms. This paper describes the publication language SuperPascal by examples. SuperPascal extends Pascal with deterministic statements for parallel processes and synchronous message communication. The language permits unrestricted combinations of recursive procedures and parallel statements. SuperPascal omits ambiguous and insecure features of Pascal. Restrictions on the use of variables enable a single-pass compiler to check that parallel processes are disjoint, even if the processes use procedures with global variables. A portable implementation of SuperPascal has been developed on a Sun workstation under Unix.

1 Introduction

One of the major challenges in computer science today is to develop effective programming tools for the next generation of parallel computers. It is equally important to design educational programming tools for the future users of parallel computers. Since the 1960s, computer scientists have recognized the distinction between *publication languages* that emphasize clarity of concepts, and *implementation languages* that reflect pragmatic concerns and historical traditions (Forsythe 1966; Perlis 1966). I believe that parallel computers will not become widely used until scientists and engineers adopt a common programming language for publication of parallel scientific algorithms.

---

[*]P. Brinch Hansen, SuperPascal—A publication language for parallel scientific computing. *Concurrency—Practice and Experience 6*, 5 (August 1994), 461–483. Copyright © 1994, John Wiley & Sons, Ltd. Reprinted by permission.

It is instructive to consider the historical role of Pascal as a publication language for sequential computing. The first paper on Pascal appeared in 1971 (Wirth 1971). At that time, there were not very many textbooks on computer science. A few years later, universities began to use Pascal as the standard programming language for computer science courses. The spreading of Pascal motivated authors to use the language in textbooks for a wide variety of computer science courses: introductory programming (Wirth 1973), operating systems (Brinch Hansen 1973), program verification (Alagić 1978), compilers (Welsh 1980), programming languages (Tennent 1981), and algorithms (Aho 1983). In 1983, IEEE acknowledged the status of Pascal as the *lingua franca* of computer science by publishing a Pascal standard (IEEE 1983). Pascal was no longer just another programming tool for computer users. It had become a thinking tool for researchers exploring new fields in computer science.

We now face a similar need for a common programming language for students and researchers in computational science. To understand the requirements of such a language, I spent three years developing a collection of *model programs* that illustrate the use of structured programming in parallel scientific computing (Brinch Hansen 1993a). These programs solve regular problems in science and engineering: linear equations, n-body simulation, matrix multiplication, shortest paths in graphs, sorting, fast Fourier transforms, simulated annealing, primality testing, Laplace's equation, and forest fire simulation. I wrote these programs in *occam* and tested their performance on a *Computing Surface* configured as a pipeline, a tree, a cube, or a matrix of *transputers* (Inmos 1988; McDonald 1991).

This practical experience led me to the following conclusions about the future of parallel scientific computing (Forsythe 1966; Dunham 1982; May 1989; Brinch Hansen 1993a):

1. A *general-purpose parallel computer* of the near future will probably be a multicomputer with tens to thousands of processors with local memories only. The computer will support automatic routing of messages between any pair of processors. The hardware architecture will be transparent to programmers, who will be able to connect processors arbitrarily by virtual communication channels. Such a parallel computer will enable programmers to think in terms of problem-oriented process configurations. There will be no need to map these configurations onto a fixed architecture, such as a hypercube.

2. The regular problems in computational science can be solved efficiently by *deterministic parallel computations*. I have not found it necessary to use a statement that enables a parallel process to poll several channels until a communication takes place on one of them. Nondeterministic communication is necessary at the hardware level in a routing network, but appears to be of minor importance in parallel programs for computational science.

3. Parallel scientific algorithms can be developed in an *elegant publication language* and tested on a sequential computer. When an algorithm works, it can easily be moved to a particular multicomputer by rewriting the algorithm in another programming language chosen for pragmatic rather than intellectual reasons. Subtle parallel algorithms should be published in their entirety as executable programs written in a publication language. Such programs may serve as models for other scientists, who wish to study them with the assurance that every detail has been considered, explained, and tested.

A publication language for computational science should, in my opinion, have the following properties:

1. The language should extend a widely used standard language with *deterministic parallelism* and *message communication*. The extensions should be defined in the spirit of the standard language.

2. The language should make it possible to program *arbitrary configurations* of parallel processes connected by communication channels. These configurations may be defined iteratively or recursively and created dynamically.

3. The language should enable a single-pass compiler to check that parallel processes do not interfere in a time-dependent manner. This check is known as *syntactic interference control*.

The following describes *SuperPascal*—a publication language for parallel scientific computing. *SuperPascal* extends Pascal with deterministic statements for parallel processes and synchronous communication. The language permits unrestricted combinations of recursive procedures and parallel statements. *SuperPascal* omits ambiguous and insecure features of Pascal. Restrictions on the use of variables permit a single-pass compiler to check that parallel processes are disjoint, even if the processes use procedures with global variables.

Since the model programs cover a broad spectrum of algorithms for scientific computing, I have used them as a guideline for language design. *SuperPascal* is based on well-known language features (Dijkstra 1968; Hoare 1971, 1972, 1985; Ambler 1977; Lampson 1977; IEEE 1983; Brinch Hansen 1987; Inmos 1988). My only contribution has been to select the smallest number of concepts that enable me to express the model programs elegantly. This paper illustrates the parallel features of *SuperPascal* by examples. The *SuperPascal* language report defines the syntax and semantics concisely and explains the differences between *SuperPascal* and Pascal (Brinch Hansen 1994a). The interference control is further discussed in (Brinch Hansen 1994b).

A *portable implementation* of *SuperPascal* has been developed on a Sun workstation under Unix. It consists of a compiler and an interpreter written in Pascal. The *SuperPascal* compiler is based on the Pascal compiler described and listed in (Brinch Hansen 1985). The compiler and interpreter are in the public domain. You can obtain the *SuperPascal* software by using anonymous FTP from the directory *pbh* at *top.cis.syr.edu*. The software has been used to rewrite the model programs for computational science in *SuperPascal*.

2   A Programming Example

I will use pieces of a model program to illustrate the features of *SuperPascal*. The Miller-Rabin algorithm is used for *primality testing* of a large integer (Rabin 1980). The model program performs p probabilistic tests of the same integer simultaneously on p processors. Each test either proves that the integer is composite, or it fails to prove anything. However, if, say, 40 trials of a 160-digit decimal number all fail, the number is prime with virtual certainty (Brinch Hansen 1992a, 1992b).

The program performs multiple-length arithmetic on natural numbers represented by arrays of w digits (plus an overflow digit):

type number = **array** [0..w] **of** integer;

A single trial is defined by a procedure with the heading

procedure test(a: number; seed: real;
        var composite: boolean)

Each trial initializes a random number generator with a distinct seed.

The parallel computation is organized as a ring network consisting of a master process and a pipeline connected by two communication channels (Fig. 1).

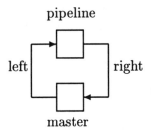

Figure 1 A ring network.

The pipeline consists of p identical, parallel nodes connected by $p+1$ communication channels (Fig. 2).

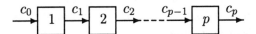

Figure 2 A pipeline.

The master sends a number through the pipeline and receives p boolean values from the pipeline. The booleans are the results of p independent trials performed in parallel by the nodes.

3   Message Communication

3.1   Communication channels

The communication channels of *SuperPascal* are *deterministic synchronous channels:*

1. A channel can transmit one message at a time in either direction between two parallel processes.

2. Before a communication, a process makes a deterministic selection of a communication channel, a communication direction, and a message type.

3. A communication takes place when one process is ready to send a message of some type through a channel, and another process is ready to receive a message of the same type through the same channel.

3.2   Channel and message types

A channel is not a variable, but a communication medium shared by two parallel processes. Each channel is created dynamically and identified by a distinct value, known as a *channel reference*. A variable that holds a channel reference is called a *channel variable*. An expression that denotes a channel reference is called a *channel expression*. These concepts are borrowed from *Joyce* (Brinch Hansen 1987).

As an example, the declarations

$$\textbf{type } \text{channel} = *(\text{boolean, number});$$
$$\textbf{var } \text{left: channel};$$

define a new type, named *channel*, and a variable of this type, named *left*. The value of the variable is a reference to a channel that can transmit messages of types *boolean* and *number* only.

In general, a type definition of the form

$$\textbf{type } T = *(T_1, T_2, \ldots, T_n);$$

introduces a new *channel type* T. The values of type T are an unordered set of channel references created dynamically. Each channel reference of type T denotes a distinct channel that can transmit messages of types $T_1, T_2, \ldots, T_n$ only (the *message types*).

3.3   Channel creation

The effect of an *open* statement

$$\text{open}(v)$$

is to create a new channel and assign the corresponding channel reference to a channel variable v. The channel reference is of the same type as the channel variable.

The abbreviation

$$\text{open}(v_1, v_2, \ldots, v_n)$$

is equivalent to

$$\textbf{begin } \text{open}(v_1);\ \text{open}(v_2, \ldots, v_n) \textbf{ end}$$

As an example, two channels, *left* and *right*, can be opened as follows

$$\text{open(left, right)}$$

or as shown below

$$\textbf{begin } \text{open(left)};\ \text{open(right)} \textbf{ end}$$

A channel exists until the program execution ends.

3.4   Communication procedures

Consider a process that receives a number a through a channel, *left*, and sends it through another channel, *right:*

$$\textbf{var } \text{left, right: channel; a: number;}$$
$$\text{receive(left, a); send(right, a)}$$

The message communication is handled by two required procedures, *send* and *receive.*

In general, a *send* statement

$$\text{send}(b,\ e)$$

denotes *output* of the value of an expression e through the channel denoted by an expression b. The expression b must be of a channel type T, and the type of the expression e must be a message type of T.

A *receive* statement

$$\text{receive}(c,\ v)$$

denotes *input* of the value of a variable v through the channel denoted by an expression c. The expression c must be of a channel type T, and the type of the variable v must be a message type of T.

The send and receive operations defined by the above statements are said to *match* if they satisfy the following conditions:

1. The channel expressions b and c are of the same type T and denote the same channel.

2. The output expression e and the input variable v are of the same type, which is a message type of T.

The execution of a send operation delays a process until another process is ready to execute a matching receive operation (and vice versa). If and when this happens, a *communication* takes place as follows:

1. The sending process obtains a value by evaluating the output expression e.

2. The receiving process assigns the value to the input variable v.

After the communication, the sending and receiving processes proceed independently.

The abbrevation

$$\text{send}(b, e_1, e_2, \ldots, e_n)$$

is equivalent to

begin send(b, e_1); send$(b, e_2, \ldots, e_n)$ **end**

Similarly,

$$\text{receive}(c, v_1, v_2, \ldots, v_n)$$

is equivalent to

begin receive(c, v_1); receive$(c, v_2, \ldots, v_n)$ **end**

The following *communication errors* are detected at run-time:

1. *Undefined channel reference:* A channel expression does not denote a channel.

2. *Channel contention:* Two parallel processes both attempt to send (or receive) through the same channel at the same time.

3. *Message type error:* Two parallel processes attempt to communicate through the same channel, but the output expression and the input variable are of different message types.

Message communication is illustrated by two procedures in the primality testing program. The *master* process, shown in Fig. 1, sends a number a through its left channel, and receives p booleans through its right channel. If at least one of the booleans is true, the number is composite; otherwise, it is considered to be prime (Algorithm 1).

```
procedure master(
   a: number; var prime: boolean;
   left, right: channel);
var i: integer; composite: boolean;
begin
   send(left, a); prime := true;
   for i := 1 to p do
      begin
         receive(right, composite);
         if composite then
            prime := false
      end
end;
```

Algorithm 1 Master.

The pipeline *nodes*, shown in Fig. 2, are numbered 1 through p. Each node receives a number a through its left channel, and sends a through its right channel (unless the node is the last one in the pipeline). The node then tests the number for primality using the node index i as the seed of its random number generator. Finally, the node outputs the boolean result of its own trial, and copies the results obtained by its $i - 1$ predecessors (if any) in the pipeline (Algorithm 2).

3.5   Channel arrays

Since channel references are typed values, it is possible to define an array of channel references. A variable of such a type represents an array of channels.

The pipeline nodes in Fig. 2 are connected by a row of channels created as follows:

```
        procedure node(i: integer;
          left, right: channel);
        var a: number; j: integer;
          composite: boolean;
        begin
          receive(left, a);
          if i < p then send(right, a);
          test(a, i, composite);
          send(right, composite);
          for j := 1 to i − 1 do
            begin
              receive(left, composite);
              send(right, composite)
            end
        end;
```

Algorithm 2 Node.

```
        type channel = *(boolean, number);
          row = array [0..p] of channel;
        var c: row; i: integer;
        for i := 0 to p do open(c[i])
```

Later, I will program a matrix of processes connected by a horizontal and a vertical matrix of channels. The channel matrices, h and v, are defined and initialized as follows:

```
        type
          row = array [0..q] of channel;
          net = array [0..q] of row;
        var h, v: net; i, j: integer;
        for i := 0 to q do
          for j := 0 to q do
            open(h[i,j], v[i,j])
```

3.6   Channel variables

The value of a channel variable v of a type T is undefined, unless a channel reference of type T has been assigned to v by executing an open statement

$$open(v)$$

or an assignment statement

$$v := e$$

If the value of the expression e is a channel reference of type T, the effect of the assignment statement is to make the values of v and e denote the same channel.

If e and f are channel expressions of the same type, the boolean expression

$$e = f$$

is true, if e and f denote the same channel, and is false otherwise. The boolean expression

$$e <> f$$

is equivalent to

$$\textbf{not}\ (e = f)$$

In the following example, the references to two channels, *left* and *right*, are assigned to the first and last elements of a channel array c:

$$c[0] := \text{left};\ c[p] := \text{right}$$

After the first assignment, the value of the boolean expression

$$c[0] = \text{left}$$

is *true*.

4 Parallel Processes

4.1 Parallel statements

The effect of a *parallel statement*

$$\textbf{parallel}\ S_1|S_2|\ldots|S_n\ \textbf{end}$$

```
procedure ring(a: number;
    var prime: boolean);
var left, right: channel;
begin
  open(left, right);
  parallel
    pipeline(left, right)|
    master(a, prime, left, right)
  end
end;
```

Algorithm 3 Ring.

is to execute the *process statements* $S_1, S_2, \ldots, S_n$ as parallel processes until all of them have terminated.

Algorithm 3 defines a *ring net* that determines if a given integer a is prime. The ring, shown in Fig. 1, consists of two parallel processes, a master and a pipeline, which share two channels. The master and the pipeline run in parallel until both of them have terminated.

A parallel statement enables you to run different kinds of algorithms in parallel. This idea is useful only for a small number of processes. It is impractical to write thousands of process statements, even if they are identical.

4.2   Forall statements

To exploit parallel computing with many processors, we need the ability to run multiple instances of the same algorithm in parallel.

As an example, consider the *pipeline* for primality testing. From the abstract point of view, shown in Fig. 1, the pipeline is a single process with two external channels. At the more detailed level, shown in Fig. 2, the pipeline consists of an array of identical, parallel nodes connected by a row of channels.

Algorithm 4 defines the pipeline.

The first and last elements of the channel array c

$$c[0] = \text{left} \qquad c[p] = \text{right}$$

refer to the external channels of the pipeline. The remaining elements

```
procedure pipeline(left, right: channel);
type row = array [0..p] of channel;
var c: row; i: integer;
begin
  c[0] := left; c[p] := right;
  for i := 1 to p − 1 do
    open(c[i]);
  forall i := 1 to p do
    node(i, c[i−1], c[i])
end;
```

Algorithm 4 Iterative pipeline.

$$c[1], c[2], \ldots, c[p-1]$$

denote the internal channels.

For $p \geq 1$, the statement

```
forall i := 1 to p do
  node(i, c[i–1], c[i])
```

is equivalent to the following statement (which is too tedious to write out in full for a pipeline with more than, say, ten nodes):

```
parallel
  node(1, c[0], c[1])|
  node(2, c[1], c[2])|
      . . .
  node(p, c[p–1], c[p])
end
```

The variable i used in the *forall* statement is not the same variable as the variable i declared at the beginning of the pipeline procedure.

In the *forall* statement, the clause

$$i := 1 \text{ to } p$$

is a *declaration* of an *index variable* i that is local to the procedure statement

$$node(i, c[i–1], c[i])$$

Each node process has its own instance of this variable, which holds a distinct index in the range from 1 to p.

It is a coincidence that the control variable of the *for* statement and the index variable of the *forall* statement have the same identifier in this example. However, the scopes of these variables are different.

In general, a *forall* statement

$$\textbf{forall } i := e_1 \textbf{ to } e_2 \textbf{ do } S$$

denotes a (possibly empty) array of parallel processes, called *element processes*, and a corresponding range of values, called *process indices*. The lower and upper bounds of the index range are denoted by two expressions, e_1 and e_2, of the same simple type. Every index value corresponds to a separate element process defined by an *index variable i* and an *element statement S*.

The *index variable declaration*

$$i := e_1 \textbf{ to } e_2$$

introduces the variable i that is local to S.

A *forall* statement is executed as follows:

1. The expressions, e_1 and e_2, are evaluated. If $e_1 > e_2$, the execution of the *forall* statement terminates; otherwise, step 2 takes place.

2. $e_2 - e_1 + 1$ element processes run in parallel until all of them have terminated. Every element process creates a local instance of the index variable i, assigns the corresponding process index to the variable, and executes the element statement S. When an element process terminates, its local instance of the index variable ceases to exist.

A model program for solving *Laplace's equation* uses a *process matrix* (Brinch Hansen 1993b). Figure 3 shows a $q \times q$ matrix of parallel nodes connected by two channel matrices, h and v.

Each node process is defined by a procedure with the heading:

```
procedure node(i, j: integer;
    up, down, left, right: channel)
```

A node has a pair of indices (i, j) and is connected to its four nearest neighbors by channels, *up, down, left,* and *right*.

The process matrix is defined by nested *forall* statements:

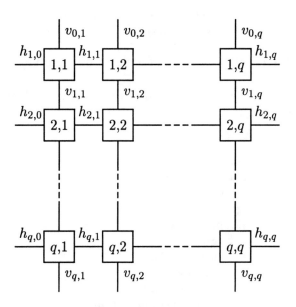

Figure 3 A process matrix.

```
forall i := 1 to q do
    forall j := 1 to q do
        node(i, j, v[i−1,j], v[i,j], h[i,j−1], h[i,j])
```

4.3   Recursive parallel processes

SuperPascal supports the beautiful concept of recursive parallel processes. Figure 4 illustrates a recursive definition of a *pipeline* with p nodes:

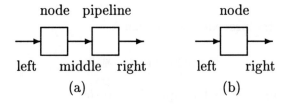

Figure 4 A recursive pipeline.

1. If $p > 1$, the pipeline consists of a single node followed by a shorter pipeline of $p - 1$ nodes (Fig. 4a).

2. If $p = 1$, the pipeline consists of a single node only (Fig. 4b).

The pipeline is defined by combining a recursive procedure with a parallel statement (Algorithm 5).

```
procedure pipeline(min, max: integer;
    left, right: channel);
var middle: channel;
begin
  if min < max then
    begin
      open(middle);
      parallel
        node(min, left, middle)|
        pipeline(min + 1, max,
          middle, right)
      end
    end
  else node(min, left, right)
end;
```

Algorithm 5 Recursive pipeline.

The pipeline consists of nodes with indices in the range from min to max (where $min \leq max$). The pipeline has a left and a right channel. If $min < max$, the pipeline opens a middle channel, and splits into a single node and a smaller pipeline running in parallel; otherwise, the pipeline behaves as a single node.

The effect of the procedure statement

pipeline(1, p, left, right)

is to activate a pipeline that is equivalent to the one shown in Fig. 2.

The recursive pipeline has a *dynamic length* defined by parameters. The nodes and channels are created by recursive parallel activations of the pipeline procedure. The iterative pipeline programmed earlier has a fixed length because it uses a channel array of fixed length (Algorithm 4).

A model program for *divide and conquer* algorithms uses a binary *process tree* (Brinch Hansen 1991a). Figure 5 shows a tree of seven parallel processes connected by seven channels.

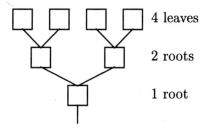

Figure 5 A specific process tree.

The bottom process of the tree inputs data from the bottom channel, and sends half of the data to its left child process, and the other half to its right child process. The splitting of data continues in parallel higher up in the tree, until the data are evenly distributed among the leaf processes at the top. Each leaf transforms its own portion of the data, and outputs the results to its parent process. Each parent combines the partial results of its children, and outputs them to its own parent. The parallel combination of results continues at lower levels in the tree, until the final results are output through the bottom channel.

A process tree can be defined recursively as illustrated by Fig. 6.

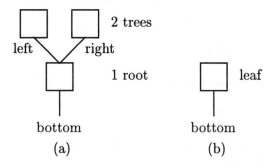

Figure 6 A recursive tree.

A binary tree is connected to its environment by a single bottom channel.

A closer look reveals that the tree takes one of two forms:

1. A tree with more than one node consists of a root process and two smaller trees running in parallel (Fig. 6a).

2. A tree with one node only is a leaf process (Fig. 6b).

The process *tree* is defined by a recursive procedure (Algorithm 6). The *depth* of the tree is the number of process layers above the bottom process. Figure 5 shows a tree of depth 2.

```
procedure tree(depth: integer;
   bottom: channel);
var left, right: channel;
begin
   if depth > 0 then
      begin
         open(left, right);
         parallel
            tree(depth − 1, left)|
            tree(depth − 1, right)|
            root(bottom, left, right)
         end
      end
   else leaf(bottom)
end;
```

Algorithm 6 Recursive tree.

The behavior of *roots* and *leaves* is defined by two procedures of the form:

procedure root(bottom, left, right: channel)

procedure leaf(bottom: channel)

These procedures vary from one application of the tree to another.
   The effect of the procedure statement

tree(2, bottom)

is to activate a binary tree of depth 2.

A notation for recursive processes is essential in a parallel programming language. The reason is simple. It is impractical to formulate thousands of processes with different behaviors. We must instead rely on repeated use of a small number of behaviors. The simplest problems that satisfy this requirement are those that can be reduced to smaller problems of the same kind and solved by combining the partial results. Recursion is the natural programming tool for these *divide and conquer* algorithms.

5 Interference Control

5.1 Disjoint processes

The relative speeds of asynchronous, parallel processes are generally unknown. If parallel processes update the same variables at unpredictable times, the combined effect of the processes is time-dependent. Similarly, if two parallel processes both attempt to send (or receive) messages through the same channel at unpredictable times, the net effect is time-dependent. Processes with *time-dependent errors* are said to *interfere* with one another due to *variable* or *channel conflicts*.

When a program with a time-dependent error is executed repeatedly with the same input, the output usually varies in an unpredictable manner from one run to another. The irreproducible behavior makes it difficult to locate interference by systematic program testing. The most effective remedy is to introduce additional restrictions, which make process interference impossible. These restrictions must be checked by a compiler before a parallel program is executed.

In the following, I concentrate on syntactic detection of variable conflicts. The basic requirement is simple: Parallel processes can only update disjoint sets of variables. A variable that is updated by a process may only be used by that process. Parallel processes may, however, share variables that are not updated by any of them. Parallel processes that satisfy this requirement are called *disjoint processes*.

5.2 Variable contexts

I will illustrate the issues of interference control by small examples only. The problem is discussed concisely in (Brinch Hansen 1994b).

In theory, syntactic detection of variable conflicts is a straightforward process. A single-pass compiler scans a program text once. For every statement S, the compiler determines the set of variables that may be updated and the set of variables that may be used as expression operands during the execution of S. These sets are called the *target* and *expression variables* of S. Together they define the *variable context* of S. If we know the variable context of every statement, it is easy to check if parallel statements define disjoint processes.

As an example, the *open* statement

$$\text{open}(h[i,j])$$

denotes creation of a component $h_{i,j}$ of a channel array h. Since the index values i and j are known during execution only, a compiler is unable to distinguish between different elements of the same array. Consequently, the entire array h is regarded as a target variable (the only one) of the open statement. The expression variables of the statement are i and j.

An *entire variable* is a variable denoted by an identifier only, such as h, i, or j above. During compilation, any operation on a component of a *structured variable* is regarded as an operation on the entire variable. The target and expression variables of a statement are therefore sets of entire variables.

A compiler cannot predict if a component of a conditional statement will be executed or skipped. To be on the safe side, the variable context of a *structured statement* is defined as the union of the variable contexts of its components.

Consider the conditional statement

$$\textbf{if } i < p \textbf{ then } \text{send}(\text{right}, a)$$

It has no target variables, but uses three expression variables, i, *right* and a (assuming that p is a constant).

5.3 Parallel statements

The choice of a notation for parallel processes is profoundly influenced by the requirement that a compiler must be able to detect process interference. The syntax of a parallel statement

$$\textbf{parallel } S_1 | S_2 | \ldots | S_n \textbf{ end}$$

clearly shows that the process statements $S_1, S_2, \ldots, S_n$ are executed in parallel.

The following restriction ensures that a parallel statement denotes disjoint processes: *A target variable of one process statement cannot be a target or an expression variable of another process statement.* This rule is enforced by a compiler.

Let me illustrate this restriction with three examples. The parallel statement

$$\textbf{parallel } \text{open(h[i,j])|open(v[i,j])} \textbf{ end}$$

defines two *open* statements executed simultaneously. The target variable h of the first process statement does not occur in the second process statement. Similarly, the target variable v of the second process statement is not used in the first process statement. Consequently, the parallel statement defines disjoint processes.

However, the parallel statement

```
parallel
    receive(left, a)|
    if i < p then send(right, a)
end
```

is incorrect, because the target variable a of the first process statement is also an expression variable of the second process statement.

Finally, the parallel statement

$$\textbf{parallel } c[0] := \text{left}|c[p] := \text{right} \textbf{ end}$$

is incorrect, since the process statements use the same target variable c.

Occasionally, a programmer may wish to override the interference control of parallel statements. This is useful when it is obvious that parallel processes update distinct elements of the same array. The previous restriction does not apply to a parallel statement prefixed by the clause [*sic*]. This is called an *unrestricted statement*. The programmer must prove that such a statement denotes disjoint processes.

The following example is taken from a model program that uses the process matrix shown in Fig. 3:

```
[sic] { 1 <= k <= m }
parallel
    receive(up, u[0,k])|
    send(down, u[m,k])|
    receive(left, u[k,0])|
    send(right, u[k,m])
end
```

This statement enables a node process to simultaneously exchange four elements of a local array u with its nearest neighbors. The initial comment implies that the two input elements are distinct and are not used as output elements.

The programmer should realize that the slightest mistake in an unrestricted statement may introduce a subtle time-dependent error. The incorrect statement

```
[sic] { 1 <= k <= m }
parallel
    receive(up, u[1,k])|
    send(down, u[m,k])|
    receive(left, u[k,1])|
    send(right, u[k,m])
end
```

is time-dependent, but only if $k = 1$.

5.4   Forall statements

The following restriction ensures that the statement

$$\textbf{forall } i := e_1 \textbf{ to } e_2 \textbf{ do } S$$

denotes disjoint processes: *In a forall statement, the element statement S cannot use target variables.* This is checked by a compiler.

This restriction implies that a process array must output its final results to another process or a file. Otherwise, the results will be lost when the element processes terminate and their local variables disappear. For technological reasons, the same restriction is necessary if the element processes run on separate processors in a parallel computer with distributed memory.

In the primality testing program, a pipeline is defined by the statement

$$\textbf{forall } i := 1 \textbf{ to } p \textbf{ do } node(i, c[i-1], c[i])$$

Since the node procedure has value parameters only, the procedure statement

$$node(i, c[i-1], c[i])$$

uses expression variables only (i and c).

The incorrect statement

forall i := 1 **to** p – 1 **do** open(c[i])

denotes element processes that attempt to update the same variable c in parallel.

If it is desirable to use the above statement, it must be turned into an *unrestricted statement*:

[**sic**] { distinct elements c[i] }
forall i := 1 **to** p – 1 **do** open(c[i])

The initial comment shows that the node processes are disjoint, since they update distinct elements of the channel array c.

Again, it needs to be said that a programming error in an unrestricted statement may cause time-dependent behavior. The incorrect statement

[**sic**] **forall** i := 1 **to** p – 1 **do** open(c[1])

denotes parallel assignments of channel references to the same array element c_1.

Needless to say, syntactic interference control is of limited value if it is frequently overridden. A programmer should make a conscientious effort to limit the use of unrestricted statements as much as possible. The thirteen model programs, that I wrote, include five unrestricted statements only; all of them denote operations on distinct array elements.

5.5   Variable parameters

To enable a compiler to recognize distinct variables, a language should have the property that distinct variable identifiers occurring in the same statement denote distinct entire variables. Due to the scope rules of Pascal, this assumption is satisfied by all entire variables except variable parameters.

The following procedure denotes parallel creation of a pair of channels:

```
procedure pair(var c, d: channel);
begin
    parallel open(c)|open(d) end
end;
```

The parallel processes are disjoint only if the formal parameters, c and d, denote distinct actual parameters.

The procedure statement

$$\text{pair(h[i,j], v[i,j])}$$

is valid, since the actual parameters are elements of different arrays, h and v.

However, the procedure statement

$$\text{pair(left, left)}$$

is incorrect, because it makes the identifiers, c and d, *aliases* of the same variable, *left*.

Aliasing of variable parameters is prevented by the following restriction: *The actual variable parameters of a procedure statement must be distinct entire variables (or components of such variables).*

An *unrestricted statement* is not subject to this restriction. A model program for *n-body simulation* computes the gravitational forces between a pair of bodies, p_i and p_j, and adds each force to the total force acting on the corresponding body (Brinch Hansen 1991b). This operation is denoted by a procedure statement

$$\text{\{ i <> j \} [sic] addforces(p[j], p[i])}$$

with two actual variable parameters. The initial comment shows that the parameters, p_i and p_j, are distinct elements of the same array variable p.

5.6   Global variables

Global variables used in procedures are another source of aliasing. Consider a procedure that updates a global seed and returns a random number (Algorithm 7).

The procedure statement

$$\text{random(x)}$$

```
    var seed: real;

    procedure random(var number: real);
    var temp: real;
    begin
      temp := a*seed;
      seed := temp − m*trunc(temp/m);
      number := seed/m
    end;
```

Algorithm 7 Random number generator.

denotes an operation that updates two distinct variables, x and *seed*.

On the other hand, the procedure statement

random(seed)

turns the identifier *number* into an alias for *seed*.

To prevent aliasing, it is necessary to regard the global variable as an *implicit parameter* of both procedure statements. Since the procedure uses the global variable as a target *and* an expression variable, it is both an *implicit variable parameter* and an *implicit value parameter* of the procedure statements.

The rule that actual variable parameters cannot be aliases applies to all variable parameters of a procedure statement, explicit as well as implicit parameters. However, since implicit value parameters can also cause trouble, we need a stronger restriction defined as follows (Brinch Hansen 1994b): The *restricted actual parameters* of a procedure statement are the explicit variable parameters that occur in the statement and the implicit parameters of the corresponding procedure block. *The restricted actual parameters of a procedure statement must be distinct entire variables (or components of such variables).*

In the primality testing program, the pipeline nodes use a random number generator. If the seed variable is global to the node procedure, then the seed is also an implicit variable parameter of the procedure statement

node(i, c[i−1], c[i])

Consequently, the statement

forall i := 1 **to** p **do** node(i, c[i–1], c[i])

denotes parallel processes that (indirectly) update the same global variable at unpredictable times. The concept of implicit parameters enables a compiler to detect this variable conflict. The problem is avoided by making the procedure, *random*, and its global variable, *seed*, local to the node procedure. The node processes will then be updating different instances of this variable.

The parallel statement

parallel write(x)|writeln **end**

is invalid because the required textfile *output* is an implicit variable parameter of both *write* statements.

Similarly, the parallel statement

parallel
    read(x)|
    if eof **then** writeln
end

is incorrect because the required textfile *input* is an implicit variable parameter of the *read* statement and an implicit value parameter of the *eof* function designator.

5.7   Functions

Functions may use global variables as implicit value parameters only. The following rules ensure that functions have no side-effects:

1. Functions cannot use implicit or explicit variable parameters.

2. Procedure statements cannot occur in the statement part of a function block.

The latter restriction implies that functions cannot use the required procedures for message communication and file input/output. This rule may seem startling at first. I introduced it after noticing that my model programs include over 40 functions, none of which violate this restriction.

Since functions have no side-effects, expressions cannot cause process interference.

5.8   Further restrictions

Syntactic detection of variable conflicts during single-pass compilation requires additional language restrictions:

1. *Pointer types* are omitted.

2. *Goto statements* and *labels* are omitted.

3. *Procedural* and *functional parameters* are omitted.

4. *Forward declarations* are omitted.

5. *Recursive functions* and *procedures* cannot use implicit parameters.

These design decisions are discussed in (Brinch Hansen 1994b).

5.9   Channel conflicts

Due to the use of channel references, a compiler is unable to detect process interference caused by channel conflicts. From a theoretical point of view, I have serious misgivings about this flaw. In practice, I have found it to be a minor problem only. Some channel conflicts are detected by the run-time checking of communication errors mentioned earlier. For regular process configurations, such as pipelines, trees, and matrices, the remaining channel conflicts are easy to locate by proofreading the few procedures that define how parallel processes are connected by channels.

6   SuperPascal versus Occam

occam2 is an admirable implementation language for transputer systems (Inmos 1988). It achieves high efficiency by relying on static allocation of processors and memory. The occam notation is somewhat bulky and not sufficiently general for a publication language:

1. Key words are capitalized.

2. A real constant requires eight additional characters to define the length of its binary representation.

3. Simple statements must be written on separate lines.

4. An *if* statement requires two additional lines to describe an empty *else* statement.

5. Array types cannot be named.

6. Record types cannot be used.

7. Process arrays must have constant lengths.

8. Functions and procedures cannot be recursive.

occam3 includes type definitions, but is considerably more complicated than occam2 (Kerridge 1993).

occam was an invaluable source of inspiration for *SuperPascal*. Years ahead of its time, occam set a standard of simplicity and security against which future parallel languages will be measured. The parallel features of *SuperPascal* are a subset of occam2 with the added generality of dynamic process arrays and recursive parallel processes. This generality enables you to write parallel algorithms that cannot be expressed in occam.

7   Final Remarks

Present multicomputers are quite difficult to program. To achieve high performance, each program must be tailored to the configuration of a particular computer. Scientific users, who are primarily interested in getting numerical results, constantly have to reprogram new parallel architectures and are getting increasingly frustrated at having to do this (Sanz 1989).

As educators, we should ignore this short-term problem and teach our students to write programs for the next generation of parallel computers. These will probably be general-purpose multicomputers that can run portable scientific programs written in parallel programming languages.

In this paper, I have suggested that universities should adopt a common programming language for publication of papers and textbooks on parallel scientific algorithms. The language Pascal has played a major role as a publication language for sequential computing. Building on that tradition, I have developed *SuperPascal* as a publication language for computational science. *SuperPascal* extends Pascal with deterministic statements for parallel processes and message communication. The language enables you to define arbitrary configurations of parallel processes, both iteratively and recursively. The number of processes may vary dynamically.

I have used the *SuperPascal* notation to write portable programs for regular problems in computational science. I found it easy to express these programs in three different programming languages (*SuperPascal*, Joyce, and occam2) and run them on three different architectures (a Unix workstation, an Encore Multimax, and a Meiko Computing Surface).

Acknowledgements

While writing this paper, I have benefited from the perceptive comments of James Allwright, Jonathan Greenfield and Peter O'Hearn.

References

Aho, A.V., Hopcroft, J.E., and Ullman, J.D. 1983. *Data Structures and Algorithms.* Addison-Wesley, Reading, MA.

Alagić, S., and Arbib, M.A. 1978. *The Design of Well-Structured and Correct Programs.* Springer-Verlag, New York.

Ambler, A.L., Good, D.I., Browne, J.C., Burger, W.F., Cohen, R.M., and Wells, R.E. 1977. Gypsy: a language for specification and implementation of verifiable programs. *ACM SIGPLAN Notices 12*, 2, 1–10.

Brinch Hansen, P. 1973. *Operating System Principles.* Prentice-Hall, Englewood Cliffs, NJ.

Brinch Hansen, P. 1985. *Brinch Hansen on Pascal Compilers.* Prentice-Hall, Englewood Cliffs, NJ.

Brinch Hansen, P. 1987. Joyce—A programming language for distributed systems. *Software Practice and Experience 17*, 1 (January), 29–50. *Article 18.*

Brinch Hansen, P. 1991a. Parallel divide and conquer. School of Computer and Information Science, Syracuse University, Syracuse, NY.

Brinch Hansen, P. 1991b. The *n*-body pipeline. School of Computer and Information Science, Syracuse University, Syracuse, NY.

Brinch Hansen, P. 1992a. Primality testing. School of Computer and Information Science, Syracuse University, Syracuse, NY.

Brinch Hansen, P. 1992b. Parallel Monte Carlo trials. School of Computer and Information Science, Syracuse University, Syracuse, NY.

Brinch Hansen, P. 1993a. Model programs for computational science: A programming methodology for multicomputers. *Concurrency—Practice and Experience 5*, 5 (August), 407–423. *Article 22.*

Brinch Hansen, P. 1993b. Parallel cellular automata: A model program for computational science. *Concurrency—Practice and Experience 5*, 5 (August) 425–448. *Article 23.*

Brinch Hansen, P. 1994a. The programming language SuperPascal. *Software—Practice and Experience 24*, 5 (May), 467–483.

Brinch Hansen, P. 1994b. Interference control in SuperPascal—A block-structured parallel language. *Computer Journal 37*, 5, 399–406.

Dijkstra, E.W. 1968. Cooperating sequential processes. In *Programming Languages*, F. Genuys, Ed. Academic Press, New York, 43–112.

Dunham, C.B. 1982. The necessity of publishing programs. *Computer Journal 25*, 1, 61–62.

Forsythe, G.E. 1966. Algorithms for scientific computing. *Communications of the ACM 9*, 4 (April), 255–256.

Hoare, C.A.R. 1971. Procedures and parameters: an axiomatic approach. *Lecture Notes in Mathematics 188*, 102–171.

Hoare, C.A.R. 1972. Towards a theory of parallel programming. In *Operating Systems Techniques*, C.A.R. Hoare and R.H. Perrott, Eds. Academic Press, New York, 61–71.

Hoare, C.A.R. 1985. *Communicating Sequential Processes*. Prentice Hall, Englewood Cliffs, NJ.

IEEE 1983. *IEEE Standard Pascal Computer Programming Language*, Institute of Electrical and Electronics Engineers, New York.

Inmos, Ltd. 1988. *occam 2 Reference Manual*, Prentice Hall, Englewood Cliffs, NJ.

Kerridge, J. 1993. Using occam3 to build large parallel systems: Part 1, occam3 features. *Transputer Communications 1* (to appear).

Lampson, B.W., Horning, J.J., London, R.L., Mitchell, J.G., and Popek, G.J. 1977. Report on the programming language Euclid. *ACM SIGPLAN Notices 12*, 2 (February).

McDonald, N. 1991. Meiko Scientific, Ltd. In *Past, Present, Parallel: A Survey of Available Parallel Computing Systems*, A. Trew and G. Wilson, Eds. Springer-Verlag, New York, 165–175.

May, D. 1989. Discussion. In *Scientific Applications of Multiprocessors*, R. Elliott and C.A.R. Hoare, Eds. Prentice-Hall, Englewood Cliffs, NJ, 54.

Perlis, A.J. 1966. A new policy for algorithms? *Communications of the ACM 9*, 4 (April), 255.

Rabin, M.O. 1980. Probabilistic algorithms for testing primality. *Journal of Number Theory 12*, 128–138.

Sanz, J.L.C., Ed. 1989. *Opportunities and Constraints of Parallel Computing*, Springer-Verlag, New York.

Tennent, R.D. 1981. *Principles of Programming Languages*, Prentice-Hall, Englewood Cliffs, NJ.

Welsh, J., and McKeag, M. 1980. *Structured System Programming*, Prentice-Hall, Englewood Cliffs, NJ.

Wirth, N. 1971. The programming language Pascal. *Acta Informatica 1*, 35–63.

Wirth, N. 1973. *Systematic Programming: An Introduction*. Prentice-Hall, Englewood Cliffs, NJ.

Efficient Parallel Recursion*

(1995)

A simple mechanism is proposed for dynamic memory allocation of a parallel recursive program with Algol-like scope rules. The method is about as fast as the traditional stack discipline for sequential languages. It has been used to implement the parallel programming language SuperPascal.

1 Introduction

I will describe a memory allocation scheme for block structured programming languages that support unbounded activation of parallel processes and recursive procedures. This technique has been used to implement the parallel programming language SuperPascal (Brinch Hansen 1994).

Three decades ago, Dijkstra (1960) proposed the standard method of dynamic memory allocation for recursive procedures in block structured, sequential languages, such as Algol 60 (Naur 1963), Pascal (Wirth 1971) and C (Kernighan 1978).

The scope rules of Algol-like languages support stack allocation of memory for sequential programs. All variables are kept in a single stack. When a block is activated, an *activation record* (a data segment of fixed length) is pushed on the stack. The activation record holds a fresh instance of every local variable of the block. At the end of the activation, the activation record is popped from the stack. Since each activation creates a new instance of the local variables, stack allocation works for both recursive and nonrecursive procedures. The crucial assumption behind stack allocation is that dynamically nested block activations always terminate in last-in, first-out order.

After two decades of research in parallel programming languages, there is still no efficient standard method for dynamic memory allocation of parallel

---

recursion. When you add parallelism to a block structured language, the variable instances form a tree structured stack with branches that grow and shrink simultaneously. If dynamic parallelism is combined with unbounded recursion, the number and extent of the stack branches are unpredictable.

In a parallel recursive program, there is no simple relationship between the order in which blocks are entered and exited. So, you cannot use the traditional last-in, first-out allocation. This makes it more difficult to reclaim and reuse the memory space of activation records efficiently.

With few exceptions, language designers have ignored the thorny problems of parallel memory allocation by outlawing recursion and restricting parallelism to the point where it is possible to use static memory allocation.

In many languages, it is impossible to reclaim the memory space of parallel processes. These include Concurrent Pascal (Brinch Hansen 1975), Simone (Kaubisch 1976), Modula (Wirth 1977), Distributed Processes (Brinch Hansen 1978), Pascal Plus (Welsh 1979), StarMod (Cook 1980), SR (Andrews 1981), Concurrent Euclid (Holt 1983), Planet (Crookes 1984) and Pascal-FC (Davies 1990).

CSP (Hoare 1978), Edison (Brinch Hansen 1981), and occam (Inmos 1988) support process activation and termination, but only of a fixed number of parallel nonrecursive processes determined during compilation.

Static memory allocation is adequate for many parallel computations (Fox 1988). However, parallel recursion is the natural programming tool for parallel versions of divide-and-conquer algorithms, such as quicksort, the fast Fourier transform and the Barnes-Hut algorithm for n-body simulation (Fox 1994).

Parallel recursion requires dynamic allocation and release of activation records in a tree structured stack. B6700 Algol (Organick 1973) and Mesa (Lampson, 1980) demonstrate that it is possible to support both parallelism and recursion in systems programming languages. The substantial overhead of parallel processes in these languages is acceptable in operating systems, which support slowly changing configurations of user processes. It is, however, too inefficient for highly parallel computations.

Is there a memory allocation method that makes parallel recursion as efficient as sequential recursion for all systems and user programs? I don't know any. Parallel recursion can probably only be implemented efficiently at the expense of some generality.

As a reasonable compromise, I will confine myself to the problem of allocating activation records of different lengths for a single parallel program in a memory of fixed size. The proposed technique is more ambitious than previous methods in the following sense: *it succeeds in making the activation and termination of parallel processes and recursive procedures equally fast!*

Joyce (Brinch Hansen 1989) was my first attempt to simplify memory allocation for parallel recursion. The multiprocessor implementation of Joyce uses a stack-like scheme for parallel block activation in a single memory heap. On entry to a block, an activation record is allocated at the top of the heap. On exit from the block, the activation record is marked as free. Free space is reclaimed only when it is at the top of the heap. This method works well for many parallel recursive programs. However, it fails if a program continues to demand space for parallel block activations before previously released space can be reclaimed. In that situation, the heap grows until it runs out of memory.

The occasional failure of the Joyce heap made me look for a more robust memory allocation for SuperPascal. After solving this problem, I found that I had reinvented a simplified version of the *Quick Fit* allocator, which was used for heap management in the sequential programming language Bliss (Weinstock 1988).

The main contribution of this paper is the discovery that Quick Fit is an efficient memory allocator for a parallel recursive language that requires an *unbounded, tree structured stack* of activation records. The consistent omission of efficient parallel recursion in previous block structured languages shows that this insight only seems obvious once you know the solution.

2 Assumptions

I will state the assumptions behind the method in general terms. However, I will use the implementation of block structured parallel languages to motivate the assumptions.

The general problem is to allocate and release segments of different lengths in a memory of fixed size under the following assumptions:

- *Each segment occupies a contiguous memory area of fixed length.*

In a block structured program, the unit of memory allocation is an activation record of fixed length that holds the local variable instances of a single activation of a block.

- *A segment is never relocated in memory.*

During program execution, the activation records in use are linked by pointers representing variable parameters, nested blocks, and activation sequences. Dynamic relocation of linked activation records would be complicated and time-consuming.

- *A segment is released only when no other segment in use points to it.*

The scope rules enable a compiler to check that the local variable instances of a block activation are accessed only during the activation. Consequently, the corresponding activation record can safely be released on exit from the block.

- *Segments are generally allocated and released in unpredictable order.*

The nondeterministic nature of parallel recursion complicates the dynamic memory allocation considerably.

- *There is a fixed number of segment lengths.*

A block structured program consists of a fixed number of blocks. (In Super-Pascal, a block is either a process statement or a procedure.) Each activation of the same block allocates an activation record of the same fixed length.

- *A program tends to use segments of the same lengths repeatedly.*

This is a plausible hypothesis about any program that uses the same procedures numerous times to transform different parts of large data structures sequentially or in parallel. The measurements in Section 4 strongly support this assumption.

The above assumptions are satisfied by a single block structured program that runs in a fixed memory area. However, they are not realistic for an operating system, which allocates an unbounded number of segments, most of which are unique to particular user jobs.

3   Implementation

Algorithm 1 defines the allocation of activation records for a parallel program that runs on a single processor in a memory area of fixed size. On a multicomputer with distributed memory, each processor must manage its own

```
var pool: array [1..limit] of integer;
  memory: array [min..max] of integer;
  top: integer;

procedure initialize;
var index: integer;
begin
  for index := 1 to limit do
     pool[index] := empty;
  top := min − 1
end;

procedure allocate( index, length: integer;
  var address: integer);
begin
  address := pool[index];
  if address <> empty then
    pool[index] := memory[address]
  else
    begin
      address := top + 1;
      top := top + length;
      assume top <= max
    end
end;

procedure release( index, address: integer);
begin
  memory[address] := pool[index];
  pool[index] := address
end;
```

Algorithm 1 Memory allocation.

memory for local processes. On a multiprocessor with shared memory, the allocation and release of activation records must be indivisible operations.

I assume that an operating system allocates a fixed amount of memory for the execution of a parallel program. The allocation method used by the operating system is beyond the scope of this discussion. My only concern is the algorithms used by a running program to allocate activation records within its own memory.

A dynamic boundary divides the program memory into two contiguous parts. One part is the heap, which holds all past and present activation records. The rest is free space. During program execution, the heap can only grow, and the free space can only shrink. A register holds the current top address of the heap.

The blocks in a program have consecutive indices and fixed activation record lengths determined by a compiler. For each block, a running program maintains a pool consisting of all free activation records reclaimed after previous activations of the block. Each pool is represented by an address, which either denotes an empty pool or is the first link in a list of free activation records of the same length.

Initially, the entire memory is free and every pool is empty.

On entry to a block with a given index and length, an attempt is made to allocate a free activation record from the corresponding pool. If the pool is empty, a new activation record of the given length is allocated in the free space, which is reduced accordingly.

On exit from the block, the activation record is released and added to the corresponding pool.

The algorithms for allocating and releasing an activation record are not intended to be implemented as separate procedures. They are part of the machine code executed at the beginning and end of every process statement and procedure. An activation record is allocated or released in constant time. Most processors can perform these simple operations by executing three or four machine instructions.

When the execution of a program ends, its memory area is still divided into pools of free activation records and the remaining free space. However, that does not matter, since the operating system will reclaim the entire memory area as a single unit.

4   Performance

The heap allocation method described here has been used to implement the block structured parallel language SuperPascal. So far, I have written parallel SuperPascal programs for a dozen standard problems in computational science (Brinch Hansen 1995).

Table 1 shows the ability of the heap allocator to recycle previous activation records during the execution of three parallel programs on a single processor.

Table 1   Measurements.

Parallel program	Quicksort tree	N-body pipeline	Laplace matrix
Number of blocks	16	24	28
Process activations	11	300	25,609
Procedure activations	18,120	513,553	67,156
New activation records	51	27	64
Reused activation records	18,080	513,826	92,701

The quicksort tree uses both parallel recursion (to create a binary tree of processes) and sequential recursion (to quicksort in parallel). The program consists of 16 blocks which are activated a total of 18,131 times (eleven process activations plus 18,120 procedure activations). These block activations create 51 new activation records, which are reused 18,080 times.

The n-body pipeline is a parallel nonrecursive program that repeatedly recreates a pipeline to perform force calculation for n gravitational bodies. During an n-body simulation the program activates parallel processes 300 times and procedures 513,553 times. These activations are handled by reusing the same 27 activation records over and over again.

The Laplace matrix is a highly parallel nonrecursive program. It creates parallel processes 25,609 times and calls procedures 67,156 times. These 92,765 block activations require only 64 activation records.

When these parallel program solve larger problems, the two nonrecursive programs run longer, but do not require more activation records. The number of activation records used by the quicksort tree increases slightly when the depth of the sequential recursion increases.

If no procedure is activated recursively or in parallel, the heap allocation uses the same amount of memory as static allocation (one activation record per block). In general, each block requires separate activation records for all activations of the block that may be in progress simultaneously (due to recursion or parallelism, or both).

5   Conclusions

I have described a simple heap mechanism for dynamic memory allocation of a parallel recursive program with Algol-like scope rules.

The mechanism has the following *advantages*:

- The heap allocation supports unbounded dynamic activation and termination of parallel processes and recursive procedures.

- The activation and termination of parallel processes and recursive procedures are equally fast.

- The heap allocation for parallel recursion is as efficient in reusing memory as the traditional stack discipline for sequential recursion.

- On a multicomputer with distributed memory, heap allocation is about as fast as stack allocation.

In its simplest form (presented here), the method has only two *limitations*:

- An activation record used to activate a block can only be reused by activating the same block again. This compromise makes it easy to release and reallocate the memory space of block activations.

- On a multiprocessor with shared memory, the need to lock and unlock the heap twice during a block activation makes the method less attractive.

Both limitations can probably be removed by more complicated variants of the basic idea. I leave that as an exercise for the reader.

Acknowledgements

It is a pleasure to acknowledge the comments of Art Bernstein, Ole-Johan Dahl, Ric Holt, Butler Lampson, Peter O'Hearn, Ron Perrott, Jørgen Staunstrup, and Peter O'Hearn.

References

Andrews, G.R. 1981. Synchronizing resources. *ACM Transactions on Programming Languages and Systems 3*, 4 (October), 405–430.

Brinch Hansen, P. 1975. The programming language Concurrent Pascal. *IEEE Transactions on Software Enginering 1*, 2 (June), 199–207. *Article 7.*

Brinch Hansen, P. 1978. Distributed processes: A concurrent programming concept. *Communications of the ACM 21*, 11 (November), 934–941. *Article 14.*

Brinch Hansen, P. 1981. Edison—a multiprocessor language. *Software—Practice and Experience 11*, 4 (April), 325–361.

Brinch Hansen, P. 1989. A multiprocessor implementation of Joyce. *Software—Practice and Experience 9*, 6 (June), 579–592. *Article 19.*

Brinch Hansen, P. 1994. The programming language SuperPascal. *Software—Practice and Experience 24*, 5 (May), 467–483.

Brinch Hansen, P. 1995. *Studies in Computational Science: Parallel Programming Paradigms.* Prentice Hall, Englewood Cliffs, NJ, (March).

Cook, R. 1980. *Mod—a language for distributed programming. *IEEE Transactions on Software Engineering 6*, 6 (November), 563–571.

Crookes, D. and Elder, J.W.G. 1984. An experiment in language design for distributed systems. *Software—Practice and Experience 14*, 10 (October), 957–971.

Davies G.L. and Burns, A. 1990. The teaching language Pascal-FC. *Computer Journal 33*, 147–154.

Dijkstra, E.W. 1960. Recursive programming. *Numerische Mathematik 2*, 312–318.

Fox, G.C., Johnson, M.A., Lyzenga, G.A., Otto, S.W., Salmon, J.K. and Walker, D.W. 1988. *Solving Problems on Concurrent Processors*, Vol. I. Prentice Hall, Englewood Cliffs, NJ.

Fox, G.C., Messina, P.C. and Williams, R.D. 1994. *Parallel Computing Works!* Morgan Kaufman, San Francisco, CA.

Hoare, C.A.R. 1978. Communicating sequential processes. *Communications of the ACM 21*, 8 (August), 666–677.

Holt, R.C. 1983. *Concurrent Euclid, the Unix Operating System and Tunis.* Addison-Wesley, Reading, MA.

Inmos Ltd. 1988. *occam 2 Reference Manual.* Prentice Hall, Englewood Cliffs, NJ.

Kaubisch, W.H., Perrott, R.H. and Hoare, C.A.R. 1976. Quasiparallel programming. *Software—Practice and Experience 6*, 3 (July–September), 341–356.

Kernighan, B.W. and Ritchie, D.M. 1978. *The C Programming Language.* Prentice Hall, Englewood Cliffs, NJ.

Lampson, B.W. and Redell, D.D. 1980. Experience with processes and monitors in Mesa. *Communications of the ACM 23*, 2 (February), 105–117.

Naur, P. 1963. Revised report on the algorithmic language Algol 60. *Communications of the ACM 6*, 1 (January), 1–17.

Organick, E.I. 1973. *Computer System Organization: The B5700/B6700 Series.* Academic Press, New York.

Weinstock, C.B., and Wulf, W.A. 1988. Quick Fit: an efficient algorithm for heap storage management. *SIGPLAN Notices 23*, 10 (October), 141–148.

Welsh, J. and Bustard, D.W. 1979. Pascal-Plus—another language for modular multipro-
    gramming. *Software—Practice and Experience 9*, 11 (November), 947–957.

Wirth, N. 1971. The programming language Pascal. *Acta Informatica 1*, 1, 35–63.

Wirth, N. 1977. Modula: a programming language for modular multiprogramming.
    Software—Practice and Experience 7, 1 (January–February), 3–35.

Index

519

IEEE COMPUTER SOCIETY
50 YEARS OF SERVICE • 1946-1996

http://www.computer.org

Press Activities Board

IEEE Computer Society Press Publications

The world-renowned Computer Society Press publishes, promotes, and distributes a wide variety of authoritative computer science and engineering texts. These books are available in two formats: 100 percent original material by authors preeminent in their field who focus on relevant topics and cutting-edge research, and reprint collections consisting of carefully selected groups of previously published papers with accompanying original introductory and explanatory text.

Submission of proposals: For guidelines and information on CS Press books, send e-mail to csbooks@computer.org or write to the Acquisitions Editor, IEEE Computer Society Press, P.O. Box 3014, 10662 Los Vaqueros Circle, Los Alamitos, CA 90720-1264. Telephone +1 714-821-8380. FAX +1 714-761-1784.

IEEE Computer Society Press Proceedings

The Computer Society Press also produces and actively promotes the proceedings of more than 130 acclaimed international conferences each year in multimedia formats that include hard and softcover books, CD-ROMs, videos, and on-line publications.

For information on CS Press proceedings, send e-mail to csbooks@computer.org or write to Proceedings, IEEE Computer Society Press, P.O. Box 3014, 10662 Los Vaqueros Circle, Los Alamitos, CA 90720-1264. Telephone +1 714-821-8380. FAX +1 714-761-1784.

Additional information regarding the Computer Society, conferences and proceedings, CD-ROMs, videos, and books can also be accessed from our web site at www.computer.org.

3/11/96